COPELAND'S
TREASURY FOR BOOKLOVERS

EDWIN BOOTH

From the painting by John Singer Sargent in the Players Club, New York

COPELAND'S TREASURY FOR BOOKLOVERS

A PANORAMA OF ENGLISH
AND AMERICAN POETRY AND PROSE FROM THE
EARLIEST TIMES TO THE PRESENT

SELECTED AND EDITED

BY

CHARLES TOWNSEND COPELAND

BOYLSTON PROFESSOR OF
ORATORY AND RHETORIC AT HARVARD UNIVERSITY

VOLUME IV

NEW YORK
CHARLES SCRIBNER'S SONS
1929

CONTENTS

CONTENTS

ILLUSTRATIONS

COPELAND'S
TREASURY FOR BOOKLOVERS

COPELAND'S
TREASURY FOR BOOKLOVERS

JOHN GALSWORTHY

A Stoic

I

1 §

"Aequam memento rebus in arduis
Servare mentem."—HORACE.

IN the City of Liverpool, on a January day of 1905, the Boardroom of "The Island Navigation Company" rested, as it were, after the labors of the afternoon. The long table was still littered with the ink, pens, blotting-paper, and abandoned documents of six persons—a deserted battlefield of the brain. And, lonely, in his chairman's seat at the top end old Sylvanus Heythorp sat, with closed eyes, still and heavy as an image. One puffy, feeble hand, whose fingers quivered, rested on the arm of his chair; the thick white hair on his massive head glistened in the light from a green-shaded lamp. He was not asleep, for every now and then his sanguine cheeks filled, and a sound, half sigh, half grunt, escaped his thick lips between a white moustache and the tiny tuft of white hairs above his cleft chin. Sunk in the chair, that square thick trunk of a body in short black-braided coat seemed divested of all neck.

Young Gilbert Farney, secretary of "The Island Navigation Company," entering his hushed Board-room, stepped briskly to the table, gathered some papers, and stood looking at his chairman. Not more than thirty-five, with the bright hues of the optimist in his hair, beard, cheeks, and eyes, he had a nose and lips which curled ironically. For, in his view, he *was* the Company; and its Board did but exist to chequer his importance. Five days in the week for seven hours a day he wrote, and thought, and wove the threads of its business, and this lot came down once a week for two or three hours, and taught their grandmother to suck eggs. But watching that red-cheeked, white-haired, somnolent figure, his smile was not so contemptuous as might have been expected. For after all, the chairman was a wonderful old boy. A man of go and insight could not but respect him. Eighty! Half paralyzed, over head and ears in debt, having gone the pace all his life—or so they said!— till at last that mine in Ecuador had done for him—before the secretary's day, of course, but he had heard of it. The old chap had bought it up on spec'—*"de l'audace, toujours de l'audace,"* as he was so fond of saying—paid for it half in cash and half in promises, and then—the thing

I

had turned out empty, and left him with £20,000 worth of the old shares
unredeemed. The old boy had weathered it out without a bankruptcy
so far. Indomitable old buffer; and never fussy like the rest of them!
Young Farney, though a secretary, was capable of attachment; and his
eyes expressed a pitying affection. The Board meeting had been long
and "snaggy"—a final settling of that Pillin business. Rum go the
chairman forcing it on them like this! And with quiet satisfaction the
secretary thought: 'And he never would have got it through if I hadn't
made up my mind that it really is good business!' For to expand the
Company was to expand himself. Still, to buy four ships with the freight
market so depressed was a bit startling, and there would be opposition
at the general meeting. Never mind! He and the chairman could put
it through—put it through. And suddenly he saw the old man looking
at him.

Only from those eyes could one appreciate the strength of life yet
flowing underground in that well-nigh helpless carcase—deep-colored
little blue wells, tiny, jovial, round windows.

A sigh travelled up through layers of flesh, and he said almost
inaudibly:

"Have they come, Mr. Farney?"

"Yes, sir. I've put them in the transfer office; said you'd be with
them in a minute; but I wasn't going to wake you."

"Haven't been asleep. Help me up."

Grasping the edge of the table with his trembling hands, the old man
pulled, and, with Farney heaving him behind, attained his feet. He stood
about five feet ten, and weighed fully fourteen stone; not corpulent, but
very thick all through; his round and massive head alone would have
outweighed a baby. With eyes shut, he seemed to be trying to get the
better of his own weight, then he moved with the slowness of a barnacle
towards the door. The secretary, watching him, thought: 'Marvellous
old chap! How he gets about by himself is a miracle! And he can't
retire, they say—lives on his fees!'

But the chairman was through the green baize door. At his tortoise
gait he traversed the inner office, where the youthful clerks suspended
their figuring—to grin behind his back—and entered the transfer office,
where eight gentlemen were sitting. Seven rose, and one did not. Old
Heythorp raised a saluting hand to the level of his chest and moving to an
arm-chair, lowered himself into it.

"Well, gentlemen?"

One of the eight gentlemen got up again.

"Mr. Heythorp, we've appointed Mr. Brownbee to voice our views. Mr. Brownbee!" And down he sat.

Mr. Brownbee rose—a stoutish man some seventy years of age, with little grey side whiskers, and one of those utterly steady faces only to be seen in England, faces which convey the sense of business from father to son for generations; faces which make wars, and passion, and free thought seem equally incredible; faces which inspire confidence, and awaken in one a desire to get up and leave the room. Mr. Brownbee rose, and said in a suave voice:

"Mr. Heythorp, we here represent about £14,000. When we had the pleasure of meeting you last July, you will recollect that you held out a prospect of some more satisfactory arrangement by Christmas. We are now in January, and I am bound to say we none of us get younger."

From the depths of old Heythorp a preliminary rumble came travelling, reached the surface, and materialized:

"Don't know about you—feel a boy, myself."

The eight gentlemen looked at him. Was he going to try and put them off again? Mr. Brownbee said with unruffled calm:

"I'm sure we're very glad to hear it. But to come to the point. We have felt, Mr. Heythorp, and I'm sure you won't think it unreasonable, that—er—bankruptcy would be the most satisfactory solution. We have waited a long time, and we want to know definitely where we stand; for, to be quite frank, we don't see any prospect of improvement; indeed, we fear the opposite."

"You think I'm going to join the majority."

This plumping out of what was at the back of their minds produced in Mr. Brownbee and his colleagues a sort of chemical disturbance. They coughed, moved their feet, and turned away their eyes, till the one who had not risen, a solicitor named Ventnor, said bluffly:

"Well, put it that way if you like."

Old Heythorp's little deep eyes twinkled.

"My grandfather lived to be a hundred; my father ninety-six—both of them rips. I'm only eighty, gentlemen; blameless life compared with theirs."

"Indeed," Mr. Brownbee said, "we hope you have many years of this life before you."

"More of this than of another." And a silence fell, till old Heythorp added: "You're getting a thousand a year out of my fees. Mistake to kill the goose that lays the golden eggs. I'll make it twelve hundred. If you force me to resign my directorships by bankruptcy, you won't get a rap, you know."

Mr. Brownbee cleared his throat:

"We think, Mr. Heythorp, you should make it at least fifteen hundred. In that case we might perhaps consider——"

Old Heythorp shook his head.

"We can hardly accept your assertion that we should get nothing in the event of bankruptcy. We fancy you greatly underrate the possibilities. Fifteen hundred a year is the least you can do for us."

"See you d——d first."

Another silence followed, then Ventnor, the solicitor, said irascibly:

"We know where we are, then."

Mr. Brownbee added almost nervously:

"Are we to understand that twelve hundred a year is your—your last word?"

Old Heythorp nodded. "Come again this day month, and I'll see what I can do for you;" and he shut his eyes.

Round Mr. Brownbee six of the gentlemen gathered, speaking in low voices; Mr. Ventnor nursed a leg and glowered at old Heythorp, who sat with his eyes closed. Mr. Brownbee went over and conferred with Mr. Ventnor, then clearing his throat, he said:

"Well, sir, we have considered your proposal; we agree to accept it for the moment. We will come again, as you suggest, in a month's time. We hope that you will by then have seen your way to something more substantial, with a view to avoiding what we should all regret, but which I fear will otherwise become inevitable."

Old Heythorp nodded. The eight gentlemen took their hats, and went out one by one, Mr. Brownbee courteously bringing up the rear.

The old man, who could not get up without assistance, stayed musing in his chair. He had diddled 'em for the moment into giving him another month, and when that month was up—he would diddle 'em again! A month ought to make the Pillin business safe, with all that hung on it. That poor funky chap Joe Pillin! A gurgling chuckle escaped his red lips. What a shadow the fellow had looked, trotting in that evening just a month ago, behind his valet's announcement: "Mr. Pillin, sir."

What a parchmenty, precise, threadpaper of a chap, with his bird's claw of a hand, and his muffled-up throat, and his quavery:

"How do you do, Sylvanus? I'm afraid you're not——"

"First rate. Sit down. Have some port."

"Port! I never drink it. Poison to me! Poison!"

"Do you good!"

"Oh! I know, that's what you always say. You've a monstrous constitution, Sylvanus. If I drank port and smoked cigars and sat up till one o'clock, I should be in my grave to-morrow. I'm not the man I was. The fact is I've come to see if you can help me. I'm getting old; I'm growing nervous——"

"You always were as chickeny as an old hen, Joe."

"Well, my nature's not like yours. To come to the point, I want to sell my ships and retire. I need rest. Freights are very depressed. I've got my family to think of."

"Crack on, and go broke: buck you up like anything!"

"I'm quite serious, Sylvanus."

"Never knew you anything else, Joe."

A quavering cough, and out it had come:

"Now—in a word—won't your 'Island Navigation Company' buy my ships?"

A pause, a twinkle, a puff of smoke. "Make it worth my while!" He had said it in jest; and then, in a flash, the idea had come to him. Rosamund and her youngsters! What a chance to put something between them and destitution when he had joined the majority! And so he said: "We don't want your silly ships."

That claw of a hand waved in deprecation. "They're very good ships —doing quite well. It's only my wretched health. If I were a strong man I shouldn't dream——"

"What d'you want for 'em?" Good Lord! how he jumped if you asked him a plain question. The chap was as nervous as a guinea-fowl!

"Here are the figures—for the last four years. I think you'll agree that I couldn't ask less than seventy thousand."

Through the smoke of his cigar old Heythorp had digested those figures slowly, Joe Pillin feeling his teeth and sucking lozenges the while; then he said:

"Sixty thousand! And out of that you pay me ten per cent, if I get it through for you. Take it or leave it."

"My dear Sylvanus, that's almost—cynical."

"Too good a price—you'll never get it without me."

"But a—but a commission! You could never disclose it!"

"Arrange that all right. Think it over. Freights'll go lower yet. Have some port."

"No, no! Thank you. No! So you think freights will go lower?"

"Sure of it."

"Well, I'll be going. I'm sure I don't know. It's—it's—I must think."

"Think your hardest."

"Yes, yes. Good-bye. I can't imagine how you still go on smoking those things and drinking port."

"See you in your grave yet, Joe." What a feeble smile the poor fellow had! Laugh—he couldn't! And, alone again, he had browsed, developing the idea which had come to him.

Though, to dwell in the heart of shipping, Sylvanus Heythorp had lived at Liverpool twenty years, he was from the Eastern Counties, of a family so old that it professed to despise the Conquest. Each of its generations occupied nearly twice as long as those of less tenacious men. Traditionally of Danish origin, its men folk had as a rule bright reddish-brown hair, red cheeks, large round heads, excellent teeth and poor morals. They had done their best for the population of any county in which they had settled; their offshoots swarmed. Born in the early twenties of the nineteenth century, Sylvanus Heythorp, after an education broken by escapades both at school and college, had fetched up in that simple London of the late forties, where claret, opera, and eight per cent. for your money ruled a cheery roost. Made partner in his shipping firm well before he was thirty, he had sailed with a wet sheet and a flowing tide; dancers, claret, Clicquot, and piquet; a cab with a tiger; some travel —all that delicious early-Victorian consciousness of nothing save a golden time. It was all so full and mellow that he was forty before he had his only love affair of any depth—with the daughter of one of his own clerks, a *liaison* so awkward as to necessitate a sedulous concealment. The death of that girl, after three years, leaving him a natural son, had been the chief, perhaps the only real, sorrow of his life. Five years later he married. What for? God only knew! as he was in the habit of remarking. His wife had been a hard, worldly, well-connected woman, who presented him with two unnatural children, a girl and a boy, and grew harder, more worldly, less handsome, in the process. The migration to Liverpool, which took place when he was sixty and she forty-two, broke what she still had of heart, but she lingered on twelve years, finding solace in bridge, and being haughty towards Liverpool. Old Heythorp saw her to her rest without regret. He had felt no love for her whatever, and practically none for her two children—they were in his view colorless, pragmatical, very unexpected characters. His son Ernest—in the Admiralty—he thought a poor, careful stick. His daughter Adela, an excellent manager, delighting in spiritual conversation and the society of tame men, rarely failed to show him that she considered him a hopeless heathen. They saw as little as need be of each other. She was provided for under that settlement he had made on her mother fifteen years ago, well before the not altogether unexpected crisis in his affairs. Very different was the feeling he had bestowed on that son of his "under the rose." The boy, who had always gone by his mother's name of Larne, had on her death been sent to some relations of hers in Ireland, and there brought up. He had been called to the Dublin bar, and married, young, a girl half Cornish and half Irish; presently, having cost old Heythorp in all a pretty penny, he had died impecunious, leaving his fair Rosamund at thirty with a girl of eight and a boy of five. She had not spent six months of widowhood before coming over from Dublin to claim the old man's guardianship. A remarkably pretty woman, like a full-blown rose, with greenish hazel eyes, she had turned up one morning at the offices of "The Island Navigation Company," accompanied by her two children—for he had never divulged to them his private address. And since then they had always been more or less on his hands, occupying a small house in a suburb of Liverpool. He visited them there, but never asked them to the house in Sefton Park, which was in fact his daughter's; so that his proper family and friends were unaware of their existence.

Rosamund Larne was one of those precarious ladies who make uncertain incomes by writing full-bodied storyettes. In the most dismal circumstances she enjoyed a buoyancy bordering on the indecent, which always amused old Heythorp's cynicism. But of his grandchildren Phyllis and Jock (wild as colts) he had become fond. And this chance of getting six thousand pounds settled on them at a stroke had seemed to him nothing but heaven-sent. As things were, if he "went off"— and, of course, he might at any moment—there wouldn't be a penny for them; for he would "cut up" a good fifteen thousand to the bad. He was now giving them some three hundred a year out of his fees; and dead directors unfortunately earned no fees! Six thousand pounds at four and a half per cent., settled so that their mother couldn't "blue it," would give them a certain two hundred and fifty pounds a year—better than beggary. And the more he thought the better he liked it, if only that shaky chap, Joe Pillin, didn't shy off when he'd bitten his nails short over it!

Four evenings later, the "shaky chap" had again appeared at his house in Sefton Park.

"I've thought it over, Sylvanus. I don't like it."

"No; but you'll do it."

"It's a sacrifice. Fifty-four thousand for four ships—it means a considerable reduction in my income."

"It means security, my boy."

"Well, there is that; but you know, I really can't be party to a secret commission. If it came out, think of my name and goodness knows what."

"It won't come out."

"Yes, yes, so you say, but——"

"All you've got to do's to execute a settlement on some third parties that I'll name. I'm not going to take a penny of it myself. Get your own lawyer to draw it up and make him trustee. You can sign it when the purchase has gone through. I'll trust you, Joe. What stock have you got that gives four and a half per cent.?"

"Midland——"

"That'll do. You needn't sell."

"Yes, but who *are* these people?"

"Woman and her children I want to do a good turn to." What a face the fellow had made! "Afraid of being connected with a woman, Joe?"

"Yes, you may laugh—I *am* afraid of being connected with some-one else's woman. I don't like it—I don't like it at all. I've not led your life, Sylvanus."

"Lucky for you; you'd have been dead long ago. Tell your lawyer it's an old flame of yours—you old dog!"

"Yes, there it is at once, you see. I might be subject to blackmail."

"Tell him to keep it dark, and just pay over the income, quarterly."

"I don't like it, Sylvanus—I don't like it."

"Then leave it, and be hanged to you. Have a cigar?"

"You know I never smoke. Is there no other way?"

"Yes. Sell stock in London, bank the proceeds there, and bring me six thousand pounds in notes. I'll hold 'em till after the general meeting. If the thing doesn't go through, I'll hand 'em back to you."

"No; I like that even less."

"Rather I trusted *you*, eh!"

"No, not at all, Sylvanus, not at all. But it's all playing round the law."

"There's no law to prevent you doing what you like with your money. What I do's nothing to you. And mind you, I'm taking nothing from it—not a mag. You assist the widowed and the fatherless—just your line, Joe!"

"What a fellow you are, Sylvanus; you don't seem capable of taking anything seriously."

"Care killed the cat!"

Left alone after this second interview he had thought: 'The beggar'll jump.'

And the beggar *had*. That settlement was drawn and only awaited signature. The Board to-day had decided on the purchase; and all that remained was to get it ratified at the general meeting. Let him but get that over, and this provision for his grandchildren made, and he would snap his fingers at Brownbee and his crew—the canting humbugs! "Hope you have many years of this life before you!" As if they cared for anything but his money—*their* money rather! And becoming conscious of the length of his reverie, he grasped the arms of his chair, heaved at his own bulk, in an effort to rise, growing redder and redder in face and neck. It was one of the hundred things his doctor had told him not to do for fear of apoplexy, the humbug! Why didn't Farney or one of those young fellows come and help him up? To call out was undignified. But was he to sit there all night? Three times he failed, and after each failure sat motionless again, crimson and exhausted; the fourth time he succeeded, and slowly made for the office. Passing through, he stopped and said in his extinct voice:

"You young gentlemen had forgotten me."

"Mr. Farney said you didn't wish to be disturbed, sir."

"Very good of him. Give me my hat and coat."

"Yes, sir."

"Thank you. What time is it?"

"Six o'clock, sir."

"Tell Mr. Farney to come and see me to-morrow at noon, about my speech for the general meeting."

"Yes, sir."

"Good-night to you."

"Good-night, sir."

At his tortoise gait he passed between the office stools to the door, opened it feebly, and slowly vanished.

Shutting the door behind him, a clerk said:

"Poor old chairman! He's on his last!"

Another answered:

"Gosh! He's a tough old hulk. He'll go down fightin'."

2 §

Issuing from the offices of "The Island Navigation Company," Sylvanus Heythorp moved towards the corner whence he always took tram to Sefton Park. The crowded street had all that prosperous air of catching or missing something which characterizes the town where London and New York and Dublin meet. Old Heythorp had to cross to the far side, and he sallied forth without regard to traffic. That snail-like passage had in it a touch of the sublime; the old man seemed saying: "Knock me down and be d——d to you—I'm not going to hurry." His life was saved perhaps ten times a day by the British character at large, compounded of phlegm and a liking to take something under its protection. The tram conductors on that line were especially used to him, never failing to catch him under the arms and heave him like a sack of coals, while with trembling hands he pulled hard at the rail and strap.

"All right, sir?"

"Thank you."

He moved into the body of the tram, where somebody would always get up from kindness and the fear that he might sit down on them; and there he stayed motionless, his little eyes tight closed. With his red face, tuft of white hairs above his square cleft block of shaven chin, and his big high-crowned bowler hat, which yet seemed too petty for his head with its thick hair—he looked like some kind of an idol dug up and decked out in gear a size too small.

One of those voices of young men from public schools and exchanges where things are bought and sold, said:

"How de do, Mr. Heythorp?"

Old Heythorp opened his eyes. That sleek cub, Joe Pillin's son! What a young pup—with his round eyes, and his round cheeks, and his little moustache, his fur coat, his spats, his diamond pin!

"How's your father?" he said.

"Thanks, rather below par, worryin' about his ships. Suppose you haven't any news for him, sir?"

Old Heythorp nodded. The young man was one of his pet abominations, embodying all the complacent, little-headed mediocrity of this new generation; natty fellows all turned out of the same mould, sippers and tasters, chaps without drive or capacity, without even vices; and he did not intend to gratify the cub's curiosity.

"Come to my house," he said; "I'll give you a note for him."

"Tha—anks; I'd like to cheer the old man up."

The old man! Cheeky brat! And closing his eyes he relapsed into immobility. The tram wound and ground its upward way, and he mused. When he was that cub's age—twenty-eight or whatever it might be—he had done most things; been up Vesuvius, driven four-in-hand, lost his last penny on the Derby and won it back on the Oaks, known all the dancers and operatic stars of the day, fought a duel with a Yankee at Dieppe and winged him for saying through his confounded nose that

Old England was played out; been a controlling voice already in his shipping firm; drunk five other of the best men in London under the table; broken his neck steeplechasing; shot a burglar in the legs; been nearly drowned, for a bet; killed snipe in Chelsea; been to Court for his sins; stared a ghost out of countenance; and travelled with a lady of Spain. If this young pup had done the last, it would be all he had; and yet, no doubt, he would call himself a "spark."

The conductor touched his arm.

" 'Ere you are, sir."

"Thank you."

He lowered himself to the ground, and moved in the bluish darkness towards the gate of his daughter's house. Bob Pillin walked beside him, thinking: 'Poor old josser, he *is* gettin' a back number!' And he said: "I should have thought you ought to drive, sir. My old guv-nor would knock up at once if he went about at night like this."

The answer rumbled out into the misty air:

"Your father's got no chest; never had."

Bob Pillin gave vent to one of those fat cackles which come so readily from a certain type of man; and old Heythorp thought: 'Laughing at his father! Parrot!'

They had reached the porch.

A woman with dark hair and a thin, straight face and figure was arranging some flowers in the hall. She turned and said:

"You really ought not to be so late, Father! It's wicked at this time of year. Who is it—oh! Mr. Pillin, how do you do? Have you had tea? Won't you come to the drawing-room; or do you want to see my father?"

"Tha—anks! I believe your father——" And he thought: 'By Jove! the old chap *is* a caution!' For old Heythorp was crossing the hall without having paid the faintest attention to his daughter. Murmuring again:

"Tha—anks awfully; he wants to give me something," he followed. Miss Heythorp was not his style at all; he had a kind of dread of that thin woman who looked as if she could never be unbuttoned. They said she was a great churchgoer and all that sort of thing.

In his sanctum old Heythorp had moved to his writing-table, and was evidently anxious to sit down.

"Shall I give you a hand, sir?"

Receiving a shake of the head, Bob Pillin stood by the fire and watched. The old "sport" liked to paddle his own canoe. Fancy having to lower yourself into a chair like that! When an old Johnny got to such a state it was really a mercy when he snuffed out, and made way for younger men. How his Companies could go on putting up with such a fossil for chairman was a marvel! The fossil rumbled and said in that almost inaudible voice:

"I suppose you're beginning to look forward to your father's shoes?"

Bob Pillin's mouth opened. The voice went on:

"Dibs and no responsibility. Tell him from me to drink port—add five years to his life."

To this unwarranted attack Bob Pillin made no answer save a laugh; he perceived that a manservant had entered the room.

"A Mrs. Larne, sir. Will you see her?"

At this announcement the old man seemed to try and start; then he nodded, and held out the note he had written. Bob Pillin received it together with the impression of a murmur which sounded like: "Scratch a poll, Poll!" and passing the fine figure of a woman in a fur coat, who seemed to warm the air as she went by, he was in the hall again before he perceived that he had left his hat.

A young and pretty girl was standing on the bearskin before the fire, looking at him with round-eyed innocence. He thought: 'This is better; I mustn't disturb them for my hat'; and approaching the fire, he said:

"Jolly cold, isn't it?"

The girl smiled: "Yes—jolly."

He noticed that she had a large bunch of violets at her breast, a lot of fair hair, a short straight nose, and round blue-grey eyes very frank and open. "Er——" he said, "I've left my hat in there."

"What larks!" And at her little clear laugh something moved within Bob Pillin.

"You know this house well?"

She shook her head. "But it's rather scrummy, isn't it?"

Bob Pillin, who had never yet thought so, answered:

"Quite O.K."

The girl threw up her head to laugh again. "O.K.? What's that?"

Bob Pillin saw her white round throat, and thought: 'She *is* a ripper!' And he said with a certain desperation:

"My name's Pillin. Yours is Larne, isn't it? Are you a relation here?"

"He's our Guardy. Isn't he a chook?"

That rumbling whisper like "Scratch a poll, Poll!" recurring to Bob Pillin, he said with reservation:

"You know him better than I do."

"Oh! Aren't you his grandson, or something?"

Bob Pillin did not cross himself.

"Lord! No! My dad's an old friend of his; that's all."

"Is your dad like him?"

"Not much."

"What a pity! It would have been lovely if they'd been Tweedles."

Bob Pillin thought: 'This bit is something new. I wonder what her Christian name is.' And he said:

"What did your godfather and godmothers in your baptism——?"

The girl laughed; she seemed to laugh at everything.

"Phyllis."

Could he say: "Is my only joy"? Better keep it! But—for what? He wouldn't see her again if he didn't look out! And he said:

"I live at the last house in the park—the red one. D'you know it? Where do you?"

"Oh! a long way—23, Millicent Villas. It's a poky little house. I hate it. We have awful larks, though."

"Who are we?"

"Mother, and myself, and Jock—he's an awful boy. You can't conceive what an awful boy he is. He's got nearly red hair; I think he'll be just like Guardy when he gets old. He's *awful!*"

Bob Pillin murmured:

"I should like to see him."

"Would you? I'll ask mother if you can. You won't want to again; he goes off all the time like a squib." She threw back her head, and again Bob Pillin felt a little giddy. He collected himself, and drawled:

"Are you going in to see your Guardy?"

"No. Mother's got something special to say. We've never been here before, you see. Isn't he fun, though?"

"Fun!"

"I think he's the greatest lark: but he's awfully nice to me. Jock calls him the last of the Stoic'uns."

A voice called from old Heythorp's den:

"Phyllis!" It had a particular ring, that voice, as if coming from beautifully formed red lips, of which the lower one must curve the least bit over; it had, too, a caressing vitality, and a kind of warm falsity.

The girl threw a laughing look back over her shoulder, and vanished through the door into the room.

Bob Pillin remained with his back to the fire and his puppy round eyes fixed on the air that her figure had last occupied. He was experiencing a sensation never felt before. Those travels with a lady of Spain, charitably conceded him by old Heythorp, had so far satisfied the emotional side of this young man; they had stopped short at Brighton and Scarborough, and been preserved from even the slightest intrusion of love. A calculated and hygienic career had caused no anxiety either to himself or his father; and this sudden swoop of something more than admiration gave him an uncomfortable choky feeling just above his high round collar, and in the temples a sort of buzzing—those first symptoms of chivalry. A man of the world does not, however, succumb without a struggle; and if his hat had not been out of reach, who knows whether he would not have left the house hurriedly, saying to himself: "No, no, my boy; Millicent Villas is hardly your form, when your intentions are honorable"? For somehow that round and laughing face, bob of glistening hair, those wide-opened grey eyes, refused to awaken the beginnings of other intentions—such is the effect of youth and innocence on even the steadiest young men. With a kind of moral stammer, he was thinking: 'Can I—dare I offer to see them to their tram? Couldn't I even nip out and get the car round and send them home in it? No, I might miss them—better stick it out here! What a jolly laugh! What a ripping face—strawberries and cream, hay, and all that! Millicent Villas!' And he wrote it on his cuff.

The door was opening; he heard that warm vibrating voice: "Come along, Phyllis!"—the girl's laugh so high and fresh: "Right-o! Coming!" And with, perhaps, the first real tremor he had ever known, he crossed to the front door. All the more chivalrous to escort them to the tram without a hat! And suddenly he heard: "I've got your hat, young man!" And her mother's voice, warm, and simulating shock: "Phyllis, you awful gairl! Did you ever see such an awful gairl, Mr.——"

"Pillin, Mother."

And then—he did not quite know how—insulated from the January air by laughter and the scent of fur and violets, he was between them walking to their tram. It was like an experience out of the "Arabian Nights," or something of that sort, an intoxication which made one say one was going their way, though one would have to come all the way back in the same beastly tram. Nothing so warming had ever happened to him as sitting between them on that drive, so that he forgot the note in his pocket, and his desire to relieve the anxiety of the "old man," his father. At the tram's terminus they all got out. There issued a purr of invitation to come and see them some time; a clear: "Jock'll love to see you!" A low laugh: "You awful gairl!"

And a flash of cunning zigzagged across his brain. Taking off his hat, he said:

"Thanks awfully; rather!" and put his foot back on the step of the tram. Thus did he delicately expose the depths of his chivalry!

"Oh! you *said* you were going our way! What one-ers you do tell! Oh!" The words were as music; the sight of those eyes growing rounder, the most perfect he had ever seen; and Mrs. Larne's low laugh, so warm yet so preoccupied, and the tips of the girl's fingers waving back above her head. He heaved a sigh and knew no more till he was seated at his club before a bottle of champagne. Home! Not he! He wished to drink and dream. "The old man" would get his news all right to-morrow!

3 §

The words: "A Mrs. Larne to see you, sir," had been of a nature to astonish weaker nerves. What had brought her here? She knew she mustn't come! Old Heythorp had watched her entrance with cynical amusement. The way she whiffed herself at that young pup in passing, the way her eyes slid round! He had a very just appreciation of his son's widow; and a smile settled deep between his chin tuft and his moustache. She lifted his hand, kissed it, pressed it to her splendid bust, and said:

"So here I am at last, you see. Aren't you surprised?"

Old Heythorp shook his head.

"I really had to come and see you, Guardy; we haven't had a sight of you for such an age. And in this awful weather! How are you, dear old Guardy?"

"Never better." And, watching her green-grey eyes, he added: "Haven't a penny for you!"

Her face did not fall; she gave her feather-laugh.

"How dreadful of you to think I came for that! But I *am* in an awful fix, Guardy."

"Never knew you not to be."

"Just let me tell you, dear; it'll be some relief. I'm having the most terrible time."

She sank into a low chair, disengaging an overpowering scent of violets, while melancholy struggled to subdue her face and body.

"The most awful fix. I expect to be sold up any moment. We may be on the streets to-morrow. I daren't tell the children; they're so happy, poor darlings. I shall be obliged to take Jock away from school. And Phyllis will have to stop her piano and dancing; it's an absolute

crisis. And all due to those Midland Syndicate people. I've been counting on at least two hundred for my new story, and the wretches have
refused it."

With a tiny handkerchief she removed one tear from the corner of
one eye. "It *is* hard, Guardy; I worked my brain silly over that story."

From old Heythorp came a mutter which sounded suspiciously like
"Rats!"

Heaving a sigh, which conveyed nothing but the generosity of her
breathing apparatus, Mrs. Larne went on:

"You couldn't, I suppose, let me have just one hundred?"

"Not a bob."

She sighed again, her eyes slid round the room; then in her warm
voice she murmured:

"Guardy, you *were* my dear Philip's father, weren't you? I've never
said anything; but *of course* you were. He was so like you, and so
is Jock."

Nothing moved in old Heythorp's face. No pagan image consulted
with flowers and song and sacrifice could have returned less answer.
Her dear Philip! She had led him the devil of a life, or he was a
Dutchman! And what the deuce made her suddenly trot out the skeleton
like this? But Mrs. Larne's eyes were still wandering.

"What a lovely house! You know, I think you ought to help me,
Guardy. Just imagine if your grandchildren were thrown out into the
street!"

The old man grinned. He was not going to deny his relationship
—it was her look-out, not his. But neither was he going to let her
rush him.

"And they will be; you *couldn't* look on and see it. Do come to
my rescue this once. You really might do something for them."

With a rumbling sigh he answered:

"Wait. Can't give you a penny now. Poor as a church mouse."

"Oh! Guardy!"

"Fact."

Mrs. Larne heaved one of her most buoyant sighs. She certainly
did not believe him.

"Well!" she said; "you'll be sorry when we come round one night
and sing for pennies under your window. Wouldn't you like to see
Phyllis? I left her in the hall. She's growing such a sweet gairl.
Guardy—just fifty!"

"Not a rap."

Mrs. Larne threw up her hands. "Well! You'll repent it. I'm at my last gasp." She sighed profoundly, and the perfume of violets escaped in a cloud. Then, getting up, she went to the door and called: "Phyllis!"

When the girl entered old Heythorp felt the nearest approach to a flutter of the heart for many years. She had put her hair up! She was like a spring day in January; such a relief from that scented humbug, her mother. Pleasant, the touch of her lips on his forehead, the sound of her clear voice, the sight of her slim movements, the feeling that she did him credit—clean-run stock, she and that young scamp Jock—better than the holy woman, his daughter Adela, would produce if anyone were ever fool enough to marry her, or that pragmatical fellow, his son Ernest.

And when they were gone he reflected with added zest on the six thousand pounds he was getting for them out of Joe Pillin and his ships. He would have to pitch it strong in his speech at the general meeting. With freights so low, there was bound to be opposition. No dash nowadays; nothing but flabby caution! They were a scrim-shanking lot on the Board—he had had to pull them round one by one—the deuce of a tug getting this thing through! And yet, the business was sound enough. Those ships would earn money, properly handled—good money!

His valet, coming in to prepare him for dinner, found him asleep. He had for the old man as much admiration as may be felt for one who cannot put his own trousers on. He would say to the housemaid Molly: "He's a game old blighter—must have been a rare one in his day. Cocks his hat at you, even now, I see!" To which the girl, Irish and pretty, would reply: "Well, an' sure I don't mind, if it gives um a pleasure. 'Tis better annyway than the sad eye I get from herself."

At dinner, old Heythorp always sat at one end of the rosewood table and his daughter at the other. It was the eminent moment of the day. With napkin tucked high into his waistcoat, he gave himself to the meal with passion. His palate was undimmed, his digestion unimpaired. He could still eat as much as two men, and drink more than one. And while he savored each mouthful he never spoke if he could help it. The holy woman had nothing to say that he cared to hear, and he nothing to say that she cared to listen to. She had a horror, too, of what she called "the pleasures of the table"—those lusts of the flesh! She was always longing to dock his grub, he knew. Would see her further first! What other pleasures were there at his age? Let her wait till *she* was eighty. But she never would be; too thin and holy!

This evening, however, with the advent of the partridge she *did* speak.

"Who were your visitors, Father?"

Trust her for nosing anything out! Fixing his little blue eyes on her, he mumbled with a very full mouth: "Ladies."

"So I saw; what ladies?"

He had a longing to say: 'Part of one of my families under the rose.' As a fact it was the best part of the only one, but the temptation to multiply exceedingly was almost overpowering. He checked himself, however, and went on eating partridge, his secret irritation crimsoning his cheeks; and he watched her eyes, those cold precise and round grey eyes, noting it, and knew she was thinking: "He eats too much."

She said: "Sorry I'm not considered fit to be told. You ought not to be drinking hock."

Old Heythorp took up the long green glass, drained it, and repressing fumes and emotion went on with his partridge. His daughter pursed her lips, took a sip of water, and said:

"I know their name is Larne, but it conveyed nothing to me; perhaps it's just as well."

The old man, mastering a spasm, said with a grin:

"My daughter-in-law and my granddaughter."

"What! Ernest married—Oh! nonsense!"

He chuckled, and shook his head.

"Then do you mean to say, Father, that you were married before you married my mother?"

"No."

The expression on her face was as good as a play!

She said with a sort of disgust: "Not married! I see. I suppose those people are hanging round your neck, then; no wonder you're always in difficulties. Are there any more of them?"

Again the old man suppressed that spasm, and the veins in his neck and forehead swelled alarmingly. If he had spoken he would infallibly have choked. He ceased eating, and putting his hands on the table tried to raise himself. He could not, and subsiding in his chair sat glaring at the stiff, quiet figure of his daughter.

"Don't be silly, Father, and make a scene before Meller. Finish your dinner."

He did not answer. He was not going to sit there to be dragooned and insulted! His helplessness had never so weighed on him before. It was like a revelation. A log—that had to put up with anything! A log! And, waiting for his valet to return, he cunningly took up his fork.

In that saintly voice of hers she said:

"I suppose you don't realize that it's a shock to me. I don't know what Ernest will think——"

"Ernest be d——d."

"I do wish, Father, you wouldn't swear."

Old Heythorp's rage found vent in a sort of rumble. How the devil had he gone on all these years in the same house with that woman, dining with her day after day! But the servant had come back now, and putting down his fork he said:

"Help me up!"

The man paused, thunderstruck, with the *soufflé* balanced.

To leave dinner unfinished—it was a portent!

"Help me up!"

"Mr. Heythorp's not very well, Meller; take his other arm."

The old man shook off her hand.

"I'm very well. Help me up. Dine in my own room in future."

Raised to his feet, he walked slowly out; but in his sanctum he did not sit down, obsessed by this first overwhelming realization of his helplessness. He stood swaying a little, holding on to the table, till the servant, having finished serving dinner, brought in his port.

"Are you waiting to sit down, sir?"

He shook his head. Hang it, he could do that for himself, anyway. He must think of something to fortify his position against that woman. And he said:

"Send me Molly!"

"Yes, sir." The man put down the port and went.

Old Heythorp filled his glass, drank, and filled again. He took a cigar from the box and lighted it. The girl came in, a grey-eyed, dark-haired damsel, and stood with her hands folded, her head a little to one side, her lips a little parted. The old man said:

"You're a human being."

"I would hope so, sirr."

"I'm going to ask you something as a human being——not a servant —see?"

"No, sirr; but I will be glad to do annything you like."

"Then put your nose in here every now and then, to see if I want anything. Meller goes out sometimes. Don't say anything; just put your nose in."

"Oh! an' I will; 'tis a pleasure 'twill be to do ut."

He nodded, and when she had gone lowered himself into his chair with a sense of appeasement. Pretty girl! Comfort to see a pretty face—not a pale, peeky thing like Adela's. His anger burned up anew.

So she counted on his helplessness, had begun to count on that, had she? She should see that there was life in the old dog yet! And his sacrifice of the uneaten *soufflé*, the still less eaten mushrooms, the peppermint sweet with which he usually concluded dinner, seemed to consecrate that purpose. They all thought he was a hulk, without a shot left in the locker! He had seen a couple of them at the Board that afternoon shrugging at each other, as though saying: "Look at him!" And young Farney pitying him. Pity, forsooth! And that coarse-grained solicitor chap at the creditors' meeting curling his lips as much to say: "One foot in the grave!" He had seen the clerks dowsing the glim of their grins; and that young pup Bob Pillin screwing up his supercilious mug over his dog-collar. He knew that scented humbug Rosamund was getting scared that he'd drop off before she'd squeezed him dry. And his valet was always looking him up and down queerly. As to that holy woman——! Not quite so fast! Not quite so fast! And filling his glass for the fourth time, he slowly sucked down the dark red fluid, with the "old boots" flavor which his soul loved, and, drawing deep at his cigar, closed his eyes.

II

I §

The room in the hotel where the general meetings of "The Island Navigation Company" were held was nearly full when the secretary came through the door which as yet divided the shareholders from their directors. Having surveyed their empty chairs, their ink and papers, and nodded to a shareholder or two, he stood, watch in hand, contemplating the congregation. A thicker attendance than he had ever seen! Due, no doubt, to the lower dividend, and this Pillin business. And his tongue curled. For if he had a natural contempt for his Board, with the exception of the chairman, he had a still more natural contempt for his shareholders. Amusing spectacle when you come to think of it, a general meeting! Unique! Eighty or a hundred men, and five women, assembled through sheer devotion to their money. Was any other function in the world so single-hearted? Church was nothing to it—so many motives were mingled there with devotion to one's soul. A well-educated young man—reader of Anatole France, and other writers—he enjoyed ironic speculation. What earthly good did they think they got by coming here? Half-past two! He put his watch back into his pocket, and passed into the Board-room.

There, the fumes of lunch and of a short preliminary meeting made

cosey the February atmosphere. By the fire four directors were convers-
ing rather restlessly; the fifth was combing his beard; the chairman sat
with eyes closed and red lips moving rhythmically in the sucking of a
lozenge, the slips of his speech ready in his hand. The secretary said
in his cheerful voice: "Time, sir."

Old Heythorp swallowed, lifted his arms, rose with help, and walked
through to his place at the centre of the table. The five directors followed. And, standing at the chairman's right, the secretary read the
minutes, forming the words precisely with his curling tongue. Then,
assisting the chairman to his feet, he watched those rows of faces, and
thought: 'Mistake to let them see he can't get up without help. He
ought to have let me read his speech—I wrote it.'

The chairman began to speak:

"It is my duty and my pleasure, ladies and gentlemen, for the nineteenth consecutive year to present to you the directors' report and the
accounts for the past twelve months. You will all have had special
notice of a measure of policy on which your Board has decided, and to
which you will be asked to-day to give your adherence—to that I shall
come at the end of my remarks. . . ."

"Excuse me, sir; we can't hear a word down here."

'Ah!' thought the secretary, 'I was expecting that.'

The chairman went on, undisturbed. But several shareholders now
rose, and the same speaker said testily: "We might as well go home.
If the chairman's got no voice, can't somebody read for him?"

The chairman took a sip of water, and resumed. Almost all in the
last six rows were now on their feet, and amid a hubbub of murmurs
the chairman held out to the secretary the slips of his speech, and fell
heavily back into his chair.

The secretary re-read from the beginning; and as each sentence fell
from his tongue, he thought: 'How good that is!' 'That's very clear!'
'A neat touch!' 'This is getting them.' It seemed to him a pity they
could not know it was all his composition. When at last he came to
the Pillin sale he paused for a second.

"I come now to the measure of policy to which I made allusion at
the beginning of my speech. Your Board has decided to expand your
enterprise by purchasing the entire fleet of Pillin & Co., Ltd. By this
transaction we become the owners of the four steamships *Smyrna*,
Damascus, *Tyre*, and *Sidon*, vessels in prime condition with a total
freight-carrying capacity of fifteen thousand tons, at the low inclusive
price of sixty thousand pounds. Gentlemen, *'Vestigia nulla retrorsum!'* "
—it was the chairman's phrase, his bit of the speech, and the secretary

did it more than justice. "Times are bad, but your Board is emphatically of the opinion that they are touching bottom; and this, in their view, is the psychological moment for a forward stroke. They confidently recommend your adoption of their policy and the ratification of this purchase, which they believe will, in the not far distant future, substantially increase the profits of the Company." The secretary sat down with reluctance. The speech should have continued with a number of appealing sentences which he had carefully prepared, but the chairman had cut them out with the simple comment: "They ought to be glad of the chance." It was, in his view, an error.

The director who had combed his beard now rose—a man of presence, who might be trusted to say nothing long and suavely. While he was speaking the secretary was busy noting whence opposition was likely to come. The majority were sitting owl-like—a good sign; but some dozen were studying their copies of the report, and three at least were making notes—Westgate, for instance, who wanted to get on the Board, and was sure to make himself unpleasant—the time-honored method of vinegar; and Batterson, who also desired to come on, and might be trusted to support the Board—the time-honored method of oil; while, if one knew anything of human nature, the fellow who had complained that he might as well go home would have something uncomfortable to say. The director finished his remarks, combed his beard with his fingers, and sat down.

A momentary pause ensued. Then Messieurs Westgate and Batterson rose together. Seeing the chairman nod towards the latter, the secretary thought: 'Mistake! He should have humored Westgate by giving him precedence.' But that was the worst of the old man, he had no notion of the *suaviter in modo!* Mr. Batterson—thus unchained —would like, if he might be so allowed, to congratulate the Board on having piloted their ship so smoothly through the troublous waters of the past year. With their worthy chairman still at the helm, he had no doubt that in spite of the still low—he would not say falling—barometer, and the—er—unseasonable climacteric, they might rely on weathering the—er—he would not say storm. He would confess that the present dividend of four per cent. was not one which satisfied every aspiration ("Hear, hear!"), but speaking for himself, and he hoped for others— and here Mr. Batterson looked round—he recognized that in all the circumstances it was as much as they had the right—er—to expect. But following the bold but to *his* mind prudent development which the Board proposed to make, he thought that they might reasonably, if not sanguinely, anticipate a more golden future. ("No, no!") A shareholder said, "No, no!" That might seem to indicate a certain lack of confidence in the special proposal before the meeting. ("Yes!") From that lack of confidence he would like at once to dissociate himself. Their chairman, a man of foresight and acumen, and valor proved on many a field and—er—sea, would not have committed himself to this policy without good reason. In his opinion they were in safe hands, and he was glad to register his support of the measure proposed. The chairman had well said in his speech: *"Vestigia nulla retrorsum!"* Shareholders would agree with him that there could be no better motto for Englishmen. Ahem!

Mr. Batterson sat down. And Mr. Westgate rose: He wanted— he said—to know more, much more, about this proposition, which to his mind was of a very dubious wisdom . . . 'Ah!' thought the secretary, 'I told the old boy he must tell them more.' . . . To whom, for instance, had the proposal first been made? To him!—the chairman said. Good! But why were Pillins selling, if freights were to go up, as they were told?

"Matter of opinion."

"Quite so; and in my opinion they are going lower, and Pillins were right to sell. It follows that we are wrong to buy." ("Hear, hear!" "No, no!") "Pillins are shrewd people. What does the chairman say? Nerves! Does he mean to tell us that this sale was the result of nerves?"

The chairman nodded.

"That appears to me a somewhat fantastic theory; but I will leave that and confine myself to asking the grounds on which the chairman bases his confidence; in fact, what it is which is actuating the Board in pressing on us at such a time what I have no hesitation in stigmatizing as a rash proposal. In a word, I want light as well as leading in this matter."

Mr. Westgate sat down.

What would the chairman do now? The situation was distinctly awkward—seeing his helplessness and the luke-warmness of the Board behind him. And the secretary felt more strongly than ever the absurdity of his being an underling, he who in a few well-chosen words could so easily have twisted the meeting round his thumb. Suddenly he heard the long, rumbling sigh which preluded the chairman's speeches.

"Has any other gentleman anything to say before I move the adoption of the report?"

Phew! That would put their backs up. Yes, sure enough it had brought that fellow, who had said he might as well go home, to his feet! Now for something nasty!

"Mr. Westgate requires answering. I don't like this business. I don't impute anything to anybody; but it looks to me as if there were something behind it which the shareholders ought to be told. Not only that; but, to speak frankly, I'm not satisfied to be ridden over roughshod in this fashion by one who, whatever he may have been in the past, is obviously not now in the prime of his faculties."

With a gasp the secretary thought: "I knew that was a plain-spoken man!"

He heard again the rumbling beside him. The chairman had gone crimson, his mouth was pursed, his little eyes were very blue.

"Help me up," he said.

The secretary helped him, and waited, rather breathless.

The chairman took a sip of water, and his voice, unexpectedly loud, broke an ominous hush:

"Never been so insulted in my life. My best services have been at your disposal for nineteen years; you know what measure of success this Company has attained. I am the oldest man here, and my experience of shipping is, I hope, a little greater than that of the two gentlemen who spoke last. I have done my best for you, ladies and gentlemen, and we shall see whether you are going to endorse an indictment of my judgment and of my honour, if I am to take the last speaker seriously. This purchase is for your good. 'There is a tide in the affairs of men'—and I for one am not content, never have been, to stagnate. If that is what you want, however, by all means give your support to these gentlemen and have done with it. I tell you freights will go up before the end of the year; the purchase is a sound one, more than a sound one—I, at any rate, stand or fall by it. Refuse to ratify it, if you like; if you do, I shall resign."

He sank back into his seat. The secretary, stealing a glance, thought with a sort of enthusiasm: 'Bravo! Who'd have thought he could rally his voice like that? A good touch, too, about his honor! I believe he's knocked them. It's still dicky, though, if that fellow at the back gets up again; the old chap can't work that stop a second time.' Ah! here was 'old Applepie' on his hind legs. That was all right!

"I do not hesitate to say that I am an old friend of the chairman; we are, many of us, old friends of the chairman, and it has been painful to me, and I doubt not to others, to hear an attack made on him. If he is old in body, he is young in mental vigor and courage. I wish we were all as young. We ought to stand by him; I say, we ought to stand by him." ("Hear, hear! Hear, hear!") And the secretary thought: 'That's done it!' And he felt a sudden odd emotion, watching the chairman bobbing his body, like a wooden top, at old Appleby; and old Appleby bobbing back. Then, seeing a shareholder close to the door get up, thought: 'What's that? I know his face—Ah! yes; Ventnor, the solicitor—he's one of the chairman's creditors that are coming again this afternoon. What now?'

"I can't agree that we ought to let sentiment interfere with our judgment in this matter. The question is simply: How are our pockets going to be affected? I came here with some misgivings, but the attitude of the chairman has been such as to remove them; and I shall support the proposition." The secretary thought: 'That's all right—only, he said it rather queerly—rather queerly.'

Then, after a long silence, the chairman, without rising, said:

"I move the adoption of the report and accounts."

"I second that."

"Those in favor signify the same in the usual way. Contrary? Carried." The secretary noted the dissentients, six in number, and that Mr. Westgate did not vote.

A quarter of an hour later he stood in the body of the emptying room supplying names to one of the gentlemen of the Press.

The passionless fellow said: "Haythorp, with an 'a'; oh! an 'e'; he seems an old man. Thank you. I may have the slips? Would you like to see a proof? With an 'a' you said—oh! an 'e.' Good afternoon!" And the secretary thought: 'Those fellows, what *does* go on inside them? Fancy not knowing the old chairman by now!' . . .

2 §

Back in the proper office of "The Island Navigation Company" old Heythorp sat smoking a cigar and smiling like a purring cat. He was dreaming a little of his triumph, sifting with his old brain, still subtle, the wheat from the chaff of the demurrers: Westgate—nothing in that—professional discontent till they silenced him with a place on the Board—but not while *he* held the reins! That chap at the back—an ill-conditioned fellow: "Something behind!" Suspicious brute! There *was* something—but—hang it! they might think themselves lucky to get four ships at that price, and all due to him! It was on the last speaker that his mind dwelt with a doubt. That fellow Ventnor, to whom he owed money—there had been something just a little queer about his tone—as much as to say, "I smell a rat." Well! one would see that at the creditors' meeting in half an hour.

"Mr. Pillin, sir."

"Show him in!"

In a fur coat which seemed to extinguish his thin form, Joe Pillin entered. It was snowing, and the cold had nipped and yellowed his meagre face between its slight grey whiskering. He said thinly:

"How are you, Sylvanus? Aren't you perished in this cold?"

"Warm as toast. Sit down. Take off your coat."

"Oh! I should be lost without it. You must have a fire inside you. So—so it's gone through?"

Old Heythorp nodded; and Joe Pillin, wandering like a spirit, scrutinized the shut door. He came back to the table, and said in a low voice:

"It's a great sacrifice."

Old Heythorp smiled.

"Have you signed the deed poll?"

Producing a parchment from his pocket, Joe Pillin unfolded it with caution to disclose his signature, and said:

"I don't like it—it's irrevocable."

A chuckle escaped old Heythorp.

"As death."

Joe Pillin's voice passed up into the treble clef.

"I can't bear irrevocable things. I consider you stampeded me, playing on my nerves."

Examining the signatures old Heythorp murmured:

"Tell your lawyer to lock it up. He must think you a sad dog, Joe."

"Ah! Suppose on my death it comes to the knowledge of my wife!"

"She won't be able to make it hotter for you than you'll be already."

Joe Pillin replaced the deed within his coat, emitting a queer thin noise. He simply could not bear joking on such subjects.

"Well," he said, "you've got your way; you always do. Who is this Mrs. Larne? You oughtn't to keep me in the dark. It seems my boy met her at your house. You told me she didn't come there."

Old Heythorp said with relish:

"Her husband was my son by a woman I was fond of before I married; her children are my grandchildren. You've provided for them. Best thing you ever did."

"I don't know—I don't know. I'm sorry you told me. It makes it all the more doubtful. As soon as the transfer's complete, I shall get away abroad. This cold's killing me. I wish you'd give me your recipe for keeping warm."

"Get a new inside."

Joe Pillin regarded his old friend with a sort of yearning. "And yet," he said, "I suppose, with your full-blooded habit, your life hangs by a thread, doesn't it?"

"A stout one, my boy!"

"Well, good-bye, Sylvanus. You're a Job's comforter; I must be getting home." He put on his hat, and, lost in his fur coat, passed out into the corridor. On the stairs he met a man who said:

"How do you do, Mr. Pillin? I know your son. Been seeing the chairman? I see your sale's gone through all right. I hope that'll do us some good, but I suppose you think the other way?"

Peering at him from under his hat, Joe Pillin said:

"Mr. Ventnor, I think? Thank you! It's very cold, isn't it?" And, with that cautious remark, he passed on down.

Alone again, old Heythorp thought: 'By George! What a wavering, quavering, thread-paper of a fellow! What misery life must be to a chap like that! He walks in fear—he wallows in it. Poor devil!' And a curious feeling swelled his heart, of elation, of lightness such as he had not known for years. Those two young things were safe now from penury—safe! After dealing with those infernal creditors of his he would go round and have a look at the children. With a hundred and twenty a year the boy could go into the Army—best place for a young scamp like that. The girl would go off like hot cakes, of course, but she needn't take the first calf that came along. As for their mother, she must look after herself; nothing under two thousand a year would keep *her* out of debt. But trust her for wheedling and bluffing her way out of any scrape! Watching his cigar-smoke curl and disperse he was conscious of the strain he had been under these last six weeks, aware suddenly of how greatly he had balked at thought of to-day's general meeting. Yes! It might have turned out nasty. He knew well enough the forces on the Board, and off, who would be only too glad to shelve him. If he were shelved here his other two Companies would be sure to follow suit, and bang would go every penny of his income—he would be a pauper dependent on that holy woman. Well! Safe now for another year if he could stave off these sharks once more. It might be a harder job this time, but he was in luck—in luck, and it must hold. And taking a luxurious pull at his cigar, he rang the handbell.

"Bring 'em in here, Mr. Farney. And let me have a cup of China tea as strong as you can make it."

"Yes, sir. Will you see the proof of the press report, or will you leave it to me?"

"To you."

"Yes, sir. It was a good meeting, wasn't it?"

Old Heythorp nodded.

"Wonderful how your voice came back just at the right moment. I was afraid things were going to be difficult. The insult did it, I think, It was a monstrous thing to say. I could have punched his head."

Again old Heythorp nodded; and, looking into the secretary's fine blue eyes, he repeated: "Bring 'em in."

The lonely minute before the entrance of his creditors passed in the thought: 'So that's how it struck him! Short shrift I should get if it came out.'

The gentlemen, who numbered ten this time, bowed to their debtor, evidently wondering why the deuce they troubled to be polite to an old man who kept them out of their money. Then, the secretary reappearing with a cup of China tea, they watched while their debtor drank it. The feat was tremulous. Would he get through without spilling it all down his front, or choking? To those unaccustomed to his private life it was slightly miraculous. He put the cup down empty, tremblingly removed some yellow drops from the little white tuft below his lip, relit his cigar, and said:

"No use beating about the bush, gentlemen; I can offer you four- teen hundred a year so long as I live and hold my directorships, and not a penny more. If you can't accept that, you must make me bankrupt and get about sixpence in the pound. My qualifying shares will fetch a couple of thousand at market price. I own nothing else. The house I live in, and everything in it, barring my clothes, my wine, and my cigars, belong to my daughter under a settlement fifteen years old. My solicitors and bankers will give you every information. That's the posi- tion in a nutshell."

In spite of business habits the surprise of the ten gentlemen was only partially concealed. A man who owed them so much would nat- urally say he owned nothing, but would he refer them to his solicitors and bankers unless he were telling the truth? Then Mr. Ventnor said:

"Will you submit your pass books?"

"No, but I'll authorize my bankers to give you a full statement of my receipts for the last five years—longer, if you like."

The strategic stroke of placing the ten gentlemen round the Board table had made it impossible for them to consult freely without being overheard, but the low-voiced transference of thought travelling round was summed up at last by Mr. Brownbee.

"We think, Mr. Heythorp, that your fees and dividends should en- able you to set aside for us a larger sum. Sixteen hundred, in fact, is what we think you should give us yearly. Representing, as we do, six-teen thousand pounds, the prospect is not cheering, but we hope you have some good years before you yet. We understand your income to be two thousand pounds."

Old Heythorp shook his head. "Nineteen hundred and thirty pounds in a good year. Must eat and drink; must have a man to look after me—not as active as I was. Can't do on less than five hundred pounds. Fourteen hundred's all I can give you, gentlemen; it's an advance of two hundred pounds. That's my last word."

The silence was broken by Mr. Ventnor.

"And it's my last word that I'm not satisfied. If these other gentle-man accept your proposition I shall be forced to consider what I can do on my own account."

The old man stared at him, and answered:

"Oh! you will, sir; we shall see."

The others had risen and were gathered in a knot at the end of the table; old Heythorp and Mr. Ventnor alone remained seated. The old man's lower lip projected till the white hairs below stood out like bristles. 'You ugly dog,' he was thinking, 'you think you've got something up your sleeve. Well, do your worst!' The "ugly dog" rose abruptly and joined the others. And old Heythorp closed his eyes, sitting per-fectly still, with his cigar, which had gone out, sticking up between his teeth. Mr. Brownbee turning to voice the decision come to, cleared his throat.

"Mr. Heythorp," he said, "if your bankers and solicitors bear out your statements, we shall accept your offer *faute de mieux*, in considera-tion of your——" but meeting the old man's eyes, which said so very plainly: "Blow your consideration!" he ended with a stammer. "Per-haps you will kindly furnish us with the authorization you spoke of?"

Old Heythorp nodded, and Mr. Brownbee, with a little bow, clasped his hat to his breast and moved towards the door. The nine gentlemen followed. Mr. Ventnor, bringing up the rear, turned and looked back. But the old man's eyes were already closed again.

The moment his creditors were gone, old Heythorp sounded the hand-bell.

"Help me up, Mr. Farney. That Ventnor—what's his holding?"

"Quite small. Only ten shares, I think."

"Ah! What time is it?"

"Quarter to four, sir."

"Get me a taxi."

After visiting his bank and his solicitors he struggled once more into his cab and caused it to be driven towards Millicent Villas. A kind of sleepy triumph permeated his whole being, bumped and shaken by the cab's rapid progress. So! He was free of those sharks now so long as he could hold on to his Companies; and he would still have a hundred a year or more to spare for Rosamund and her youngsters. He could live on four hundred, or even three-fifty, without losing his independence, for there would be no standing life in that holy woman's house unless he could pay his own scot! A good day's work! The best for many a long month!

The cab stopped before the villa.

3 §

There are rooms which refuse to give away their owners, and rooms which seem to say: 'They really are like this.' Of such was Rosamund Larne's—a sort of permanent confession, seeming to remark to anyone who entered: 'Her taste? Well, you can see—cheerful and exuberant; her habits—yes, she sits here all the morning in a dressing-gown, smoking cigarettes and dropping ink; kindly observe my carpet. Notice the piano —it has a look of coming and going, according to the exchequer. This very deep-cushioned sofa is permanent, however; the water-colors on the walls are safe, too—they're by herself. Mark the scent of mimosa— she likes flowers, and likes them strong. No clock, of course. Examine the bureau—she is obviously always ringing for "the drumstick," and saying: "Where's this, Ellen, and where's that? You naughty gairl, you've been tidying." Cast an eye on that pile of manuscript—she has evidently a genius for composition; it flows off her pen—like Shakespeare, she never blots a line. See how she's had the electric light put in, instead of that horrid gas; but try and turn either of them on—you can't; last quarter isn't paid, of course; and she uses an oil lamp, you can tell that by the ceiling. The dog over there, who will not answer to the name of "Carmen," a Pekinese spaniel like a little Djin, all prominent eyes rolling their blacks, and no nose between—yes, Carmen looks as if she didn't know what was coming next; she's right—it's a pet-and-slap-again life! Consider, too, the fittings of the tea-tray, rather soiled, though not quite tin, but I say unto you that no millionaire's in all its glory ever had a liqueur bottle on it.'

When old Heythorp entered this room, which extended from back to front of the little house, preceded by the announcement "Mr. Æsop," it was resonant with a very clatter-bodandigo of noises, from Phyllis playing the Machiche; from the boy Jock on the hearthrug, emitting at short intervals the most piercing notes from an ocarina; from Mrs. Larne on the sofa, talking with her trailing volubility to Bob Pillin; from Bob Pillin muttering: "Ye—es! Qui-ite! Ye—es!" and gazing at Phyllis over his collar. And, on the window-sill, as far as she could get from all this noise, the little dog Carmen was rolling her eyes. At sight of their visitor Jock blew one rending screech, and bolting behind the sofa, placed his chin on its top, so that nothing but his round pink unmoving face was visible, and the dog Carmen tried to climb the blind cord.

Encircled from behind by the arms of Phyllis, and preceded by the gracious perfumed bulk of Mrs. Larne, old Heythorp was escorted to the sofa. It was low, and when he had plumped down on to it, the boy Jock emitted a hollow groan. Bob Pillin was the first to break the silence.

"How are you, sir? I hope it's gone through."

Old Heythorp nodded. His eyes were fixed on the liqueur, and Mrs. Larne murmured:

"Guardy, you *must* try our new liqueur. Jock, you awful boy, get up and bring Guardy a glass."

The boy Jock approached the tea-table, took up a glass, put it to his eye and filled it rapidly.

"You horrible boy, you could see that glass has been used."

In a high round voice rather like an angel's, Jock answered:

"All right, Mother; I'll get rid of it," and rapidly swallowing the yellow liqueur, took up another glass.

Mrs. Larne laughed.

"What *am* I to do with him?"

A loud shriek prevented a response. Phyllis, who had taken her brother by the ear to lead him to the door, let him go to clasp her injured self. Bob Pillin went hastening towards her; and following the young man with her chin, Mrs. Larne said, smiling:

"Aren't those children awful? He's such a nice fellow. We like him so much, Guardy."

The old man grinned. So she was making up to that young pup! Rosamund Larne, watching him, murmured:

"Oh! Guardy, you're as bad as Jock. He takes after you terribly. Look at the shape of his head. Jock, come here!" The innocent boy approached; with his girlish complexion, his flowery blue eyes, his perfect mouth, he stood before his mother like a large cherub. And suddenly he blew his ocarina in a dreadful manner. Mrs. Larne launched a box at his ears, and receiving the wind of it he fell prone.

"That's the way he behaves. Be off with you, you awful boy. I want to talk to Guardy."

The boy withdrew on his stomach, and sat against the wall cross-legged, fixing his innocent round eyes on old Heythorp. Mrs. Larne sighed.

"Things are worse and worse, Guardy. I'm at my wit's end to tide over this quarter. You wouldn't advance me a hundred on my new story? I'm sure to get two for it in the end."

The old man shook his head.

"I've done something for you and the children," he said. "You'll get notice of it in a day or two; ask no questions."

"Oh! Guardy! Oh, you dear!" And her gaze rested on Bob Pillin, leaning over the piano, where Phyllis again sat.

Old Heythorp snorted. "What are you cultivating that young gaby for? She mustn't be grabbed up by any fool who comes along."

Mrs. Larne murmured at once:

"Of course, the dear gairl is *much* too young. Phyllis, come and talk to Guardy!"

When the girl was installed beside him on the sofa, and he had felt that little thrill of warmth the proximity of youth can bring, he said:

"Been a good girl?"

She shook her head.

"Can't when Jock's not at school. Mother can't pay for him this term."

Hearing his name, the boy Jock blew his ocarina till Mrs. Larne drove him from the room, and Phyllis went on:

"He's more awful than anything you can think of. Was my dad at all like him, Guardy? Mother's always so mysterious about him. I suppose you knew him well."

Old Heythorp, incapable of confusion, answered stolidly:

"Not very."

"Who was *his* father? I don't believe even mother knows."

"Man about town in my day."

"Oh! your day must have been jolly. Did you wear peg-top trousers, and dundrearies?"

Old Heythorp nodded.

"What larks! And I suppose you had lots of adventures with opera dancers and gambling. The young men are all so good now." Her eyes rested on Bob Pillin. "That young man's a perfect stick of goodness."

Old Heythorp grunted.

"You wouldn't know how good he was," Phyllis went on musingly, "unless you'd sat next him in a tunnel. The other day he had his waist squeezed and he simply sat still and did nothing. And then when the tunnel ended, it was Jock after all, not me. His face was—Oh! ah! ha! ha! Ah! ha!" She threw back her head, displaying all her white, round throat. Then edging near, she whispered:

"He likes to pretend, of course, that he's fearfully lively. He's promised to take mother and me to the theatre and supper afterwards. Won't it be scrummy! Only, I haven't anything to go in."

Old Heythorp said: "What do you want? Irish poplin?"

Her mouth opened wide: "Oh! Guardy! Soft white satin!"

"How many yards'll go round you?"

"I should think about twelve. We could make it ourselves. You *are* a chook!"

A scent of hair, like hay, enveloped him, her lips bobbed against his nose, and there came a feeling in his heart as when he rolled the first sip of a special wine against his palate. This little house was a rumpty-too affair, her mother was a humbug, the boy a cheeky young rascal, but there was a warmth here he never felt in that big house which had been his wife's and was now his holy daughter's. And once more he rejoiced at his day's work, and the success of his breach of trust, which put some little ground beneath these young feet, in a hard and un-scrupulous world. Phyllis whispered in his ear:

"Guardy, do look; he *will* stare at me like that. Isn't it awful—like a boiled rabbit?"

Bob Pillin, attentive to Mrs. Larne, was gazing with all his might over her shoulder at the girl. The young man was moonstruck, that was clear! There was something almost touching in the stare of those puppy-dog's eyes. And he thought: 'Young beggar—wish I were his age!' The utter injustice of having an old and helpless body, when your desire for enjoyment was as great as ever! They said a man was as old as he felt Fools! A man was as old as his legs and arms, and not a day younger. He heard the girl beside him utter a discomfortable sound, and saw her face cloud as if tears were not far off; she jumped up, and going to the window, lifted the little dog and buried her face in its brown and white fur. Old Heythorp thought: 'She sees that her humbugging mother is using her as a decoy.' But she had come back, and the little dog, rolling its eyes horribly at the strange figure on the sofa, in a desperate effort to escape succeeded in reaching her shoulder, where it stayed perched like a cat, held by one paw and trying to back away into space. Old Heythorp said abruptly:

"Are you very fond of your mother?"

"Of course I am, Guardy. I adore her."

"H'm! Listen to me. When you come of age or marry, you'll have a hundred and twenty a year of your own that you can't get rid of. Don't ever be persuaded into doing what you don't want. And remember: Your mother's a sieve, no good giving her money; keep what you'll get for yourself—it's only a pittance, and you'll want it all—every penny."

Phyllis's eyes had opened very wide; so that he wondered if she had taken in his words.

"Oh! Isn't money horrible, Guardy?"

"The want of it."

"No, it's beastly altogether. If only we were like birds. Or if one could put out a plate overnight, and have just enough in the morning to use during the day."

Old Heythorp sighed.

"There's only one thing in life that matters—independence. Lose that, and you lose everything. That's the value of money. Help me up."

Phyllis stretched out her hands, and the little dog, running down her back, resumed its perch on the windowsill, close to the blind cord.

Once on his feet, old Heythorp said:

"Give me a kiss. You'll have your satin to-morrow."

Then looking at Bob Pillin, he remarked:

"Going my way? I'll give you a lift."

The young man, giving Phyllis one appealing look, answered dully: "Tha—anks!" and they went out together to the taxi. In that draughtless vehicle they sat, full of who knows what contempt of age for youth, and youth for age; the old man resenting this young pup's aspiration to his granddaughter; the young man annoyed that this old image had dragged him away before he wished to go. Old Heythorp said at last:

"Well?"

Thus expected to say something, Bob Pillin muttered:

"Glad your meetin' went off well, sir. You scored a triumph I should think."

"Why?"

"Oh! I don't know. I thought you had a good bit of opposition to contend with."

Old Heythorp looked at him.

"Your grandmother!" he said; then, with his habitual instinct of attack, added: "You make the most of your opportunities, I see."

At this rude assault Bob Pillin's red-cheeked face assumed a certain dignity. "I don't know what you mean, sir. Mrs. Larne is very kind to me."

"No doubt. But don't try to pick the flowers."

Thoroughly upset, Bob Pillin preserved a dogged silence. This fortnight, since he had first met Phyllis in old Heythorp's hall, had been the most singular of his existence up to now. He would never have believed that a fellow could be so quickly and completely bowled, could succumb without a kick, without even wanting to kick. To one with his philosophy of having a good time and never committing himself too far, it was in the nature of "a fair knock-out," and yet so pleasurable, except for the wear and tear about one's chances. If only he knew how far the old boy really counted in the matter! To say: "My intentions are strictly honorable" would be old-fashioned; besides—the old fellow might have no right to hear it. They called him Guardy, but without knowing more he did not want to admit the old curmudgeon's right to interfere.

"Are you a relation of theirs, sir?"

Old Heythorp nodded.

Bob Pillin went on with desperation:

"I should like to know what your objection to me is."

The old man turned his head so far as he was able; a grim smile bristled the hairs about his lips, and twinkled in his eyes. What did he object to? Why—everything! Object to! That sleek head, those puppy-dog eyes, fattish red cheeks, high collars, pearl pin, spats, and drawl—pah! the imbecility, the smugness of his mug; no go, no devil in any of his sort, in any of these fish-veined, coddled-up young bloods; nothing but playing for safety! And he wheezed out:

"Milk and water masquerading as port wine."

Bob Pillin frowned.

It was almost too much for the composure even of a man of the world. That this paralytic old fellow should express contempt for his virility was really the last thing in jests. Luckily he could not take it seriously. But suddenly he thought: 'What if he really has the power to stop my going there, and means to turn them against me!' And his heart quailed.

"Awfully sorry, sir," he said, "if you don't think I'm wild enough. Anything I can do for you in that line——"

The old man grunted; and realizing that he had been quite witty, Bob Pillin went on:

"I know I'm not in debt, no entanglements, got a decent income, pretty good expectations and all that; but I can soon put that all right if I'm not fit without."

It was perhaps his first attempt at irony, and he could not help thinking how good it was.

But old Heythorp preserved a deadly silence. He looked like a stuffed man, a regular Aunt Sally sitting there, with the fixed red in his cheeks, his stivered hair, square block of a body, and no neck that you could see—only wanting the pipe in his mouth! Could there really be danger from such an old idol? The idol spoke:

"I'll give you a word of advice. Don't hang around there, or you'll burn your fingers. Remember me to your father. Good-night!"

The taxi had stopped before the house in Sefton Park. An insensate impulse to remain seated and argue the point fought in Bob Pillin with an impulse to leap out, shake his fist in at the window, and walk off. He merely said, however:

"Thanks for the lift. Good-night!" And, getting out deliberately, he walked off.

Old Heythorp, waiting for the driver to help him up, thought:

"Fatter, but no more guts than his father!"

In his sanctum he sank at once into his chair. It was wonderfully still there every day at this hour; just the click of the coals, just the faintest ruffle from the wind in the trees of the park. And it was cosily warm, only the fire lightening the darkness. A drowsy beatitude pervaded the old man. A good day's work! A triumph—that young pup had said. Yes! Something of a triumph! He had held on, and won. And dinner to look forward to, yet. A nap—a nap! And soon, rhythmic, soft, sonorous, his breathing rose, with now and then that pathetic twitching of the old who dream.

III

1 §

When Bob Pillin emerged from the little front garden of 23, Millicent Villas ten days later, his sentiments were ravelled, and he could not get hold of an end to pull straight the stuff of his mind.

He had found Mrs. Larne and Phyllis in the sitting-room, and Phyllis had been crying; he was sure she had been crying; and that memory still infected the sentiments evoked by later happenings. Old Heythorp had said: "You'll burn your fingers." The process had begun. Having sent her daughter away on a pretext really a bit too thin, Mrs. Larne had installed him beside her scented bulk on the sofa, and poured into his ear such a tale of monetary woe and entanglement, such a mass of present difficulties and rosy prospects, that his brain still whirled, and only one thing emerged clearly—that she wanted fifty pounds, which she would repay him on quarter-day; for their Guardy had made a settlement by which, until the dear children came of age, she would have sixty pounds every quarter. It was only a question of a few weeks; he might ask Messrs. Scriven and Coles; they would tell him the security was quite safe. He certainly might ask Messrs. Scriven and Coles—they happened to be his father's solicitors; but it hardly seemed to touch the point. Bob Pillin had a certain shrewd caution, and the point was whether he was going to begin to lend money to a woman who, he could see, might borrow up to seventy times seven on the strength of his infatuation for her daughter. That was rather too strong! Yet, if he didn't—she might take a sudden dislike to him, and where would he be then? Besides, would not a loan make his position stronger? And then—such is the effect of love even on the younger generation—that thought seemed to him unworthy. If he lent at all, it would be from chivalry—ulterior motives might go hang! And the memory of the tear-marks on Phyllis's pretty pale-pink cheeks; and her petulantly mournful: "Oh! young man, isn't money beastly!" scraped his heart, and ravished his judgment. All the same, fifty pounds was fifty pounds, and goodness knew how much more; and what did he know of Mrs. Larne, after all, except that she was a relative of old Heythorp's, and wrote stories—told them too, if he was not mistaken? Perhaps it would be better to see Scrivens'. But again that absurd nobility assaulted him. Phyllis! Phyllis! Besides, were not settlements always drawn so that they refused to form security for anything? Thus, hampered and troubled, he hailed a cab. He was dining with the Ventnors on the Cheshire side, and would be late if he didn't get home sharp to dress.

Driving, white-tied and waistcoated, in his father's car, he thought with a certain contumely of the younger Ventnor girl, whom he had been wont to consider pretty before he knew Phyllis. And seated next her at dinner, he quite enjoyed his new sense of superiority to her charms, and the ease with which he could chaff and be agreeable. And all the time he suffered from the suppressed longing which scarcely ever left him now, to think and talk of Phyllis. Ventnor's fizz was good and plentiful, his old Madeira absolutely first chop, and the only other man present a teetotal curate, who withdrew with the ladies to talk his parish shop. Favored by these circumstances, and the perception that

Ventnor was an agreeable fellow, Bob Pillin yielded to his secret itch to get near the subject of his affections.

"Do you happen," he said airily, "to know a Mrs. Larne—relative of old Heythorp's—rather a handsome woman—she writes stories."

Mr. Ventnor shook his head. A closer scrutiny than Bob Pillin's would have seen that he also moved his ears.

"Of old Heythorp's? Didn't know he had any, except his daughter, and that son of his in the Admiralty."

Bob Pillin felt the glow of his secret hobby spreading within him.

"She is, though—lives rather out of town; got a son and daughter. I thought you might know her stories—clever woman."

Mr. Ventnor smiled.

"Ah!" he said enigmatically, "these lady novelists! Does she make any money by them?"

Bob Pillin knew that to make money by writing meant success, but that not to make money by writing was artistic, and implied that you had private means, which perhaps was even more distinguished. And he said:

"Oh! she has private means, I know."

Mr. Ventnor reached for the Madeira.

"So she's a relative of old Heythorp's," he said. "He's a very old friend of your father's. He ought to go bankrupt, you know."

To Bob Pillin, glowing with passion and Madeira, the idea of bankruptcy seemed discreditable in connection with a relative of Phyllis. Besides, the old boy was far from that! Had he not just made this settlement on Mrs. Larne? And he said:

"I think you're mistaken. That's of the past."

Mr. Ventnor smiled.

"Will you bet?" he said.

Bob Pillin also smiled. "I should be bettin' on a certainty."

Mr. Ventnor passed his hand over his whiskered face. "Don't you believe it; he hasn't a mag to his name. Fill your glass."

Bob Pillin said, with a certain resentment:

"Well, I happen to know he's just made a settlement of five or six thousand pounds. Don't know if you call that being bankrupt."

"What! On this Mrs. Larne?"

Confused, uncertain whether he had said something derogatory or indiscreet, or something which added distinction to Phyllis, Bob Pillin hesitated, then gave a nod.

Mr. Ventnor rose and extended his short legs before the fire.

"No, my boy," he said. "No!"

Unaccustomed to flat contradiction, Bob Pillin reddened.

"I'll bet you a tenner. Ask Scrivens'."

Mr. Ventnor ejaculated:

"Scrivens'—but they're not——" then, staring rather hard he added: "I won't bet. You may be right. Scrivens' are your father's solicitors too, aren't they? Always been sorry he didn't come to me. Shall we join the ladies?" And to the drawing-room he preceded a young man more uncertain in his mind than on his feet. . . .

Charles Ventnor was not one to let you see that more was going on within than met the eye. But there was a good deal going on that evening, and after his conversation with young Bob he had occasion more than once to turn away and rub his hands together. When, after that second creditors' meeting, he had walked down the stairway which led to the offices of "The Island Navigation Company," he had been deep in thought. Short, squarely built, rather stout, with moustache and large mutton-chop whiskers of a red-brown, and a faint floridity in face and dress, he impressed at first sight only by a certain truly British vulgarity. One felt that here was a hail-fellow-well-met man who liked lunch and dinner, went to Scarborough for his summer holidays, sat on his wife, took his daughters out in a boat and was never sick. One felt that he went to church every Sunday morning, looked upwards as he moved through life, disliked the unsuccessful, and expanded with his second glass of wine. But then a clear look into his well-clothed face and red-brown eyes would give the feeling: 'There's something fulvous here; he might be a bit too foxy.' A third look brought the thought: 'He's certainly a bully.' He was not a large creditor of old Heythorp. With interest on the original, he calculated his claim at three hundred pounds—unredeemed shares in that old Ecuador mine. But he had waited for his money eight years, and could never imagine how it came about that he had been induced to wait so long. There had been, of course, for one who liked "big pots," a certain glamour about the personality of old Heythorp, still a bit of a swell in shipping circles, and a bit of an aristocrat in Liverpool. But during the last year Charles Ventnor had realized that the old chap's star had definitely set—when that happens, of course, there is no more glamour, and the time has come to get your money. Weakness in oneself and others is despicable! Besides, he had food for thought, and descending the stairs he chewed it. He smelt a rat—creatures for which both by nature and profession he had a nose. Through Bob Pillin, on whom he sometimes dwelt in connection with his younger daughter, he knew that old Pillin and old Heythorp had been friends for thirty years and more. That, to an astute mind, suggested something behind this sale. The thought had already occurred to him when he read his copy of the report. A commission would be a breach of trust, of course, but there were ways of doing things; the old chap was devilish hard pressed, and human nature was human nature! His lawyerish mind habitually put two and two together. The old fellow had deliberately appointed to meet his creditors again just after the general meeting which would decide the purchase— had said he might do something for them then. Had that no significance?

In these circumstances Charles Ventnor had come to the meeting with eyes wide open and mouth tight closed. And he had watched. It was certainly remarkable that such an old and feeble man with no neck at all, who looked indeed as if he might go off with apoplexy any moment, should actually say that he "stood or fell" by this purchase, knowing that if he fell he would be a beggar. Why should the old chap be so keen on getting it through? It would do him personally no good, unless—Exactly! He had left the meeting, therefore, secretly confident that old Heythorp had got something out of this transaction which would enable him to make a substantial proposal to his creditors. So that when the old man had declared that he was going to make none, something was turned sour in his heart, and he had said to himself: "All right, you old rascal! You don't know C. V." The cavalier manner of that beggarly old rip, the defiant look of his deep little eyes, had put a polish on the rancor of one who prided himself on letting no man get the better of him. All that evening, seated on one side of the fire, while Mrs. Ventnor sat on the other, and the younger daughter played Gounod's Serenade on the violin—he cogitated. And now and again he smiled, but not too much. He did not see his way as yet, but had little doubt that before long he would. It would not be hard to knock that chipped old idol off his perch. There was already a healthy feeling among the shareholders that he was past work and should be scrapped. The old chap should find that Charles V. was not to be defied; that when he got his teeth into a thing, he did not let it go. By hook or crook he would have the old man off his Boards, or his debt out of him as the price of leaving him alone. His life or his money— and the old fellow should determine which. With the memory of that defiance fresh within him, he almost hoped it might come to be the first, and turning to Mrs. Ventnor, he said abruptly:

"Have a little dinner Friday week, and ask young Pillin and the curate." He specified the curate, a teetotaller, because he had two daughters, and males and females must be paired, but he intended to pack him off after dinner to the drawing-room to discuss parish matters while he and Bob Pillin sat over their wine. What he expected to get out of the young man he did not as yet know.

On the day of the dinner, before departing for the office, he had gone to his cellar. Would three bottles of Perrier Jouet do the trick, or must he add one of the old Madeira? He decided to be on the safe side. A bottle or so of champagne went very little way with him personally, and young Pillin might be another.

The Madeira having done its work by turning the conversation into such an admirable channel, he had cut it short for fear young Pillin might drink the lot or get wind of the rat. And when his guests were gone, and his family had retired, he stood staring into the fire, putting together the pieces of the puzzle. Five or six thousand pounds—six would be ten per cent. on sixty! Exactly! Scrivens'—young Pillin had said! But Crow & Donkin, not Scriven & Coles, were old Heythorp's solicitors. What could that mean, save that the old man wanted to cover the tracks of a secret commission, and had handled the matter through solicitors who did not know the state of his affairs! But why Pillin's solicitors? With this sale just going through, it must look deuced fishy to them too. Was it all a mare's nest, after all? In such circumstances he himself would have taken the matter to a London firm who knew nothing of anybody. Puzzled, therefore, and rather disheartened, feeling too that touch of liver which was wont to follow his old Madeira, he went up to bed and woke his wife to ask her why the dickens they couldn't always have soup like that!

Next day he continued to brood over his puzzle, and no fresh light came; but having a matter on which his firm and Scrivens' were in touch, he decided to go over in person, and see if he could surprise something out of them. Feeling, from experience, that any really delicate matter would only be entrusted to the most responsible member of the firm, he had asked to see Scriven himself, and just as he had taken his hat to go, he said casually:

"By the way, you do some business for old Mr. Heythorp, don't you?"

Scriven, raising his eyebrows a little, muttered: "Er—no," in exactly the tone Mr. Ventnor himself used when he wished to imply that though he didn't as a fact do business, he probably soon would. He knew therefore that the answer was a true one. And nonplussed, he hazarded:

"Oh! I thought you did, in regard to a Mrs. Larne."

This time he had certainly drawn blood of sorts, for down came Scriven's eyebrows, and he said:

"Mrs. Larne—we know a Mrs. Larne, but not in that connection. Why?"

"Oh! Young Pillin told me——"

"Young Pillin! Why, it's his——!" A little pause, and then: "Old Mr. Heythorp's solicitors are Crow & Donkin, I believe."

Mr. Ventnor held out his hand. "Yes, yes," he said; "good-bye. Glad to have got that matter settled up," and out he went, and down the street, important, smiling. By George! He had got it! "It's his father"—Scriven had been going to say. What a plant! Exactly! Oh! neat! Old Pillin had made the settlement direct; and the solicitors were in the dark; that disposed of his difficulty about *them.* No money had passed between old Pillin and old Heythorp—not a penny. Oh! neat! But not neat enough for Charles Ventnor, who had that nose for rats. Then his smile died, and with a little chill he perceived that it was all based on supposition—not quite good enough to go on! What then? Somehow he must see this Mrs. Larne, or better—old Pillin himself. The point to ascertain was whether she had any connection of her own with Pillin. Clearly young Pillin didn't know of it; for, according to him, old Heythorp had made the settlement. By Jove! That old rascal was deep—all the more satisfaction in proving that he was not as deep as C. V. To unmask the old cheat was already beginning to seem in the nature of a public service. But on what pretext could he visit Pillin? A subscription to the Windeatt almshouses! That would make him talk in self-defence and he would take care to press the request to the actual point of getting a subscription. He caused himself to be driven to the Pillin residence in Sefton Park. Ushered into a room on the ground floor, heated in American fashion, Mr. Ventnor unbuttoned his coat. A man of sanguine constitution, he found this hot-house atmosphere a little trying. And having sympathetically obtained Joe Pillin's reluctant refusal—Quite so! One could not indefinitely extend one's subscriptions even for the best of causes!—he said gently:

"By the way, you know Mrs. Larne, don't you?"

The effect of that simple shot surpassed his highest hopes. Joe Pillin's face, never highly colored, turned a sort of grey; he opened his thin lips, shut them quickly, as birds do, and something seemed to pass with difficulty down his scraggy throat. The hollows, which nerve exhaustion delves in the cheeks of men whose cheek-bones are not high, increased alarmingly. For a moment he looked deathly; then, moistening his lips, he said:

"Larne—Larne? No, I don't seem——"

Mr. Ventnor, who had taken care to be drawing on his gloves, murmured:

"Oh! I thought—your son knows her; a relation of old Heythorp's," and he looked up.

Joe Pillin had his handkerchief to his mouth; he coughed feebly, then with more and more vigor:

"I'm in very poor health," he said, at last. "I'm getting abroad at once. This cold's killing me. What name did you say?" And he remained with his handkerchief against his teeth.

Mr. Ventnor repeated:

"Larne. Writes stories."

Joe Pillin muttered into his handkerchief:

"Ah! H'm! No—I—no! My son knows all sorts of people. I shall have to try Mentone. Are you going? Good-bye! Good-bye! I'm sorry; oh! ha! My cough—ah! ha h'h'm! Very distressing. Ye-hes! My cough—ah! ha h'h'm! Most distressing. Ye-hes!"

Out in the drive Mr. Ventnor took a deep breath of the frosty air. Not much doubt now! The two names had worked like charms. This weakly old fellow would make a pretty witness, would simply crumple under cross-examination. What a contrast to that hoary old sinner Heythorp, whose brazenness nothing could affect. The rat was as large as life! And the only point was how to make the best use of it. Then —for his experience was wide—the possibility dawned on him, that after all, this Mrs. Larne might only have been Old Pillin's mistress— or be his natural daughter, or have some other black-mailing hold on him. Any such connection would account for his agitation, for his denying her, for his son's ignorance. Only it wouldn't account for young Pillin's saying that old Heythorp had made the settlement. He could only have got that from the woman herself. Still, to make absolutely sure, he had better try and see her. But how? It would never do to ask Bob Pillin for an introduction, after this interview with his father. He would have to go on his own and chance it. Wrote stories did she? Perhaps a newspaper would know her address; or the Directory would give it—not a common name! And, hot on the scent, he drove to a post office. Yes, there it was, right enough! "Larne, Mrs. R.—23, Millicent Villas." And thinking to himself: 'No time like the present,' he turned in that direction. The job was delicate. He must be careful not to do anything which might compromise his power of making public use of his knowledge. Yes—ticklish! What he did now must have a proper legal bottom. Still, anyway you looked at it, he had a *right* to investigate a fraud on himself as a shareholder of "The Island Navigation Company," and a fraud on himself as a creditor of old Heythorp. Quite! But suppose this Mrs. Larne was really entangled with old Pillin, and the settlement a mere reward of virtue, easy or otherwise. Well! in that case there'd be no secret commission to make public, and he needn't go further. So that, in either event, he would be all right. Only—how to introduce himself? He might pretend he was a newspaper man wanting a story. No, that wouldn't do! He must not represent that he was what he was not, in case he had afterwards to justify his actions publicly, always a difficult thing, if you were not careful! At that moment there came into his mind a question Bob Pillin had asked the other night. "By the way, you can't borrow on a settlement, can you? Isn't there generally some clause against it?" Had this woman been trying to borrow from him on that settlement? But at this moment he reached the house, and got out of his cab still undecided as to how he was going to work the oracle. Impudence, constitutional and professional, sustained him in saying to the little maid:

"Mrs. Larne at home? Say Mr. Charles Ventnor, will you?"

His quick brown eyes took in the apparel of the passage which served for hall—the deep blue paper on the walls, lilac-patterned curtains over the doors, the well-known print of a nude young woman looking over her shoulder, and he thought: "H'm! Distinctly tasty!" They noted, too, a small brown-and-white dog cowering in terror at the very end of the passage, and he murmured affably: "Fluffy! Come here, Fluffy!" till Carmen's teeth chattered in her head.

"Will you come in, sir?"

Mr. Ventnor ran his hand over his whiskers, and, entering a room, was impressed at once by its air of domesticity. On a sofa a handsome woman and a pretty young girl were surrounded by sewing apparatus and some white material. The girl looked up, but the elder lady rose.

Mr. Ventnor said easily:

"You know my young friend, Mr. Robert Pillin, I think."

The lady, whose bulk and bloom struck him to the point of admiration, murmured in a full sweet drawl:

"Oh! Ye—es. Are you from Messrs. Scrivens'?"

With the swift reflection: 'As I thought!' Mr. Ventnor answered:

"Er—not exactly. I *am* a solicitor though; came just to ask about a certain settlement that Mr. Pillin tells me you're entitled under."

"Phyllis dear!"

Seeing the girl about to rise from underneath the white stuff, Mr. Ventnor said quickly:

"Pray don't disturb yourself—just a formality!" It had struck him at once that the lady would have to speak the truth in the presence of this third party, and he went on: "Quite recent, I think. This'll be your first interest—on six thousand pounds? Is that right?" And at the limpid assent of that rich, sweet voice, he thought: 'Fine woman; what eyes!'

Thank you; that's quite enough. I can go to Scrivens' for any detail. Nice young fellow, Bob Pillin, isn't he?" He saw the girl's chin tilt, and Mrs. Larne's full mouth curling in a smile.

"Delightful young man; we're very fond of him."

And he proceeded:

"I'm quite an old friend of his; have you known him long?"

"Oh! no. How long, Phyllis, since we met him at Guardy's? About a month. But he's so unaffected—quite at home with us. A *nice* fellow."

Mr. Ventnor murmured:

"Very different from his father, isn't he?"

"Is he! We don't know his father; he's a shipowner, I think."

Mr. Ventnor rubbed his hands: "Ye—es," he said, "just giving up —a warm man. Young Pillin's a lucky fellow—only son. So you met him at old Mr. Heythorp's. I know him too—relation of yours, I believe."

"Our dear Guardy—such a wonderful man."

Mr. Ventnor echoed: "Wonderful—regular old Roman."

"Oh! but he's so *kind!*" Mrs. Larne lifted the white stuff: "Look what he's given this naughty gairl!"

Mr. Ventnor murmured: "Charming! Charming! Bob Pillin said, I think, that Mr. Heythorp was your settlor."

One of those little clouds which visit the brows of women who have owed money in their time passed swiftly athwart Mrs. Larne's eyes. For a moment they seemed saying: 'Don't you want to know too much?' Then they slid from under it.

"Won't you sit down?" she said. "You must forgive our being at work."

Mr. Ventnor, who had need of sorting his impressions, shook his head.

"Thank you; I must be getting on. Then Messrs. Scriven can— a mere formality! Good-bye! Good-bye, Miss Larne. I'm sure the dress will be most becoming."

And with memories of a too clear look from the girl's eyes, of a warm firm pressure from the woman's hand, Mr. Ventnor backed

towards the door and passed away just in time to avoid hearing in two
voices:

"What a nice lawyer!"

"What a horrid man!"

Back in his cab, he continued to rub his hands. No, she *didn't* know
old Pillin! That was certain; not from her words, but from her face.
She wanted to know him, or about him, anyway. She was trying to
hook young Bob for that sprig of a girl—it was clear as mud. H'm!
it would astonish his young friend to hear that he had called. Well,
let it! And a curious mixture of emotions beset Mr. Ventnor. He saw
the whole thing now so plainly, and really could not refrain from a certain admiration. The law had been properly diddled! There was nothing to prevent a man from settling money on a woman he had never
seen; and so old Pillin's settlement could probably not be upset. But
old Heythorp could. It was neat, though, oh! neat! And that was a
fine woman—remarkably! He had a sort of feeling that if only the
settlement had been in danger, it might have been worth while to have
made a bargain—a woman like that could have made it worth while!
And he believed her quite capable of entertaining the proposition! Her
eye! Pity—quite a pity! Mrs. Ventnor was not a wife who satisfied
every aspiration. But alas! the settlement was safe. This baulking of
the sentiment of love, whipped up, if anything, the longing for justice
in Mr. Ventnor. That old chap should feel his teeth now. As a piece
of investigation it was not so bad—not so bad at all! He had had a
bit of luck, of course—no, not luck—just that knack of doing the right
thing at the right moment which marks a real genius for affairs.

But getting into his train to return to Mrs. Ventnor, he thought:
'A woman like that would have been——!' And he sighed.

2 §

With a neatly written cheque for fifty pounds in his pocket Bob
Pillin turned in at 23, Millicent Villas on the afternoon after Mr. Ventnor's visit. Chivalry had won the day. And he rang the bell with an
elation which astonished him, for he knew he was doing a soft thing.

"Mrs. Larne is out, sir; Miss Phyllis is at home."

His heart leaped.

"Oh—h! I'm sorry. I wonder if she'd see me?"

The little maid answered:

"I think she's been washin' 'er 'air, sir, but it may be dry be now.
I'll see."

Bob Pillin stood stock still beneath the young woman on the wall. He could scarcely breathe. If her hair were not dry—how awful! Suddenly he heard, floating down a clear but smothered: "Oh! Gefoozleme!" and other words which he could not catch. The little maid came running down.

"Miss Phyllis says, sir, she'll be with you in a jiffy. And I was to tell you that Master Jock is loose, sir."

Bob Pillin answered "Tha—anks," and passed into the drawing-room. He went to the bureau, took an envelope, enclosed the cheque, and addressing it: "Mrs. Larne," replaced it in his pocket. Then he crossed over to the mirror. Never till this last month had he really doubted his own face; but now he wanted for it things he had never wanted. It had too much flesh and color. It did not reflect his passion. This was a handicap. With a narrow white piping round his waistcoat opening, and a button-hole of tuberoses, he had tried to repair its deficiencies. But do what he would, he was never easy about himself nowadays, never up to that pitch which could make him confident in her presence. And until this month to lack confidence had never been his wont. A clear, high, mocking voice said:

"Oh—h! Conceited young man!"

And spinning round he saw Phyllis in the doorway. Her light brown hair was fluffed out on her shoulders, so that he felt a kind of fainting-sweet sensation, and murmured inarticulately:

"Oh! I say—how jolly!"

"Lawks! It's awful! Have you come to see mother?"

Balanced between fear and daring, conscious of a scent of hay and verbena and camomile, Bob Pillin stammered:

"Ye—es. I—I'm glad she's not in, though."

Her laugh seemed to him terribly unfeeling.

"Oh! oh! Don't be foolish. Sit down. Isn't washing one's head awful?"

Bob Pillin answered feebly:

"Of course, I haven't much experience."

Her mouth opened.

"Oh! You *are*—aren't you?"

And he thought desperately: "Dare I—oughtn't I—couldn't I somehow take her hand or put my arm round her, or something?" Instead, he sat very rigid at his end of the sofa, while she sat lax and lissom at the other, and one of those crises of paralysis which beset would-be lovers fixed him to the soul.

Sometimes during this last month memories of a past existence, when chaff and even kisses came readily to the lips, and girls were fair game, would make him think: 'Is she really such an innocent? Does she really want me to kiss her?" Alas! such intrusions lasted but a moment before a blast of awe and chivalry withered them, and a strange and tragic delicacy—like nothing he had ever known—resumed its sway. And suddenly he heard her say:

"Why do you know such awful men?"

"What? I don't know any *awful* men."

"Oh yes, you do; one came here yesterday; he had whiskers, and he was awful."

"Whiskers?" His soul revolted in disclaimer. "I believe I only know one man with whiskers—a lawyer."

"Yes—that was him; a perfectly horrid man. Mother didn't mind him, but *I* thought he was a beast."

"Ventnor! Came here? How d'you mean?"

"He did; about some business of yours, too." Her face had clouded over. Bob Pillin had of late been harassed by the still-born beginning of a poem:

> "I rode upon my way and saw
> A maid who watched me from the door."

It never grew longer, and was prompted by the feeling that her face was like an April day. The cloud which came on it now was like an April cloud, as if a bright shower of rain must follow. Brushing aside the two distressful lines, he said:

"Look here, Miss Larne—Phyllis—look here!"

"All right, I'm looking!"

"What does it mean—how did he come? What did he say?"

She shook her head, and her hair quivered; the scent of camomile, verbena, hay, was wafted; then looking at her lap, she muttered:

"I wish you wouldn't—I wish mother wouldn't—I hate it. Oh! Money! Beastly—beastly!" and a tearful sigh shivered itself into Bob Pillin's reddening ears.

"I say—don't! And do tell me, because——"

"Oh! you *know.*"

"I don't—I don't know anything at all. I never——"

Phyllis looked up at him. "Don't tell fibs; you know mother's borrowing money from you, and it's hateful!"

A desire to lie roundly, a sense of the cheque in his pocket, a feeling of injustice, the emotion of pity, and a confused and black astonishment about Ventnor, caused Bob Pillin to stammer:

"Well, I'm d——d!" and to miss the look which Phyllis gave him through her lashes—a look saying:

"Ah! that's better!"

"I *am* d——d! Look here! D'you mean to say that Ventnor came here about my lending money? I never said a word to him——"

"There you see—you *are* lending!"

He clutched his hair.

"We've got to have this out," he added.

"Not by the roots! Oh! you do look funny. I've never seen you with your hair untidy. Oh! oh!"

Bob Pillin rose and paced the room. In the midst of his emotion he could not help seeing himself sidelong in the mirror; and on pretext of holding his head in both his hands, tried earnestly to restore his hair. Then coming to a halt he said:

"Suppose I *am* lending money to your mother, what does it matter? It's only till quarter-day. Anybody might want money."

Phyllis did not raise her face.

"Why are you lending it?"

"Because—because—why shouldn't I?" and diving suddenly, he seized her hands.

She wrenched them free; and with the emotion of despair, Bob Pillin took out the envelope.

"If you like," he said, "I'll tear this up. I don't want to lend it, if you don't want me to; but I thought—I thought——" It was for her alone he had been going to lend this money!

Phyllis murmured through her hair:

"Yes! You thought that *I*—that's what's so hateful!"

Apprehension pierced his mind.

"Oh? I never—I swear I never——"

"Yes, you did; you thought I wanted you to lend it."

She jumped up, and brushed past him into the window.

So she thought she was being used as a decoy! That was awful—especially since it was true. He knew well enough that Mrs. Larne was working his admiration for her daughter for all that it was worth. And he said with simple fervor:

"What rot!" It produced no effect, and at his wits' end, he almost shouted: "Look, Phyllis! If you don't want me to—here goes!" Phyllis turned. Tearing the envelope across he threw the bits into the fire. "There it is," he said.

Her eyes grew round; she said in an awed voice: "Oh!"

In a sort of agony of honesty he said:

"It was only a cheque. Now you've got your way."

Staring at the fire she answered slowly:

"I expect you'd better go before mother comes."

Bob Pillin's mouth fell ajar; he secretly agreed, but the idea of sacrificing a moment alone with her was intolerable, and he said hardily:

"No, I shall stick it!"

Phyllis sneezed.

"My hair isn't a bit dry," and she sat down on the fender with her back to the fire.

A certain spirituality had come into Bob Pillin's face. If only he could get that wheeze off: "Phyllis is my only joy!" or even: "Phyllis —do you—won't you—mayn't I?" But nothing came—nothing.

And suddenly she said:

"Oh! don't breathe so loud; it's awful!"

"Breathe? I wasn't!"

"You were; just like Carmen when she's dreaming."

He had walked three steps towards the door, before he thought: 'What does it matter? I can stand anything from her'; and walked the three steps back again.

She said softly:

"Poor young man!"

He answered gloomily:

"I suppose you realize that this may be the last time you'll see me?"

"Why? I thought you were going to take us to the theatre."

"I don't know whether your mother will—after——"

Phyllis gave a little clear laugh.

"You don't know mother. Nothing makes any difference to her."

And Bob Pillin muttered:

"I see." He did not, but it was of no consequence. Then the thought of Ventnor again ousted all others. What on earth—how on earth! He searched his mind for what he could possibly have said the other night. Surely he had not asked him to do anything; certainly not given him their address. There was something very odd about it that had jolly well got to be cleared up! And he said:

"Are you sure the name of that johnny who came here yesterday was Ventnor?"

Phyllis nodded.

"And he was short, and had whiskers?"

"Yes; red, and red eyes."

He murmured reluctantly:

"It must be him. Jolly good cheek; I simply can't understand. I shall go and see him. How on earth did he know your address?"

"I expect you gave it him."

"I did not. I won't have you thinking me a squirt."

Phyllis jumped up. "Oh! Lawks! Here's mother!" Mrs. Larne was coming up the garden. Bob Pillin made for the door. "Good-bye," he said; "I'm going." But Mrs. Larne was already in the hall. Enveloping him in fur and her rich personality, she drew him with her into the drawing-room, where the back window was open and Phyllis gone.

"I hope," she said, "those naughty children have been making you comfortable. That nice lawyer of yours came yesterday. He seemed quite satisfied."

Very red above his collar, Bob Pillin stammered:

"I never told him to; he isn't my lawyer. I don't know what it means."

Mrs. Larne smiled. "My dear boy, it's all right. You needn't be so squeamish. I want it to be quite on a business footing."

Restraining a fearful inclination to blurt out: "It's not going to be on any footing!" Bob Pillin mumbled. "I must go; I'm late."

"And when will you be able——?"

"Oh! I'll—I'll send—I'll write. Good-bye!" And suddenly he found that Mrs. Larne had him by the lapel of his coat. The scent of violets and fur was overpowering, and the thought flashed through him: 'I believe she only wanted to take money off old Joseph in the Bible. I can't leave my coat in her hands; What shall I do?'

Mrs. Larne was murmuring:

"It would be *so* sweet of you if you could manage it to-day"; and her hand slid over his chest. "Oh! You *have* brought your cheque-book—what a nice boy!"

Bob Pillin took it out in desperation, and, sitting down at the bureau, wrote a cheque similar to that which he had torn and burned. A warm kiss lighted on his eyebrow, his head was pressed for a moment to a furry bosom; a hand took the cheque; a voice said: "How delightful!" and a sigh immersed him in a bath of perfume. Backing to the door, he gasped:

"Don't mention it; and—and *don't tell Phyllis, please*. Good-bye!"

Once through the garden gate, he thought: 'By gum! I've done it now. That Phyllis should know about it at all! That beast Ventnor!'

His face grew almost grim. He would go and see what that meant anyway!

3 §

Mr. Ventnor had not left his office when his young friend's card was brought to him. Tempted for a moment to deny his own presence, he thought: 'No! What's the good? Bound to see him sometime!' If he had not exactly courage, he had that particular blend of self-confidence and insensibility which must needs distinguish those who follow the law; nor did he ever forget that he was in the right.

"Show him in!" he said.

He would be quite bland, but young Pillin might whistle for an explanation; he was still tormented, too, by the memory of rich curves and moving lips, and the possibilities of better acquaintanceship.

While shaking the young man's hand his quick and fulvous eye detected at once the discomposure behind that mask of cheek and collar, and relapsing into one of those swivel chairs which give one an advantage over men more statically seated, he said:

"You look pretty bobbish. Anything I can do for you?"

Bob Pillin, in the fixed chair of the consulter, nursed his bowler on his knee.

"Well, yes, there is. I've just been to see Mrs. Larne."

Mr. Ventnor did not flinch.

"Ah! Nice woman; pretty daughter, too!" And into those words he put a certain meaning. He never waited to be bullied. Bob Pillin felt the pressure of his blood increasing.

"Look here, Ventnor," he said, "I want an explanation."

"What of?"

"Why, of your going there, and using my name, and God knows what."

Mr. Ventnor gave his chair two little twiddles before he said:

"Well, you won't get it."

Bob Pillin remained for a moment taken aback; then he muttered resolutely:

"It's not the conduct of a gentleman."

Every man has his illusions, and no man likes them disturbed. The gingery tint underlying Mr. Ventnor's coloring overlaid it; even the whites of his eyes grew red.

"Oh!" he said; "indeed. You mind your own business, will you?"

"It is my business—very much so. You made use of my name, and I don't choose——"

"The devil you don't! Now, I tell you what——" Mr. Ventnor

leaned forward—"you'd better hold your tongue, and not exasperate me. I'm a good-tempered man, but I won't stand your impudence."

Clenching his bowler hat, and only kept in his seat by that sense of something behind, Bob Pillin ejaculated:

"Impudence! That's good—after what you did! Look here, why did you? It's so extraordinary!"

Mr. Ventnor answered:

"Oh! is it? You wait a bit, my friend!"

Still more moved by the mystery of this affair, Bob Pillin could only mutter:

"I never gave you their address; we were only talking about old Heythorp."

And at the smile which spread between Mr. Ventnor's whiskers, he jumped up, crying:

"It's not the thing, and you're not going to put me off. I insist on an explanation."

Mr. Ventnor leaned back, crossing his stout legs, joining the tips of his thick fingers. In this attitude he was always self-possessed.

"You do—do you?"

"Yes. You must have had some reason."

Mr. Ventnor gazed up at him.

"I'll give you a piece of advice, young cock, and charge you nothing for it, too: Ask no questions, and you'll be told no lies. And here's another: Go away before you forget yourself again."

The natural stolidity of Bob Pillin's face was only just proof against this speech. He said thickly:

"If you go there again and use my name, I'll——. Well, it's lucky for you you're not my age. Anyway I'll relieve you of my acquaintance-ship in future. Good-evening!" and he went to the door. Mr. Ventnor had risen.

"Very well," he said loudly. "Good riddance! You wait and see which boot the leg is on!"

But Bob Pillin was gone, leaving the lawyer with a very red face, a very angry heart, and a vague sense of disorder in his speech. Not only Bob Pillin, but his tender aspirations had all left him; he no longer dallied with the memory of Mrs. Larne, but like a man and a Briton thought only of how to get his own back and punish evildoers. The atrocious words of his young friend, "It's not the conduct of a gentle-man," festered in the heart of one who was made gentle not merely by nature but by Act of Parliament, and he registered a solemn vow to wipe the insult out, if not with blood, with verjuice. It was his duty, and they should d——d well see him do it!

IV

⟁ §

Sylvanus Heythorp seldom went to bed before one or rose before eleven. The latter habit alone kept his valet from handling in the resignation which the former habit prompted almost every night.

Propped on his pillows in a crimson dressing-gown, and freshly shaved, he looked more Roman than he ever did, except in his bath. Having disposed of coffee, he was wont to read his letters, and *The Morning Post,* for he had always been a Tory, and could not stomach paying a halfpenny for his news. Not that there were many letters—when a man has reached the age of eighty, who should write to him, except to ask for money?

It was Valentine's Day. Through his bedroom window he could see the trees of the park, where the birds were in song, though he could not hear them. He had never been interested in Nature—full-blooded men with short necks seldom are.

This morning indeed there *were* two letters, and he opened that which smelt of something. Inside was a thing like a Christmas card, save that the naked babe had in his hands a bow and arrow, and words coming out of his mouth: "To be your Valentine." There was also a little pink note with one blue forget-me-not printed at the top. It ran:

"Dearest Guardy,—I'm sorry this is such a mangy little valentine; I couldn't go out to get it because I've got a beastly cold, so I asked Jock, and the pig bought this. The satin is simply scrumptious. If you don't come and see me in it some time soon, I shall come and show it to you. I wish I had a moustache, because my top lip feels just like a matchbox, but it's rather ripping having breakfast in bed. Mr. Pillin's taking us to the theatre the day after to-morrow evening. Isn't it nummy! I'm going to have rum and honey for my cold.

"Good-bye,
"Your Phyllis."

So this that quivered in his thick fingers, too insensitive to feel it, was a valentine for *him!* Forty years ago that young thing's grand-mother had given him his last. It made him out a very old chap! Forty years ago! Had that been himself living then? And himself, who, as a youth, came on the town in 'forty-five? Not a thought, not a feeling the same! They said you changed your body every seven years. The mind with it, too, perhaps. Well, he had come to the last of his bodies, now! And that holy woman had been urging him to take it to Bath, with her face as long as a tea-tray, and some gammon from that doctor of his. Too full a habit—dock his port—no alcohol—might go off in a coma any night! Knock off—not he! Rather die any day than turn teetotaller! When a man had nothing left in life except his dinner, his bottle, his cigar, and the dreams they gave him—these doctors forsooth must want to cut them off! No, no! *Carpe diem!* while you lived, get something out of it. And now that he had made all the provision he could for those youngsters, his life was no good to anyone but himself; and the sooner he went off the better, if he ceased to enjoy what there was left, or lost the power to say: "I'll do this and that, and you be jiggered!" Keep a stiff lip until you crashed, and then go clean! He sounded the bell beside him twice—for Molly, not his man. And when the girl came in, and stood, pretty in her print frock, her fluffy over-fine dark hair escaping from under her cap, he gazed at her in silence.

"Yes, sirr?"

"Want to look at you, that's all."

"Oh! an' I'm not tidy, sirr."

"Never mind. Had your valentine?"

"No, sirr; who would send me one, then?"

"Haven't you a young man?"

"Well, I might. But he's over in my country."

"What d'you think of this?"

He held out the little boy.

The girl took the card and scrutinized it reverently; she said in a detached voice:

"Indeed, an' ut's pretty, too."

"Would you like it?"

"Oh; if 'tis not taking ut from you."

Old Heythorp shook his head, and pointed to the dressing-table.

"Over there—you'll find a sovereign. Little present for a good girl."

She uttered a deep sigh. "Oh, sirr, 'tis too much; 'tis kingly."

"Take it."

She took it, and came back, her hands clasping the sovereign and the valentine, in an attitude as of prayer.

The old man's gaze rested on her with satisfaction.

"I like pretty faces—can't bear sour ones. Tell Meller to get my bath ready."

When she had gone he took up the other letter—some lawyer's writing—and opening it with the usual difficulty read:

"February 13th, 1905.

"SIR,—Certain facts having come to my knowledge, I deem it my duty to call a special meeting of the shareholders of 'The Island Navigation Coy.,' to consider circumstances in connection with the purchase of Mr. Joseph Pillin's fleet. And I give you notice that at this meeting your conduct will be called in question.

"I am, Sir,

"Yours faithfully,

"CHARLES VENTNOR.

"SYLVANUS HEYTHORP, Esq."

Having read this missive, old Heythorp remained some minutes without stirring. Ventnor! That solicitor chap who had made himself unpleasant at the creditors' meetings!

There are men whom a really bad bit of news at once stampedes out of all power of coherent thought and action, and men who at first simply do not take it in. Old Heythorp took it in fast enough; coming from a lawyer it was about as nasty as it could be. But, at once, with stoic wariness his old brain began casting round. What did this fellow really know? And what exactly could he do? One thing was certain; even if he knew everything, he couldn't upset that settlement. The youngsters were all right. The old man grasped the fact that only his own position was at stake. But this was enough in all conscience; a name which had been before the public fifty odd years—income, independence, more perhaps. It would take little, seeing his age and feebleness, to make his Companies throw him over. But what had the fellow got hold of? How decide whether or not to take notice; to let him do his worst, or to try and get into touch with him? And what was the fellow's motive? He held ten shares! That would never make a man take all this trouble, and over a purchase which was really first-rate business for the Company. Yes! His conscience was quite clean. He had not betrayed his Company—on the contrary, had done it a good turn, got them four sound ships at a low price—against much opposition. That he might have done the Company a better turn, and got the ships at fifty-four thousand, did not trouble him—the six thousand was a deuced sight better employed; and he had not pocketed a penny piece himself! But the fellow's motive? Spite? Looked like it. Spite, because he had been disappointed of his money, and defied into the bargain! H'm! If that were so, he might still be got to blow cold

again. His eyes lighted on the pink note with the blue forget-me-not.
It marked as it were the high-water mark of what was left to him of
life; and this other letter in his hand—by Jove!—low-water mark!
And with a deep and rumbling sigh he thought: 'No, I'm not going to
be beaten by this fellow.'

"Your bath is ready, sir."

Crumpling the two letters into the pocket of his dressing-gown, he
said:

"Help me up; and telephone to Mr. Farney to be good enough to
come round." . . .

An hour later, when the secretary entered, his chairman was sitting
by the fire perusing the articles of association. And, waiting for him
to look up, watching the articles shaking in that thick, feeble hand, the
secretary had one of those moments of philosophy not too frequent with
his kind. Some said the only happy time of life was when you had no
passions, nothing to hope and live for. But did you really ever reach
such a stage? The old chairman, for instance, still had his passion for
getting his own way, still had his prestige, and set a lot of store by it!
And he said:

"Good-morning, sir; I hope you're all right in this east wind. The
purchase is completed."

"Best thing the Company ever did. Have you heard from a shareholder called Ventnor? You know the man I mean."

"No, sir. I haven't."

"Well! You may get a letter that'll make you open your eyes. An
impudent scoundrel! Just write at my dictation."

"*February* 14*th*, 1905.

"CHARLES VENTNOR, Esq.

"SIR,—I have your letter of yesterday's date, the contents of which
I am at a loss to understand. My solicitors will be instructed to take
the necessary measures."

'Phew! What's all this about?' the secretary thought.

"Yours truly . . . I'll sign."

And the shaky letters closed the page:

"SYLVANUS HEYTHORP."

"Post that as you go."

"Anything else I can do for you, sir?"

"Nothing, except to let me know if you hear from this fellow."

When the secretary had gone the old man thought: 'So! The

ruffian hasn't called the meeting yet. That'll bring him round here fast enough if it's his money he wants—blackmailing scoundrel!'

"Mr. Pillin, sir; and will you wait lunch, or will you have it in the dining-room?"

"In the dining-room."

At the sight of that death's-head of a fellow, old Heythorp felt a sort of pity. He looked bad enough already—and this news would make him look worse. Joe Pillin glanced round at the two closed doors.

"How are you, Sylvanus? I'm very poorly." He came closer, and lowered his voice: "Why did you get me to make that settlement? I must have been mad. I've had a man called Ventnor—I didn't like his manner. He asked me if I knew a Mrs. Larne."

"Ha! What did you say?"

"What could I say? I *don't* know her. But why did he ask?"

"Smells a rat."

Joe Pillin grasped the edge of the table with both hands.

"Oh!" he murmured. "Oh, don't say that!"

Old Heythorp held out to him the crumpled letter.

When he had read it Joe Pillin sat down abruptly before the fire.

"Pull yourself together, Joe; they can't touch you, and they can't upset either the purchase or the settlement. They can upset me, that's all."

Joe Pillin answered, with trembling lips:

"How you can sit there, and look the same as ever! Are you sure they can't touch me?"

Old Heythorp nodded grimly.

"They talk of an Act, but they haven't passed it yet. They might prove a breach of trust against me. But I'll diddle them. Keep your pecker up, and get off abroad."

"Yes, yes. I must. I'm very bad. I was going to-morrow. But I don't know, I'm sure, with this hanging over me. My son knowing her makes it worse. He knows this man Ventnor, too. And I daren't say anything to Bob. What are you thinking of, Sylvanus? You look very funny."

Old Heythorp seemed to rouse himself from a sort of coma.

"I want my lunch," he said. "Will you stop and have some?"

Joe Pillin stammered out:

"Lunch! I don't know when I shall eat again. What are you going to do, Sylvanus?"

"Bluff the beggar out of it."

"But suppose you can't?"

"Buy him off. He's one of my creditors."

Joe Pillin stared at him afresh. "You always had such nerve," he said yearningly. "Do you ever wake up between two and four? I do— and everything's black."

"Put a good stiff nightcap on, my boy, before going to bed."

"Yes; I sometimes wish I was less temperate. But I couldn't stand it. I'm told your doctor forbids you alcohol."

"He does. That's why I drink it."

Joe Pillin, brooding over the fire, said: "This meeting—d'you think they mean to have it? D'you think this man really knows? If my name gets into the newspapers——" but encountering his old friend's deep little eyes, he stopped. "So you advise me to get off to-morrow, then?"

Old Heythorp nodded.

"Your lunch is served, sir."

Joe Pillin started violently, and rose.

"Well, good-bye, Sylvanus—good-bye! I don't suppose I shall be back till the summer, if I ever come back!" He sank his voice: "I shall rely on you. You won't let them, will you?"

Old Heythorp lifted his hand, and Joe Pillin put into that swollen shaking paw his pale and spindly fingers. "I wish I had your pluck," he said sadly. "Good-bye, Sylvanus," and turning, he passed out.

Old Heythorp thought: 'Poor shaky chap. All to pieces at the first shot!' And, going to his lunch, ate more heavily than usual.

2 §

Mr. Ventnor, on reaching his office and opening his letters, found, as he had anticipated, one from "that old rascal." Its contents excited in him the need to know his own mind. Fortunately this was not complicated by a sense of dignity—he only had to consider the position with an eye on not being made to *look* a fool. The point was simply whether he set more store by his money than by his desire for—er— justice. If not, he had merely to convene the special meeting, and lay before it the plain fact that Mr. Joseph Pillin, selling his ships for sixty thousand pounds, had just made a settlement of six thousand pounds on a lady whom he did not know, a daughter, ward, or what-not—of the purchasing Company's chairman, who had said, moreover, at the general meeting, that he stood or fell by the transaction; he had merely to do this, and demand that an explanation be required from the old man of such a startling coincidence. Convinced that no explanation would hold water, he felt sure that his action would be at once followed by the collapse, if nothing more, of that old image, and the infliction of a nasty slur on old Pillin and his hopeful son. On the other hand, three hundred pounds was money; and if old Heythorp were to say to him: "What do you want to make this fuss for?—here's what I owe you!" could a man of business and the world let his sense of justice—however he might itch to have it satisfied—stand in the way of what was after all also his sense of justice?—for this money had been owing to him for the deuce of a long time. In this dilemma, the words: "My solicitors will be instructed" were of a notable service in helping him to form a decision, for he had a certain dislike of other solicitors, and an intimate knowledge of the law of libel and slander; if by any remote chance there should be a slip between the cup and the lip, Charles Ventnor might be in the soup—a position which he deprecated both by nature and profession. High thinking, therefore, decided him at last to answer thus:

"February 15*th,* 1905.

"Sir,—I have received your note. I think it may be fair, before taking further steps in this matter, to ask you for a personal explanation of the circumstances to which I alluded. I therefore propose with your permission to call on you at your private residence at five o'clock to-morrow afternoon.

"Yours faithfully,
"Charles Ventnor.

"Sylvanus Heythorp, Esq."

Having sent this missive, and arranged in his mind, the damning, if circumstantial, evidence he had accumulated, he awaited the hour with confidence, for his nature was not lacking in the cock-surety of a Briton. All the same, he dressed himself particularly well that morning, putting on a blue and white striped waistcoat which, with a cream-colored tie, set off his fulvous whiskers and full blue eyes; and he lunched, if any-thing, more fully than his wont, eating a stronger cheese and taking a glass of special Club ale. He took care to be late, too, to show the old fellow that his coming at all was in the nature of an act of grace. A strong scent of hyacinths greeted him in the hall; and Mr. Ventnor, who was an amateur of flowers, stopped to put his nose into a fine bloom and think uncontrollably of Mrs. Larne. Pity! The things one had to give up in life—fine women—one thing and another. Pity! The thought inspired in him a timely anger; and he followed the servant, intending to stand no nonsense from this paralytic old rascal.

The room he entered was lighted by a bright fire, and a single electric lamp with an orange shade on a table covered by a black satin cloth. There were heavily gleaming oil paintings on the walls, a heavy old brass chandelier without candles, heavy dark red curtains, and an indefinable scent of burnt acorns, coffee, cigars, and old man. He became conscious of a candescent spot on the far side of the hearth, where the light fell on old Heythorp's thick white hair.

"Mr. Ventnor, sir."

The candescent spot moved. A voice said: "Sit down."

Mr. Ventnor sat in an armchair on the opposite side of the fire, and, finding a kind of somnolence creeping over him, pinched himself. He wanted all his wits about him.

The old man was speaking in that extinct voice of his, and Mr. Ventnor said rather pettishly:

"Beg pardon, I don't get you."

Old Heythorp's voice swelled with sudden force:

"Your letters are Greek to me."

"Oh! indeed! I think we can soon make them into plain English!"

"Sooner the better."

Mr. Ventnor passed through a moment of indecision. Should he lay his cards on the table? It was not his habit, and the proceeding was sometimes attended with risk. The knowledge, however, that he could always take them up again, seeing there was no third person here to testify that he had laid them down, decided him, and he said:

"Well, Mr. Heythorp, the long and short of the matter is this: Our friend Mr. Pillin paid you a commission of ten per cent. on the sale of his ships. Oh! yes. He settled the money not on you, but on your relative Mrs. Larne and her children. This, as you know, is a breach of trust on your part."

The old man's voice: "Where did you get hold of that cock-and-bull story?" brought him to his feet before the fire.

"It won't do, Mr. Heythorp. My witnesses are Mr. Pillin, Mrs. Larne, and Mr. Scriven."

"What have you come here for, then—blackmail?"

Mr. Ventnor straightened his waistcoat; a rush of conscious virtue had dyed his face.

"Oh! you take that tone," he said, "do you? You think you can ride roughshod over everything? Well, you're very much mistaken. I advise you to keep a civil tongue and consider your position, or I'll make a beggar of you. I'm not sure this isn't a case for a prosecution!"

"Gammon!"

The choler in Charles Ventnor kept him silent for a moment; then he burst out:

"Neither gammon nor spinach. You owe me three hundred pounds, you've owed it me for years, and you have the impudence to take this attitude with me, have you? Now, I never bluster; I say what I mean. You just listen to me. Either you pay me what you owe at once, or I call this meeting and make what I know public. You'll very soon find out where you are. And a good thing, too, for a more unscrupulous—unscrupulous——" he paused for breath.

Occupied with his own emotion, he had not observed the change in old Heythorp's face. The imperial on that lower lip was bristling, the crimson of those cheeks had spread to the roots of his white hair. He grasped the arms of his chair, trying to rise; his swollen hands trembled; a little saliva escaped one corner of his lips. And the words came out as if shaken by his teeth:

"So—so—you—you bully me!"

Conscious that the interview had suddenly passed from the phase of negotiation, Mr. Ventnor looked hard at his opponent. He saw nothing but a decrepit, passionate, crimson-faced old man at bay, and all the instincts of one with everything on his side boiled up in him. The miserable old turkey-cock—the apoplectic image! And he said:

"And you'll do no good for yourself by getting into a passion. At your age, and in your condition, I recommend a little prudence. Now just take my terms quietly, or you know what'll happen. I'm not to be intimidated by any of your airs." And seeing that the old man's rage was such that he simply could not speak, he took the opportunity of going on: "I don't care two straws which you do—I'm out to show you who's master. If you think in your dotage you can domineer any longer—well, you'll find two can play at that game. Come, now, which are you going to do?"

The old man had sunk back in his chair, and only his little deep-blue eyes seemed living. Then he moved one hand, and Mr. Ventnor saw that he was fumbling to reach the button of an electric bell at the end of a cord. "I'll show him," he thought, and stepping forward, he put it out of reach.

Thus frustrated, the old man remained motionless, staring up. The word "blackmail" resumed its buzzing in Mr. Ventnor's ears. The impudence—the consummate impudence of it from this fraudulent old ruffian with one foot in bankruptcy and one foot in the grave, if not in the dock.

"Yes," he said, "it's never too late to learn; and for once you've come up against someone a leetle bit too much for you. Haven't you now? You'd better cry 'Peccavi.'"

Then, in the deathly silence of the room, the moral force of his position, and the collapse as it seemed of his opponent, awakening a faint compunction, he took a turn over the Turkey carpet to readjust his mind.

"You're an old man, and I don't want to be too hard on you. I'm only showing you that you can't play fast and loose as if you were God Almighty any longer. You've had your own way too many years. And now you can't have it, see!" Then, as the old man again moved forward in his chair, he added: "Now, don't get into a passion again; calm yourself, because I warn you—this is your last chance. I'm a man of my word; and what I say, I do."

By a violent and unsuspected effort the old man jerked himself up and reached the bell. Mr. Ventnor heard it ring, and said sharply:

"Mind you, it's nothing to me which you do. I came for your own good. Please yourself. Well?"

He was answered by the click of the door and the old man's husky voice:

"Show this hound out! And then come back!"

Mr. Ventnor had presence of mind enough not to shake his fist. Muttering: "Very well, Mr. Heythorp! Ah! *Very* well!" he moved with dignity to the door. The careful shepherding of the servant renewed the fire of his anger. Hound! he had been called a hound!

3 §

After seeing Mr. Ventnor off the premises the man Meller returned to his master, whose face looked very odd—"all patchy-like," as he put it in the servants' hall, as though the blood driven to his head had mottled for good the snowy whiteness of the forehead. He received the unexpected order:

"Get me a hot bath ready, and put some pine stuff in it."

When the old man was seated there, the valet asked:

"How long shall I give you, sir?"

"Twenty minutes."

"Very good, sir."

Lying in that steaming brown fragrant liquid, old Heythorp heaved a stertorous sigh. By losing his temper with that ill-conditioned cur he had cooked his goose. It was done to a turn; and he was a ruined man. If only—oh! if only he could have seized the fellow by the neck and pitched him out of the room! To have lived to be so spoken to; to have been unable to lift hand or foot, hardly even his voice—he would sooner have been dead! Yes—sooner have been dead! A dumb and measureless commotion was still at work in the recesses of that thick old body, silver-brown in the dark water, whose steam he drew deep into his wheezing lungs, as though for spiritual relief. To be beaten by a cur like that! To have a common cad of a pettifogging lawyer drag him down and kick him about; tumble a name which had stood high, in the dust! The fellow had the power to make him a byword and a beggar! It was incredible! But it was a fact. And to-morrow he would begin to do it—perhaps had begun already. His tree had come down with a crash! Eighty years—eighty good years! He regretted none of them—regretted nothing; least of all this breach of trust which had provided for his grandchildren—one of the best things he had ever done. The fellow was a cowardly hound, too! The way he had snatched the bell-pull out of his reach—despicable cur! And a chap like that was to put "paid" to the account of Sylvanus Heythorp, to "scratch" him out of life—so near the end of everything, the very end. His hand raised above the surface fell back on his stomach through the dark water, and a bubble or two rose. Not so fast—not so fast! He had but to slip down a foot, let the water close over his head, and "Good-bye" to Master Ventnor's triumph! Dead men could not be kicked off the Boards of Companies. Dead men could not be beggared, deprived of their independence. He smiled and stirred a little in the bath till the water reached the white hairs on his lower lip. It smelt nice! And he took a long sniff. He had had a good life, a good life! And with the thought that he had it in his power at any moment to put Master Ventnor's nose out of joint—to beat the beggar after all, a sense of assuagement and well-being crept over him. His blood ran more evenly again. He closed his eyes. They talked about an after-life—people like that holy woman. Gammon! You went to sleep—a long sleep; no dreams. A nap after dinner! Dinner! His tongue sought his palate! Yes! he could eat a good dinner! That dog hadn't put him off his stroke! The best dinner he had ever eaten was the one he gave to Jack Herring, Chichester, Thornworthy, Nick Treffry and Jolyon Forsyte at Pole's. Good Lord! In 'sixty—yes—'sixty-five? Just before he fell in love with Alice Larne—ten years before he came to Liverpool. That *was* a dinner! Cost twenty-four pounds for the six of them—and Forsyte an absurdly moderate fellow. Only Nick Treffry and himself had been three-bottle men! Dead! Every jack man of them. And

suddenly he thought: 'My name's a good one—I was never down
before—never beaten!'

A voice above the steam said:

"The twenty minutes is up, sir."

"All right; I'll get out. Evening clothes."

And Meller, taking out dress suit and shirt, thought: 'Now, what
does the old bloomer want dressin' up again for; why can't he go to
bed and have his dinner there? When a man's like a baby, the cradle's
the place for him.'

An hour later, at the scene of his encounter with Mr. Ventnor,
where the table was already laid for dinner, old Heythorp stood and
gazed. The curtains had been drawn back, the window thrown open
to air the room, and he could see out there the shapes of the dark trees
and a sky grape-colored, in the mild, moist night. It smelt good. A
sensuous feeling stirred in him, warm from his bath, clothed from
head to foot in fresh garments. Deuce of a time since he had dined
in full fig! He would have liked a woman dining opposite—but not
the holy woman; no, by George!—would have liked to see light falling on a woman's shoulders once again, and a pair of bright eyes!
He crossed, snail-like, towards the fire. There that bullying fellow had
stood with his back to it—confound his impudence!—as if the place
belonged to him. And suddenly he had a vision of his three secretaries'
faces—especially young Farney's—as they would look when the pack
got him by the throat and pulled him down. His co-directors, too!
Old Heythorp! How are the mighty fallen! And that hound jubilant!

His valet passed across the room to shut the window and draw the
curtains. This chap too! The day he could no longer pay his wages,
and had lost the power to say "Shan't want your services any more"—
when he could no longer even pay his doctor for doing his best to kill
him off! Power, interest, independence, all—gone! To be dressed
and undressed, given pap, like a baby in arms, served as they chose
to serve him, and wished out of the way—broken, dishonored! By
money alone an old man had his being! Meat, drink, movement,
breath! When all his money was gone the holy woman would let him
know it fast enough. They would all let him know it; or if they
didn't, it would be out of pity! He had never been pitied yet—thank
God! And he said:

"Get me up a bottle of Perrier Jouet. What's the menu?"

"Germane soup, sir; filly de sole; sweetbread; cutler soubees, rum
souffly."

"Tell her to give me a *hors d'œuvre,* and put on a savoury."

"Yes, sir."

When the man had gone, he thought: 'I should have liked an oyster
—too late now!' and going over to his bureau he fumblingly pulled
out the top drawer.   There was little in it—just a few papers, business papers on his Companies, and a schedule of his debts; not even
a copy of his will—he had not made one, nothing to leave!   Letters
he had never kept.   Half a dozen bills, a few receipts, and the little
pink note with the blue forget-me-not.   That was the lot.   An old tree
gives up bearing leaves, and its roots dry up, before it comes down
in a wind; an old man's world slowly falls away from him till he
stands alone in the night.   Looking at the pink note, he thought:
'Suppose I'd married Alice—a man never had a better mistress!'   He
fumbled the drawer to; but still he strayed feebly about the room, with
a curious shrinking from sitting down, legacy from the quarter of
an hour he had been compelled to sit while that hound worried at his
throat.   He was opposite one of the pictures now.   It gleamed, dark
and oily, limning a Scots Grey who had mounted a wounded Russian
on his horse, and was bringing him back prisoner from the Balaclava
charge.   A very old friend—bought in 'fifty-nine.   It had hung in his
chambers in the Albany—hung with him ever since.   With whom
would it hang when he was gone?   For that holy woman would scrap
it, to a certainty, and stick up some Crucifixion or other, some new-
fangled high art thing!   She could even do that now if she liked—
for she owned it, owned every mortal stick in the room, to the very
glass he would drink his champagne from; all made over under the
settlement fifteen years ago, before his last big gamble went wrong.
"De l'audace, toujours de l'audace!"   The gamble which had brought
him down till his throat at last was at the mercy of a bullying hound.
The pitcher and the well!   At the mercy——!   The sound of a pop-
ping cork dragged him from reverie.   He moved to his seat, back to
the window, and sat down to his dinner.   By George!   They had got
him an oyster!   And he said:

"I've forgotten my teeth!"

While the man was gone for them, he swallowed the oysters,
methodically touching them one by one with cayenne, Chili vinegar, and
lemon.   Ummm!   Not quite what they used to be at Pimm's in the
best days, but not bad—not bad!   Then seeing the little blue bowl
lying before him, he looked up and said:

"My compliments to cook on the oysters.   Give me the champagne."
And he lifted his trembling teeth.   Thank God, he could still put 'em
in for himself!   The creaming goldenish fluid from the napkined bot-

tle slowly reached the brim of his glass, which had a hollow stem; raising it to his lips, very red between the white hairs above and below, he drank with a gurgling noise, and put the glass down—empty. Nectar! And just cold enough!

"I frapped it the least bit, sir."

"Quite right. What's that smell of flowers?"

"It's from those 'yacinths on the sideboard, sir. They come from Mrs. Larne, this afternoon."

"Put 'em on the table. Where's my daughter?"

"She's had dinner, sir; goin' to a ball, I think."

"A ball!"

"Charity ball, I fancy, sir."

"Ummm! Give me a touch of the old sherry with the soup."

"Yes, sir. I shall have to open a bottle."

"Very well, then, do!"

On his way to the cellar the man confided to Molly, who was carrying the soup:

"The Gov'nor's going it to-night! What he'll be like to-morrow I dunno."

The girl answered softly:

"Poor old man, let um have his pleasure." And, in the hall, with the soup tureen against her bosom, she hummed above the steam, and thought of the ribbons on her new chemises, bought out of the sovereign he had given her.

And old Heythorp, digesting his oysters, snuffed the scent of the hyacinths, and thought of the St. Germain, his favorite soup. It wouldn't be first-rate, at this time of year—should be made with little young home-grown peas. Paris was the place for it. Ah! The French were the fellows for eating, and—looking things in the face! Not hypocrites—not ashamed of their reason or their senses!

The soup came in. He sipped it, bending forward as far as he could, his napkin tucked in over his shirt-front like a bib. He got the bouquet of that sherry to a T—his sense of smell was very keen to-night; rare old stuff it was—more than a year since he had tasted it— but no one drank sherry nowadays, hadn't the constitution for it! The fish came up, and went down; and with the sweetbread he took his second glass of champagne. Always the best, that second glass—the stomach well warmed, and the palate not yet dulled. Umm! So that fellow thought he had him beaten, did he? And he said suddenly:

"The fur coat in the wardrobe, I've no use for it. You can take it away to-night."

With tempered gratitude the valet answered:

"Thank you, sir; much obliged, I'm sure." So the old buffer had found out there was moth in it!

"Have I worried you much?"

"No, sir; not at all, sir—that is, no more than reason."

"Afraid I have. Very sorry—can't help it. You'll find that, when you get like me."

"Yes, sir; I've always admired your pluck, sir."

"Um! Very good of you to say so."

"Always think of you keepin' the flag flyin', sir."

Old Heythorp bent his body from the waist.

"Much obliged to you."

"Not at all, sir. Cook's done a little spinach in cream with the soubees."

"Ah! Tell her from me it's a capital dinner, so far."

"Thank you, sir."

Alone again, old Heythorp sat unmoving, his brain just narcotically touched. "The flag flyin'—the flag flyin'!" He raised his glass and sucked. He had an appetite now, and finished the three cutlets, and all the sauce and spinach. Pity! he could have managed a snipe—fresh shot! A desire to delay, to lengthen dinner, was strong upon him; there were but the *soufflé* and the savoury to come. He would have enjoyed, too, someone to talk to. He had always been fond of good company—been good company himself, or so they said—not that he had had a chance of late. Even at the Boards they avoided talking to him, he had noticed for a long time. Well! that wouldn't trouble him again—he had sat through his last Board, no doubt. They shouldn't kick him off, though; he wouldn't give them that pleasure—had seen the beggars hankering after his chairman's shoes too long. The *soufflé* was before him now, and lifting his glass, he said:

"Fill up."

"These are the special glasses, sir; only four to the bottle."

"Fill up."

The servant filled, screwing up his mouth.

Old Heythorp drank, and put the glass down empty with a sigh. He had been faithful to his principles, finished the bottle before touching the sweet—a good bottle—of a good brand! And now for the *soufflé*! Delicious, flipped down with the old sherry! So that holy woman was going to a ball, was she? How deuced funny! Who would dance with a dry stick like that, all eaten up with a piety which was just sexual disappointment? Ah! yes, lots of women like that—had often noticed 'em—pitied 'em too, until you had to do with them and they made you as unhappy as themselves, and were tyrants into the bargain. And he asked:

"What's the savoury?"

"Cheese remmykin, sir."

His favorite.

"I'll have my port with it—the 'sixty-eight."

The man stood gazing with evident stupefaction. He had not expected this. The old man's face was very flushed, but that might be the bath. He said feebly:

"Are you sure you ought, sir?"

"No, but I'm going to."

"Would you mind if I spoke to Miss Heythorp, sir?"

"If you do, you can leave my service."

"Well, sir, I don't accept the responsibility."

"Who asked you to?"

"No, sir."

"Well, get it, then; and don't be an ass."

"Yes, sir." If the old man were not humored he would have a fit, perhaps!

And the old man sat quietly staring at the hyacinths. He felt happy, his whole being lined and warmed and drowsed—and there was more to come! What had the holy folk to give you compared with the comfort of a good dinner? Could they make you dream, and see life rosy for a little? No, they could only give you promissory notes which would never be cashed. A man had nothing but his pluck— they only tried to undermine it, and make him squeal for help. He could see his precious doctor throwing up his hands: "Port after a bottle of champagne—you'll die of it!" And a very good death too —none better. A sound broke the silence of the closed-up room. Music. His daughter playing the piano overhead. Singing too! What a trickle of a voice! Jenny Lind! The Swedish nightingale— he had never missed the nights when she was singing—Jenny Lind!

"It's very hot, sir. Shall I take it out of the case?"

Ah. The ramequin!

"Touch of butter, and the cayenne!"

"Yes, sir."

He ate it slowly, savouring each mouthful; had never tasted a better. With cheese—port! He drank one glass, and said:

"Help me to my chair."

And settled there before the fire with decanter and glass and hand-bell on the little low table by his side, he murmured:

"Bring coffee, and my cigar, in twenty minutes."

To-night he would do justice to his wine, not smoking till he had finished. As old Horace said:

"Aequam memento rebus in arduis
Servare mentem."

And, raising his glass, he sipped slowly, spilling a drop or two, shutting his eyes.

The faint silvery squealing of the holy woman in the room above, the scent of hyacinths, the drowse of the fire, on which a cedar log had just been laid, the feeling of the port soaking down into the crannies of his being, made up a momentary Paradise. Then the music stopped; and no sound rose but the tiny groans of the log trying to resist the fire. Dreamily he thought: 'Life wears you out, wears you out. Logs on a fire!' And he filled his glass again. That fellow had been careless; there were dregs at the bottom of the decanter and he had got down to them! Then, as the last drop from his tilted glass trickled into the white hairs on his chin, he heard the coffee tray put down, and taking his cigar he put it to his ear, rolling it in his thick fingers. In prime condition! And drawing a first whiff, he said:

"Open that bottle of the old brandy in the sideboard."

"Brandy, sir? I really daren't, sir."

"Are you my servant or not?"

"Yes, sir, but——"

A minute of silence, then the man went hastily to the sideboard, took out the bottle, and drew the cork. The tide of crimson in the old man's face had frightened him.

"Leave it there."

The unfortunate valet placed the bottle on the little table. 'I'll have to tell her,' he thought; 'but if I take away the port decanter and the glass, it won't look so bad.' And, carrying them, he left the room.

Slowly the old man drank his coffee, and the liqueur of brandy. The whole gamut! And watching his cigar-smoke wreathing blue in the orange glow, he smiled. The last night to call his soul his own, the last night of his independence. Send in his resignations to-morrow—not wait to be kicked off! Not give that fellow a chance!

A voice which seemed to come from far off, said:

"Father! You're drinking brandy! How *can* you—you know it's simple poison to you!" A figure in white, scarcely actual, loomed up close. He took the bottle to fill up his liqueur glass, in defiance; but a hand in a long white glove, with another dangling from its wrist, pulled it away, shook it at him, and replaced it in the sideboard. And, just as when Mr. Ventnor stood there accusing him, a swelling and churning in his throat prevented him from speech; his lips moved, but only a little froth came forth.

His daughter had approached again. She stood quite close, in white satin, thin-faced, sallow, with eyebrows raised, and her dark hair frizzed —yes! frizzed—the holy woman! With all his might he tried to say: 'So you bully me, do you—you bully me *to-night!*' but only the word "so" and a sort of whispering came forth. He heard her speaking. "It's no good your getting angry, Father. After champagne — it's wicked!" Then her form receded in a sort of rustling white mist; she was gone; and he heard the spluttering and growling of her taxi, bearing her to the ball. So! She tryrannized and bullied, even before she had him at her mercy, did she? She should see! Anger had brightened his eyes; the room came clear again. And slowly raising himself he sounded the bell twice, for the girl, not for that fellow Meller, who was in the plot. As soon as her pretty black and white-aproned figure stood before him, he said:

"Help me up!"

Twice her soft pulling was not enough, and he sank back. The third time he struggled to his feet.

"Thank you! that'll do." Then, waiting till she was gone, he crossed the room, fumbled open the sideboard door, and took out the bottle. Reaching over the polished oak, he grasped a sherry glass; and holding the bottle with both hands, tipped the liquor into it, put it to his lips and sucked. Drop by drop it passed over his palate—mild, very old, old as himself, colored like sunlight, fragrant. To the last drop he drank it, then hugging the bottle to his shirt-front, he moved snail-like to his chair, and fell back into its depths.

For some minutes he remained there motionless, the bottle clasped to his chest, thinking: 'This is not the attitude of a gentleman. I must put it down on the table—on the table;' but a thick cloud was between him and everything. It was with his hands he would have to put the bottle on the table! But he could not find his hands, could not feel them. His mind see-sawed in strophe and antistrophe: "You can't move!"—"I will move!" "You're beaten"—"I'm not beat." "Give up"—"I won't." That struggle to find his hands seemed to last for ever—he *must* find them! After that—go down—all standing— after that! Everything round him was red. Then the red cloud cleared just a little, and he could hear the clock—"tick—tick—tick"; a faint sensation spread from his shoulders down to his wrists, down his palms; and yes—he could feel the bottle! He redoubled his struggle to get forward in his chair; to get forward and put the bottle down. It was not dignified like this! One arm he could move now; but he could not grip the bottle nearly tight enough to put it down. Working his whole body forward, inch by inch, he shifted himself up in the chair till he could lean sideways, and the bottle, slipping down his chest, dropped slanting to the edge of the low stool-table. Then with all his might he screwed his trunk and arms an inch further, and the bottle stood. He had done it—done it! His lips twitched into a smile; his body sagged back to its old position. He had done it! And he closed his eyes. . . .

At half-past eleven the girl Molly, opening the door, looked at him and said softly: "Sirr! there's some ladies, and a gentleman!" But he did not answer. And, still holding the door, she whispered out into the hall:

"He's asleep, miss."

A voice whispered back:

"Oh! Just let me go in, I won't wake him unless he does. But I do want to show him my dress."

The girl moved aside; and on tiptoe Phyllis passed in. She walked to where, between the lamp-glow and the fire-glow, she was lighted up. White satin—her first low-cut dress—the flush of her first supper party—a gardenia at her breast, another in her fingers! Oh! what a pity he was asleep! How red he looked! How funnily old men breathed! And mysteriously, as a child might, she whispered:

"Guardy!"

No answer! And pouting, she stood twiddling the gardenia. Then suddenly she thought: 'I'll put it in his buttonhole! When he wakes up and sees it, how he'll jump!'

And stealing close, she bent and slipped it in. Two faces looked at her from round the door; she heard Bob Pillin's smothered chuckle; her mother's rich and feathery laugh. Oh! How red his forehead was! She touched it with her lips; skipped back, twirled round, danced silently a second, blew a kiss, and like quicksilver was gone.

And the whispering, the chuckling, and one little outpealing laugh rose in the hall.

But the old man slept. Nor until Meller came at his usual hour of half-past twelve, was it known that he would never wake.

RALPH HODGSON

Time, you Old Gipsy Man

TIME, you old gipsy man,
Will you not stay,
Put up your caravan
Just for one day?

All things I'll give you
Will you be my guest,
Bells for your jennet
Of silver the best,
Goldsmiths shall beat you
A great golden ring,
Peacocks shall bow to you,
Little boys sing,
Oh, and sweet girls will
Festoon you with may.
Time, you old gipsy,
Why hasten away?

Last week in Babylon,
Last night in Rome,
Morning, and in the crush
Under Paul's dome;
Under Paul's dial
You tighten your rein—
Only a moment,
And off once again;
Off to some city
Now blind in the womb,
Off to another
Ere that's in the tomb.

Time, you old gipsy man,
Will you not stay,
Put up your caravan
Just for one day?

Eve

EVE, with her basket, was
Deep in the bells and grass,
Wading in bells and grass
Up to her knees,
Picking a dish of sweet
Berries and plums to eat,
Down in the bells and grass
Under the trees.

Mute as a mouse in a
Corner the cobra lay,
Curled round a bough of the
Cinnamon tall. . . .
Now to get even and
Humble proud heaven and
Now was the moment or
Never at all.

"Eva!" Each syllable
Light as a flower fell,
"Eva!" he whispered the
Wondering maid,
Soft as a bubble sung
Out of a linnet's lung,
Soft and most silverly
"Eva!" he said.

Picture that orchard sprite,
Eve, with her body white,
Supple and smooth to her
Slim finger tips,
Wondering, listening,
Listening, wondering,
Eve with a berry
Half-way to her lips.

Oh, had our simple Eve
Seen through the make-believe!
Had she but known the
Pretender he was!
Out of the boughs he came,
Whispering still her name,
Tumbling in twenty rings
Into the grass.

Here was the strangest pair
In the world anywhere,
Eve in the bells and grass
Kneeling, and he
Telling his story low. . . .
Singing birds saw them go
Down the dark path to
The Blasphemous Tree.

Oh, what a clatter when
Titmouse and Jenny Wren
Saw him successful and
Taking his leave!
How the birds rated him,

How they all hated him!
How they all pitied
Poor motherless Eve!

Picture her crying
Outside in the lane,
Eve, with no dish of sweet
Berries and plums to eat,
Haunting the gate of the
Orchard in vain. . . .
Picture the lewd delight
Under the hill to-night—
"Eva!" the toast goes round,
"Eva!" again.

WALTER DE LA MARE

The Sleeper

As Ann came in one summer's day,
  She felt that she must creep,
So silent was the clear cool house,
  It seemed a house of sleep.
And sure, when she pushed open the door,
  Rapt in the stillness there,
Her mother sat, with stooping head,
  Asleep upon a chair;
Fast—fast asleep; her two hands laid
  Loose-folded on her knee,
So that her small unconscious face
  Looked half unreal to be:
So calmly lit with sleep's pale light
  Each feature was; so fair
Her forehead—every trouble was
  Smoothed out beneath her hair.
But though her mind in dream now
    moved,
  Still seemed her gaze to rest—
From out beneath her fast-sealed lids,
  Above her moving breast—
On Ann; as quite, quite still she stood;
  Yet slumber lay so deep
Even her hands upon her lap
  Seemed saturate with sleep.
And as Ann peeped, a childlike dread
  Stole over her, and then,
On stealthy, mouselike feet she trod,
  And tiptoed out again.

Winter Dusk

DARK frost was in the air without,
  The dusk was still with cold and gloom,
When less than even a shadow came
  And stood within the room.

But of the three around the fire,
  None turned a questioning head to look,
Still read a clear voice, on and on,
  Still stooped they o'er their book.

The children watched their mother's eyes
  Moving on softly line to line;
It seemed to listen too—that shade,
  Yet made no outward sign.

The fire-flames crooned a tiny song,
  No cold wind moved the wintry tree;
The children both in Faërie dreamed
  Beside their mother's knee.

And nearer yet that spirit drew
  Above that heedless one, intent
Only on what the simple words
  Of her small story meant.

No voiceless sorrow grieved her mind,
  No memory her bosom stirred,
Nor dreamed she, as she read to two,
  'Twas surely three who heard.

Yet when, the story done, she smiled
  From face to face, serene and clear,
A love, half dread, sprang up, as she
  Leaned close and drew them near.

The Listeners

"Is there anybody there?" said the Trav-
    eller,
  Knocking on the moonlit door;
And his horse in the silence champed the
    grasses
  Of the forest's ferny floor:
And a bird flew up out of the turret,
  Above the Traveller's head:
And he smote upon the door again a sec-
    ond time;
  "Is there anybody there?" he said.
But no one descended to the Traveller;

No head from the leaf-fringed sill
Leaned over and looked into his grey
    eyes,
  Where he stood perplexed and still.
But only a host of phantom listeners
  That dwelt in the lone house then
Stood listening in the quiet of the moon-
    light
  To that voice from the world of men:
Stood thronging the faint moonbeams on
    the dark stair,
  That goes down to the empty hall,
Hearkening in an air stirred and shaken
  By the lonely Traveller's call.
And he felt in his heart their strangeness,
  Their stillness answering his cry,
While his horse moved, cropping the dark
    turf,
  'Neath the starred and leafy sky;
For he suddenly smote on the door, even
  Louder, and lifted his head:—
"Tell them I came, and no one answered,
  That I kept my word," he said.
Never the least stir made the listeners,
  Though every word he spake
Fell echoing through the shadowiness of
    the still house
  From the one man left awake:
Ay, they heard his foot upon the stirrup,
  And the sound of iron on stone,
And how the silence surged softly back-
    ward,
  When the plunging hoofs were gone.

GILBERT KEITH CHESTERTON

From THE BALLAD OF THE WHITE
HORSE

Book VII. Ethandune: The Last Charge

King Guthrun and his Northmen
ravaged the land from Chester to the
Humber, until they came to the heights
of Wessex and the Hill of the Horse.
Here, in the Battle of Ethandune, they
were finally attacked by the hastily
mustered forces of King Alfred and
his Chiefs. In the first day's fighting
the Chiefs—Saxon, Celt, Roman, and
Norseman—all were slain, and Alfred
was driven back, with a tiny remnant
of his poor host.

AWAY in the waste of White Horse
    Down
  An idle child alone
Played some small game through hours
    that pass
And patiently would pluck the grass,
  Patiently push the stone.

On the lean, green edge for ever,
  Where the blank chalk touched the
    turf,
The child played on, alone, divine,
As a child plays on the last line
  That sunders sand and surf.

For he dwelleth in high divisions
  Too simple to understand,
Seeing on what morn of mystery
The Uncreated rent the sea
  With roarings from the land.

Through the long infant hours like days
  He built one tower in vain—
Piled up small stones to make a town,
And evermore the stones fell down,
  And he piled them up again.

And crimson kings on battle-towers,
  And saints on Gothic spires,
And hermits on their peaks of snow,
  And heroes on their pyres,

And patriots riding royally
  That rush the rocking town,
Stretch hands, and hunger and aspire,
Seeking to mount where high and higher,
The child whom Time can never tire,
  Sings over White Horse Down.

And this was the might of Alfred
  At the ending of the way;
That of such smiters wise or wild,
He was least distant from the child,
  Piling stones all day.

For Eldred fought like a frank hunter,
  That killeth and goeth home;

And Mark had fought because all arms
   Rang like the name of Rome.

And Colan fought with a double mind,
   Moody and madly gay;
But Alfred fought as gravely
   As a good child at play.

He saw wheels break and work run back,
   And all things as they were;
And his heart was orbed like victory,
   And simple like despair.

Therefore is Mark forgotten,
   That was wise with his tongue and
      brave;
And the cairn over Colan crumbled,
   And the cross on Eldred's grave.

Their great souls went on a wind away,
   And they have not tale or tomb;
And Alfred born in Wantage
   Rules England till the doom.

Because in the forest of all fears,
   Like a strange fresh gust from sea,
Struck him that ancient innocence
   That is more than mastery.

And as a child whose bricks fall down,
   Re-piles them o'er and o'er;
Came ruin and the rain that burns,
Returning as a wheel returns,
And crouching in the furze and ferns
   He began his life once more.

He took his ivory horn unslung
   And smiled, but not in scorn;
"Endeth the Battle of Ethandune
   With the blowing of a horn."

On a dark horse at the double way
   He saw great Guthrum ride;
Heard roar of brass and ring of steel,
The laughter and the trumpet peal,
   The pagan in his pride,

And Ogier's red and hated head
   Moved in some talk or task;
But the men seemed scattered in the
      brier,

And some of them had lit a fire,
   And one had broached a cask.

And waggons one or two stood up,
   Like tall ships in sight,
As if an outpost were encamped
   At the cloven ways for night.

And joyous of the sudden stay
   Of Alfred's routed few,
Sat one upon a stone to sigh;
And some slipped up the road to fly,
Till Alfred in the fern hard by
   Set horn to mouth and blew.

And they all abode like statues—
   One sitting on the stone,
One half-way through the thorn hedge
      tall,
One with a leg across a wall;
And one looked backwards, very small,
   Far up the road, alone.

Grey twilight and a yellow star
   Hung over thorn and hill.
Two spears and a cloven war-shield lay
Loose on the road as cast-away,
The horn died faint in the forests grey,
   And the fleeing men stood still.

"Brothers at arms," said Alfred,
   "On this side lies the foe;
Are slavery and starvation flowers
   That you should pluck them so?

"For whether is it better
   To be prodded with Danish poles,
Having hewn a chamber in a ditch,
And hounded like a howling witch,
   Or smoked to death in holes?

"Or that before the red cock crow,
   All we, a thousand strong,
Go down the dark road to God's house,
   Singing a Wessex song?

"To sweat a slave to a race of slaves,
   To drink up infamy?
No, brothers, by your leave, I think
Death is a better ale to drink;
And by all the stars of Christ that sink,
   The Danes shall drink with me.

"To grow old cowed in a conquered land,
  With the sun itself discrowned,
To see trees crouch and cattle slink—
Death is a better ale to drink,
And by high Death on the fell brink,
  That flagon shall go round.

"Though dead are all the paladins,
  Whom Glory had in ken,
Though all your thunder-sworded thanes
With proud hearts died among the
    Danes,
While a man remains, great war re-
    mains;
  Now is a war of men.

"The men that tear the furrows,
  The men that fell the trees;
When all their lords be lost and dead,
The bondsmen of the earth shall tread
  The tyrants of the seas.

"The wheel of the roaring stillness
  Of all labours under the sun,
Speed the wild work as well at least,
  As the whole world's work is done.

"Let Hildred hack the shield-wall,
  Clean as he hacks the hedge;
Let Gurth the Fowler stand as cool
  As he stands on the chasm's edge;

"Let Gorlias ride the sea-kings
  As Gorlias rides the sea,
Then let all hell and Denmark drive,
Yelling to all its fiends alive,
  And not a rag care we."

When Alfred's word was ended,
  Stood firm that feeble line,
Each in his place with club or spear,
And fury deeper than deep fear,
  And smiles as sour as brine.

And the King held up the horn and said,
  "See ye my father's horn,
That Egbert blew in his empery,
Once, when he rode out commonly,
Twice when he rode for venery,
  And thrice on the battle-morn.

"But heavier fates have fallen
  The horn of the Wessex kings;
And I blew once, the riding sign,
To call you to the fighting line
  And glory and all good things,

"And now two blasts, the hunting sign,
  Because we turn to bay;
But I will not blow the three blasts,
  Till we be lost or they.

"And now I blow the hunting sign,
  Charge some, by rule and rod,
But when I blow the battle sign,
  Charge all, and go to God."

Wild stared the Danes at the double
    ways
  Where they loitered, all at large,
As that dark line for the last time
  Doubled the knee to charge—

And caught their weapons clumsily,
  And marvelled how and why—
In such degree, by rule and rod,
The people of the peace of God
  Went roaring down to die.

And when the last arrow
  Was fitted and was flown,
When the broken shield hung on the
    breast,
And the hopeless lance was laid in rest,
  And the hopeless horn blown,

The King looked up, and what he saw
  Was a great light like death,
For Our Lady stood on the standards
    rent,
As lonely and as innocent
As when between white walls she went
  In the lilies of Nazareth.

One instant in a still light,
  He saw Our Lady then,
Her dress was soft as western sky,
And she was a queen most womanly—
  But she was a queen of men.

Over the iron forest
  He saw Our Lady stand;

Her eyes were sad withouten art,
And seven swords were in her heart—
But one was in her hand.

Then the last charge went blindly,
And all too lost for fear;
The Danes closed round, a roaring ring,
And twenty clubs rose o'er the King,
Four Danes hewed at him, halloing,
And Ogier of the Stone and Sling
Drove at him with a spear.

But the Danes were wild with laughter,
And the great spear swung wide,
The point stuck to a straggling tree,
And either host cried suddenly,
As Alfred leapt aside.

Short time had shaggy Ogier
To pull his lance in line—
He knew King Alfred's axe on high,
He heard it rushing through the sky,

He cowered beneath it with a cry—
It split him to the spine;
And Alfred sprang over him dead,
And blew the battle sign.

Then bursting all and blasting,
Came Christendom like death,
Kicked from such catapults of will
The staves shiver, the barrels spill,
The waggons waver and crash and kill
The waggoners beneath.

Barriers go backwards, banners rend,
Great shields groan like a gong—
Horses like horns of nightmare
Neigh horribly and long.

Horses ramp high and rock and boil
And break their golden reins,
And slide on carnage clamorously,
Down where the bitter blood doth lie,
Where Ogier went on foot to die,
In the old way of the Danes.

"The high tide!" King Alfred cried;
"The high tide and the turn!
As a tide turns on the tall grey seas,
See how they waver in the trees,

How stray their spears, how knock their
knees,
How wild their watchfires burn!

"The Mother of God goes over them,
Walking on wind and flame,
And the storm-cloud drifts from city and
dale,
And the White Horse stamps in the
White Horse Vale,
And we all shall yet drink Christian ale,
In the village of our name.

"The Mother of God goes over them,
On dreadful Cherubs borne;
And the psalm is roaring above the rune,
And the cross goes over the sun and
moon;
Endeth the Battle of Ethandune,
With the blowing of the horn."

For back indeed disorderly
The Danes went clamouring,
Too worn to take anew the tale,
Or dazed with insolence and ale,
Or stunned of heaven, or stricken pale
Before the face of the King.

For dire was Alfred in his hour
The pale scribe witnesseth,
More mighty in defeat was he
Than all men else in victory;
And behind, his men came murderously,
Dry-throated, drinking death.

And Edgar of the Golden Ship
He broke with his own hand,
Took Ludwig from his lady's bower,
And smote down Harmer in his hour,
And vain and lonely stood the tower—
The tower in Guelderland.

And Torr out of his tiny boat,
Whose eyes beheld the Nile,
Wulf with his war cry on his lips,
And Hacro born in the eclipse,
Who blocked the Seine with battle-ships
Round Paris on the Isle.

And Hacon of the Harvest-song,
And Dirck from the Elbe he slew,

And Cnut that melted Durham bell,
And Fulk and fiery Oscar fell,
And Goderic and Sigael,
   And Uriel of the Yew.

And highest sang the slaughter,
   And fastest fell the slain,
When from the wood-road's blackening
     throat
A crowning and crashing wonder smote
   The rear-guard of the Dane.

For the dregs of Colan's company—
   Lost down the other road,
Had gathered and grown and heard the
     din,
And with wild yells came pouring in
Naked as their old British kin
   And bright with blood for woad.

And bare and bloody and aloft
   They bore before their band
The body of their mighty lord,
Colan of Caerleon, and the horde,
That bore King Alfred's battle-sword
   Broken in his left hand.

And a strange music went with him,
   Loud and yet strangely far;
The wild pipes of the western land,
Too keen for the ear to understand,
Sang high and deathly on each hand
   When the dead man went to war.

Blocked between ghost and buccaneer,
   Brave men have dropped and died,
And the wild sea-lords well might quail
As the ghastly war-pipes of the Gael
Called to the horns of White Horse
     Vale,
   And all the horns replied.

And Hildred the poor hedger
   Cut down four captains dead,
And Halfgar laid seven others low,
And the great earls wavered to and fro
   For the living and the dead.

And Gorlias grasped the great flag,
   The Raven of Odin, torn;
And the eyes of Guthrum altered,
   For the first time since morn.

As a turn of the wheel of tempest
   Tilts up the whole sky tall,
And cliffs of wan cloud luminous
Lean out like great walls over us,
   As if the heavens might fall;

As such a tall and tilted sky
   Sends certain snow or light,
So did the eyes of Guthrum change,
And the turn was more certain and more
     strange
   Than a thousand men in flight.

For not till the floor of the skies is
     split
And hell-fire shines through the sea,
Or the stars look up through the rent
     earth's knees,
Cometh such rending of certainties,
As when one wise man truly sees
   What is more wise than he.

He set his horse in the battle-breach
   Even Guthrum of the Dane,
And as ever had fallen fell his brand,
A falling tower o'er many a land,
But Gurth the Fowler laid one hand
   Upon this bridle rein.

King Guthrum was a great lord,
   And higher than his gods—
He put the popes to laughter,
   He chid the saints with rods.

He took this hollow world of ours
   For a cup to hold his wine;
In the parting of the woodways
   There came to him a sign.

In Wessex in the forest,
   In the breaking of the spears,
We set a sign on Guthrum
   To blaze a thousand years.

Where the high saddles jostle
   And the horse-tails toss,
There rose to the birds flying
A roar of dead and dying;
In deafness and strong crying
   We signed him with the cross.

Far out to the winding river
  The blood ran down for days,
When we put the cross on Guthrum
  In the parting of the ways.

JOHN MASEFIELD

Cargoes

QUINQUIREME of Nineveh from distant
    Ophir,
Rowing home to haven in sunny Pales-
    tine,
With a cargo of ivory,
And apes and peacocks,
Sandalwood, cedarwood, and sweet white
    wine.

Stately Spanish galleon coming from the
    Isthmus,
Dipping through the Tropics by the palm-
    green shores,
With a cargo of diamonds,
Emeralds, amethysts,
Topazes, and cinnamon, and gold moi-
    dores.

Dirty British coaster with a salt-caked
    smoke stack,
Butting through the Channel in the mad
    March days,

With a cargo of Tyne coal,
Road-rails, pig-lead,
Firewood, iron-ware, and cheap tin trays.

O little self, within whose small- ness lies

O LITTLE SELF, within whose smallness
    lies
All that man was, and is, and will be-
    come,
Atom unseen that comprehends the
    skies
And tells the tracks by which the planets
    roam.
That, without moving, knows the joys of
    wings,
The tiger's strength, the eagle's secrecy,
And in the hovel can consort with
    kings,
Or clothe a god with his own mystery.
O with what darkness do we cloak thy
    light,
What dusty folly gather thee for food,
Thou who alone art knowledge and de-
    light,
The heavenly bread, the beautiful, the
    good.
O living self, O god, O morning star,
Give us thy light, forgive us what we are.

The Western Islands

"ONCE there were two sailors; and one of them was Joe, and the other one was Jerry, and they were fishermen. And they'd a young apprentice-feller, and his name was Jim. And Joe was a great one for his pot, and Jerry was a wonder at his pipe; and Jim did all the work, and both of them banged him. So one time Joe and Jerry were in the beer-house, and there was a young parson there, telling the folks about foreign things, about plants and that. 'Ah,' he says, 'what wonders there are in the west.'

" 'What sort of wonders, begging your pardon, sir,' says Joe. 'What sort of wonders might them be?'

" 'Why, all sorts of wonders,' says the parson. 'Why, in the west,' he says, 'there's things you wouldn't believe. No, you wouldn't believe; not till you'd seen them,' he says. 'There's diamonds growing on the trees. And great, golden, glittering pearls as common as pea-straw. And there's islands in the west. Ah, I could tell you of them. Islands? I rather guess there's islands. None of your Isles of Man. None of your Alderney and Sark. Not in them seas.'

" 'What sort of islands might they be, begging your pardon, sir?' says Jerry.

" 'Why,' he says (the parson feller says), 'ISLANDS. Islands as big as Spain. Islands with rivers of rum and streams of sarsaparilla. And none of your roses. Rubies and ame-thynes is all the roses grows in them parts. With golden stalks to them, and big diamond sticks to them, and the taste of pork-crackling if you eat them. They're the sort of roses to have in your area,' he says.

" 'And what else might there be in them parts, begging your pardon, sir?' says Joe.

" 'Why,' he says, this parson says, 'there's wonders. There's not only wonders but miracles. And not only miracles, but sperrits.'

" 'What sort of sperrits might they be, begging your pardon?' says Jerry. 'Are they rum and that?'

" 'When I says sperrits,' says the parson feller, 'I mean ghosts.'

" 'Of course ye do,' says Joe.

" 'Yes, ghosts,' says the parson. 'And by ghosts I mean sperrits. And by sperrits I mean white things. And by white things I mean things as turn your hair white. And there's red devils there, and blue devils there, and a great gold queen a-waiting for a man to kiss her. And the first man as dares to kiss that queen, why he becomes king, and all her sacks of gold become his.'

" 'Begging your pardon, sir,' said Jerry, 'but whereabouts might these here islands be?'

" 'Why, in the west,' says the parson. 'In the west, where the sun sets.'

" 'Ah,' said Joe and Jerry. 'What wonders there are in the world.'

*   *   *   *   *

"Now, after that, neither one of them could think of anything but these here western islands. So at last they take their smack, and off they go in search of them. And Joe had a barrel of beer in the bows, and Jerry had a box of twist in the waist, and pore little Jim stood and steered abaft all. And in the evenings Jerry and Joe would bang their pannikins together, and sing of the great times they meant to have when they were married to the queen. Then they would clump pore little Jim across the head, and tell him to watch out, and keep her to her course, or they'd ride him down like you would a main tack. And he'd better mind his eye, they told him, or they'd make him long to be boiled and salted. And he'd better put more sugar in the tea, they said, or they'd cut him up for cod-bait. And who was he, they asked, to be wanting meat for dinner, when there was that much weevilly biscuit in the bread-barge? And boys was going to the dogs, they said, when limbs the like of him had the heaven-born insolence to want to sleep. And a nice pass things was coming to, they said, when a lad as they'd done everything for, and saved, so to speak, from the workhouse, should go for to snivel when they hit him a clip. If they'd said a word, when they was hit, when they was boys, they told him, they'd have had their bloods drawed, and been stood in the wind to cool. But let him take heed, they said, and be a good lad, and do the work of five, and they wouldn't half wonder, they used to say, as he'd be a man before his mother. So the sun shone, and the stars came out golden, and all the sea was a sparkle of gold with them. Blue was the sea, and the wind blew, too, and it blew Joe and Jerry west as fast as a cat can eat sardines.

> *   *   *   *   *

"And one fine morning the wind fell calm, and a pleasant smell came over the water, like nutmegs on a rum-milk-punch. Presently the dawn broke. And, lo and behold, a rousing great wonderful island, all scarlet with coral and with rubies. The surf that was beating on her sands went shattering into silver coins, into dimes, and pesetas, and francs, and fourpenny bits. And the flowers on the cliffs was all one gleam and glitter. And the beauty of that island was a beauty beyond the beauty of Sally Brown, the lady as kept the beer-house. And on the beach of that island, on a golden throne, like, sat a woman so lovely that to look at her was as good as a church-service for one.

" 'That's the party I got to kiss,' said Jerry. 'Steady, and beach her, Jim, boy,' he says. 'Run her ashore, lad. That's the party is to be my queen.'

" 'You've got a neck on you, all of a sudden,' said Joe. 'You ain't the admiral of this fleet. Not by a wide road you ain't. I'll do all the kissing as there's any call for. You keep clear, my son.'

"Here the boat ran her nose into the sand, and the voyagers went ashore.

" 'Keep clear, is it?' said Jerry. 'You tell me to keep clear? You tell me again, and I'll put a head on you—'ll make you sing like a kettle. Who are you to tell me to keep clear?'

" 'I tell you who I am,' said Joe. 'I'm a better man than you are. That's what I am. I'm Joe the Tank, from Limehouse Basin, and there's no tinker's donkey-boy'll make me stand from under. Who are you to go kissing queens? Who are you that talk so proud and so mighty? You've a face on you would make a Dago tired. You look like a sea-sick Kanaka that's boxed seven rounds with a buzz-saw. You've no more manners than a hog, and you've a lip on you would fetch the enamel off a cup.'

" 'If it comes to calling names,' said Jerry, 'you ain't the only pebble on the beach. Whatever you might think, I tell you you ain't. You're the round turn and two-half hitches of a figure of fun as makes the angels weep. That's what you are. And you're the right-hand strand, and the left-hand strand, and the centre strand, and the core, and the serving, and the marling, of a three-stranded, left-handed, poorly worked junk of a half begun and never finished odds and ends of a Port Mahon soldier. You look like a Portuguese drummer. You've a whelky red nose that shines like a port side-light. You've a face like a muddy field where they've been playing football in the rain. Your hair is an insult and a shame. I blush when I look at you. You give me a turn like the first day out to a first voyager. Kiss, will you? Kiss? Man, I tell you you'd paralyze a shark if you kissed him. Paralyze him, strike him cold. That's what a kiss of yours'd do.'

" 'You ought to 'a' been a parson,' said Joe, 'that's what you'd ought. There's many would 'a' paid you for talk like that. But for all your fine talk, and for all your dandy language, you'll not come the old soldier over me. No, nor ten of you. *You* talk of kissing, when there's a handsome young man, the likes of me, around. Neither you nor ten of you. To hear you talk one'd think you was a Emperor or a Admiral. One would think you was a Bishop or a King. One might mistake you for a General or a Member of Parliament. You might. Straight, you might. A General or a Bishop or a King. And what are you? What are you? I ask you plain. What are you?—I'll tell you what you are.

" 'You're him as hired himself out as a scarecrow, acos no one'd take you as a fo'c's'le hand. You're him as give the colic to a weather-cock. You're him as turned old Mother Bomby's beer. You're him as drowned the duck and stole the monkey. You're him as got the medal give him for having a face that made the bull tame. You're——'

" 'Now don't you cast no more to me,' said Jerry. 'For I won't take no lip from a twelve-a-shilling, cent-a-corner, the likes of you are. You're the clippings of old junk, what the Dagoes smoke in cigarettes. A swab, and a-wash-deck-broom, and the half of a pint of paint'd make a handsomer figger of a man than what you are. I've seen a coir whisk, what they grooms a mule with, as had a sweeter face than you got. So

stand aside, before you're put aside. I'm the king of this here island.
You can go chase yourself for another. Stand clear, I say, or I'll give
you a jog'll make your bells ring.'

* * * * *

"Now, while they were argufying, young Jim, the young apprentice
feller, he creeps up to the queen upon the throne. She was beautiful,
she was, and she shone in the sun, and she looked straight ahead of her
like a wax-work in a show. And in her hand she had a sack full of
jewels, and at her feet she had a sack full of gold, and by her side was
an empty throne ready for the king she married. But round her right
hand there was a red snake, and round her left hand there was a blue
snake, and the snakes hissed and twisted, and they showed their teeth
full of poison. So Jim looked at the snakes, and he hit them a welt,
right and left, and he kissed the lady.

"And immediately all the bells and the birds of the world burst out
a-ringing and a-singing. The lady awoke from her sleep, and Jim's
old clothes were changed to cloth of gold. And there he was, a king,
on the throne beside the lady.

"But the red snake turned to a big red devil who took a-hold of Joe,
and the blue snake turned to a big blue devil, who took a hold of Jerry.
And 'Come you here, you brawling pugs,' they said, 'come and shovel
sand.' And Joe and Jerry took the spades that were given to them.
And 'Dig, now,' said the devils. 'Heave round. Let's see you dig.
Dig, you scarecrows. And tell us when you've dug to London.' "

WILFRID WILSON GIBSON

Flannan Isle

"THOUGH three men dwell on Flannan
  Isle
To keep the lamp alight,
As we steer'd under the lee, we caught
No glimmer through the night!"

A passing ship at dawn had brought
The news; and quickly we set sail,
To find out what strange thing might ail
The keepers of the deep-sea light.

The winter day broke blue and bright,
With glancing sun and glancing spray,
As o'er the swell our boat made way,
As gallant as a gull in flight.

But, as we near'd the lonely isle;
And look'd up at the naked height;
And saw the lighthouse towering while
With blinded lantern, that all night
Had never shot a spark
Of comfort through the dark,
So ghostly in the cold sunlight
It seem'd, that we were struck the
  while
With wonder all too dread for words.

And, as into the tiny creek
We stole beneath the hanging crag,
We saw three queer, black, ugly birds—
Too big, by far, in my belief,
For guillemot or shag—
Like seamen sitting bolt-upright
Upon a half-tide reef:

But, as we near'd, they plunged from
    sight
Without a sound, or spurt of white.

And still too mazed to speak,
We landed; and made fast the boat;
And climb'd the track in single file,
Each wishing he was safe afloat,
On any sea, however far,
So it be far from Flannan Isle:
And still we seem'd to climb, and climb,
As though we'd lost all count of time,
And so must climb for evermore.
Yet, all too soon, we reached the door—
The black, sun-blister'd lighthouse-door,
That gaped for us ajar.

As, on the threshold, for a spell,
We paused, we seem'd to breathe the
    smell
Of limewash and of tar,
Familiar as our daily breath,
As though 'twere some strange scent of
    death:
And so, yet wondering, side by side,
We stood a moment, still tongue-tied:
And each with black foreboding eyed
The door, ere we should fling it wide,
To leave the sunlight for the gloom:
Till, plucking courage up, at last,
Hard on each other's heels we pass'd
Into the living-room.

Yet, as we crowded through the door,
We only saw a table, spread
For dinner, meat and cheese and bread;
But all untouch'd; and no one there:
As though, when they sat down to eat,
Ere they could even taste,
Alarm had come; and they in haste
Had risen and left the bread and meat:
For at the table-head a chair
Lay tumbled on the floor.

We listen'd; but we only heard
The feeble cheeping of a bird
That starved upon its perch:
And, listening still, without a word,
We set about our hopeless search.

We hunted high, we hunted low,
And soon ransack'd the empty house;
Then o'er the Island, to and fro,
We ranged, to listen and to look
In every cranny, cleft or nook
That might have hid a bird or mouse:
But, though we search'd from shore to
    shore,
We found no sign in any place:
And soon again stood face to face
Before the gaping door:
And stole into the room once more
As frighten'd children steal.

Aye: though we hunted high and low,
And hunted everywhere,
Of the three men's fate we found no
    trace
Of any kind in any place,
But a door ajar, and an untouch'd meal,
And an overtoppled chair.

And, as we listen'd in the gloom
Of that forsaken living-room—
A chill clutch on our breath—
We thought how ill-chance came to all
Who kept the Flannan Light:
And how the rock had been the death
Of many a likely lad:
How six had come to a sudden end,
And three had gone stark mad:
And one whom we'd all known as friend
Had leapt from the lantern one still
    night,
And fallen dead by the lighthouse wall:
And long we thought
On the three we sought,
And of what might yet befall.

Like curs a glance has brought to heel,
We listen'd, flinching there:
And look'd, and look'd, on the untouch'd
    meal
And the overtoppled chair.

We seem'd to stand for an endless while,
Though still no word was said,
Three men alive on Flannan Isle,
Who thought on three men dead.

The Hare

My hands were hot upon a hare,
Half-strangled, struggling in a snare—
My knuckles at her warm wind-pipe—
When suddenly, her eyes shot back,
Big, fearful, staggering and black,
And ere I knew, my grip was slack;
And I was clutching empty air,
Half-mad, half-glad at my lost luck . . .
When I awoke beside the stack.

'Twas just the minute when the snipe
As though clock-wakened, every jack,
An hour ere dawn, dart in and out
The mist-wreaths filling syke and slack,
And flutter wheeling round about,
And drumming out the Summer night.
I lay star-gazing yet a bit;
Then, chilly-skinned, I sat upright,
To shrug the shivers from my back;
And, drawing out a straw to suck,
My teeth nipped through it at a bite . . .
The liveliest lad is out of pluck
An hour ere dawn—a tame cock-spar-
    row—
When cold stars shiver through his mar-
    row,
And wet mist soaks his mother-wit.

But, as the snipe dropped, one by one;
And one by one the stars blinked out;
I knew 'twould only need the sun
To send the shudders right about:
And as the clear East faded white,
I watched and wearied for the sun—
The jolly, welcome, friendly sun—
The sleepy sluggard of a sun
That still kept snoozing out of sight,
Though well he knew the night was
    done . . .
And after all, he caught me dozing,
And leapt up, laughing, in the sky
Just as my lazy eyes were closing:
And it was good as gold to lie
Full-length among the straw, and feel
The day wax warmer every minute,
As, glowing glad, from head to heel,
I soaked, and rolled rejoicing in it . . .

When from the corner of my eye,
Upon a heathery knowe hard-by,
With long lugs cocked, and eyes astare,
Yet all serene, I saw a hare.

Upon my belly in the straw,
I lay, and watched her sleek her fur,
As, daintily, with well-licked paw,
She washed her face and neck and ears:
Then, clean and comely in the sun,
She kicked her heels up, full for fun,
As if she did not care a pin
Though she should jump out of her skin,
And leapt and lolloped, free of fears,
Until my heart frisked round with her.

"And yet, if I but lift my head,
You'll scamper off, young Puss," I said.
"Still, I can't lie, and watch you play,
Upon my belly half the day.
The Lord alone knows where I'm going:
But, I had best be getting there.
Last night I loosed you from the snare—
Asleep, or waking, who's for knowing!—
So, I shall thank you now for showing
Which art to take to bring me where
My luck awaits me. When you're ready
To start, I'll follow on your track.
Though slow of foot, I'm sure and
    steady . . ."
She pricked her ears, then set them back;
And like a shot was out of sight:
And, with a happy heart and light,
As quickly I was on my feet;
And following the way she went,
Keen as a lurcher on the scent,
Across the heather and the bent,
Across the quaking moss and peat.
Of course, I lost her soon enough,
For moorland tracks are steep and
    rough;
And hares are made of nimbler stuff
Than any lad of seventeen,
However lanky-legged and tough,
However kestrel-eyed and keen:
And I'd at last to stop and eat
The little bit of bread and meat
Left in my pocket overnight.
So, in a hollow, snug and green,

I sat beside a burn, and dipped
The dry bread in an icy pool;
And munched a breakfast fresh and
    cool . . .
And then sat gaping like a fool . . .
For, right before my very eyes,
With lugs acock and eyes astare,
I saw again the selfsame hare.

So, up I jumped, and off she slipped;
And I kept sight of her until
I stumbled in a hole, and tripped,
And came a heavy, headlong spill;
And she, ere I'd the wit to rise,
Was o'er the hill, and out of sight:
And, sore and shaken with the tumbling,
And sicker at my foot for stumbling,
I cursed my luck, and went on, grum-
    bling,
The way her flying heels had fled.

The sky was cloudless overhead,
And just alive with larks asinging;
And in a twinkling I was swinging
Across the windy hills, lighthearted.
A kestrel at my footstep started,
Just pouncing on a frightened mouse,
And hung o'er head with wings a-hover;
Through rustling heath an adder darted:
A hundred rabbits bobbed to cover:
A weasel, sleek and rusty-red,
Popped out of sight as quick as winking:
I saw a grizzled vixen slinking
Behind a clucking brood of grouse
That rose and cackled at my coming:
And all about my way were flying
The peewit, with their slow wings
    creaking;
And little jack-snipe darted, drumming:
And now and then a golden plover
Or redshank piped with reedy whistle.
But never shaken bent or thistle
Betrayed the quarry I was seeking;
And not an instant, anywhere
Did I clap eyes upon a hare.

So, travelling still, the twilight caught
    me;
And as I stumbled on, I muttered:

"A deal of luck the hare has brought
    me!
The wind and I must spend together
A hungry night among the heather.
If I'd her here . . ." And as I uttered,
I tripped, and heard a frightened squeal;
And dropped my hands in time to feel
The hare just bolting 'twixt my feet.
She slipped my clutch: and I stood there
And cursed that devil-littered hare,
That left me stranded in the dark
In that wide waste of quaggy peat
Beneath black night without a spark:
When, looking up, I saw a flare
Upon a far-off hill, and said:
"By God, the heather is afire!
It's mischief at this time of year . . ."
And then, as one bright flame shot higher,
And booths and vans stood out quite
    clear,
My wits came back into my head;
And I remembered Brough Hill Fair.
And as I stumbled towards the glare
I knew the sudden kindling meant
The Fair was over for the day;
And all the cattle-folk away;
And gipsy folk and tinkers now
Were lighting supper-fires without
Each caravan and booth and tent.
And as I climbed the stiff hill-brow
I quite forgot my lucky hare.
I'd something else to think about:
For well I knew there's broken meat
For empty bellies after fair-time;
And looked to have a royal rare time
With something rich and prime to eat;
And then to lie and toast my feet
All night beside the biggest fire.

But, even as I neared the first,
A pleasant whiff of stewing burst
From out a smoking pot a-bubble:
And as I stopped behind the folk
Who sprawled around, and watched it
    seething,
A woman heard my eager breathing,
And, turning, caught my hungry eye:
And called out to me: "Draw in nigher,

Unless you find it too much trouble;
Or you've a nose for better fare,
And go to supper with the Squire . . .
You've got the hungry parson's air!"
And all looked up, and took the joke,
As I dropped gladly to the ground
Among them, when they all lay gazing
Upon the bubbling and the blazing.
My eyes were dazzled by the fire
At first; and then I glanced around;
And in those swarthy, fire-lit faces—
Though drowsing in the glare and heat
And snuffing the warm savour in,
Dead-certain of their fill of meat—
I felt the bit between the teeth,
The flying heels, the broken traces,
And heard the highroad ring beneath
The trampling hoofs; and knew them
    kin.
Then for the first time, standing there
Behind the woman who had hailed me,
I saw a girl with eyes astare
That looked in terror o'er my head;
And, all at once, my courage failed
    me . . .
For now again, and sore-adread,
My hands were hot upon a hare,
That struggled, strangling in the
    snare . . .
Then once more as the girl stood clear,
Before me—quaking cold with fear—
I saw the hare look from her eyes . . .

And when, at last, I turned to see
What held her scared, I saw a man—
A fat man with dull eyes aleer—
Within the shadow of the van;
And I was on the point to rise
To send him spinning 'mid the wheels
And stop his leering grin with mud . . .
And would have done it in a tick . . .
When, suddenly, alive with fright,
She started, with red, parted lips,
As though she guessed we'd come to
    grips,
And turned her black eyes full on
    me . . .
And as I looked into their light
My heart forgot the lust of fight,

And something shot me to the quick,
And ran like wildfire through my blood,
And tingled to my finger-tips . . .
And, in a dazzling flash, I knew
I'd never been alive before . . .
And she was mine for evermore.

While all the others slept asnore
In caravan and tent that night,
I lay alone beside the fire;
And stared into its blazing core,
With eyes that would not shut or tire,
Because the best of all was true,
And they looked still into the light
Of her eyes, burning ever bright
Within the brightest coal for me . . .
Once more, I saw her, as she started,
And glanced at me with red lips parted:
And as she looked, the frightened hare
Had fled her eyes; and merrily
She smiled, with fine teeth flashing white,
As though she, too, were happy-
    hearted . . .
Then she had trembled suddenly,
And dropped her eyes, as that fat man
Stepped from the shadow of the van,
And joined the circle, as the pot
Was lifted off, and, piping-hot,
The supper streamed in wooden bowls.
Yet, she had hardly touched a bite;
And had never raised her eyes all night
To mine again; but on the coals,
As I sat staring, she had stared—
The black curls, shining round her head
From under the red kerchief, tied
So nattily beneath her chin—
And she had stolen off to bed
Quite early, looking dazed and scared.
Then, all agape and sleepy-eyed,
Ere long the others had turned in:
And I was rid of that fat man,
Who slouched away to his own van.

And now, before her van, I lay,
With sleepless eyes, awaiting day;
And as I gazed upon the glare
I heard, behind, a gentle stir:
And, turning round, I looked on her
Where she stood on the little stair

Outside the van, with listening air—
And, in her eyes, the hunted hare . . .
And then, I saw her slip away,
A bundle underneath her arm,
Without a single glance at me.
I lay a moment wondering,
My heart a-thump like anything,
Then, fearing she should come to harm,
I rose, and followed speedily
Where she had vanished in the night.
And as she heard my step behind
She started, and stopt dead with fright;
Then blundered on as if struck blind:
And now as I caught up with her,
Just as she took the moorland track,
I saw the hare's eyes, big and black . . .
She'd made as though she'd double
    back . . .
But when she looked into my eyes,
She stood quite still and did not stir . . .
And picking up her fallen pack
I tucked it 'neath my arm; and she
Just took her luck quite quietly,
As she must take what chance might
    come,
And would not have it otherwise,
And walked into the night with me,
Without a word across the fells.

And all about us, through the night,
The mists were stealing, cold and white,
Down every rushy syke or slack:
But, soon the moon swung into sight;
And as we went my heart was light,
And singing like a burn in flood:
And in my ears were tinkling bells;
My body was a rattled drum:
And fifes were shrilling through my
    blood
That summer night, to think that she
Was walking through the world with me.

But when the air with dawn was chill,
As we were travelling down a hill,
She broke her silence with low-sobbing;
And told her tale, her bosom throbbing
As though her very heart were shaken
With fear she'd yet be overtaken . . .
She'd always lived in caravans—

Her father's, gay as any man's,
Grass-green, picked out with red and
    yellow
And glittering brave with burnished
    brass
That sparkled in the sun like flame,
And window curtains, white as snow . . .
But, they had died, ten years ago,
Her parents both, when fever came . . .
And they were buried, side by side,
Somewhere beneath the wayside
    grass . . .
In times of sickness, they kept wide
Of towns and busybodies, so
No parson's or policeman's tricks
Should bother them when in a fix . . .
Her father never could abide
A black coat or a blue, poor man . . .
And so, Long Dick, a kindly fellow,
When you could keep him from the can,
And Meg, his easy-going wife,
Had taken her into the van;
And kept her since her parents died . . .
And she had lived a happy life,
Until Fat Pete's young wife was
    taken . . .
But, ever since, he'd pestered her . . .
And she dared scarcely breathe or stir,
Lest she should see his eyes aleer . . .
And many a night she'd lain and shaken,
And very nearly died of fear—
Though safe enough within the van
With Mother Meg and her good-man—
For, since Fat Pete was Long Dick's
    friend,
And they were thick and sweet as honey,
And Dick owed Pete a lot of money,
She knew too well how it must end . . .
And she would rather lie stone dead
Beneath the wayside grass than wed
With leering Pete, and live the life,
And die the death, of his first wife . . .
And so, last night, clean-daft with dread,
She'd bundled up a pack and fled . . .

When all the sobbing tale was out,
She dried her eyes, and looked about,
As though she'd left all fear behind,
And out of sight were out of mind,

Then, when the dawn was burning red,
"I'm hungry as a hawk!" she said:
And from the bundle took out bread,
And at the happy end of night
We sat together by a burn:
And ate a thick slice, turn by turn;
And laughed and kissed between each
    bite.

Then, up again, and on our way
We went; and tramped the livelong day
The moorland trackways, steep and
    rough,
Though there was little fear enough
That they would follow on our flight.

And then again a shiny night
Among the honey-scented heather,
We wandered in the moonblaze bright,
Together through a land of light,
A lad and lass alone with life.
And merrily we laughed together,
When, starting up from sleep, we heard
The cock-grouse talking to his wife . . .
And "Old Fat Pete" she called the bird.

Six months and more have cantered by:
And, Winter past, we're out again—
We've left the fat and weatherwise
To keep their coops and reeking sties,
And eat their fill of oven-pies,
While we win free and out again
To take potluck beneath the sky
With sun and moon and wind and rain.
Six happy months . . . and yet, at night,
I've often wakened in affright,
And looked upon her lying there,
Beside me sleeping quietly,
Adread that when she waked, I'd see
The hunted hare within her eyes.

And only last night, as I slept
Beneath the shelter of a stack . . .
My hands were hot upon a hare,
Half-strangled, struggling in the snare,
When, suddenly, her eyes shot back,
Big, fearful, staggering and black;
And ere I knew, my grip was slack,
And I was clutching empty air . . .
Bolt-upright from my sleep I leapt . . .

Her place was empty in the straw . . .
And then, with quaking heart, I saw
That she was standing in the night,
A leveret cuddled to her breast . . .

I spoke no word; but as the light
Through banks of Eastern cloud was
    breaking,
She turned, and saw that I was waking:
And told me how she could not rest;
And, rising in the night, she'd found
This baby-hare crouched on the ground;
And she had nursed it quite a while;
But, now, she'd better let it go . . .
Its mother would be fretting so . . .
A mother's heart . . .
                I saw her smile
And look at me with tender eyes;
And as I looked into their light,
My foolish, fearful heart grew wise . . .
And now, I knew that never there
I'd see again the startled hare,
Or need to dread the dreams of night.

Devil's Edge

ALL night I lay on Devil's Edge,
Along an overhanging ledge
Between the sky and sea:
And as I rested 'waiting sleep,
The windless sky and soundless deep
In one dim, blue infinity
Of starry peace encompassed me.

And I remembered, drowsily,
How 'mid the hills last night I'd lain
Beside a singing moorland burn;
And waked at dawn, to feel the rain
Fall on my face, as on the fern
That drooped about my heather-bed;
And how by noon the wind had blown
The last grey shred from out the sky,
And blew my homespun jacket dry,
As I stood on the topmost stone
That crowns the cairn on Hawkshaw
    Head,
And caught a gleam of far-off sea;
And heard the wind sing in the bent
Like those far waters calling me:
When, my heart answering to the call,

I followed down the seaward stream,
By silent pool and singing fall;
Till with a quiet, keen content,
I watched the sun, a crimson ball,
Shoot through grey seas a fiery gleam,
Then sink in opal deeps from sight.

And with the coming on of night,
The wind had dropped: and as I lay,
Retracing all the happy day,
And gazing long and dreamily
Across the dim, unsounding sea,
Over the far horizon came
A sudden sail of amber flame;
And soon the new moon rode on high
Through cloudless deeps of crystal sky.

Too holy seemed the night for sleep;
And yet, I must have slept, it seems;
For, suddenly, I woke to hear
A strange voice singing, shrill and clear,
Down in a gully black and deep
That cleft the beetling crag in twain.
It seemed the very voice of dreams
That drive hag-ridden souls in fear
Through echoing, unearthly vales,
To plunge in black, slow-crawling
    streams,
Seeking to drown that cry, in vain . . .
Or some sea creature's voice that wails
Through blind, white banks of fog un-
    lifting
To God-forgotten sailors drifting
Rudderless to death . . .
And as I heard,
Though no wind stirred,
An icy breath
Was in my hair . . .
And clutched my heart with cold de-
    spair . . .
But, as the wild song died away,
There came a faltering break
That shivered to a sobbing fall;
And seemed half-human, after all . . .

And yet, what foot could find a track
In that deep gully, sheer and black . . .
And singing wildly in the night!
So, wondering, I lay awake,

Until the coming of the light
Brought day's familiar presence back.

Down by the harbour-mouth that day,
A fisher told the tale to me.
Three months before, while out at sea,
Young Philip Burn was lost, though how,
None knew, and none would ever know.
The boat becalmed at noonday lay . . .
And not a ripple on the sea . . .
And Philip standing in the bow,
When his six comrades went below
To sleep away an hour or so,
Dog-tired with working day and night,
While he kept watch . . . and not a
    sound
They heard, until, at set of sun
They woke; and coming up they found
The deck was empty, Philip gone . . .
Yet not another boat in sight . . .
And not a ripple on the sea.
How he had vanished, none could tell.
They only knew the lad was dead
They'd left but now, alive and well . . .
And he, poor fellow, newly-wed . . .
And when they broke the news to her,
She spoke no word to anyone:
But sat all day, and would not stir—
Just staring, staring in the fire,
With eyes that never seemed to tire;
Until, at last, the day was done,
And darkness came; when she would rise,
And seek the door with queer, wild eyes;
And wander singing all the night
Unearthly songs beside the sea:
But always the first blink of light
Would find her back at her own door.

'Twas Winter when I came once more
To that old village by the shore;
And as, at night, I climbed the street,
I heard a singing, low and sweet,
Within a cottage near at hand:
And I was glad awhile to stand
And listen by the glowing pane:
And as I hearkened, that sweet strain
Brought back the night when I had lain
Awake on Devil's Edge . . .
And now I knew the voice again,

So different, free of pain and fear—
Its terror turned to tenderness—
And yet the same voice none the less,
Though singing now so true and clear:
And drawing nigh the window-ledge,
I watched the mother sing to rest
The baby snuggling to her breast.

PADRAIC COLUM

An Old Woman of the Roads

O, TO have a little house!
To own the hearth and stool and all!
The heaped up sods upon the fire,
The pile of turf against the wall!

To have a clock with weights and chains
And pendulum swinging up and down!
A dresser filled with shining delph,
Speckled and white and blue and brown!

I could be busy all the day
Clearing and sweeping hearth and floor,
And fixing on their shelf again
My white and blue and speckled store!

I could be quiet there at night
Beside the fire and by myself,
Sure of a bed and loth to leave
The ticking clock and the shining delph!

Och! but I'm weary of mist and dark,
And roads where there's never a house
    nor bush,
And tired I am of bog and road,
And the crying wind and the lonesome
    hush!

And I am praying to God on high,
And I am praying Him night and day,
For a little house—a house of my own—
Out of the wind's and the rain's way.

JAMES STEPHENS

The Snare

I HEAR a sudden cry of pain!
    There is a rabbit in a snare:
Now I hear the cry again,
    But I cannot tell from where.

But I cannot tell from where
    He is calling out for aid;
Crying on the frightened air,
    Making everything afraid.

Making everything afraid,
    Wrinkling up his little face,
As he cries again for aid;
    And I cannot find the place!

And I cannot find the place
    Where his paw is in the snare:
Little one! Oh, little one!
    I am searching everywhere.

JAMES ELROY FLECKER
(1884-1915)

Gates of Damascus

FOUR great gates has the city of Da-
    mascus,
    And four Grand Wardens, on their
    spears reclining,
All day long stand like tall stone men
    And sleep on the towers when the
    moon is shining.

*This is the song of the East Gate
    Warden*
*When he locks the great gate and smokes
    in his garden.*

Postern of Fate, the Desert Gate, Dis-
    aster's Cavern, Fort of Fear,
The Portal of Bagdad am I, the Door-
    way of Diarbekir.

The Persian Dawn with new desires may
    net the flushing mountain spires:
But my gaunt buttress still rejects the
    suppliance of those mellow fires.

Pass not beneath, O Caravan, or pass
    not singing. Have you heard
That silence where the birds are dead yet
    something pipeth like a bird?

Pass not beneath! Men say there blows
    in stony deserts still a rose
But with no scarlet to her leaf—and
    from whose heart no perfume flows.

Wilt thou bloom red where she buds pale,
    thy sister rose? Wilt thou not fail
When noonday flashes like a flail? Leave
    nightingale the caravan!

Pass then, pass all! "Bagdad!" ye cry,
    and down the billows of blue sky
Ye beat the bell that beats to hell, and
    who shall thrust ye back? Not I.

The Sun who flashes through the head
    and paints the shadows green and
    red,—
The Sun shall eat thy fleshless dead, O
    Caravan, O Caravan!

And one who licks his lips for thirst with
    fevered eyes shall face in fear
The palms that wave, the streams that
    burst, his last mirage, O Caravan!

And one—the bird-voiced Singing-man—
    shall fall behind thee, Caravan!
And God shall meet him in the night, and
    he shall sing as best he can.

And one the Bedouin shall slay, and one,
    sand-stricken on the way,
Go dark and blind; and one shall say—
    "How lonely is the Caravan!"

Pass out beneath, O Caravan, Doom's
    Caravan, Death's Caravan!
I had not told ye, fools, so much, save
    that I heard your Singing-man.

This was sung by the West Gate's keeper
When heaven's hollow dome grew deeper.

I am the gate toward the sea: O sailor
    men, pass out from me!
I hear you high on Lebanon, singing the
    marvels of the sea.

The dragon-green, the luminous, the
    dark, the serpent-haunted sea,
The snow-besprinkled wine of earth, the
    white-and-blue-flower foaming sea.

Beyond the sea are towns with towers,
    carved with lions and lily flowers,
And not a soul in all those lonely streets
    to while away the hours.

Beyond the towns, an isle where, bound,
    a naked giant bites the ground:
The shadow of a monstrous wing looms
    on his back: and still no sound.

Beyond the isle a rock that screams like
    madmen shouting in their dreams,
From whose dark issues night and day
    blood crashes in a thousand streams.

Beyond the rock is Restful Bay, where no
    wind breathes or ripple stirs,
And there on Roman ships, they say,
    stand rows of metal mariners.

Beyond the bay in utmost West old Solo-
    mon the Jewish King
Sits with his beard upon his breast, and
    grips and guards his magic ring:

And when that ring is stolen, he will rise
    in outraged majesty,
And take the World upon his back, and
    fling the World beyond the sea.

This is the song of the North Gate's
master,
Who singeth fast, but drinketh faster.

I am the gay Aleppo Gate: a dawn, a
    dawn and thou art there:
Eat not thy heart with fear and care, O
    brother of the beast we hate!

Thou hast not many miles to tread, nor
    other foes than fleas to dread;
Homs shall behold thy morning meal and
    Hama see thee safe in bed.

Take to Aleppo filigrane, and take them
    paste of apricots,
And coffee tables botched with pearl, and
    little beaten brassware pots:

And thou shalt sell thy wares for thrice
    the Damascene retailers' price,
And buy a fat Armenian slave who
    smelleth odorous and nice.

Some men of noble stock were made:
    some glory in the murder-blade:
Some praise a Science or an Art, but I
    like honourable Trade!

Sell them the rotten, buy the ripe! Their
 heads are weak; their pockets burn.
Aleppo men are mighty fools. Salaam
 Aleikum! Safe return!

*This is the song of the South Gate
 Holder,*
A silver man, but his song is older.

I am the Gate that fears no fall: the
 Mihrab of Damascus wall,
The bridge of booming Sinai: the Arch
 of Allah all in all.

O spiritual pilgrim rise: the night has
 grown her single horn:
The voices of the souls unborn are half
 adream with Paradise.

To Meccah thou hast turned in prayer
 with aching heart and eyes that
 burn:
Ah Hajji, whither wilt thou turn when
 thou art there, when thou art there?

God be thy guide from camp to camp:
 God be thy shade from well to well;
God grant beneath the desert stars thou
 hear the Prophet's camel bell.

And God shall make thy body pure, and
 give thee knowledge to endure
This ghost-life's piercing phantom-pain,
 and bring thee out to Life again.

And God shall make thy soul a Glass
 where eighteen thousand Æons pass,
And thou shalt see the gleaming Worlds
 as men see dew upon the grass.

And son of Islam, it may be that thou
 shalt learn at journey's end
Who walks thy garden eve on eve, and
 bows his head, and calls thee Friend.

The Burial in England

THESE then we honour: these in fragrant
 earth
Of their own country in great peace forget
Death's lion-roar and gust of nostril-
 flame

Breathing souls across to the Evening
 Shore.
Soon over these the flowers of our hill-
 sides
Shall wake and wave and nod beneath
 the bee
And whisper love to Zephyr year on year,
Till the red war gleam like a dim red
 rose
Lost in the garden of the Sons of Time.
But ah what thousands no such friendly
 doom
Awaits,—whom silent comrades in full
 night
Gazing right and left shall bury swiftly
By the cold flicker of an alien moon.
 Ye veilèd women, ye with folded
 hands,
Mourning those you half hoped for
 Death too dear,
I claim no heed of you. Broader than
 earth
Love stands eclipsing nations with his
 wings,
While Pain, his shadow, delves as black
 and deep
As he e'er flamed or flew. Citizens draw
Back from their dead awhile. Salute the
 flag!
 If this flag though royally always
 borne,
Deceived not dastard, ever served base
 gold;
If the dark children of the old Forest
Once feared it, or ill Sultans mocked it
 furled,
Yet now as on a thousand death-reaped
 days
It takes once more the unquestionable
 road.
O bright with blood of heroes, not a star
Of all the north shines purer on the sea!
 Our foes—the hardest men a state can
 forge,
An army wrenched and hammered like a
 blade
Toledo-wrought neither to break nor
 bend,

Dipped in that ice the pedantry of power,
And toughened with wry gospels of dismay;
Such are these who brake down the door of France,
Wolves worrying at the old World's honour,
Hunting Peace not to prison but her tomb.
But ever as some brown song-bird whose torn nest
Gapes robbery, darts on the hawk like fire,
So Peace hath answered, angry and in arms.
And from each grey hamlet and bright town of France
From where the apple or the olive grows
Or thin tall strings of poplars on the plains,
From the rough castle of the central hills,
From the three coasts—of mist and storm and sun,
And meadows of the four deep-rolling streams,
From every house whose windows hear God's bell
Crowding the twilight with the wings of prayer
And flash their answer in a golden haze,
Stream the young soldiers who are never tired.
For all the foul mists vanished when that land
Called clear, as in the sunny Alpine morn
The jodeler awakes the frosty slopes
To thunderous replies,—soon fading far
Among the vales like songs of dead children.
But the French guns' answer, ne'er to echoes weak
Diminished, bursts from the deep trenches yet;
And its least light vibration blew to dust
The weary factions,—priest's or guild's or king's,
And side by side troop up the old partisans,

The same laughing, invincible, tough men
Who gave Napoleon Europe like a loaf,
For slice and portion,—not so long ago!
Either to Alsace or loved lost Lorraine
They pass, or inexpugnable Verdun
Ceintured with steel, or stung with faith's old cry
Assume God's vengeance for his temple stones.
But you maybe best wish them for the north
Beside you 'neath low skies in loamèd fields,
Or where the great line hard on the duned shore
Ends and night leaps to England's sea-borne flame.
Never one drop of Lethe's stagnant cup
Dare dim the fountains of the Marne and Aisne
Since still the flowers and meadow-grass unmown
Lie broken with the imprint of those who fell,
Briton and Gaul—but fell immortal friends
And fell victorious and like tall trees fell.
  But young men, you who loiter in the town,
Need you be roused with overshouted words,
Country, Empire, Honour, Liége, Louvain?
Pay your own Youth the duty of her dreams.
For what sleep shall keep her from the thrill
Of War's star-smiting music, with its swell
Of shore and forest and horns high in the wind,
(Yet pierced with that too sharp piping which if man
Hear and not fear he shall face God unscathed)?
What, are you poets whose vain souls contrive

Sorties and sieges spun of the trickling
　　moon
And such a rousing ghost-catastrophe
You need no concrete marvels to be
　　saved?
Or live you here too lustily for change?
Sail you such pirate seas on such high
　　quests,
Hunt you thick gold or striped and spot-
　　ted beasts,
Or tread the lone ways of the swan-like
　　mountains?
Excused.　But if, as I think, breeched in
　　blue,
Stalled at a counter, cramped upon a
　　desk,
You drive a woman's pencraft—or a
　　slave's,
What chain shall hold you when the
　　trumpets play,
Calling from the blue hill behind your
　　town,
Calling over the seas, calling for you!
"But"—do you murmur?—"we'd not be
　　as those.
Death is a dour recruiting-sergeant:
　　see,
These women weep, we celebrate the
　　dead."
Boys, drink the cup of warning dry.
　　Face square
That old grim hazard, "Glory-or-the-
　　Grave."
Not we shall trick your pleasant years
　　away,
Yet is not Death the great adventure
　　still,
And is it all loss to set ship clean anew
When heart is young and life an eagle
　　poised?
Choose, you're no cowards.　After all,
　　think some,
Since we are men and shrine immortal
　　souls
Surely for us as for these nobly dead
The Kings of England lifting up their
　　swords
Shall gather at the gate of Paradise.

RUPERT BROOKE (1887-1915)

The Great Lover

I HAVE been so great a lover: filled my
　　days
So proudly with the splendour of Love's
　　praise,
The pain, the calm, and the astonish-
　　ment,
Desire illimitable, and still content,
And all dear names men use, to cheat
　　despair,
For the perplexed and viewless streams
　　that bear
Our hearts at random down the dark of
　　life.
Now, ere the unthinking silence on that
　　strife
Steals down, I would cheat drowsy Death
　　so far,
My night shall be remembered for a star
That outshone all the suns of all men's
　　days.
Shall I not crown them with immortal
　　praise
Whom I have loved, who have given me,
　　dared with me
High secrets, and in darkness knelt to see
The inenarrable godhead of delight?
Love is a flame;—we have beaconed the
　　world's night.
A city:—and we have built it, these
　　and I.
An emperor:—we have taught the world
　　to die.
So, for their sakes I loved, ere I go
　　hence,
And the high cause of Love's magnifi-
　　cence,
And to keep loyalties young, I'll write
　　those names
Golden for ever, eagles, crying flames,
And set them as a banner, that men may
　　know,
To dare the generations, burn, and
　　blow
Out on the wind of Time, shining and
　　streaming. . . .

These I have loved:
  White plates and cups, clean-gleaming,
Ringed with blue lines; and feathery,
    faery dust;
Wet roofs, beneath the lamp-light; the
    strong crust
Of friendly bread; and many-tasting
    food;
Rainbows; and the blue bitter smoke of
    wood;
And radiant raindrops couching in cool
    flowers;
And flowers themselves, that sway
    through sunny hours,
Dreaming of moths that drink them
    under the moon;
Then, the cool kindliness of sheets, that
    soon
Smooth away trouble; and the rough
    male kiss
Of blankets; grainy wood; live hair
    that is
Shining and free; blue-massing clouds;
    the keen
Unpassioned beauty of a great machine;
The benison of hot water; furs to
    touch;
The good smell of old clothes; and other
    such—
The comfortable smell of friendly fingers,
Hair's fragrance, and the musty reek that
    lingers
About dead leaves and last year's
    ferns. . . .
                    Dear names,
And thousand other throng to me!
    Royal flames;
Sweet water's dimpling laugh from tap
    or spring;
Holes in the ground; and voices that do
    sing;
Voices in laughter, too; and body's pain,
Soon turned to peace; and the deep-
    panting train;
Firm sands; the little dulling edge of
    foam
That browns and dwindles as the wave
    goes home;

And washen stones, gay for an hour; the
    cold
Graveness of iron; moist black earthen
    mould;
Sleep; and high places; footprints in the
    dew;
And oaks; and brown horse-chestnuts,
    glossy-new;
And new-peeled sticks; and shining pools
    on grass;—
All these have been my loves. And these
    shall pass,
Whatever passes not, in the great hour,
Nor all my passion, all my prayers, have
    power
To hold them with me through the gate
    of Death.
They'll play deserter, turn with the
    traitor breath,
Break the high bond we made, and sell
    Love's trust
—Oh, never a doubt but, somewhere, I
    shall wake,
And give what's left of love again, and
    make
New friends, now strangers. . . .
                But the best I've known,
Stays here, and changes, breaks, grows
    old, is blown
About the winds of the world, and fades
    from brains
Of living men, and dies.
                    Nothing remains.

O dear my loves, O faithless, once again
This one last gift I give: that after men
Shall know, and later lovers, far-
    removed,
Praise you, "All these were lovely"; say,
    "He loved."

The Soldier

IF I should die, think only this of me:
That there's some corner of a foreign
    field
That is for ever England. There shall
    be

In that rich earth a richer dust concealed;
A dust whom England bore, shaped,
made aware,
Gave, once, her flowers to love, her ways
to roam,
A body of England's, breathing English
air,
Washed by the rivers, blest by suns of
home.

And think, this heart, all evil shed away,
A pulse in the eternal mind, no less
Gives somewhere back the thoughts by
England given;
Her sights and sounds; dreams happy as
her day;
And laughter, learnt of friends; and gen-
tleness,
In hearts at peace, under an English
heaven.

JULIAN GRENFELL (1888-1915)

Into Battle

THE naked earth is warm with Spring,
And with green grass and bursting trees
Leans to the sun's gaze glorying,
And quivers in the sunny breeze;

And life is Colour and Warmth and
Light,
And a striving evermore for these;
And he is dead who will not fight,
And who dies fighting has increase.

The fighting man shall from the sun
Take warmth, and life from the glowing
earth;
Speed with the light-foot winds to run
And with the trees to newer birth;

And find, when fighting shall be done,
Great rest, and fulness after dearth.

All the bright company of Heaven
Hold him in their high comradeship,
The Dog star, and the Sisters Seven,
Orion's belt and sworded hip:

The woodland trees that stand together,
They stand to him each one a friend;
They gently speak in the windy weather;
They guide to valley and ridge's end.

The kestrel hovering by day,
And the little owls that call by night,
Bid him be swift and keen as they,
As keen of ear, as swift of sight.

The blackbird sings to him: "Brother,
brother,
If this be the last song you shall sing,
Sing well, for you may not sing another;
Brother, sing."

In dreary doubtful waiting hours,
Before the brazen frenzy starts,
The horses show him nobler powers;—
O patient eyes, courageous hearts!

And when the burning moment breaks,
And all things else are out of mind,
And only joy of battle takes
Him by the throat and makes him blind,

Through joy and blindness he shall know,
Not caring much to know, that still
Nor lead nor steel shall reach him, so
That it be not the Destined Will.

The thundering line of battle stands,
And in the air Death moans and sings;
But Day shall clasp him with strong
hands,
And Night shall fold him in soft wings.

III. AMERICAN SELECTIONS

BENJAMIN FRANKLIN (1706-1790)

From THE AUTOBIOGRAPHY

Franklin Arrives in Philadelphia

I WAS in my working dress, my best clothes being to come round by sea. I was dirty from my journey; my pockets were stuff'd out with shirts and stockings, and I knew no soul nor where to look for lodging. I was fatigued with travelling, rowing, and want of rest, I was very hungry; and my whole stock of cash consisted of a Dutch dollar, and about a shilling in copper. The latter I gave the people of the boat for my passage, who at first refus'd it, on account of my rowing; but I insisted on their taking it. A man being sometimes more generous when he has but a little money than when he has plenty, perhaps thro' fear of being thought to have but little.

Then I walked up the street, gazing about till near the market-house I met a boy with bread. I had made many a meal on bread, and, inquiring where he got it, I went immediately to the baker's he directed me to, in Second-street, and ask'd for bisket, intending such as we had in Boston; but they, it seems, were not made in Philadelphia. Then I asked for a three-penny loaf, and was told they had none such. So not considering or knowing the difference of money, and the greater cheapness nor the names of his bread, I bad him give me three-penny worth of any sort. He gave me, accordingly, three great puffy rolls. I was surpriz'd at the quantity, but took it, and, having no room in my pockets, walk'd off with a roll under each arm, and eating the other. Thus I went up Market-street as far as Fourth-street, passing by the door of Mr. Read, my future wife's father; when she, standing at the door, saw me, and thought I made, as I certainly did, a most awkward, ridiculous appearance. Then I turned and went down Chestnut-street and part of Walnut-street, eating my roll all the way, and, coming round, found myself again at Market-street wharf, near the boat I came in, to which I went for a draught of the river water; and, being filled with one of my rolls, gave the other two to a woman and her child that came down the river in the boat with us, and were waiting to go farther.

Thus refreshed, I walked again up the street, which by this time had many clean-dressed people in it, who were all walking the same way. I joined them, and thereby was led into the great meeting-house of the Quakers near the market. I sat down among them, and, after looking round awhile and hearing nothing said, being very drowsy thro' labor and want of rest the preceding night, I fell fast asleep, and continued so till the meeting broke up, when one was kind enough to rouse me. This was, therefore, the first house I was in, or slept in, in Philadelphia.

Walking down again toward the river, and, looking in the faces of people, I met a young Quaker man, whose countenance I lik'd, and, accosting him, requested he would tell me where a stranger could get lodging. We were then near the sign of the Three Mariners. "Here," says he, "is one place that entertains strangers, but it is not a reputable house; if thee wilt walk with me, I'll show thee a better." He brougl me to the Crooked Billet in Water-street. Here I got a dinner; and, while I was eating it, several sly questions were asked me, as it seemed to be suspected from my youth and appearance, that I might be some runaway.

After dinner, my sleepiness return'd, and being shown to a bed, I lay down without undressing, and slept till six in the evening, was call'd to supper, went to bed again very early, and slept soundly till next morning. Then I made myself as tidy as I could, and went to Andrew Bradford the printer's. I found in the shop the old man his father, whom I had seen at New York, and who, travelling on horseback, had got to Philadelphia before me. He introduc'd me to his son, who receiv'd me civilly, gave me a breakfast, but told me he did not at present want a hand, being lately suppli'd with one; but there was another printer in town, lately set up, one Keimer, who, perhaps, might employ me; if not, I should be welcome to lodge at his house, and he would give me a little work to do now and then till fuller business should offer.

The old gentleman said he would go with me to the new printer; and when we found him, "Neighbor," says Bradford, "I have brought to see you a young man of your business; perhaps you may want such a one." He ask'd me a few questions, put a composing stick in my hand to see how I work'd, and then said he would employ me soon, though he had just then nothing for me to do; and, taking old Bradford, whom he had never seen before, to be one of the town's people that had a good will for him, enter'd into a conversation on his present undertaking and prospects; while Bradford, not discovering that he was the other printer's father, on Keimer's saying he expected soon to get the greatest part of the business into his own hands, drew him on by artful questions, and starting little doubts, to explain all his views, what interest he reli'd on, and in what manner he intended to proceed. I, who stood by and heard all, saw immediately that one of them was a crafty old sophister, and the other a mere novice. Bradford left me with Keimer, who was greatly surprised when I told him who the old man was.

Keimer's printing-house, I found, consisted of an old shatter'd press, and one small, worn-out font of English, which he was then using himself, composing an Elegy on Aquila Rose, before mentioned, an ingenious young man, of excellent character, much respected in the town, clerk of the Assembly, and a pretty poet. Keimer made verses too, but very indifferently. He could not be said to write them, for his manner was to compose them in the types directly out of his head. So there being no copy, but one pair of cases, and the Elegy likely to require all the letters no one could help him. I endeavor'd to put his press (which he had not yet us'd, and of which he understood nothing) into order fit to be work'd with; and, promising to come and print off his Elegy as soon as he should have got it ready, I return'd to Bradford's, who gave me a little job to do for the present, and there I lodged and dieted. A few days after, Keimer sent for me to print off the Elegy. And now he had got another pair of cases, and a pamphlet to reprint, on which he set me to work.

These two printers I found poorly qualified for their business. Bradford had not been bred to it, and was very illiterate; and Keimer, tho' something of a scholar, was a mere compositor, knowing nothing of presswork. He had been one of the French prophets, and could act their enthusiastic agitations. At this time he did not profess any particular religion, but something of all on occasion; was very ignorant of the world, and had, as I afterwards found, a good deal of the knave in his composition. He did not like my lodging at Bradford's while I work'd with him. He had a house, indeed, but without furniture, so he could not lodge me; but he got me a lodging at Mr. Read's, before mentioned, who was the owner of his house; and, my chest and clothes being come by this time, I made rather a more respectable appearance in the eyes of Miss Read than I had done when she first happen'd to see me eating my roll in the street.

Collins Refuses to Row

AT New York I found my friend Collins, who had arriv'd there some time before me. We had been intimate from children, and had read the same books together; but he had the advantage of more time for reading and studying, and a wonderful genius for mathematical learning, in which he far outstript me. While I liv'd in Boston, most of my hours of leisure for conversation were spent with him, and he continu'd a sober as well as an industrious lad; was much respected for his learning by several of the clergy and other gentlemen, and seemed to promise making a good figure in life. But, during my absence, he had acquir'd a habit of sotting with brandy; and I found by his own account, and what I heard from others, that he had been drunk every day since his arrival at New York, and behav'd very oddly. He had gam'd, too, and lost his money, so that I was oblig'd to discharge his lodgings, and defray his expenses to and at Philadelphia, which prov'd extremely inconvenient to me.

The then governor of New York, Burnet (son of Bishop Burnet), hearing from the captain that a young man, one of his passengers, had a great many books, desir'd he would bring me to see him. I waited upon him accordingly, and should have taken Collins with me but that he was not sober. The gov'r. treated me with great civility, show'd me his library, which was a very large one, and we had a good deal of conversation about books and authors. This was the second governor who had done me the honor to take notice of me; which, to a poor boy like me, was very pleasing.

We proceeded to Philadelphia. I received on the way Vernon's money, without which we could hardly have finish'd our journey. Collins wished to be employ'd in some counting-house; but, whether they discover'd his dramming by his breath, or by his behavior, tho he had some recommendations, he met with no success in any application, and continu'd lodging and boarding at the same house with me, and at my expense. Knowing I had that money of Vernon's, he was continually borrowing of me, still promising repayment as soon as he should be in business. At length he had got so much of it that I was distress'd to think what I should do in case of being call'd on to remit it.

His drinking continu'd, about which we sometimes quarrell'd; for, when a little intoxicated, he was very fractious. Once, in a boat on the Delaware with some other young men, he refused to row in his turn. "I will be row'd home," says he. "We will not row you," says I. "You must, or stay all night on the water," says he, "just as you please." The others said, "Let us row; what signifies it?" But, my mind being soured with his other conduct, I continu'd to refuse. So he swore he would make me row, or throw me overboard; and coming along, stepping on the thwarts, toward me, when he came up and struck at me, I clapped my hand under his crutch, and, rising, pitched him head-foremost into the river. I knew he was a good swimmer, and so was under little concern about him; but before he could get round to lay hold of the boat, we had with a few strokes pull'd her out of his reach; and ever when he drew near the boat, we ask'd if he would row, striking a few strokes to slide her away from him. He was ready to die with vexation, and obstinately would not promise to row. However, seeing him at last beginning to tire, we lifted him in and brought him home dripping wet in the evening. We hardly exchang'd a civil word afterwards, and a West India captain, who had a commission to procure a tutor for the sons of a gentleman at Barbadoes, happening to meet with him, agreed to carry him thither. He left me then, promising to remit me the first money he should receive in order to discharge the debt; but I never heard of him after.

Mr. Whitefield's Preaching

IN 1739 arrived among us from Ireland the Reverend Mr. White-field, who had made himself remarkable there as an itinerant preacher. He was at first permitted to preach in some of our churches; but the clergy, taking a dislike to him, soon refus'd him their pulpits, and he was oblig'd to preach in the fields. The multitudes of all sects and denominations that attended his sermons were enormous, and it was matter of speculation to me, who was one of the number, to observe the extraordinary influence of his oratory on his hearers, and how much they admir'd and respected him, notwithstanding his common abuse of them, by assuring them they were naturally *half beasts and half devils*. It was wonderful to see the change soon made in the manners of our inhabitants. From being thoughtless or indifferent about religion, it seem'd as if all the world were growing religious, so that one could not walk thro' the town in an evening without hearing psalms sung in different families of every street.

And it being found inconvenient to assemble in the open air, subject to its inclemencies, the building of a house to meet in was no sooner propos'd, and persons appointed to receive contributions, but sufficient sums were soon receiv'd to procure the ground and erect the building, which was one hundred feet long and seventy broad, about the size of Westminster Hall; and the work was carried on with such spirit as to be finished in a much shorter time than could have been expected. Both house and ground were vested in trustees, expressly for the use of any preacher of any religious persuasion who might desire to say something to the people at Philadelphia; the design in building not being to accommodate any particular sect, but the inhabitants in general; so that even if the Mufti of Constantinople were to send a missionary to preach Mohammedanism to us, he would find a pulpit at his service.

Mr. Whitefield, in leaving us, went preaching all the way thro' the colonies to Georgia. The settlement of that province had lately been begun, but, instead of being made with hardy, industrious husbandmen, accustomed to labor, the only people fit for such an enterprise, it was with families of broken shop-keepers and other insolvent debtors, many of indolent and idle habits, taken out of the jails, who, being set down in the woods, unqualified for clearing land, and unable to endure the hardships of a new settlement, perished in numbers, leaving many helpless children unprovided for. The sight of their miserable situation inspir'd the benevolent heart of Mr. Whitefield with the idea of building an Orphan House there, in which they might be supported and educated. Returning northward, he preach'd up this charity, and made large collections, for his eloquence had a wonderful power over the hearts and purses of his hearers, of which I myself was an instance.

I did not disapprove of the design, but, as Georgia was then destitute of materials and workmen, and it was proposed to send them from Philadelphia at a great expense, I thought it would have been better to have built the house here, and brought the children to it. This I advis'd; but he was resolute in his first project, rejected my counsel, and I therefore refus'd to contribute. I happened soon after to attend one of his sermons, in the course of which I perceived he intended to finish with a collection, and I silently resolved he should get nothing from me. I had in my pocket a handful of copper money, three or four silver dollars, and five pistoles in gold. As he proceeded I began to soften, and concluded to give the coppers. Another stroke of his oratory made me asham'd of that, and determin'd me to give the silver; and he finish'd so admirably, that I empty'd my pocket wholly into the collector's dish, gold and all. At this sermon there was also one of our club, who, being of my sentiments respecting the building in Georgia, and suspecting a collection might be intended, had, by precaution, emptied his pockets before he came from home. Towards the conclusion of the discourse, however, he felt a strong desire to give, and apply'd to a neighbour, who stood near him, to borrow some money for the purpose. The application was unfortunately [made] to perhaps the only man in the company who had the firmness not to be affected by the preacher. His answer was, *"At any other time, Friend Hopkinson, I would lend to thee freely; but not now, for thee seems to be out of thy right senses."*

Some of Mr. Whitefield's enemies affected to suppose that he would apply these collections to his own private emolument; but I, who was intimately acquainted with him (being employed in printing his Sermons and Journals, etc.), never had the least suspicion of his integrity, but am to this day decidedly of opinion that he was in all his conduct a perfectly *honest man;* and methinks my testimony in his favor ought to have the more weight, as we had no religious connection. He us'd, indeed, sometimes to pray for my conversion, but never had the satisfaction of believing that his prayers were heard. Ours was a mere civil friendship, sincere on both sides, and lasted to his death.

The following instance will show something of the terms on which we stood. Upon one of his arrivals from England at Boston, he wrote to me that he should come soon to Philadelphia, but knew not where he could lodge when there, as he understood his old friend and host, Mr. Benezet, was removed to Germantown. My answer was, "You know my house; if you can make shift with its scanty accommodations, you will be most heartily welcome." He reply'd, that if I made that kind offer for Christ's sake, I should not miss of a reward. And I returned, *"Don't let me be mistaken; it was not for Christ's sake, but for your sake."* One of our common acquaintance jocosely remark'd, that, knowing it to be the custom of the saints, when they received any favour, to shift the burden of the obligation from off their own shoulders, and place it in heaven, I had contriv'd to fix it on earth.

The last time I saw Mr. Whitefield was in London, when he consulted me about his Orphan House concern, and his purpose of appropriating it to the establishment of a college.

He had a loud and clear voice, and articulated his words and sentences so perfectly, that he might be heard and understood at a great distance, especially as his auditories, however numerous, observ'd the most exact silence. He preach'd one evening from the top of the Courthouse steps, which are in the middle of Market-street, and on the west side of Second-street, which crosses it at right angles. Both streets were fill'd with his hearers to a considerable distance. Being among the hindmost in Market-street, I had the curiosity to learn how far he could be heard, by retiring backwards down the street towards the river; and I found his voice distinct till I came near Front-street, when some noise in that street obscur'd it. Imagining then a semi-circle, of which my distance should be the radius, and that it were fill'd with auditors, to each of whom I allow'd two square feet, I computed that he might well be heard by more than thirty thousand. This reconcil'd me to the newspaper accounts of his having preach'd to twenty-five thousand people in the fields, and to the antient histories of generals haranguing whole armies, of which I had sometimes doubted.

WASHINGTON IRVING (1783-1859)

Rip Van Winkle

[THE following Tale was found among the papers of the late Diedrich Knicker-bocker, an old gentleman of New York, who was very curious in the Dutch history of the province, and the manners of the descendants from its primitive settlers. His historical researches, however, did not lie so much among books as among men; for the former are lamentably scanty on his favorite topics, whereas he found the old burghers, and still more their wives, rich in that legendary lore so invaluable to true history. Whenever, therefore, he happened upon a genuine Dutch family, snugly shut up in its low-roofed farmhouse, under a spreading sycamore, he looked upon it as a little clasped volume of black letter, and studied it with the zeal of a book-worm.

The result of all these researches was a history of the province during the reign of the Dutch governors, which he published some years since. There have been various opinions as to the literary character of his work, and, to tell the truth, it is not a whit better than it should be. Its chief merit is its scrupulous accuracy, which indeed was a little questioned on its first appearance, but has since been completely established; and it is now admitted into all historical collections as a book of unquestionable authority.

The old gentleman died shortly after the publication of his work, and now that he is dead and gone, it cannot do much harm to his memory to say, that his time might have been much better employed in weightier labors. He, how-ever, was apt to ride his hobby his own way; and though it did now and then kick up the dust a little in the eyes of his neighbors, and grieve the spirit of some friends, for whom he felt the truest deference and affection; yet his errors and follies are remembered "more in sorrow than in anger," and it begins to be suspected that he never intended to injure or offend. But however his memory may be appreciated by critics, it is still held dear by many folk whose good opinion is well worth having, particularly by certain biscuit-bakers, who have gone so far as to imprint his likeness on their New-year cakes, and have thus given him a chance for immortality, almost equal to the being stamped on a Waterloo medal or a Queen Anne's farthing.]

RIP VAN WINKLE:

A POSTHUMOUS WRITING OF DIEDRICH KNICKERBOCKER

By Woden, God of Saxons,
From whence comes Wensday, that is Wodensday,
Truth is a thing that ever I will keep
Unto thylke day in which I creep into
My sepulchre———   CARTWRIGHT.

WHOEVER has made a voyage up the Hudson must remember the Kaatskill mountains. They are a dismembered branch of the great Appalachian family, and are seen away to the west of the river, swelling up to a noble height, and lording it over the surrounding country. Every change of season, every change of weather, indeed, every hour of the day, produces some change in the magical hues and shapes of these mountains, and they are regarded by all the good wives, far and near, as perfect barometers. When the weather is fair and settled, they are clothed in blue and purple, and print their bold outlines on the clear evening sky; but sometimes, when the rest of the landscape is cloudless, they will gather a hood of gray vapors about their summits, which, in the last rays of the setting sun, will glow and light up like a crown of glory.

At the foot of these fairy mountains, the voyager may have descried the light smoke curling up from a village, whose shingle-roofs gleam among the trees, just where the blue tints of the upland melt away into the fresh green of the nearer landscape. It is a little village, of great antiquity, having been founded by some of the Dutch colonists, in the early times of the province, just about the beginning of the government of the good Peter Stuyvesant (may he rest in peace!) and there were some of the houses of the original settlers standing within a few years, built of small yellow bricks brought from Holland, having latticed windows and gable fronts, surmounted with weathercocks.

In that same village and in one of these very houses (which, to tell the precise truth, was sadly time-worn and weather-beaten), there lived many years since, while the country was yet a province of Great Britain, a simple good-natured fellow, of the name of Rip Van Winkle. He was a descendant of the Van Winkles who figured so gallantly in the chivalrous days of Peter Stuyvesant, and accompanied him to the siege of Fort Christina. He inherited, however, but little of the martial character of his ancestors. I have observed that he was a simple good-natured man; he was, moreover, a kind neighbor, and an obedient hen-pecked husband. Indeed, to the latter circumstance might be owing that meekness of spirit which gained him such universal popularity; for those men are most apt to be obsequious and conciliating abroad, who are under the discipline of shrews at home. Their tempers, doubtless, are rendered pliant and malleable in the fiery furnace of domestic tribulation, and a curtain lecture is worth all the sermons in the world for teaching the virtues of patience and long-suffering. A termagant wife may, therefore, in some respects, be considered a tolerable blessing; and if so, Rip Van Winkle was thrice blessed.

Certain it is that he was a great favorite among all the good wives of the village, who, as usual with the amiable sex, took his part in all family squabbles; and never failed, whenever they talked those matters over in their evening gossipings, to lay all the blame on Dame Van Winkle. The children of the village, too, would shout with joy whenever he approached. He assisted at their sports, made their playthings, taught them to fly kites and shoot marbles, and told them long stories of ghosts, witches, and Indians. Whenever he went dodging about the village, he was surrounded by a troop of them hanging on his skirts, clambering on his back, and playing a thousand tricks on him with impunity; and not a dog would bark at him throughout the neighbourhood.

The great error in Rip's composition was an insuperable aversion to all kinds of profitable labour. It could not be from the want of assiduity or perseverance; for he would sit on a wet rock, with a rod as long and heavy as a Tartar's lance, and fish all day without a murmur, even though he should not be encouraged by a single nibble. He would carry a fowling-piece on his shoulder for hours together, trudging through woods and swamps, and up hill and down dale, to shoot a few squirrels or wild pigeons. He would never refuse to assist a neighbour even in the roughest toil, and was a foremost man at all country frolics for husking Indian corn, or building stone fences; the women of the village, too, used to employ him to run their errands, and to do such little odd jobs as their less obliging husbands would not do for them. In a word, Rip was ready to attend to anybody's business but his own; but as to doing family duty, and keeping his farm in order, he found it impossible.

In fact, he declared it was of no use to work on his farm; it was the most pestilent little piece of ground in the whole country; everything about it went wrong, and would go wrong, in spite of him. His fences were continually falling to pieces; his cow would either go astray, or get among the cabbages; weeds were sure to grow quicker in his fields than anywhere else; the rain always made a point of setting in just as he had some out-door work to do; so that though his patrimonial estate had dwindled away under his management, acre by acre, until there was little more left than a mere patch of Indian corn and potatoes, yet it was the worst conditioned farm in the neighbourhood.

His children, too, were as ragged and wild as if they belonged to nobody. His son Rip, an urchin begotten in his own likeness, promised to inherit the habits, with the old clothes of his father. He was generally seen trooping like a colt at his mother's heels, equipped in a pair of his father's cast-off galligaskins, which he had much ado to hold up with one hand, as a fine lady does her train in bad weather.

Rip Van Winkle, however, was one of those happy mortals, of foolish, well-oiled dispositions, who take the world easy, eat white bread or brown, whichever can be got with least thought or trouble, and would rather starve on a penny than work for a pound. If left to himself, he would have whistled life away in perfect contentment; but his wife kept continually dinning in his ears about his idleness, his carelessness, and the ruin he was bringing on his family. Morning, noon, and night, her tongue was incessantly going, and everything he said or did was sure to produce a torrent of household eloquence. Rip had but one way of replying to all lectures of the kind, and that, by frequent use, had grown into a habit. He shrugged his shoulders, shook his head, cast up his eyes, but said nothing. This, however, always provoked a fresh volley from his wife; so that he was fain to draw off his forces, and take to the outside of the house—the only side which, in truth, belongs to a hen-pecked husband.

Rip's sole domestic adherent was his dog Wolf, who was as much hen-pecked as his master; for Dame Van Winkle regarded them as companions in idleness, and even looked upon Wolf with an evil eye, as the cause of his master's going so often astray. True it is, in all points of spirit befitting an honourable dog, he was as courageous an animal as ever scoured the woods—but what courage can withstand the ever-during and all-besetting terrors of a woman's tongue? The moment Wolf entered the house, his crest fell, his tail drooped to the ground, or curled between his legs, he sneaked about with a gallows air, casting many a side-long glance at Dame Van Winkle, and at the least flourish of a broomstick or ladle, he would fly to the door with yelping precipitation.

Times grew worse and worse with Rip Van Winkle as years of matrimony rolled on; a tart temper never mellows with age, and a sharp tongue is the only edged tool that grows keener with constant use. For a long while he used to console himself, when driven from home, by frequenting a kind of perpetual club of the sages, philosophers, and other idle personages of the village; which held its sessions on a bench before a small inn, designated by a rubicund portrait of his Majesty George the Third. Here they used to sit in the shade through a long lazy summer's day, talking listlessly over village gossip, or telling endless sleepy stories about nothing. But it would have been worth any statesman's money to have heard the profound discussions that sometimes took place, when by chance an old newspaper fell into their hands from some passing traveller. How solemnly they would listen to the contents, as drawled out by Derrick Van Bummel, the schoolmaster, a dapper learned little man, who was not to be daunted by the most gigantic word in the dictionary; and how sagely they would deliberate upon public events some months after they had taken place.

The opinions of this junto were completely controlled by Nicholas Vedder, a patriarch of the village, and landlord of the inn, at the door of which he took his seat from morning till night, just moving sufficiently to avoid the sun and keep in the shade of a large tree; so that the neighbours could tell the hour by his movements as accurately as by a sundial. It is true he was rarely heard to speak, but smoked his pipe incessantly. His adherents, however (for every great man has his adherents), perfectly understood him, and knew how to gather his opinions. When anything that was read or related displeased him, he was observed to smoke his pipe vehemently, and to send forth short, frequent, and angry puffs, but when pleased he would inhale the smoke slowly and tranquilly, and emit it in light and placid clouds; and sometimes, taking the pipe from his mouth, and letting the fragrant vapor curl about his nose, would gravely nod his head in token of perfect approbation.

From even this stronghold the unlucky Rip was at length routed by his termagant wife, who would suddenly break in upon the tranquillity of the assemblage and call the members all to naught; nor was that august personage, Nicholas Vedder himself, sacred from the daring tongue of this terrible virago, who charged him outright with encouraging her husband in habits of idleness.

Poor Rip was at last reduced almost to despair; and his only alternative, to escape from the labor of the farm and clamor of his wife, was to take gun in hand and stroll away into the woods. Here he would sometimes seat himself at the foot of a tree, and share the contents of his wallet with Wolf, with whom he sympathized as a fellow-sufferer in persecution. "Poor Wolf," he would say, "thy mistress leads thee a dog's life of it; but never mind, my lad, whilst I live thou shalt never want a friend to stand by thee!" Wolf would wag his tail, look wistfully in his master's face, and if dogs can feel pity, I verily believe he reciprocated the sentiment with all his heart.

In a long ramble of the kind on a fine autumnal day, Rip had unconsciously scrambled to one of the highest parts of the Kaatskill mountains. He was after his favorite sport of squirrel-shooting, and the still solitudes had echoed and re-echoed with the reports of his gun. Panting and fatigued, he threw himself, late in the afternoon, on a green knoll, covered with mountain herbage, that crowned the brow of a precipice. From an opening between the trees he could overlook all the lower country for many a mile of rich woodland. He saw at a distance the lordly Hudson, far, far below him, moving on its silent but majestic course, with the reflection of a purple cloud, or the sail of a lagging bark, here and there sleeping on its glassy bosom, and at last losing itself in the blue highlands.

On the other side he looked down into a deep mountain glen, wild, lonely, and shagged, the bottom filled with fragments from the impending cliffs, and scarcely lighted by the reflected rays of the setting sun.

For some time Rip lay musing on this scene; evening was gradually advancing; the mountains began to throw their long blue shadows over the valleys; he saw that it would be dark long before he could reach the village, and he heaved a heavy sigh when he thought of encountering the terrors of Dame Van Winkle.

As he was about to descend, he heard a voice from a distance, hallooing, "Rip Van Winkle! Rip Van Winkle!" He looked round, but could see nothing but a crow winging its solitary flight across the mountain. He thought his fancy must have deceived him, and turned again to descend, when he heard the same cry ring through the still evening air: "Rip Van Winkle! Rip Van Winkle!"—at the same time Wolf bristled up his back, and, giving a loud growl, skulked to his master's side, looking fearfully down into the glen. Rip now felt a vague apprehension stealing over him; he looked anxiously in the same direction, and perceived a strange figure slowly toiling up the rocks, and bending under the weight of something he carried on his back. He was surprised to see any human being in this lonely and unfrequented place; but supposing it to be some one of the neighbourhood in need of his assistance, he hastened down to yield it.

On nearer approach he was still more surprised at the singularity of the stranger's appearance. He was a short, square-built old fellow, with thick bushy hair and a grizzled beard. His dress was of the antique Dutch fashion—a cloth jerkin, strapped round the waist—several pair of breeches, the outer one of ample volume, decorated with rows of buttons down the sides, and bunches at the knees. He bore on his shoulder a stout keg, that seemed full of liquor, and made signs for Rip to approach and assist him with the load. Though rather shy and distrustful of this new acquaintance, Rip complied with his usual alacrity; and mutually relieving each other, they clambered up a narrow gully, apparently the dry bed of a mountain torrent. As they ascended, Rip every now and then heard long rolling peals, like distant thunder, that seemed to issue out of a deep ravine, or rather cleft, between the lofty rocks, toward which their rugged path conducted. He paused for an instant, but supposing it to be the muttering of one of those transient thunder-showers which often take place in mountain heights, he proceeded. Passing through the ravine, they came to a hollow, like a small amphitheatre, surrounded by perpendicular precipices, over the brinks of which impending trees shot their branches, so that you only caught glimpses of the azure sky and the bright evening cloud. During the whole time Rip and his companion had labored on in silence, for though the former marvelled greatly what could be the object of carrying a keg of liquor up this wild mountain; yet there was something strange and incomprehensible about the unknown, that inspired awe and checked familiarity.

On entering the amphitheatre, new objects of wonder presented themselves. On a level spot in the centre was a company of odd-looking personages playing at nine-pins. They were dressed in a quaint outlandish fashion; some wore short doublets, others jerkins, with long knives in their belts, and most of them had enormous breeches, of similar style with that of the guide's. Their visages, too, were peculiar; one had a large head, broad face, and small piggish eyes; the face of another seemed to consist entirely of nose, and was surmounted by a white sugarloaf hat, set off with a little red cock's tail. They all had beards, of various shapes and colors. There was one who seemed to be the commander. He was a stout old gentleman, with a weather-beaten countenance; he wore a laced doublet, broad belt and hanger, high-crowned hat and feather, red stockings, and high-heeled shoes, with roses in them. The whole group reminded Rip of the figures in an old Flemish painting, in the parlor of Dominie Van Shaick, the village parson, and which had been brought over from Holland at the time of the settlement.

What seemed particularly odd to Rip was, that though these folks were evidently amusing themselves, yet they maintained the gravest faces, the most mysterious silence, and were, withal, the most melancholy party of pleasure he had ever witnessed. Nothing interrupted the stillness of the scene but the noise of the balls, which, whenever they were rolled, echoed along the mountains like rumbling peals of thunder.

As Rip and his companion approached them, they suddenly desisted from their play, and stared at him with such fixed, statue-like gaze, and such strange, uncouth, lack-lustre countenances, that his heart turned within him, and his knees smote together. His companion now emptied the contents of the keg into large flagons, and made signs to him to wait upon the company. He obeyed with fear and trembling; they quaffed the liquor in profound silence, and then returned to their game.

By degrees Rip's awe and apprehension subsided. He even ventured, when no eye was fixed upon him, to taste the beverage, which he found had much of the flavor of excellent Hollands. He was naturally a thirsty soul, and was soon tempted to repeat the draught. One taste provoked another; and he reiterated his visits to the flagon so often, that at length his senses were overpowered, his eyes swam in his head, his head gradually declined, and he fell into a deep sleep.

On waking, he found himself on the green knoll whence he had first seen the old man of the glen. He rubbed his eyes—it was a bright sunny morning. The birds were hopping and twittering among the bushes, and the eagle was wheeling aloft, and breasting the pure mountain breeze. "Surely," thought Rip, "I have not slept here all night." He recalled the occurrences before he fell asleep. The strange man with a keg of liquor—the mountain ravine—the wild retreat among the rocks—the woe-begone party at nine-pins—the flagon—"Oh! that flagon! that wicked flagon!" thought Rip; "what excuse shall I make to Dame Van Winkle?"

He looked round for his gun, but in place of the clean well-oiled fowling-piece, he found an old firelock lying by him, the barrel incrusted with rust, the lock falling off, and the stock worm-eaten. He now suspected that the grave roysters of the mountain had put a trick upon him, and, having dosed him with liquor, had robbed him of his gun. Wolf, too, had disappeared, but he might have strayed away after a squirrel or partridge. He whistled after him, and shouted his name, but all in vain; the echoes repeated his whistle and shout, but no dog was to be seen.

He determined to revisit the scene of the last evening's gambol, and, if he met with any of the party, to demand his dog and gun. As he rose to walk he found himself stiff in the joints, and wanting in his usual activity. "These mountain beds do not agree with me," thought Rip; "and if this frolic should lay me up with a fit of the rheumatism, I shall have a blessed time with Dame Van Winkle." With some difficulty he got down into the glen: he found the gully up which he and his companion had ascended the preceding evening; but, to his astonishment, a mountain stream was now foaming down it—leaping from rock to rock, and filling the glen with babbling murmurs. He, however, made shift to scramble up its sides, working his toilsome way through thickets of birch, sassafras, and witch-hazel, and sometimes tripped up or entangled by the wild grape-vines that twisted their coils or tendrils from tree to tree, and spread a kind of network in his path.

At length he reached to where the ravine had opened through the cliffs to the amphitheatre; but no traces of such opening remained. The rocks presented a high impenetrable wall, over which the torrent came tumbling in a sheet of feathery foam, and fell into a broad, deep basin, black from the shadows of the surrounding forest. Here, then, poor Rip was brought to a stand. He again called and whistled after his dog; he was only answered by the cawing of a flock of idle crows, sporting high in air about a dry tree that overhung a sunny precipice; and who, secure in their elevation, seemed to look down and scoff at the poor man's perplexities. What was to be done?—the morning was passing away, and Rip felt famished for want of his breakfast. He grieved to give up his dog and his gun; he dreaded to meet his wife; but it would not do to starve among the mountains. He shook his head, shouldered the rusty firelock, and, with a heart full of trouble and anxiety, turned his steps homeward.

As he approached the village he met a number of people, but none whom he knew, which somewhat surprised him, for he had thought himself acquainted with everyone in the country round. Their dress, too, was of a different fashion from that to which he was accustomed. They all stared at him with equal marks of surprise, and, whenever they cast their eyes upon him, invariably stroked their chins. The constant recurrence of this gesture induced Rip, involuntarily, to do the same—when, to his astonishment, he found his beard had grown a foot long!

He had now entered the skirts of the village. A troop of strange children ran at his heels, hooting after him, and pointing at his gray beard. The dogs, too, not one of which he recognized for an old acquaintance, barked at him as he passed. The very village was altered; it was larger and more populous. There were rows of houses which he had never seen before, and those which had been his familiar haunts had disappeared. Strange names were over the doors—strange faces at the windows—everything was strange. His mind now misgave him; he began to doubt whether both he and the world around him were not bewitched. Surely this was his native village, which he had left but the day before. There stood the Kaatskill mountains—there ran the silver Hudson at a distance—there was every hill and dale precisely as it had always been. Rip was sorely perplexed. "That flagon last night," thought he, "has addled my poor head sadly!"

It was with some difficulty that he found the way to his own house, which he approached with silent awe, expecting every moment to hear the shrill voice of Dame Van Winkle. He found the house gone to decay —the roof fallen in, the windows shattered, and the doors off the hinges. A half-starved dog that looked like Wolf, was skulking about it. Rip called him by name, but the cur snarled, showed his teeth, and passed on. This was an unkind cut indeed—"My very dog," sighed poor Rip, "has forgotten me!"

He entered the house, which, to tell the truth, Dame Van Winkle had always kept in neat order. It was empty, forlorn, and apparently abandoned. The desolateness overcame all his connubial fears—he called loudly for his wife and children—the lonely chambers rang for a moment with his voice, and then all again was silence.

He now hurried forth, and hastened to his old resort, the village inn— but it too was gone. A large, rickety, wooden building stood in its place, with great gaping windows, some of them broken and mended with old hats and petticoats, and over the door was painted, "The Union Hotel, by Jonathan Doolittle." Instead of the great tree that used to shelter the quiet little Dutch inn of yore, there was now reared a tall naked pole, with something on the top that looked like a red nightcap, and from it was fluttering a flag, on which was a singular assemblage of stars and stripes—all this was strange and incomprehensible. He recognized on the sign, however, the ruby face of King George, under which he had smoked so many a peaceful pipe; but even this was singularly metamorphosed. The red coat was changed for one of blue and buff, a sword was held in the hand instead of a sceptre, the head was decorated with a cocked hat, and underneath was painted in large characters, GENERAL WASHINGTON.

There was, as usual, a crowd of folks about the door, but none that Rip recollected. The very character of the people seemed changed. There was a busy, bustling, disputatious tone about it, instead of the accustomed phlegm and drowsy tranquillity. He looked in vain for the sage Nicholas Vedder, with his broad face, double chin, and fair long pipe, uttering clouds of tobacco-smoke instead of idle speeches; or Van Bummel, the schoolmaster, doling forth the contents of an ancient newspaper. In place of these, a lean, bilious-looking fellow, with his pockets full of hand-bills, was haranguing vehemently about rights of citizens—elections—members of Congress—liberty—Bunker's Hill—heroes of seventy-six—and other words, which were a perfect Babylonish jargon to the bewildered Van Winkle.

The appearance of Rip, with his long grizzled beard, his rusty fowling-piece, his uncouth dress, and an army of women and children at his heels, soon attracted the attention of the tavern politicians. They crowded round him, eyeing him from head to foot with great curiosity. The orator bustled up to him, and, drawing him partly aside, inquired "on which side he voted?" Rip stared in vacant stupidity. Another short but busy little fellow pulled him by the arm, and, rising on tiptoe, inquired in his ear, "Whether he was Federal or Democrat?" Rip was equally at a loss to comprehend the question; when a knowing, self-important old gentleman, in a sharp cocked hat, made his way through the crowd, putting them to the right and left with his elbows as he passed, and planting himself before Van Winkle, with one arm akimbo, the other resting on his cane, his keen eyes and sharp hat penetrating, as it were, into his very soul, demanded in an austere tone, "What brought him to the election with a gun on his shoulder, and a mob at his heels, and whether he meant to breed a riot in the village?"—"Alas! gentlemen," cried Rip, somewhat dismayed, "I am a poor quiet man, a native of the place, and a loyal subject of the king, God bless him!"

Here a general shout burst from the bystanders—"A tory! a tory! a spy! a refugee! hustle him! away with him!" It was with great difficulty that the self-important man in the cocked hat restored order; and, having assumed a tenfold austerity of brow, demanded again of the unknown culprit, what he came there for, and whom he was seeking? The poor man humbly assured him that he meant no harm, but merely came there in search of some of his neighbors, who used to keep about the tavern.

"Well—who are they?—name them."

Rip bethought himself a moment, and inquired, "Where's Nicholas Vedder?"

There was a silence for a little while, when an old man replied in a thin piping voice, "Nicholas Vedder! why, he is dead and gone these eighteen years! There was a wooden tombstone in the churchyard that used to tell all about him, but that's rotten and gone too."

"Where's Brom Dutcher?"

"Oh, he went off to the army in the beginning of the war; some say he was killed at the storming of Stony Point—others say he was drowned in a squall at the foot of Antony's Nose. I don't know—he never came back again."

"Where's Van Bummell, the schoolmaster?"

"He went off to the wars too, was a great militia general, and is now in Congress."

Rip's heart died away at hearing of these sad changes in his home and friends, and finding himself thus alone in the world. Every answer puzzled him too, by treating of such enormous lapses of time, and of matters which he could not understand; war—Congress—Stony Point; —he had no courage to ask after any more friends, but cried out in despair, "Does anybody here know Rip Van Winkle?"

"Oh, Rip Van Winkle!" exclaimed two or three. "Oh, to be sure! that's Rip Van Winkle yonder, leaning against the tree."

Rip looked, and beheld a precise counterpart of himself, as he went up the mountain: apparently as lazy, and certainly as ragged. The poor fellow was now completely confounded. He doubted his own identity, and whether he was himself or another man. In the midst of his bewilderment, the man in the cocked hat demanded who he was, and what was his name?

"God knows," exclaimed he, at his wits' end; "I'm not myself—I'm somebody else—that's me yonder—no—that's somebody else got into my shoes—I was myself last night, but I fell asleep on the mountain, and they've changed my gun, and everything's changed, and I'm changed, and I can't tell what's my name, or who I am!"

The bystanders began now to look at each other, nod, wink significantly, and tap their fingers against their foreheads. There was a whisper, also, about securing the gun, and keeping the old fellow from doing mischief, at the very suggestion of which the self-important man in the cocked hat retired with some precipitation. At this critical moment a fresh, comely woman pressed through the throng to get a peep at the gray-bearded man. She had a chubby child in her arms, which, frightened at his looks, began to cry. "Hush, Rip," cried she, "hush, you little fool; the old man won't hurt you." The name of the child, the air of the mother, the tone of her voice, all awakened a train of recollections in his mind.

"What is your name, my good woman?" asked he.

"Judith Gardenier."

"And your father's name?"

"Ah, poor man, Rip Van Winkle was his name, but it's twenty years since he went away from home with his gun, and never has been heard of since—his dog came home without him; but whether he shot himself, or was carried away by the Indians, nobody can tell. I was then but a little girl."

Rip had but one question more to ask; but he put it with a faltering voice,—

"Where's your mother?"

"Oh, she too had died but a short time since; she broke a blood-vessel in a fit of passion at a New-England pedler."

There was a drop of comfort, at least, in this intelligence. The honest man could contain himself no longer. He caught his daughter and her child in his arms. "I am your father!" cried he—"Young Rip Van Winkle once—old Rip Van Winkle now!—Does nobody know poor Rip Van Winkle?"

All stood amazed, until an old woman, tottering out from among the crowd, put her hand to her brow, and peering under it in his face for a moment, exclaimed, "Sure enough! it is Rip Van Winkle—it is himself! Welcome home again, old neighbor—Why, where have you been these twenty long years?"

Rip's story was soon told, for the whole twenty years had been to him but as one night. The neighbors stared when they heard it; some were seen to wink at each other, and put their tongues in their cheeks: and the self-important man in the cocked hat, who, when the alarm was over, had returned to the field, screwed down the corners of his mouth, and shook his head—upon which there was a general shaking of the head throughout the assemblage.

It was determined, however, to take the opinion of old Peter Vander-donk, who was seen slowly advancing up the road. He was a descendant of the historian of that name, who wrote one of the earliest accounts of the province. Peter was the most ancient inhabitant of the village, and well versed in all the wonderful events and traditions of the neighborhood. He recollected Rip at once, and corroborated his story in the most satisfactory manner. He assured the company that it was a fact, handed down from his ancestor the historian, that the Kaatskill mountains had always been haunted by strange beings. That it was affirmed that the great Hendrick Hudson, the first discoverer of the river and country, kept a kind of vigil there every twenty years, with his crew of the *Half-moon;* being permitted in this way to revisit the scenes of his enterprise, and keep a guardian eye upon the river, and the great city called by his name. That his father had once seen them in their old Dutch dresses playing at nine-pins in a hollow of the mountain; and that he himself had heard, one summer afternoon, the sound of their balls, like distant peals of thunder.

To make a long story short, the company broke up, and returned to the more important concerns of the election. Rip's daughter took him home to live with her; she had a snug, well-furnished house, and a stout cheery farmer for her husband, whom Rip recollected for one of the urchins that used to climb upon his back. As to Rip's son and heir, who was the ditto of himself, seen leaning against the tree, he was employed to work on the farm; but evinced an hereditary disposition to attend to anything else but his business.

Rip now resumed his old walks and habits; he soon found many of his former cronies, though all rather the worse for the wear and tear of time; and preferred making friends among the rising generation, with whom he soon grew into great favor.

Having nothing to do at home, and being arrived at that happy age when a man can be idle with impunity, he took his place once more on the bench at the inn door, and was reverenced as one of the patriarchs of the village, and a chronicle of the old times "before the war." It was some time before he could get into the regular track of gossip, or could be made to comprehend the strange events that had taken place during his torpor. How that there had been a revolutionary war—that the country had thrown off the yoke of Old England—and that, instead of being a subject of His Majesty George the Third, he was now a free citizen of the United States. Rip, in fact, was no politician; the changes of states and empires made but little impression on him; but there was one species of despotism under which he had long groaned, and that was—

petticoat government. Happily that was at an end; he had got his neck out of the yoke of matrimony, and could go in and out whenever he pleased without dreading the tyranny of Dame Van Winkle. Whenever her name was mentioned, however, he shook his head, shrugged his shoulders, and cast up his eyes; which might pass either for an expression of resignation to his fate, or joy at his deliverance.

He used to tell his story to every stranger that arrived at Mr. Doolittle's hotel. He was observed at first to vary on some points every time he told it, which was, doubtless, owing to his having so recently awaked. It at last settled down precisely to the tale I have related, and not a man, woman, or child in the neighborhood but knew it by heart. Some always pretended to doubt the reality of it, and insisted that Rip had been out of his head, and that this was one point on which he always remained flighty. The old Dutch inhabitants, however, almost universally gave it full credit. Even to this day they never hear a thunderstorm of a summer afternoon about the Kaatskill, but they say Hendrick Hudson and his crew are at their game of nine-pins; and it is a common wish of all henpecked husbands in the neighborhood, when life hangs heavy on their hands, that they might have a quieting draught out of Rip Van Winkle's flagon.

NOTE.—The foregoing tale, one would suspect, had been suggested to Mr. Knickerbocker by a little German superstition about the Emperor Frederick *der Rothbart,* and the Kypphaüser mountain; the subjoined note, however, which he had appended to the tale, shows that it is an absolute fact, narrated with his usual fidelity:—

"The story of Rip Van Winkle may seem incredible to many, but nevertheless I give it my full belief, for I know the vicinity of our old Dutch settlements to have been very subject to marvellous events and appearances. Indeed, I have heard many stranger stories than this in the villages along the Hudson, all of which were too well authenticated to admit of a doubt. I have even talked with Rip Van Winkle myself, who, when I last saw him, was a very venerable old man and so perfectly rational and consistent on every other point, that I think no conscientious person could refuse to take this into the bargain; nay, I have seen a certificate on the subject, taken before a country justice, and signed with a cross, in the justice's own handwriting. The story, therefore, is beyond the possibility of doubt.   D. K."

POSTSCRIPT.—The following are travelling notes from a memorandum-book of Mr. Knickerbocker:—

"The Kaatsberg, or Catskill Mountains, have always been a region full of fable. The Indians considered them the abode of spirits, who influenced the weather, spreading sunshine or clouds over the landscape, and sending good or bad hunting seasons. They were ruled by an old squaw spirit, said to be their mother. She dwelt on the highest peak of the Catskills, and had charge of the doors of day and night, to open and shut them at the proper hour. She hung up the new moons in the skies, and cut up the old ones into stars. In times of drought, if properly propitiated, she would spin light summer clouds out of cobwebs and morning dew, and send them off from the crest of the mountain, flake after flake, like flakes of carded cotton, to float in the air, until, dissolved by the heat of the sun, they would fall in gentle showers, causing the grass to spring, the fruits to ripen, and the corn to grow an inch an hour. If displeased, however, she would brew up clouds black as ink, sitting in the midst of them like a bottle-bellied spider in the midst of its web; and when these clouds broke, woe betide the valleys!

"In old times, say the Indian traditions, there was a kind of Manitou or Spirit, who kept about the wildest recesses of the Catskill Mountains, and took a mischievous pleasure in wreaking all kinds of evils and vexations upon the red men. Sometimes he would assume the form of a bear, a panther, or a deer, lead the bewildered hunter a weary chase through tangled forests and among ragged rocks, and then spring off with a loud ho! ho! leaving him aghast on the brink of a beetling precipice or raging torrent.

"The favorite abode of this Manitou is still shown. It is a great rock or cliff on the loneliest part of the mountains, and, from the flowering vines which clamber about it, and the wild flowers, which abound in its neighborhood, is known by the name of the Garden Rock. Near the foot of it is a small lake, the haunt of the solitary bittern, with water-snakes basking in the sun on the leaves of the pond-lilies which lie on the surface. This place was held in great awe by the Indians, insomuch that the boldest hunter would not pursue his game within its precincts. Once upon a time, however, a hunter who had lost his way penetrated to the Garden Rock, where he beheld a number of gourds placed in the crotches of trees. One of these he seized and made off with, but in the hurry of his retreat he let it fall among the rocks, when a great stream gushed forth, which washed him away and swept him down precipices, where he was dashed to pieces, and the stream made its way to the Hudson, and continues to flow to the present day, being the identical stream known by the name of the Kaaterskill."

WILLIAM CULLEN BRYANT
(1794-1878)

To a Waterfowl

WHITHER, midst falling dew,
While glow the heavens with the last
    steps of day,
Far, through their rosy depths, dost thou
    pursue
    Thy solitary way?

Vainly the fowler's eye
Might mark thy distant flight to do thee
    wrong,
As, darkly seen against the crimson sky,
    Thy figure floats along.

Seek'st thou the plashy brink
Of weedy lake, or marge of river wide,
Or where the rocking billows rise and
    sink
    On the chafed ocean-side?

There is a Power whose care
Teaches thy way along that pathless
    coast—
The desert and illimitable air—
    Lone wandering, but not lost.

All day thy wings have fanned,
At that far height, the cold, thin atmos-
    phere,
Yet stoop not, weary, to the welcome
    land,
    Though the dark night is near.

And soon that toil shall end;
Soon shalt thou find a summer home, and
    rest,
And scream among thy fellows; reeds
    shall bend,
    Soon, o'er thy sheltered nest.

Thou'rt gone, the abyss of heaven
Hath swallowed up thy form; yet on my
    heart
Deeply hath sunk the lesson thou hast
    given,
    And shall not soon depart:

He who, from zone to zone,
Guides through the boundless sky thy
    certain flight,
In the long way that I must tread alone,
    Will lead my steps aright.

WILLIAM HICKLING PRESCOTT (1796–1859)

From THE HISTORY OF THE CONQUEST OF MEXICO

The Storming of the Great Temple

OPPOSITE to the Spanish quarters, at only a few rods' distance, stood the great *teocalli* of Huitzilopotchli. This pyramidal mound, with the sanctuaries that crowned it, rising altogether to the height of near a hundred and fifty feet, afforded an elevated position that completely commanded the palace of Axayacatl, occupied by the Christians. A body of five or six hundred Mexicans, many of them nobles and warriors of the highest rank, had got possession of the *teocalli*, whence they discharged such a tempest of arrows on the garrison, that no one could leave his defences for a moment without imminent danger; while the Mexicans, under shelter of the sanctuaries, were entirely covered from the fire of the besieged. It was obviously necessary to dislodge the enemy, if the Spaniards would remain longer in their quarters.

Cortés assigned this service to his chamberlain, Escobar, giving him a hundred men for the purpose, with orders to storm the *teocalli,* and set fire to the sanctuaries. But that officer was thrice repulsed in the attempt, and, after the most desperate efforts, was obliged to return with considerable loss, and without accomplishing his object.

Cortés, who saw the immediate necessity of carrying the place, determined to lead the storming party himself. He was then suffering much from the wound in his left hand, which had disabled it for the present. He made the arm serviceable, however, by fastening his buckler to it, and, thus crippled, sallied out at the head of three hundred chosen cavaliers, and several thousand of his auxiliaries.

In the courtyard of the temple he found a numerous body of Indians prepared to dispute his passage. He briskly charged them, but the flat, smooth stones of the pavement were so slippery, that the horses lost their footing, and many of them fell. Hastily dismounting, they sent back the animals to their quarters, and, renewing the assault, the Spaniards succeeded without much difficulty in dispersing the Indian warriors, and opening a free passage for themselves to the *teocalli*. This building, as the reader may remember, was a huge pyramidal structure, about three hundred feet square at the base. A flight of stone steps on the outside, at one of the angles of the mound, led to a platform, or terraced walk, which passed round the building until it reached a similar flight of stairs directly over the preceding, that conducted to another landing as before. As there were five bodies or divisions of the *teocalli,* it became necessary to pass round its whole extent four times, or nearly a mile, in order to reach the summit, which, it may be recollected, was an open area, crowned only by the two sanctuaries dedicated to the Aztec deities.

Cortés, having cleared a way for the assault, sprang up the lower stairway, followed by Alvarado, Sandoval, Ordaz, and the other gallant cavaliers of his little band, leaving a file of arquebusiers and a strong corps of Indian allies to hold the enemy in check at the foot of the monument. On the first landing, as well as on the several galleries above, and on the summit, the Aztec warriors were drawn up to dispute his passage. From their elevated position they showered down volleys of lighter missiles, together with heavy stones, beams, and burning rafters, which, thundering along the stairway, overturned the ascending Spaniards, and carried desolation through their ranks. The more fortunate, eluding or springing over these obstacles, succeeded in gaining the first terrace; where, throwing themselves on their enemies, they compelled them, after a short resistance, to fall back. The assailants pressed on, effectually supported by a brisk fire of the musketeers from below, which so much galled the Mexicans in their exposed situation, that they were glad to take shelter on the broad summit of the *teocalli.*

Cortés and his comrades were close upon their rear, and the two parties soon found themselves face to face on this aërial battle-field, engaged in mortal combat in presence of the whole city, as well as of the troops in the courtyard, who paused, as if by mutual consent, from their own hostilities, gazing in silent expectation on the issue of those above. The area, though somewhat smaller than the base of the *teocalli,* was large enough to afford a fair field of fight for a thousand combatants. It was paved with broad, flat stones. No impediment occurred over its surface, except the huge sacrificial block, and the temples of stone which rose to the height of forty feet, at the further extremity of the arena. One of these had been consecrated to the Cross. The other was still occupied by the Mexican war-god. The Christian and the Aztec contended for their religions under the very shadow of their respective shrines; while the Indian priests, running to and fro, with their hair wildly streaming over their sable mantles, seemed hovering in mid air, like so many demons of darkness urging on the work of slaughter!

The parties closed with the desperate fury of men who had no hope but in victory. Quarter was neither asked nor given; and to fly was impossible. The edge of the area was unprotected by parapet or battlement. The least slip would be fatal; and the combatants, as they struggled in mortal agony, were sometimes seen to roll over the sheer sides of the precipice together. Cortés himself is said to have had a narrow escape from this dreadful fate.

Two warriors, of strong, muscular frames, seized on him, and were dragging him violently towards the brink of the pyramid. Aware of their intention, he struggled with all his force, and, before they could accomplish their purpose, succeeded in tearing himself from their grasp, and hurling one of them over the wall with his own arm! The story is not improbable in itself, for Cortés was a man of uncommon agility and strength. It has been often repeated; but not by contemporary history.

The battle lasted with unintermitting fury for three hours. The number of the enemy was double that of the Christians; and it seemed as if it were a contest which must be determined by numbers and brute force, rather than by superior science. But it was not so. The invulnerable armor of the Spaniard, his sword of matchless temper, and his skill in the use of it, gave him advantages which far outweighed the odds of physical strength and numbers. After doing all that the courage of despair could enable men to do, resistance grew fainter and fainter on the side of the Aztecs. One after another they had fallen. Two or three priests only survived to be led away in triumph by the victors. Every other combatant was stretched a corpse on the bloody arena, or had been hurled from the giddy heights. Yet the loss of the Spaniards was not inconsiderable. It amounted to forty-five of their best men, and nearly all the remainder were more or less injured in the desperate conflict.

The victorious cavaliers now rushed towards the sanctuaries. The lower story was of stone; the two upper were of wood. Penetrating into their recesses, they had the mortification to find the image of the Virgin and the Cross removed. But in the other edifice they still beheld the grim figure of Huitzilopotchli, with his censer of smoking-hearts, and the walls of his oratory reeking with gore,—not improbably of their own countrymen. With shouts of triumph the Christians tore the uncouth monster from his niche, and tumbled him, in the presence of the horror-struck Aztecs, down the steps of the *teocalli*. They then set fire to the accursed building. The flames speedily ran up the sanctuary walls, sending forth an ominous light over city, lake, and valley, to the remotest hut among the mountains. It was the funeral pyre of Paganism and proclaimed the fall of the sanguinary religion which had so long hung like a dark cloud over the fair regions of Anahuac.

Having accomplished this good work, the Spaniards descended the winding slopes of the *teocalli* with more free and buoyant step, as if conscious that the blessing of Heaven now rested on their arms. They passed through the dusky files of Indian warriors in the courtyard, too much dismayed by the appalling scenes they had witnessed to offer resistance; and reached their own quarters in safety. That very night they followed up the blow by a sortie on the sleeping town, and burned three hundred houses, the horrors of conflagration being made still more impressive by occurring at the hour when the Aztecs, from their own system of warfare, were least prepared for them.

Hoping to find the temper of the natives somewhat subdued by these reverses, Cortés now determined, with his usual policy, to make them a vantage-ground for proposing terms of accommodation. He accordingly invited the enemy to a parley, and, as the principal chiefs, attended by their followers, assembled in the great square, he mounted the turret before occupied by Montezuma, and made signs that he would address them. Marina, as usual, took her place by his side, as his interpreter. The multitude gazed with earnest curiosity on the Indian girl, whose influence with the Spaniards was well-known, and whose connection with the general, in particular, had led the Aztecs to designate him by her Mexican name of Malinche. Cortés, speaking through the soft, musical tones of his mistress, told his audience they must now be convinced, that they had nothing further to hope from opposition to the Spaniards. They had seen their gods trampled in the dust, their altars broken, their dwellings burned, their warriors falling on all sides. "All this," continued he, "you have brought on yourselves by your rebellion. Yet for the affection the sovereign, whom you have so unworthily treated, still bears you, I would willingly stay my hand, if you will lay down your arms, and return once more to your obedience. But, if you do not," he concluded, "I will make your city a heap of ruins, and leave not a soul alive to mourn over it!"

But the Spanish commander did not yet comprehend the character of the Aztecs, if he thought to intimidate them by menaces. Calm in their exterior and slow to move, they were the more difficult to pacify when roused; and now that they had been stirred to their inmost depths, it was no human voice that could still the tempest. It may be, however, that Cortés did not so much misconceive the character of the people. He may have felt that an authoritative tone was the only one he could assume with any chance of effect, in his present position, in which milder and more conciliatory language would, by intimating a consciousness of inferiority, have too certainly defeated its own object.

It was true, they answered, he had destroyed their temples, broken in pieces their gods, massacred their countrymen. Many more, doubtless, were yet to fall under their terrible swords. But they were content so long as for every thousand Mexicans they could shed the blood of a single white man! "Look out," they continued, "on our terraces and streets, see them still thronged with warriors as far as your eyes can reach. Our numbers are scarcely diminished by our losses. Yours, on the contrary, are lessening every hour. You are perishing from hunger and sickness. Your provisions and water are failing. You must soon fall into our hands. *The bridges are broken down, and you cannot escape!* There will be too few of you left to glut the vengeance of our Gods!" As they concluded, they sent a volley of arrows over the battlements, which compelled the Spaniards to descend and take refuge in their defences.

The fierce and indomitable spirit of the Aztecs filled the besieged with dismay. All, then, that they had done and suffered, their battles by day, their vigils by night, the perils they had braved, even the victories they had won, were of no avail. It was too evident that they had no longer the spring of ancient superstition to work upon, in the breasts of the natives, who, like some wild beast that has burst the bonds of his keeper, seemed now to swell and exult in the full consciousness of their strength. The annunciation respecting the bridges fell like a knell on the ears of the Christians. All that they had heard was too true,—and they gazed on one another with looks of anxiety and dismay.

The same consequences followed, which sometimes take place among the crew of a shipwrecked vessel. Subordination was lost in the dreadful sense of danger. A spirit of mutiny broke out, especially among the recent levies drawn from the army of Narvaez. They had come into the country from no motive of ambition, but attracted simply by the glowing reports of its opulence, and they had fondly hoped to return in a few months with their pockets well lined with the gold of the Aztec monarch. But how different had been their lot! From the first hour of their landing, they had experienced only trouble and disaster, privations of every description, sufferings unexampled, and they now beheld in perspective a fate yet more appalling. Bitterly did they lament the hour when they left the sunny fields of Cuba for these cannibal regions! And heartily did they curse their own folly in listening to the call of Velasquez, and still more, in embarking under the banner of Cortés!

They now demanded with noisy vehemence to be led instantly from the city, and refused to serve longer in defence of a place where they were cooped up like sheep in the shambles, waiting only to be dragged to slaughter. In all this they were rebuked by the more orderly, soldierlike conduct of the veterans of Cortés. These latter had shared with their general the day of his prosperity, and they were not disposed to desert him in the tempest. It was, indeed, obvious, on a little reflection, that the only chance of safety, in the existing crisis, rested on subordination and union; and that even this chance must be greatly diminished under any other leader than their present one.

Thus pressed by enemies without and by factions within, that leader was found, as usual, true to himself. Circumstances so appalling, as would have paralyzed a common mind, only stimulated his to higher action, and drew forth all its resources. He combined what is most rare, singular coolness and constancy of purpose, with a spirit of enterprise that might well be called romantic. His presence of mind did not now desert him. He calmly surveyed his condition, and weighed the difficulties which surrounded him, before coming to a decision. Independently of the hazard of a retreat in the face of a watchful and desperate foe, it was a deep mortification to surrender up the city, where he had so long lorded it as a master; to abandon the rich treasures which he had secured to himself and his followers; to forego the very means by which he had hoped to propitiate the favor of his sovereign, and secure an amnesty for his irregular proceedings. This, he well knew, must, after all, be dependent on success. To fly now was to acknowledge himself further removed from the conquest than ever. What a close was this to a career so auspiciously begun! What a contrast to his magnificent vaunts! What a triumph would it afford to his enemies! The governor of Cuba would be amply revenged.

But, if such humiliating reflections crowded on his mind, the alternative of remaining, in his present crippled condition, seemed yet more desperate. With his men daily diminishing in strength and numbers, their provisions reduced so low that a small daily ration of bread was all the sustenance afforded to the soldier under his extraordinary fatigues, with the breaches every day widening in his feeble fortifications, with his ammunition, in fine, nearly expended, it would be impossible to maintain the place much longer— and none but men of iron constitutions and tempers, like the Spaniards, could have held it out so long—against the enemy. The chief embarrassment was as to the time and manner in which it would be expedient to evacuate the city. The best route seemed to be that of Tlacopan (Tacuba). For the causeway, the most dangerous part of the road, was but two miles long in that direction and would, therefore, place the fugitives, much sooner than either of the other great avenues, on terra firma. Before his final departure, however, he proposed to make another sally in that direction, in order to reconnoitre the ground, and, at the same time, divert the enemy's attention from his real purpose by a show of active operations.

For some days his workmen had been employed in constructing a military machine of his own invention. It was called a *manta* and was contrived somewhat on the principle of the mantelets used in the wars of the Middle Ages. It was, however, more complicated, consisting of a tower made of light beams and planks, having two chambers, one over the other. These were to be filled with musketeers, and the sides were provided with loopholes, through which a fire could be kept up on the enemy. The great advantage proposed by this contrivance was, to afford a defence to the troops against the missiles hurled from the terraces. These machines, three of which were made, rested on rollers, and were provided with strong ropes, by which they were to be dragged along the streets by the Tlascalan auxiliaries.

The Mexicans gazed with astonishment on this warlike machinery, and, as the rolling fortresses advanced, belching forth fire and smoke from their entrails, the enemy, incapable of making an impression on those within, fell back in dismay. By bringing the *mantas* under the walls of the houses, the Spaniards were enabled to fire with effect on the mischievous tenants of the *azoteas,* and when this did not silence them, by letting a ladder, or light draw-bridge, fall on the roof from the top of the *manta* they opened a passage to the terrace, and closed with the combatants hand to hand. They could not, however, thus approach the higher buildings, from which the Indian warriors threw down such heavy masses of stone and timber as dislodged the planks that covered the machines, or, thundering against their sides, shook the frail edifices to their foundations, threatening all within with indiscriminate ruin. Indeed, the success of the experiment was doubtful, when the intervention of a canal put a stop to their further progress.

The Spaniards now found the assertion of their enemies too well confirmed. The bridge which traversed the opening had been demolished; and, although the canals which intersected the city were, in general, of no great width or depth, the removal of the bridges not only impeded the movements of the general's clumsy machines, but effectually disconcerted those of his cavalry. Resolving to abandon the *mantas,* he gave orders to fill up the chasm with stone, timber, and other rubbish drawn from the ruined buildings, and to make a new passage-way for the army. While this labor was going on, the Aztec slingers and archers on the other side of the opening kept up a galling discharge on the Christians, the more defenceless from the nature of their occupation. When the work was completed, and a safe passage secured, the Spanish cavaliers rode briskly against the enemy, who, unable to resist the shock of the steel-clad column, fell back with precipitation to where another canal afforded a similar strong position for defence.

There were no less than seven of these canals, intersecting the great street of Tlacopan, and at every one the same scene was renewed, the Mexicans making a gallant stand and inflicting some loss, at each, on their persevering antagonists. These operations consumed two days, when, after incredible toil, the Spanish general had the satisfaction to find the line of communication completely reëstablished through the whole length of the avenue, and the principal bridges placed under strong detachments of infantry. At this juncture, when he had driven the foe before him to the furthest extremity of the street, where it touches on the causeway, he was informed, that the Mexicans, disheartened by their reverses, desired to open a parley with him respecting the terms of an accommodation, and that their chiefs awaited his return for that purpose at the fortress. Overjoyed at the intelligence, he instantly rode back, attened by Alvarado, Sandoval, and about sixty of the cavaliers, to his quarters.

The Mexicans proposed that he should release the two priests captured in the temple, who might be the bearers of his terms, and serve as agents for conducting the negotiation. They were accordingly sent with the requisite instructions to their countrymen. But they did not return. The whole was an artifice of the enemy, anxious to procure the liberation of their religious leaders, one of whom was their *teoteuctli,* or high-priest, whose presence was indispensable in the probable event of a new coronation.

Cortés, meanwhile, relying on the prospects of a speedy arrangement, was hastily taking some refreshments with his officers after the fatigues of the day; when he received the alarming tidings, that the enemy were in arms again, with more fury than ever; that they had overpowered the detachments posted under Alvarado at three of the bridges, and were busily occupied in demolishing them. Stung with shame at the facility with which he had been duped by his wily foe, or rather by his own sanguine hopes, Cortés threw himself into the saddle, and, followed by his brave companions, galloped back at full speed to the scene of action. The Mexicans recoiled before the impetuous charge of the Spaniards. The bridges were again restored; and Cortés and his chivalry rode down the whole extent of the great street, driving the enemy, like frightened deer, at the points of their lances. But, before he could return on his steps, he had the mortification to find that the indefatigable foe, gathering from the adjoining lanes and streets, had again closed on his infantry, who, worn down by fatigue, were unable to maintain their position at one of the principal bridges. New swarms of warriors now poured in on all sides, overwhelming the little band of Christian cavaliers with a storm of stones, darts, and arrows, which rattled like hail on their armor and on that of their well-barbed horses. Most of the missiles, indeed, glanced harmless from the good panoplies of steel, or thick quilted cotton, but, now and then, one better aimed penetrated the joints of the harness, and stretched the rider on the ground.

The confusion became greater around the broken bridge. Some of the horsemen were thrown into the canal, and their steeds floundered wildly about without a rider. Cortés himself, at this crisis, did more than any other to cover the retreat of his followers. While the bridge was repairing, he plunged boldly into the midst of the barbarians, striking down an enemy at every vault of his charger, cheering on his own men, and spreading terror through the ranks of his opponents by the well-known sound of his battle-cry. Never did he display greater hardihood, or more freely expose his person, emulating, says an old chronicler, the feats of the Roman Cocles. In this way he stayed the tide of assailants, till the last man had crossed the bridge, when, some of the planks having given way, he was compelled to leap a chasm of full six feet in width, amidst a cloud of missiles, before he could place himself in safety. A report ran through the army that the general was slain. It soon spread through the city, to the great joy of the Mexicans, and reached the fortress, where the besieged were thrown into no less consternation. But, happily for them, it was false. He, indeed, received two severe contusions on the knee, but in other respects remained uninjured. At no time, however, had he been in such extreme danger; and his escape, and that of his companions, were esteemed little less than a miracle. More than one grave historian refers the preservation of the Spaniards to the watchful care of their patron Apostle, St. James, who, in these desperate conflicts, was beheld careering on his milk-white steed at the head of the Christian squadrons, with his sword flashing lightning, while a lady robed in white—supposed to be the Virgin—was distinctly seen by his side, throwing dust in the eyes of the infidel! The fact is attested both by Spaniards and Mexicans,—by the latter after their conversion to Christianity. Surely, never was there a time when the interposition of their tutelar saint was more strongly demanded.

The coming of night dispersed the Indian battalions, which vanishing like birds of ill omen from the field, left the well-contested pass in possession of the Spaniards. They returned, however, with none of the joyous feelings of conquerors to their citadel, but with slow step and dispirited, with weapons hacked, armor battered, and fainting under the loss of blood, fasting, and fatigue. In this condition they had yet to learn the tidings of a fresh misfortune in the death of Montezuma.

The Indian monarch had rapidly declined, since he had received his injury, sinking, however, quite as much under the anguish of a wounded spirit, as under disease. He continued in the same moody state of insensibility as that already described; holding little communication with those around him, deaf to consolation, obstinately rejecting all medical remedies as well as nourishment. Perceiving his end approach, some of the cavaliers present in the fortress, whom the kindness of his manners had personally attached to him, were anxious to save the soul of the dying prince from the sad doom of those who perish in the darkness of unbelief. They accordingly waited on him, with Father Olmedo at their head, and in the most earnest manner implored him to open his eyes to the error of his creed, and consent to be baptized. But Montezuma—whatever may have been suggested to the contrary—seems never to have faltered in his hereditary faith, or to have contemplated becoming an apostate; for surely he merits that name in its most odious application, who, whether Christian or Pagan, renounces his religion without conviction of its falsehood. Indeed, it was a too implicit reliance on its oracles, which had led him to give such easy confidence to the Spaniards. His intercourse with them had, doubtless, not sharpened his desire to embrace their communion; and the calamities of his country he might consider as sent by his gods to punish him for his hospitality to those who had desecrated and destroyed their shrines.

When Father Olmedo, therefore, kneeling at his side with the uplifted crucifix, affectionately besought him to embrace the sign of man's redemption, he coldly repulsed the priest, exclaiming, "I have but a few moments to live; and will not at this hour desert the faith of my fathers." One thing, however, seemed to press heavily on Montezuma's mind. This was the fate of his children, especially of three daughters, whom he had by his two wives; for there were certain rites of marriage, which distinguished the lawful wife from the concubine. Calling Cortés to his bedside, he earnestly commended these children to his care, as "the most precious jewels that he could leave him." He besought the general to interest his master, the emperor, in their behalf, and to see that they should not be left destitute, but be allowed some portion of their rightful inheritance. "Your lord will do this," he concluded, "if it were only for the friendly offices I have rendered the Spaniards, and for the love I have shown them,—though it has brought me to this condition! But for this I bear them no ill-will." Such, according to Cortés himself, were the words of the dying monarch. Not long after, on the 30th June, 1520, he expired in the arms of some of his own nobles, who still remained faithful in their attendance on his person. "Thus," exclaims a native historian, one of his enemies, a Tlascalan, "thus died the unfortunate Montezuma, who had swayed the sceptre with such consummate policy and wisdom; and who was held in greater reverence and awe than any other prince of his lineage, or any, indeed, that ever sat on a throne in this Western World. With him may be said to have terminated the royal line of the Aztecs, and the glory to have passed away from the empire, which under him had reached the zenith of its prosperity." "The tidings of his death," says the old Castilian chronicler, Diaz, "were received with real grief by every cavalier and soldier in the army who had had access to his person; for we all loved him as a father—and no wonder, seeing how good he was." This simple, but emphatic, testimony to his desert, at such a time, is in itself the best refutation of the suspicions occasionally entertained of his fidelity to the Christians.

It is not easy to depict the portrait of Montezuma in its true colors, since it has been exhibited to us under two aspects, of the most opposite and contradictory character. In the accounts gathered of him by the Spaniards, on coming into the country, he was uniformly represented as bold and warlike, unscrupulous as to the means of gratifying his ambition, hollow and perfidious, the terror of his foes, with a haughty bearing which made him feared even by his own people. They found him, on the contrary, not merely affable and gracious, but disposed to waive all the advantages of his own position, and to place them on a footing with himself; making their wishes his law; gentle even to effeminacy in his deportment, and constant in his friendship, while his whole nation was in arms against them.—Yet these traits, so contradictory, were truly enough drawn. They are to be explained by the extraordinary circumstances of his position.

When Montezuma ascended the throne, he was scarcely twenty-three years of age. Young, and ambitious of extending his empire, he was continually engaged in war, and is said to have been present himself in nine pitched battles. He was greatly renowned for his martial prowess, for he belonged to the *Quachictin,* the highest military order of his nation, and one into which but few even of its sovereigns had been admitted. In later life, he preferred intrigue to violence, as more consonant to his character and priestly education. In this he was as great an adept as any prince of his time, and, by arts not very honorable to himself, succeeded in filching away much of the territory of his royal kinsman of Tezcuco. Severe in the administration of justice, he made important reforms in the arrangement of the tribunals. He introduced other innovations in the royal household, creating new offices, introducing a lavish magnificence and forms of courtly etiquette unknown to his ruder predecessors. He was, in short, most attentive to all that concerned the exterior and pomp of royalty. Stately and decorous he was careful of his own dignity, and might be said to be as great an "actor of majesty" among the barbarian potentates of the new world, as Louis the Fourteenth was among the polished princes of Europe.

He was deeply tinctured, moreover, with that spirit of bigotry, which threw such a shade over the latter days of the French monarch. He received the Spaniards as the beings predicted by his oracles. The anxious dread, with which he had evaded their proffered visit, was founded on the same feelings which led him so blindly to resign himself to them on their approach. He felt himself rebuked by their superior genius. He at once conceded all that they demanded,—his treasures, his power, even his person. For their sake, he forsook his wonted occupations, his pleasures, his most familiar habits. He might be said to forego his nature; and, as his subjects asserted, to change his sex and become a woman. If we cannot refuse our contempt for the pusillanimity of the Aztec monarch, it should be mitigated by the consideration, that his pusillanimity sprung from his superstition, and that superstition in the savage is the substitute for religious principle in the civilized man.

It is not easy to contemplate the fate of Montezuma without feelings of the strongest compassion;—to see him thus borne along the tide of events beyond his power to avert or control; to see him, like some stately tree, the pride of his own Indian forests, towering aloft in the pomp and majesty of its branches, by its very eminence a mark for the thunderbolt, the first victim of the tempest which was to sweep over its native hills! When the wise king of Tezcuco addressed his royal relative at his coronation, he exclaimed, "Happy the empire, which is now in the meridian of its prosperity, for the sceptre is given to one whom the Almighty has in his keeping; and the nations shall hold him in reverence!" Alas! the subject of this auspicious invocation lived to see his empire melt away like the winter's wreath; to see a strange race drop, as it were, from the clouds on his land; to find himself a prisoner in the palace of his fathers, the companion of those who were the enemies of his gods and his people; to be insulted, reviled, trodden in the dust, by the meanest of his subjects, by those who, a few months previous, had trembled at his glance; drawing his last breath in the halls of the stranger, —a lonely outcast in the heart of his own capital! He was the sad victim of destiny,—a destiny as dark and irresistible in its march, as that which broods over the mythic legends of Antiquity!

Montezuma, at the time of his death, was about forty-one years old, of which he reigned eighteen. His person and manners have been already described. He left a numerous progeny by his various wives, most of whom, having lost their consideration after the Conquest, fell into obscurity, as they mingled with the mass of the Indian population. Two of them, however, a son and a daughter, who embraced Christianity, became the founders of noble houses in Spain. The government willing to show its gratitude for the large extent of empire derived from their ancestor, conferred on them ample estates, and important hereditary honors; and the Counts of Montezuma and Tula, intermarrying with the best blood of Castile, intimated by their names and titles their illustrious descent from the royal dynasty of Mexico.

Montezuma's death was a misfortune to the Spaniards. While he lived, they had a precious pledge in their hands, which in extremity, they might possibly have turned to account. Now the last link was snapped which connected them with the natives of the country. But independently of interested feelings, Cortés and his officers were much affected by his death from personal considerations, and, when they gazed on the cold remains of the ill-starred monarch, they may have felt a natural compunction, as they contrasted his late flourishing condition with that to which his friendship for them had now reduced him.

RALPH WALDO EMERSON (1803–1882)

From LITERARY ETHICS

THE youth, intoxicated with his admiration of a hero, fails to see that it is only a projection of his own soul which he admires. In solitude, in a remote village, the ardent youth loiters and mourns. With inflamed eye, in this sleeping wilderness, he has read the story of the Emperor Charles the Fifth, until his fancy has brought home to the surrounding woods the faint roar of cannonades in the Milanese, and marches in Germany. He is curious concerning that man's day. What filled it? the crowded orders, the stern decisions, the foreign despatches, the Castilian etiquette? The soul answers —Behold his day here! In the sighing of these woods, in the quiet of these gray fields, in the cool breeze that sings out of these northern mountains; in the workmen, the boys, the maidens you meet,—in the hopes of the morning, the ennui of noon, and sauntering of the afternoon; in the disquieting comparisons; in the regrets at want of vigor; in the great idea and the puny execution;—behold Charles the Fifth's day; another, yet the same; behold Chatham's, Hampden's, Bayard's, Alfred's, Scipio's, Pericles's day,— day of all that are born of women. The difference of circumstance is merely costume. I am tasting the self-same life,—its sweetness, its greatness, its pain, which I so admire in other men. Do not foolishly ask of the inscrutable, obliterated past, what it cannot tell,—the details of that nature, of that day, called Byron, or Burke;—but ask it of the enveloping Now; the more quaintly you inspect its evanescent beauties, its wonderful details, its spirtual causes, its astounding whole,—so much the more you master the biography of this hero, and that, and every hero.

All men, in the abstract, are just and good; what hinders them in the particular is the momentary predominance of the finite and individual over the general truth. The condition of our incarnation in a private self seems to be a perpetual tendency to prefer the private law, to obey the private impulse, to the exclusion of the law of universal being. The hero is great by means of the predominance of the universal nature; he has only to open his mouth, and it speaks; he has only to be forced to act, and it acts. All men catch the word, or embrace the deed, with the heart, for it is verily theirs as much as his; but in them this disease of an excess of organization cheats them of equal issues. Nothing is more simple than greatness; indeed, to be simple is to be great. The vision of genius comes by renouncing the too officious activity of the understanding, and giving leave and amplest privilege to the spontaneous sentiment. Out of this must all that is alive and genial in thought go. Men grind and grind in the mill of a truism, and nothing comes out but what was put in. But the moment they desert the tradition for a spontaneous thought, then poetry, wit, hope, virtue, learning, anecdote, all flock to their aid. Observe the phenomenon of extempore debate. A man of cultivated mind but reserved habits, sitting silent, admires the miracle of free, impassioned, picturesque speech, in the man addressing an assembly;—a state of being and power how unlike his own! Presently his own emotion rises to his lips, and overflows in speech. He must also rise and say somewhat. Once embarked, once having overcome the novelty of the situation, he finds it just as easy and natural to speak,—to speak with thoughts, with pictures, with rhythmical balance of sentences,—as it was to sit silent; for it needs not to do, but to suffer; he only adjusts himself to the free spirit which gladly utters itself through him; and motion is as easy as rest.

We assume that all thought is already long ago adequately set down in books,—all imaginations in poems; and what we say we only throw in as confirmatory of this supposed complete body of literature. A very shallow assumption. Say rather all literature is yet to be written. Poetry has scarce chanted its first song. The perpetual admonition of nature to us, is, 'The world is new, untried. Do not believe the past. I give you the universe a virgin to-day.'

By Latin and English poetry we were born and bred in an oratorio of praises of nature,—flowers, birds, mountains, sun, and moon;—yet the naturalist of this hour finds that he knows nothing, by all their poems, of any of these fine things; that he has conversed with the mere surface and show of them all; and of their essence, or of their history, knowing nothing. Further inquiry will discover that nobody,—that not these chanting poets themselves, knew anything sincere of these handsome natures they so commended; that they contented themselves with the passing chirp of a bird, that they saw one or two mornings, and listlessly looked at sunsets, and repeated idly these few glimpses in their song. But go into the forest, you shall find all new and undescribed. The honking of the wild geese flying by night; the thin note of the companionable titmouse in the winter day; the fall of swarms of flies, in autumn, from combats high in the air, pattering down on the leaves like rain; the angry hiss of the wood-birds; the pine throwing out its pollen for the benefit of the next century; the turpentine exuding from the tree;—and indeed any vegetation, any animation, any and all, are alike unattempted. The man who stands on the seashore, or who rambles in the woods, seems to be the first man that ever stood on the shore, or entered a grove, his sensations and his world are so novel and strange. Whilst I read the poets, I think that nothing new can be said about morning and evening. But when I see the daybreak I am not reminded of these Homeric, or Shakspearian, or Miltonic, or Chaucerian pictures. No, but I feel perhaps the pain of an alien world; a world not yet subdued by the thought; or I am cheered by the moist, warm, glittering, budding, melodious hour, that takes down the narrow walls of my soul, and extends its life and pulsation to the very horizon. .*That* is morning, to cease for a bright hour to be a prisoner of this sickly body, and to become as large as nature.

The noonday darkness of the American forest, the deep, echoing, aboriginal woods, where the living columns of the oak and fir tower up from the ruins of the trees of the last millennium; where, from year to year, the eagle and the crow see no intruder; the pines, bearded with savage moss, yet touched with grace by the violets at their feet; the broad, cold lowland which forms its coat of vapor with the stillness of subterranean crystallization; and where the traveller, amid the repulsive plants that are native in the swamp, thinks with pleasing terror of the distant town; this beauty,—haggard and desert beauty, which the sun and the moon, the snow and the rain, repaint and vary, has never been recorded by art, yet is not indifferent to any passenger. All men are poets at heart. They serve nature for bread, but her loveliness overcomes them sometimes. What mean these journeys to Niagara; these pilgrims to the White Hills? Men believe in the adaptations of utility, always: in the mountains, they may believe in the adaptations of the eye. Undoubtedly the changes of geology have a relation to the prosperous sprouting of the corn and peas in my kitchen garden; but not less is there a relation of beauty between my soul and the dim crags of Agiochook up there in the clouds. Every man, when this is told, hearkens with joy, and yet his own conversation with nature is still unsung.

He must embrace solitude as a bride. He must have his glees and his glooms alone. His own estimate must be measure enough, his own praise reward enough for him. And why must the student be solitary and silent? That he may become acquainted with his thoughts. If he pines in a lonely place, hankering for the crowd, for display, he is not in the lonely place; his heart is in the market; he does not see; he does not hear; he does not think. But go cherish your soul; expel companions; set your habits to a life of solitude; then will the faculties rise fair and full within, like forest trees and field flowers; you will have results, which, when you meet your fellowmen, you can communicate, and they will gladly receive. Do not go into solitude only that you may presently come into public. Such solitude denies itself; is public and stale. The public can get public experience, but they wish the scholar to replace to them those private, sincere, divine experiences of which they have been defrauded by dwelling in the street. It is the noble, manlike, just thought, which is the superiority demanded of you, and not crowds but solitude confers this elevation. Not insulation of place, but independence of spirit is essential, and it is only as the garden, the cottage, the forest, and the rock, are a sort of mechanical aids to this, that they are of value. Think alone, and all places are friendly and sacred. The poets who have lived in cities have been hermits still. Inspiration makes solitude anywhere.

You can very soon learn all that society can teach you for one while. Its foolish routine, an indefinite multiplication of balls, concerts, rides, theatres, can teach you no more than a few can. Then accept the hint of shame, of spiritual emptiness and waste which true nature gives you, and retire and hide; lock the door; shut the shutters; then welcome falls the imprisoning rain,—dear hermitage of nature. Re-collect the spirits. Have solitary prayer and praise. Digest and correct the past experience; and blend it with the new and divine life.

You will pardon me, Gentlemen, if I say I think that we have need of a more rigorous scholastic rule; such an asceticism, I mean, as only the hardihood and devotion of the scholar himself can enforce. We live in the sun and on the surface,—a thin, plausible, superficial existence, and talk of muse and prophet, of art and creation. But out of our shallow and frivolous way of life, how can greatness ever grow? Come now, let us go and be dumb. Let us sit with our hands on our mouths, a long, austere, Pythagorean lustrum. Let us live in corners, and do chores, and suffer, and weep, and drudge, with eyes and hearts that love the Lord. Silence, seclusion, austerity, may pierce deep into the grandeur and secret of our being, and so diving, bring up out of secular darkness the sublimities of the moral constitution. How mean to go blazing, a gaudy butterfly, in fashionable or political *salons,* the fool of society, the fool of notoriety, a topic for newspapers, a piece of the street, and forfeiting the real prerogative of the russet coat, the privacy, and the true and warm heart of the citizen!

Not the least instructive passage in modern history seems to me a trait of Napoleon exhibited to the English when he became their prisoner. On coming on board the Bellerophon, a file of English soldiers drawn up on deck gave him a military salute. Napoleon observed that their manner of handling their arms differed from the French exercise, and, putting aside the guns of those nearest him, walked up to a soldier, took his gun, and himself went through the motion in the French mode. The English officers and men looked on with astonishment, and inquired if such familiarity was usual with the Emperor.

In this instance, as always, that man, with whatever defects or vices, represented performance in lieu of pretension. Feudalism and Orientalism had long enough thought it majestic to do nothing; the modern majesty consists in work. He belonged to a class fast growing in the world, who think that what a man can do is his greatest ornament, and that he always consults his dignity by doing it. He was not a believer in luck; he had a faith, like sight, in the application of means to ends. Means to ends, is the motto of all his behavior. He believed that the great captains of antiquity performed their exploits only by correct combinations, and by justly comparing the relation between means and consequences, efforts and obstacles. The vulgar call good fortune that which really is produced by the calculations of genius. But Napoleon, thus faithful to facts, had also this crowning merit, that whilst he believed in number and weight, and omitted no part of prudence, he believed also in the freedom and quite incalculable force of the soul. A man of infinite caution, he neglected never the least particular of preparation, of patient adaptation; yet nevertheless he had a sublime confidence, as in his all, in the sallies of the courage, and the faith in his destiny, which, at the right moment, repaired all losses, and demolished cavalry, infantry, king, and kaiser, as with irresistible thunderbolts. As they say the bough of the tree has the character of the leaf, and the whole tree of the bough, so, it is curious to remark, Bonaparte's army partook of this double strength of the captain; for, whilst strictly supplied in all its appointments, and everything expected from the valor and discipline of every platoon, in flank and centre, yet always remained his total trust in the prodigious revolutions of fortune which his reserved Imperial Guard were capable of working, if, in all else, the day was lost. Here he was sublime. He no longer calculated the chance of the cannon ball. He was faithful to tactics to the uttermost,—and when all tactics had come to an end then he dilated and availed himself of the mighty salutations of the most formidable soldiers in nature.

The man of genius should occupy the whole space between God or pure mind and the multitude of uneducated men. He must draw from the infinite Reason, on one side; and he must penetrate into the heart and sense of the crowd, on the other. From one, he must draw his strength; to the other, he must owe his aim. The one yokes him to the real; the other, to the apparent. At one pole is Reason; at the other, Common Sense. If he be defective at either extreme of the scale, his philosophy will seem low and utilitarian, or it will appear too vague and indefinite for the uses of life.

The student, as we all along insist, is great only by being passive to the superincumbent spirit. Let this faith then dictate all his action. Snares and bribes abound to mislead him; let him be true nevertheless. His success has its perils too. There is somewhat inconvenient and injurious in his position. They whom his thoughts have entertained or inflamed, seek him before yet they have learned the hard conditions of thought. They seek him, that he may turn his lamp on the dark riddles whose solution they think is inscribed on the walls of their being. They find that he is a poor, ignorant man, in a white-seamed, rusty coat, like themselves, nowise emitting a continuous stream of light, but now and then a jet of luminous thought followed by total darkness; moreover, that he cannot make of his infrequent illumination a portable taper to carry whither he would, and explain now this dark riddle, now that. Sorrow ensues. The scholar regrets to damp the hope of ingenuous boys; and the youth has lost a star out of his new flaming firmament. Hence the temptation to the scholar to mystify, to hear the question, to sit upon it, to make an answer of words in lack of the oracle of things. Not the less let him be cold and true, and wait in patience, knowing that truth can make even silence eloquent and memorable. Truth shall be policy enough for him. Let him open his breast to all honest inquiry, and be an artist superior to tricks of art. Show frankly as a saint would do, your experience, methods, tools, and means. Welcome all comers to the freest use of the same. And out of this superior frankness and charity you shall learn higher secrets of your nature, which gods will bend and aid you to communicate.

Gentlemen, I have ventured to offer you these considerations upon the scholar's place and hope, because I thought that standing, as many of you now do, on the threshold of this College, girt and ready to go and assume tasks, public and private, in your country, you would not be sorry to be admonished of those primary duties of the intellect whereof you will seldom hear from the lips of your new companions. You will hear every day the maxims of a low prudence. You will hear that the first duty is to get land and money, place and name. 'What is this Truth you seek? what is this Beauty?' men will ask, with derision. If nevertheless God have called any of you to explore truth and beauty, be bold, be firm, be true. When you shall say, 'As others do, so will I: I renounce, I am sorry for it, my early visions; I must eat the good of the land and let learning and romantic expectations go, until a more convenient season;'—then dies the man in you; then once more perish the buds of art, and poetry, and science, as they have died already in a thousand thousand men. The hour of that choice is the crisis of your history, and see that you hold yourself fast by the intellect. It is this domineering temper of the sensual world that creates the extreme need of the priests of science; and it is the office and right of the intellect to make and not take its estimate. Bend to the persuasion which is flowing to you from every object in nature, to be its tongue to the heart of man, and to show the besotted world how passing fair is wisdom. Forewarned that the vice of the times and the country is an excessive pretension, let us seek the shade, and find wisdom in neglect. Be content with a little light, so it be your own. Explore, and explore. Be neither chided nor flattered out of your position of perpetual inquiry. Neither dogmatize, nor accept another's dogmatism. Why should you renounce your right to traverse the star-lit deserts of truth, for the premature comforts of an acre, house, and barn? Truth also has its roof, and bed, and board. Make yourself necessary to the world, and mankind will give you bread, and if not store of it, yet such as shall not take away your property in all men's possessions, in all men's affections, in art, in nature, and in hope.

You will not fear that I am enjoining too stern an asceticism. Ask not, Of what use is a scholarship that systematically retreats? or, Who is the better for the philosopher who conceals his accomplishments, and hides his thoughts from the waiting world? Hides his thoughts! Hide the sun and moon. Thought is all light, and publishes itself to the universe. It will speak, though you were dumb, by its own miraculous organ. It will flow out of your actions, your manners, and your face. It will bring you friendships. It will impledge you to truth by the love and expectation of generous minds. By virtue of the laws of that Nature which is one and perfect, it shall yield every sincere good that is in the soul to the scholar beloved of earth and heaven.

The Rhodora:

ON BEING ASKED, WHENCE IS THE FLOWER?

In May, when sea-winds pierced our solitudes,
I found the fresh Rhodora in the woods,
Spreading its leafless blooms in a damp nook,
To please the desert and the sluggish brook.
The purple petals, fallen in the pool,
Made the black water with their beauty gay;
Here might the red-bird come his plumes to cool,
And court the flower that cheapens his array.
Rhodora! if the sages ask thee why
This charm is wasted on the earth and sky,
Tell them, dear, that if eyes were made for seeing,
Then Beauty is its own excuse for being:
Why thou wert there, O rival of the rose!
I never thought to ask, I never knew:
But, in my simple ignorance, suppose
The self-same Power that brought me there brought you.

The Snow-Storm

Announced by all the trumpets of the sky,
Arrives the snow, and, driving o'er the fields,
Seems nowhere to alight: the whited air
Hides hills and woods, the river, and the heaven,
And veils the farm-nouse at the garden's end.

The sled and traveller stopped, the
    courier's feet
Delayed, all friends shut out, the house-
    mates sit
Around the radiant fireplace, enclosed
In a tumultuous privacy of storm.

Come see the north wind's masonry.
Out of an unseen quarry evermore
Furnished with tile, the fierce artificer
Curves his white bastions with projected
    roof
Round every windward stake, or tree, or
    door.
Speeding, the myriad-handed, his wild
    work
So fanciful, so savage, nought cares he
For number or proportion. Mockingly,
On coop or kennel he hangs Parian
    wreaths;
A swan-like form invests the hidden
    thorn;
Fills up the farmer's lane from wall to wall,
Maugre the farmer's sighs; and at the gate
A tapering turret overtops the work.
And when his hours are numbered, and
    the world
Is all his own, retiring, as he were not,
Leaves, when the sun appears, astonished
    Art
To mimic in slow structures, stone by
    stone,
Built in an age, the mad wind's night-
    work,
The frolic architecture of the snow.

Fable

THE mountain and the squirrel
Had a quarrel,
And the former called the latter 'Little
    Prig';
Bun replied,
'You are doubtless very big;
But all sorts of things and weather
Must be taken in together,
To make up a year
And a sphere.
And I think it no disgrace
To occupy my place.

If I'm not so large as you,
You are not so small as I,
And not half so spry.
I'll not deny you make
A very pretty squirrel track;
Talents differ; all is well and wisely put;
If I cannot carry forests on my back,
Neither can you crack a nut.'

Days

DAUGHTERS of Time, the hypocritic Days,
Muffled and dumb like barefoot dervishes,
And marching single in an endless file,
Bring diadems and fagots in their hands.
To each they offer gifts after his will,
Bread, kingdoms, stars, and sky that
    holds them all.
I, in my pleached garden, watched the
    pomp,
Forgot my morning wishes, hastily
Took a few herbs and apples, and the
    Day
Turned and departed silent. I, too late,
Under her solemn fillet saw the scorn.

Concord Hymn

SUNG AT THE COMPLETION OF THE BATTLE
    MONUMENT, JULY 4, 1837

By the rude bridge that arched the flood,
    Their flag to April's breeze unfurled,
Here once the embattled farmers stood
    And fired the shot heard round the
    world.

The foe long since in silence slept;
    Alike the conqueror silent sleeps;
And Time the ruined bridge has swept
    Down the dark stream which seaward
    creeps.

On this green bank, by this soft stream,
    We set to-day a votive stone;
That memory may their deed redeem,
    When, like our sires, our sons are gone.

Spirit, that made those heroes dare
    To die, and leave their children free,
Bid Time and Nature gently spare
    The shaft we raise to them and thee.

NATHANIEL HAWTHORNE (1804-1864)

The Great Stone Face

ONE afternoon, when the sun was going down, a mother and her little boy sat at the door of their cottage, talking about the Great Stone Face. They had but to lift their eyes, and there it was plainly to be seen, though miles away, with the sunshine brightening all its features.

And what was the Great Stone Face?

Embosomed amongst a family of lofty mountains, there was a valley so spacious that it contained many thousand inhabitants. Some of these good people dwelt in log-huts, with the black forest all around them, on the steep and difficult hill-sides. Others had their homes in comfortable farm-houses, and cultivated the rich soil on the gentle slopes or level surfaces of the valley. Others, again, were congregated into populous villages, where some wild, highland rivulet, tumbling down from its birthplace in the upper mountain region, had been caught and tamed by human cunning, and compelled to turn the machinery of cotton-factories. The inhabitants of this valley, in short, were numerous, and of many modes of life. But all of them, grown people and children, had a kind of familiarity with the Great Stone Face, although some possessed the gift of distinguishing this grand natural phenomenon more perfectly than many of their neighbors.

The Great Stone Face, then, was a work of Nature in her mood of majestic playfulness, formed on the perpendicular side of a mountain by some immense rocks, which had been thrown together in such a position as, when viewed at a proper distance, precisely to resemble the features of the human countenance. It seemed as if an enormous giant, or a Titan, had sculptured his own likeness on the precipice. There was the broad arch of the forehead, a hundred feet in height; the nose, with its long bridge; and the vast lips, which, if they could have spoken, would have rolled their thunder accents from one end of the valley to the other. True it is, that if the spectator approached too near, he lost the outline of the gigantic visage, and could discern only a heap of ponderous and gigantic rocks, piled in chaotic ruin one upon another. Retracing his steps, however, the wondrous features would again be seen; and the farther he withdrew from them, the more like a human face, with all its original divinity intact, did they appear; until, as it grew dim in the distance, with the clouds and glorified vapor of the mountains clustering about it, the Great Stone Face seemed positively to be alive.

It was a happy lot for children to grow up to manhood or womanhood with the Great Stone Face before their eyes, for all the features were noble, and the expression was at once grand and sweet, as if it were the glow of a vast, warm heart, that embraced all mankind in its affections, and had room for more. It was an education only to look at it. According to the belief of many people, the valley owed much of its fertility to this benign aspect that was continually beaming over it, illuminating the clouds, and infusing its tenderness into the sunshine.

As we began with saying, a mother and her little boy sat at their cottage-door, gazing at the Great Stone Face, and talking about it. The child's name was Ernest.

"Mother," said he, while the Titanic visage smiled on him, "I wish that it could speak, for it looks so very kindly that its voice must needs be pleasant. If I were to see a man with such a face, I should love him dearly."

"If an old prophecy should come to pass," answered his mother, "we may see a man, some time or other, with exactly such a face as that."

"What prophecy do you mean, dear mother?" eagerly inquired Ernest. "Pray tell me all about it!"

So his mother told him a story that her own mother had told to her, when she herself was younger than little Ernest; a story, not of things that were past, but of what was yet to come; a story, nevertheless, so very old, that even the Indians, who formerly inhabited this valley, had heard it from their forefathers, to whom, as they affirmed, it had been murmured by the mountain streams, and whispered by the wind among the tree-tops. The purport was, that, at some future day, a child should be born hereabouts, who was destined to become the greatest and noblest personage of his time, and whose countenance, in manhood, should bear an exact resemblance to the Great Stone Face. Not a few old-fashioned people, and young ones likewise, in the ardor of their hopes, still cherished an enduring faith in this old prophecy. But others, who had seen more of the world, had watched and waited till they were weary, and had beheld no man with such a face, nor any man that proved to be much greater or nobler than his neighbors, concluded it to be nothing but an idle tale. At all events, the great man of the prophecy had not yet appeared.

"O mother, dear mother!" cried Ernest, clapping his hands above his head, "I do hope that I shall live to see him!"

His mother was an affectionate and thoughtful woman, and felt that it was wisest not to discourage the generous hopes of her little boy. So she only said to him, "Perhaps you may."

And Ernest never forgot the story that his mother told him. It was always in his mind, whenever he looked upon the Great Stone Face. He spent his childhood in the log-cottage where he was born, and was dutiful to his mother, and helpful to her in many things, assisting her much with his little hands, and more with his loving heart. In this manner, from a happy yet often pensive child, he grew up to be a mild, quiet, unobtrusive boy, and sun-browned with labor in the fields, but with more intelligence brightening his aspect than is seen in many lads who have been taught at famous schools. Yet Ernest had had no teacher, save only that the great Stone Face became one to him. When the toil of the day was over, he would gaze at it for hours, until he began to imagine that those vast features recognized him, and gave him a smile of kindness and encouragement, responsive to his own look of veneration. We must not take upon us to affirm that this was a mistake, although the Face may have looked no more kindly at Ernest than at all the world besides. But the secret was that the boy's tender and confiding simplicity discerned what other people could not see; and thus the love, which was meant for all, became his peculiar portion.

About this time there went a rumor throughout the valley, that the great man, foretold from ages long ago, who was to bear a resemblance to the Great Stone Face, had appeared at last. It seems that, many years before, a young man had migrated from the valley and settled at a distant seaport, where, after getting together a little money, he had set up as a shopkeeper. His name—but I could never learn whether it was his real one, or a nickname that had grown out of his habits and success in life— was Gathergold. Being shrewd and active, and endowed by Providence with that inscrutable faculty which develops itself in what the world calls luck, he became an exceedingly rich merchant, and owner of a whole fleet of bulky-bottomed ships. All the countries of the globe appeared to join hands for the mere purpose of adding heap after heap to the mountainous accumulation of this one man's wealth. The cold regions of the north, almost within the gloom and shadow of the Arctic Circle, sent him their tribute in the shape of furs; hot Africa sifted for him the golden sands of her rivers, and gathered up the ivory tusks of her great elephants out of the forests; the East came bringing him the rich shawls, and spices, and teas, and the effulgence of diamonds, and the gleaming purity of large pearls. The ocean, not to be behindhand with the earth, yielded up her mighty whales, that Mr. Gathergold might sell their oil, and make a profit on it. Be the original commodity what it might, it was gold within his grasp. It might be said of him, as of Midas in the fable, that whatever he touched with his finger immediately glistened, and grew yellow, and was changed at once into sterling metal, or, which suited him still better, into piles of coin. And, when Mr. Gathergold had become so very rich that it would have taken him a hundred years only to count his wealth, he bethought himself of his native valley, and resolved to go back thither, and end his days where he was born. With this purpose in view, he sent a skilful architect to build him such a palace as should be fit for a man of his vast wealth to live in.

As I have said above, it had already been rumored in the valley that Mr. Gathergold had turned out to be the prophetic personage so long and vainly looked for, and that his visage was the perfect and undeniable similitude of the Great Stone Face. People were the more ready to believe that this must needs be the fact, when they beheld the splendid edifice that rose, as if by enchantment, on the site of his father's old weather-beaten farm-house. The exterior was of marble, so dazzlingly white that it seemed as though the whole structure might melt away in the sunshine, like those humbler ones which Mr. Gathergold, in his young play-days, before his fingers were gifted with the touch of transmutation, had been accustomed to build of snow. It had a richly ornamented portico, supported by tall pillars, beneath which was a lofty door, studded with silver knobs, and made of a kind of variegated wood that had been brought from beyond the sea. The windows, from the floor to the ceiling of each stately apartment, were composed, respectively, of but one enormous pane of glass, so transparently pure that it was said to be a finer medium than even the vacant atmosphere. Hardly anybody had been permitted to see the interior of this palace; but it was reported, and with good semblance of truth, to be far more gorgeous than the outside, insomuch that whatever was iron or brass in other houses was silver or gold in this; and Mr. Gathergold's bedchamber, especially, made such a glittering appearance that no ordinary man would have been able to close his eyes there. But, on the other hand, Mr. Gathergold was now so inured to wealth, that perhaps he could not have closed his eyes unless where the gleam of it was certain to find its way beneath his eyelids.

In due time, the mansion was finished; next came the upholsterers, with magnificent furniture; then, a whole troop of black and white servants, the harbingers of Mr. Gathergold, who, in his own majestic person, was expected to arrive at sunset. Our friend Ernest, meanwhile, had been deeply stirred by the idea that the great man, the noble man, the man of prophecy, after so many ages of delay, was at length to be made manifest to his native valley. He knew, boy as he was, that there were a thousand ways in which Mr. Gathergold, with his vast wealth, might transform himself into an angel of beneficence, and assume a control over human affairs as wide and benignant as the smile of the Great

Stone Face. Full of faith and hope, Ernest doubted not that what the people said was true, and that now he was to behold the living likeness of those wondrous features on the mountain-side. While the boy was still gazing up the valley, and fancying, as he always did, that the Great Stone Face returned his gaze and looked kindly at him, the rumbling of wheels was heard, approaching swiftly along the winding road.

"Here he comes!" cried a group of people who were assembled to witness the arrival. "Here comes the great Mr. Gathergold!"

A carriage, drawn by four horses, dashed round the turn of the road. Within it, thrust partly out of the window, appeared the physiognomy of the old man, with a skin as yellow as if his own Midas-hand had transmuted it. He had a low forehead, small, sharp eyes, puckered about with innumerable wrinkles, and very thin lips, which he made still thinner by pressing them forcibly together.

"The very image of the Great Stone Face!" shouted the people. "Sure enough, the old prophecy is true; and here we have the great man come, at last!"

And, what greatly perplexed Ernest, they seemed actually to believe that here was the likeness which they spoke of. By the roadside there chanced to be an old beggar-woman and two little beggar-children, stragglers from some far-off region, who, as the carriage rolled onward, held out their hands and lifted up their doleful voices, most piteously beseeching charity. A yellow claw—the very same that had clawed together so much wealth—poked itself out of the coach-window, and dropt some copper coins upon the ground; so that, though the great man's name seems to have been Gathergold, he might just as suitably have been nicknamed Scattercopper. Still, nevertheless, with an earnest shout, and evidently with as much good faith as ever, the people bellowed,—

"He is the very image of the Great Stone Face!"

But Ernest turned sadly from the wrinkled shrewdness of that sordid visage, and gazed up the valley, where, amid a gathering mist, gilded by the last sunbeams, he could still distinguish those glorious features which had impressed themselves into his soul. Their aspect cheered him. What did the benign lips seem to say?

"He will come! Fear not, Ernest; the man will come!"

The years went on, and Ernest ceased to be a boy. He had grown to be a young man now. He attracted little notice from the other inhabitants of the valley; for they saw nothing remarkable in his way of life, save that, when the labor of the day was over, he still loved to go apart and gaze and meditate upon the Great Stone Face. According to their idea of the matter, it was a folly, indeed, but pardonable, inasmuch as Ernest was industrious, kind, and neighborly, and neglected no duty for the sake of indulging this idle habit. They knew not that the Great Stone Face had become a teacher to him, and that the sentiment which was expressed in it would enlarge the young man's heart, and fill it with wider and deeper sympathies than other hearts. They knew not that thence would come a better wisdom than could be learned from books, and a better life than could be moulded on the defaced example of other human lives. Neither did Ernest know that the thoughts and affections which came to him so naturally, in the fields and at the fireside, and wherever he communed with himself, were of a higher tone than those which all men shared with him. A simple soul,—simple as when his mother first taught him the old prophecy,—he beheld the marvellous features beaming adown the valley, and still wondered that their human counterpart was so long in making his appearance.

By this time poor Mr. Gathergold was dead and buried; and the oddest part of the matter was, that his wealth, which was the body and spirit of his existence, had disappeared before his death, leaving nothing of him but a living skeleton, covered over with a wrinkled, yellow skin. Since the melting away of his gold, it had been very generally conceded that there was no such striking resemblance, after all, betwixt the ignoble features of the ruined merchant and that majestic face upon the mountain-side. So the people ceased to honor him during his lifetime, and quietly consigned him to forgetfulness after his decease. Once in a while, it is true, his memory was brought up in connection with the magnificent palace which he had built, and which had long ago been turned into a hotel for the accommodation of strangers, multitudes of whom came, every summer, to visit that famous natural curiosity, the Great Stone Face. Thus, Mr. Gathergold being discredited and thrown into the shade, the man of prophecy was yet to come.

It so happened that a native-born son of the valley, many years before, had enlisted as a soldier, and, after a great deal of hard fighting, had now become an illustrious commander. Whatever he may be called in history, he was known in camps and on the battle-field under the nickname of Old Blood-and-Thunder. This war-worn veteran, being now infirm with age and wounds, and weary of the turmoil of a military life, and of the roll of the drum and the clangor of the trumpet, that had so long been ringing in his ears, had lately signified a purpose of returning to his native valley, hoping to find repose where he remembered to have left it. The inhabitants, his old neighbors and their grown-up children, were resolved to welcome the renowned warrior with a salute of cannon and a public dinner; and all the more enthusiastically, it being affirmed that now, at last, the likeness of the Great Stone Face had actually appeared. An aide-de-camp of Old Blood-and-Thunder, travelling through the valley, was said to have been struck with the resemblance. Moreover the school-mates and early acquaintances of the general were ready to testify, on oath, that, to the best of their recollection, the aforesaid general had been exceedingly like the majestic image, even when a boy, only that the idea had never occurred to them at that period. Great, therefore, was the excitement throughout the valley; and many people, who had never once thought of glancing at the Great Stone Face for years before, now spent their time in gazing at it, for the sake of knowing exactly how General Blood-and-Thunder looked.

On the day of the great festival, Ernest, with all the other people of the valley, left their work, and proceeded to the spot where the sylvan banquet was prepared. As he approached, the loud voice of the Rev. Dr. Battleblast was heard, beseeching a blessing on the good things set before them, and on the distinguished friend of peace in whose honor they were assembled. The tables were arranged in a cleared space of the woods, shut in by the surrounding trees, except where a vista opened eastward, and afforded a distant view of the Great Stone Face. Over the general's chair, which was a relic from the home of Washington, there was an arch of verdant boughs, with the laurel profusely inter-mixed, and surmounted by his country's banner, beneath which he had won his victories. Our friend Ernest raised himself on his tiptoes, in hopes to get a glimpse of the celebrated guest; but there was a mighty crowd about the tables anxious to hear the toasts and speeches, and to catch any word that might fall from the general in reply; and a volunteer company, doing duty as a guard, pricked ruthlessly with their bayonets at any particularly quiet person among the throng. So Ernest, being of an unobtrusive character, was thrust quite into the background, where he could see no more of Old Blood-and-Thunder's physiognomy than if it had been still blazing on the battle-field. To console himself, he turned towards the Great Stone Face, which, like a faithful and long-remem-bered friend, looked back and smiled upon him through the vista of the forest. Meantime, however, he could overhear the remarks of various individuals, who were comparing the features of the hero with the face on the distant mountain-side.

"'Tis the same face, to a hair!" cried one man, cutting a caper for joy.

"Wonderfully like, that's a fact!" responded another.

"Like! why, I call it Old Blood-and-Thunder himself, in a monstrous looking-glass!" cried a third. "And why not? He's the greatest man of this or any other age, beyond a doubt."

And then all three of the speakers gave a great shout, which communicated electricity to the crowd, and called forth a roar from a thousand voices, that went reverberating for miles among the mountains, until you might have supposed that the Great Stone Face had poured its thunder-breath into the cry. All these comments, and this vast enthusiasm, served the more to interest our friend; nor did he think of questioning that now, at length, the mountain-visage had found its human counterpart. It is true, Ernest had imagined that this long-looked-for personage would appear in the character of a man of peace, uttering wisdom, and doing good, and making people happy. But, taking an habitual breadth of view, with all his simplicity, he contended that Providence should choose its own method of blessing mankind, and could conceive that this great end might be effected even by a warrior and a bloody sword, should inscrutable wisdom see fit to order matters so.

"The general! the general!" was now the cry. "Hush! silence! Old Blood-and-Thunder's going to make a speech."

Even so; for, the cloth being removed, the general's health had been drunk, amid shouts of applause, and he now stood upon his feet to thank the company. Ernest saw him. There he was, over the shoulders of the crowd, from the two glittering epaulets and embroidered collar upward, beneath the arch of green boughs with intertwined laurel, and the banner drooping as if to shade his brow! And there, too, visible in the same glance, through the vista of the forest, appeared the Great Stone Face! And was there, indeed, such a resemblance as the crowd had testified? Alas, Ernest could not recognize it! He beheld a war-worn and weather-beaten countenance, full of energy, and expressive of an iron will; but the gentle wisdom, the deep, broad, tender sympathies, were altogether wanting in Old Blood-and-Thunder's visage; and even if the Great Stone Face had assumed his look of stern command, the milder traits would still have tempered it.

"This is not the man of prophecy," sighed Ernest to himself, as he made his way out of the throng. "And must the world wait longer yet?"

The mists had congregated about the distant mountain-side, and there were seen the grand and awful features of the Great Stone Face, awful but benignant, as if a mighty angel were sitting among the hills, and enrobing himself in a cloud-vesture of gold and purple. As he looked, Ernest could hardly believe but that a smile beamed over the whole visage, with a radiance still brightening, although without motion of the lips. It was probably the effect of the western sunshine, melting through the thinly diffused vapors that had swept between him and the object that he gazed at. But—as it always did—the aspect of his marvellous friend made Ernest as hopeful as if he had never hoped in vain.

"Fear not, Ernest," said his heart, even as if the Great Face were whispering him,—"fear not, Ernest; he will come."

More years sped swiftly and tranquilly away. Ernest still dwelt in his native valley, and was now a man of middle age. By imperceptible degrees, he had become known among the people. Now, as heretofore, he labored for his bread, and was the same simple-hearted man that he had always been. But he had thought and felt so much, he had given so many of the best hours of his life to unworldly hopes for some great good to mankind, that it seemed as though he had been talking with the angels, and had imbibed a portion of their wisdom unawares. It was visible in the calm and well-considered beneficence of his daily life, the quiet stream of which had made a wide green margin all along its course. Not a day passed by, that the world was not the better because this man, humble as he was, had lived. He never stepped aside from his own path, yet would always reach a blessing to his neighbor. Almost involuntarily, too, he had become a preacher. The pure and high simplicity of his thought, which, as one of its manifestations, took shape in the good deeds that dropped silently from his hand, flowed also forth in speech. He uttered truths that wrought upon and moulded the lives of those who heard him. His auditors, it may be, never suspected that Ernest, their own neighbor and familiar friend, was more than an ordinary man; least of all did Ernest himself suspect it; but, inevitably as the murmur of a rivulet, came thoughts out of his mouth that no other human lips had spoken.

When the people's minds had had a little time to cool, they were ready enough to acknowledge their mistake in imagining a similarity between General Blood-and-Thunder's truculent physiognomy and the benign visage on the mountain-side. But now, again, there were reports and many paragraphs in the newspapers, affirming that the likeness of the Great Stone Face had appeared upon the broad shoulders of a certain eminent statesman. He, like Mr. Gathergold and Old Blood-and-Thunder, was a native of the valley, but had left it in his early days, and taken up the trades of law and politics. Instead of the rich man's wealth and the warrior's sword, he had but a tongue, and it was mightier than both together. So wonderfully eloquent was he, that whatever he might choose to say, his auditors had no choice but to believe him; wrong looked like right, and right like wrong; for when it pleased him, he could make a kind of illuminated fog with his mere breath, and obscure the natural daylight with it. His tongue, indeed, was a magic instrument: sometimes it rumbled like the thunder; sometimes it warbled like the sweetest music. It was the blast of war,—the song of peace; and it seemed to have a heart in it, when there was no such matter. In good truth, he was a wondrous man; and when his tongue had acquired him all other imaginable success,—when it had been heard in halls of state, and in the courts of princes and potentates,—after it had made him known all over the world, even as a voice crying from shore to shore,—it finally persuaded his countrymen to select him for the Presidency. Before this time,—indeed, as soon as he began to grow celebrated,—his admirers had found out the resemblance between him and the Great Stone Face; and so much were they struck by it, that throughout the country this distinguished gentleman was known by the name of Old Stony Phiz. The phrase was considered as giving a highly favorable aspect to his political prospects; for, as is likewise the case with the Popedom, nobody ever becomes President without taking a name other than his own.

While his friends were doing their best to make him President, Old Stony Phiz, as he was called, set out on a visit to the valley where he was born. Of course, he had no other object than to shake hands with his fellow-citizens, and neither thought nor cared about any effect which his progress through the country might have upon the election. Magnificent preparations were made to receive the illustrious statesman; a cavalcade of horsemen set forth to meet him at the boundary line of the state, and all the people left their business and gathered along the wayside to see him pass. Among these was Ernest. Though more than once disappointed, as we have seen, he had such a hopeful and confiding nature, that he was always ready to believe in whatever seemed beautiful and good. He kept his heart continually open, and thus was sure to catch the blessing from on high when it should come. So now again, as buoyantly as ever, he went forth to behold the likeness of the Great Stone Face.

The cavalcade came prancing along the road, with a great clattering of hoofs and a mighty cloud of dust, which rose up so dense and high that the visage of the mountain-side was completely hidden from Ernest's eyes. All the great men of the neighborhood were there on horseback; militia officers, in uniform; the member of Congress; the sheriff of the county; the editors of newspapers; and many a farmer, too, had mounted his patient steed, with his Sunday coat upon his back. It really was a very brilliant spectacle, especially as there were numerous banners flaunting over the cavalcade, on some of which were gorgeous portraits of the illustrious statesman and the Great Stone Face, smiling familiarly at one another, like two brothers. If the pictures were to be trusted, the mutual resemblance, it must be confessed, was marvellous. We must not forget to mention that there was a band of music, which made the echoes of the mountains ring and reverberate with the loud triumph of its strains; so that airy and soul-thrilling melodies broke out among all the heights and hollows, as if every nook of his native valley had found a voice, to welcome the distinguished guest. But the grandest effect was when the far-off mountain precipice flung back the music; for then the Great Stone Face itself seemed to be swelling the triumphant chorus, in acknowledgment that, at length, the man of prophecy was come.

All this while the people were throwing up their hats and shouting, with enthusiasm so contagious that the heart of Ernest kindled up, and he likewise threw up his hat, and shouted, as loudly as the loudest, "Huzza for the great man! Huzza for Old Stony Phiz!" But as yet he had not seen him.

"Here he is, now!" cried those who stood near Ernest. "There! There! Look at Old Stony Phiz and then at the Old Man of the Mountain, and see if they are not as like as two twin-brothers!"

In the midst of all this gallant array came an open barouche, drawn by four white horses; and in the barouche, with his massive head uncovered, sat the illustrious statesman, Old Stony Phiz himself.

"Confess it," said one of Ernest's neighbors to him, "the Great Stone Face has met its match at last!"

Now, it must be owned that, at his first glimpse of the countenance which was bowing and smiling from the barouche, Ernest did fancy that there was a resemblance between it and the old familiar face upon the mountain-side. The brow, with its massive depth and loftiness, and all the other features, indeed, were boldly and strongly hewn, as if in emulation of a more than heroic, of a Titanic model. But the sublimity and stateliness, the grand expression of a divine sympathy, that illuminated the mountain visage and etherealized its ponderous granite substance into spirit, might here be sought in vain. Something had been originally left out, or had departed. And therefore the marvellously gifted statesman had always a weary gloom in the deep caverns of his eyes, as of a child that has outgrown its playthings or a man of mighty faculties and little aims, whose life, with all its high performances, was vague and empty, because no high purpose had endowed it with reality.

Still, Ernest's neighbor was thrusting his elbow into his side, and pressing him for an answer.

"Confess! confess! Is not he the very picture of your Old Man of the Mountain?"

"No!" said Ernest, bluntly, "I see little or no likeness."

"Then so much the worse for the Great Stone Face!" answered his neighbor; and again he set up a shout for Old Stony Phiz.

But Ernest turned away, melancholy, and almost despondent: for this was the saddest of his disappointments, to behold a man who might have fulfilled the prophecy, and had not willed to do so. Meantime, the cavalcade, the banners, the music, and the barouches swept past him, with the vociferous crowd in the rear, leaving the dust to settle down, and the Great Stone Face to be revealed again, with the grandeur that it had worn for untold centuries.

"Lo, here I am, Ernest!" the benign lips seemed to say. "I have waited longer than thou, and am not yet weary. Fear not; the man will come."

The years hurried onward, treading in their haste on one another's heels. And now they began to bring white hairs, and scatter them over the head of Ernest; they made reverend wrinkles across his forehead, and furrows in his cheeks. He was an aged man. But not in vain had he grown old: more than the white hairs on his head were the sage thoughts in his mind; his wrinkles and furrows were inscriptions that Time had graved, and in which he had written legends of wisdom that had been tested by the tenor of a life. And Ernest had ceased to be obscure. Unsought for, undesired, had come the fame which so many seek, and made him known in the great world, beyond the limits of the valley in which he had dwelt so quietly. College professors, and even the active men of cities, came from far to see and converse with Ernest; for the report had gone abroad that this simple husbandman had ideas unlike those of other men, not gained from books, but of a higher tone,—a tranquil and familiar majesty, as if he had been talking with the angels as his daily friends. Whether it were sage, statesman, or philanthropist, Ernest received these visitors with the gentle sincerity that had characterized him from boyhood, and spoke freely with them of whatever came uppermost, or lay deepest in his heart or their own. While they talked together, his face would kindle, unawares, and shine upon them, as with a mild evening light. Pensive with the fulness of such discourse, his guests took leave and went their way; and passing up the valley, paused to look at the Great Stone Face, imagining that they had seen its likeness in a human countenance, but could not remember where.

While Ernest had been growing up and growing old, a bountiful Providence had granted a new poet to this earth. He, likewise, was a native of the valley, but had spent the greater part of his life at a distance from that romantic region, pouring out his sweet music amid the bustle and din of cities. Often, however, did the mountains which had been familiar to him in his childhood lift their snowy peaks into the clear atmosphere of his poetry.   Neither was the Great Stone Face forgotten, for the poet had celebrated it in an ode, which was grand enough to have been uttered by its own majestic lips.   This man of genius, we may say, had come down from heaven with wonderful endowments.   If he sang of a mountain, the eyes of all mankind beheld a mightier grandeur reposing on its breast, or soaring to its summit, than had before been seen there.   If his theme were a lovely lake, a celestial smile had now been thrown over it, to gleam forever on its surface.   If it were the vast old sea, even the deep immensity of its dread bosom seemed to swell the higher, as if moved by the emotions of the song.   Thus the world assumed another and a better aspect from the hour that the poet blessed it with his happy eyes.   The Creator had bestowed him, as the last best touch to his own handiwork.   Creation was not finished till the poet came to interpret, and so complete it.

The effect was no less high and beautiful, when his human brethren were the subject of his verse.   The man or woman, sordid with the common dust of life, who crossed his daily path, and the little child who played in it, were glorified if he beheld them in his mood of poetic faith. He showed the golden links of the great chain that intertwined them with an angelic kindred; he brought out the hidden traits of a celestial birth that made them worthy of such kin.   Some, indeed, there were, who thought to show the soundness of their judgment by affirming that all the beauty and dignity of the natural world existed only in the poet's fancy. Let such men speak for themselves, who undoubtedly appear to have been spawned forth by Nature with a contemptuous bitterness; she having plastered them up out of her refuse stuff, after all the swine were made. As respects all things else, the poet's ideal was the truest truth.

The songs of this poet found their way to Ernest.   He read them after his customary toil, seated on the bench before his cottage-door, where for such a length of time he had filled his repose with thought, by gazing at the Great Stone Face.   And now as he read stanzas that caused the soul to thrill within him, he lifted his eyes to the vast countenance beaming on him so benignantly.

"O majestic friend," he murmured, addressing the Great Stone Face, "is not this man worthy to resemble thee?"

The Face seemed to smile, but answered not a word.

Now it happened that the poet, though he dwelt so far away, had not only heard of Ernest, but had meditated much upon his character, until he deemed nothing so desirable as to meet this man, whose untaught wisdom walked hand in hand with the noble simplicity of his life.   One summer morning, therefore, he took passage by the railroad, and, in the decline of the afternoon, alighted from the cars at no great distance from Ernest's cottage. The great hotel, which had formerly been the palace of Mr. Gathergold, was close at hand, but the poet, with his carpet-bag on his arm, inquired at once where Ernest dwelt, and was resolved to be accepted as his guest.

Approaching the door, he there found the good old man, holding a volume in his hand, which alternately he read, and then, with a finger between the leaves, looked lovingly at the Great Stone Face.

"Good evening," said the poet. "Can you give a traveller a night's lodging?"

"Willingly," answered Ernest; and then he added, smiling, "Methinks I never saw the Great Stone Face look so hospitably at a stranger."

The poet sat down on the bench beside him, and he and Ernest talked together. Often had the poet held intercourse with the wittiest and the wisest, but never before with a man like Ernest, whose thoughts and feelings gushed up with such a natural freedom, and who made great truths so familiar by his simple utterance of them. Angels, as had been so often said, seemed to have wrought with him at his labor in the fields; angels seemed to have sat with him by the fireside; and, dwelling with angels as friend with friend, he had imbibed the sublimity of their ideas, and imbued it with the sweet and lowly charm of household words. So thought the poet. And Ernest, on the other hand, was moved and agitated by the living images which the poet flung out of his mind, and which peopled all the air about the cottage-door with shapes of beauty, both gay and pensive. The sympathies of these two men instructed them with a profounder sense than either could have attained alone. Their minds accorded into one strain, and made delightful music which neither of them could have claimed as all his own, nor distinguished his own share from the other's. They led one another, as it were, into a high pavilion of their thoughts, so remote, and hitherto so dim, that they had never entered it before, and so beautiful that they desired to be there always.

As Ernest listened to the poet, he imagined that the Great Stone Face was bending forward to listen too. He gazed earnestly into the poet's glowing eyes.

"Who are you, my strangly gifted guest?" he said.

The poet laid his finger on the volume that Ernest had been reading.

"You have read these poems," said he. "You know me, then,—for I wrote them."

Again, and still more earnestly than before, Ernest examined the poet's features; then turned towards the Great Stone Face; then back, with an uncertain aspect, to his guest. But his countenance fell; he shook his head, and sighed.

"Wherefore are you sad?" inquired the poet.

"Because," replied Ernest, "all through life I have awaited the fulfilment of a prophecy; and, when I read these poems, I hoped that it might be fulfilled in you."

"You hoped," answered the poet, faintly smiling, "to find in me the likeness of the Great Stone Face. And you are disappointed, as formerly with Mr. Gathergold, and Old Blood-and-Thunder, and Old Stony Phiz. Yes Ernest, it is my doom. You must add my name to the illustrious three, and record another failure of your hopes. For—in shame and sadness do I speak it, Ernest—I am not worthy to be typified by yonder benign and majestic image."

"And why?" asked Ernest. He pointed to the volume. "Are not those thoughts divine?"

"They have a strain of the Divinity," replied the poet. "You can hear in them the far-off echo of a heavenly song. But my life, dear Ernest, has not corresponded with my thought. I have had grand dreams, but they have been only dreams, because I have lived—and that, too, by my own choice—among poor and mean realities. Sometimes even—shall I dare to say it?—I lack faith in the grandeur, the beauty, and the goodness, which my own works are said to have made more evident in nature and in human life. Why, then, pure seeker of the good and true, shouldst thou hope to find me, in yonder image of the divine?"

The poet spoke sadly, and his eyes were dim with tears. So, likewise, were those of Ernest.

At the hour of sunset, as had long been his frequent custom, Ernest was to discourse to an assemblage of the neighboring inhabitants in the open air. He and the poet, arm in arm, still talking together as they went along, proceeded to the spot. It was a small nook among the hills, with a gray precipice behind, the stern front of which was relieved by the pleasant foliage of many creeping plants that made a tapestry for the naked rock, by hanging their festoons from all its rugged angles. At a small elevation above the ground, set in a rich framework of verdure, there appeared a niche, spacious enough to admit a human figure, with freedom for such gestures as spontaneously accompany earnest thought and genuine emotion. Into this natural pulpit Ernest ascended, and threw a look of familiar kindness around upon his audience. They stood, or sat, or reclined upon the grass, as seemed good to each, with the departing sunshine falling obliquely over them, and mingling its subdued cheerfulness with the solemnity of a grove of ancient trees, beneath and amid the boughs of which the golden rays were constrained to pass. In another direction was seen the Great Stone Face, with the same cheer, combined with the same solemnity, in its benignant aspect.

Ernest began to speak, giving to the people of what was in his heart and mind. His words had power, because they accorded with his thoughts; and his thoughts had reality and depth, because they harmonized with the life which he had always lived. It was not mere breath that this preacher uttered; they were the words of life, because a life of good deeds and holy love was melted into them. Pearls, pure and rich, had been dissolved into this precious draught. The poet, as he listened, felt that the being and character of Ernest were a nobler strain of poetry than he had ever written. His eyes glistening with tears, he gazed reverentially at the venerable man, and said within himself that never was there an aspect so worthy of a prophet and a sage as that mild, sweet, thoughtful countenance, with the glory of white hair diffused about it. At a distance, but distinctly to be seen, high up in the golden light of the setting sun, appeared the Great Stone Face, with hoary mists around it, like the white hairs around the brow of Ernest. Its look of grand beneficence seemed to embrace the world.

At that moment, in sympathy with a thought which he was about to utter, the face of Ernest assumed a grandeur of expression, so imbued with benevolence, that the poet, by an irresistible impulse, threw his arms aloft, and shouted,—

"Behold! Behold! Ernest is himself the likeness of the Great Stone Face!"

Then all the people looked, and saw that what the deep-sighted poet said was true. The prophecy was fulfilled. But Ernest, having finished what he had to say, took the poet's arm, and walked slowly homeward, still hoping that some wiser and better man than himself would by and by appear, bearing a resemblance to the GREAT STONE FACE.

David Swan

WE can be but partially acquainted even with the events which actually influence our course through life, and our final destiny. There are innumerable other events, if such they may be called, which come close upon us, yet pass away without actual results, or even betraying their near approach, by the reflection of any light or shadow across our minds. Could we know all the vicissitudes of our fortunes, life would be too full of hope and fear, exultation or disappointment, to afford us a single hour of true serenity. This idea may be illustrated by a page from the secret of David Swan.

We have nothing to do with David until we find him, at the age of twenty, on the high road from his native place to the city of Boston, where his uncle, a small dealer in the grocery line, was to take him behind the counter. Be it enough to say, that he was a native of New Hampshire, born of respectable parents, and had received an ordinary school education, with a classic finish by a year at Gilmanton Academy. After journeying on foot from sunrise till nearly noon of a summer's day, his weariness and the increasing heat determined him to sit down in the first convenient shade, and await the coming up of the stagecoach. As if planted on purpose for him, there soon appeared a little tuft of maples, with a delightful recess in the midst, and such a fresh bubbling spring, that it seemed never to have sparkled for any wayfarer but David Swan. Virgin or not, he kissed it with his thirsty lips, and then flung himself along the brink, pillowing his head upon some shirts and a pair of pantaloons, tied up in a striped cotton handkerchief. The sunbeams could not reach him; the dust did not yet rise from the road, after the heavy rain of yesterday; and his grassy lair suited the young man better than a bed of down. The spring murmured drowsily beside him; the branches waved dreamily across the blue sky overhead; and a deep sleep, perchance hiding dreams within its depths, fell upon David Swan. But we are to relate events which he did not dream of.

While he lay sound asleep in the shade, other people were wide awake, and passed to and fro, afoot, on horseback, and in all sorts of vehicles, along the sunny road by his bed-chamber. Some looked neither to the right hand nor the left, and knew not that he was there; some merely glanced that way, without admitting the slumberer among their busy thoughts; some laughed to see how soundly he slept; and several, whose hearts were brimming full of scorn, ejected their venomous superfluity on David Swan. A middle-aged widow, when nobody else was near, thrust her head a little way into the recess, and vowed that the young fellow looked charming in his sleep. A temperance lecturer saw him, and wrought poor David into the texture of his evening's discourse, as an awful instance of dead drunkenness by the road-side. But censure, praise, merriment, scorn, and indifference, were all one, or rather all nothing, to David Swan.

He had slept only a few moments when a brown carriage, drawn by a handsome pair of horses, bowled easily along, and was brought to a standstill nearly in front of David's resting place. A linchpin had fallen out, and permitted one of the wheels to slide off. The damage was slight, and occasioned merely a momentary alarm to an elderly merchant and his wife, who were returning to Boston in the carriage. While the coachman and a servant were replacing the wheel, the lady and gentleman sheltered themselves beneath the maple-trees and there espied the bubbling fountain, and David Swan asleep beside it. Impressed with the awe which the humblest sleeper usually sheds around him, the merchant trod as lightly as the gout would allow; and his spouse took good heed not to rustle her silk gown, lest David should start up, all of a sudden.

"How soundly he sleeps!" whispered the old gentleman. "From what a depth he draws that easy breath! Such sleep as that, brought on without an opiate, would be worth more to me than half my income, for it would suppose health and an untroubled mind."

"And youth besides," said the lady. "Healthy and quiet age does not sleep thus. Our slumber is no more like his than our wakefulness."

The longer they looked the more did this elderly couple feel interested in the unknown youth, to whom the wayside and the maple shade was as a secret chamber, with the rich gloom of damask curtains brooding over him. Perceiving that a stray sunbeam glimmered down upon his face, the lady contrived to twist a branch aside, so as to intercept it. And having done this little act of kindness, she began to feel like a mother to him.

"Providence seems to have laid him here," whispered she to her husband, "and to have brought us hither to find him, after our disappointment in our cousin's son. Methinks I can see a likeness to our departed Henry. Shall we waken him?"

"To what purpose?" said the merchant, hesitating. "We know nothing of the youth's character."

"That open countenance!" replied his wife, in the same hushed voice, yet earnestly. "This innocent sleep!"

While these whispers were passing, the sleeper's heart did not throb, nor his breath become agitated, nor his features betray the least token of interest. Yet Fortune was bending over him, just ready to let fall a burthen of gold. The old merchant had lost his only son, and had no heir to his wealth, except a distant relative, with whose conduct he was dissatisfied. In such cases, people sometimes do stranger things than to act the magician, and awaken a young man to splendor, who fell asleep in poverty.

"Shall we not waken him?" repeated the lady, persuasively.

"The coach is ready, sir," said the servant, behind.

The old couple started, reddened, and hurried away, mutually wondering that they should ever have dreamed of doing anything so very ridiculous. The merchant threw himself back in the carriage, and occupied his mind with the plan of a magnificent asylum for unfortunate men of business. Meanwhile, David Swan enjoyed his nap.

The carriage could not have gone above a mile or two, when a pretty young girl came along with a tripping pace, which showed precisely how her little heart was dancing in her bosom. Perhaps it was this merry kind of motion that caused—is there any harm in saying it? —her garter to slip its knot. Conscious that the silken girth, if silk it were, was relaxing its hold, she turned aside into the shelter of the maple-trees, and there found a young man asleep by the spring! Blushing as red as any rose, that she should have intruded into a gentleman's bedchamber, and for such a purpose too, she was about to make her escape on tiptoe. But there was peril near the sleeper. A monster of a bee had been wandering overhead—buzz, buzz, buzz—now among the leaves, now flashing through the strips of sunshine, and now lost in the dark shade, till finally he appeared to be settling on the eyelid of David Swan. The sting of a bee is sometimes deadly. As free-hearted as she was innocent, the girl attacked the intruder with her handkerchief, brushed him soundly, and drove him from the maple shade. How sweet a picture! This good deed accomplished, with quickened breath, and a deeper blush, she stole a glance at the youthful stranger, for whom she had been battling with a dragon in the air.

"He is handsome!" thought she, and blushed redder yet.

How could it be that no dream of bliss grew so strong within him, that, shattered by its very strength, it should part asunder and allow him to perceive the girl among its phantoms? Why, at least, did no smile of welcome brighten upon his face? She was come, the maid whose soul, according to the old and beautiful idea, had been severed from his own, and whom, in all his vague but passionate desires, he yearned to meet. Her only could he love with a perfect love—him only could she receive into the depths of her heart—and now her image was faintly blushing in the fountain by his side; should it pass away, its happy lustre would never gleam upon his life again.

"How sound he sleeps!" murmured the girl.

She departed, but did not trip along the road so lightly as when she came.

Now, this girl's father was a thriving country merchant in the neighborhood, and happened, at that identical time, to be looking out for just such a young man as David Swan. Had David formed a wayside acquaintance with the daughter, he would have become the father's clerk, and all else in natural succession. So here, again, had good fortune—the best of fortunes—stolen so near that her garments brushed against him, and he knew nothing of the matter.

The girl was hardly out of sight when two men turned aside beneath the maple shade. Both had dark faces, set off by cloth caps, which were drawn down aslant over their brows. Their dresses were shabby, yet had a certain smartness. These were a couple of rascals, who got their living by whatever the devil sent them, and now, in the interim of other business, had staked the joint profits of their next piece of villainy on a game of cards, which was to have been decided here under the trees. But finding David asleep by the spring, one of the rogues whispered to his fellow—

"Hist!—Do you see that bundle under his head!"

The other villain nodded, winked, and leered.

"I'll bet you a horn of brandy," said the first, "that the chap has either a pocket-book or a snug little hoard of small change, stowed away amongst his shirts. And if not there, we shall find it in his pantaloons' pocket."

"But how if he wakes?" said the other.

His companion thrust aside his waistcoat, pointed to the handle of a dirk, and nodded.

"So be it!" muttered the second villain.

They approached the unconscious David, and, while one pointed the dagger towards his heart, the other began to search the bundle beneath his head. Their two faces, grim, wrinkled, and ghastly with guilt and fear, bent over their victim, looking horrible enough to be mistaken for fiends, should he suddenly awake. Nay, had the villains glanced aside into the spring, even they would hardly have known themselves, as reflected there. But David Swan had never worn a more tranquil aspect, even when asleep on his mother's breast.

"I must take away the bundle," whispered one.

"If he stirs, I'll strike," muttered the other.

But, at this moment, a dog, scenting along the ground, came in beneath the maple trees, and gazed alternately at each of these wicked men, and then at the quiet sleeper. He then lapped out of the fountain.

"Pshaw!" said one villain. "We can do nothing now. The dog's master must be close behind."

"Let's take a drink, and be off," said the other.

The man with the dagger thrust back the weapon into his bosom, and drew forth a pocket-pistol, but not of that kind which kills by a single discharge. It was a flask of liquor, with a block-tin tumbler screwed upon the mouth. Each drank a comfortable dram, and left the spot, with so many jests and such laughter at their unaccomplished wickedness that they might be said to have gone on their way rejoicing. In a few hours they had forgotten the whole affair, nor once imagined that the recording angel had written down the crime of murder against their souls in letters as durable as eternity. As for David Swan, he still slept quietly, neither conscious of the shadow of death when it hung over him, nor of the glow of renewed life when that shadow was withdrawn.

He slept, but no longer so quietly as at first. An hour's repose had snatched from his elastic frame the weariness with which many hours of toil had burthened it. Now he stirred—now moved his lips, without a sound—now talked in an inward tone to the noonday spectres of his dream. But a noise of wheels came rattling louder and louder along the road, until it dashed through the dispersing mist of David's slumber —and there was the stage-coach. He started up, with all his ideas about him.

"Halloo, driver!—Take a passenger?" shouted he.

"Room on top!" answered the driver.

Up mounted David, and bowled away merrily towards Boston, without so much as a parting glance at that fountain of dreamlike vicissitude. He knew not that a phantom of Wealth had thrown a golden hue upon its waters—nor that one of Love had sighed softly to their murmur— nor that one of Death had threatened to crimson them with his blood— all, in the brief hour since he lay down to sleep. Sleeping or waking, we hear not the airy footsteps of the strange things that almost happen. Does it not argue a superintending Providence, that, while viewless and unexpected events thrust themselves continually athwart our path, there should still be regularity enough in mortal life to render foresight even partially available?

From OUR OLD HOME

Dr. Johnson's Birthplace and the Site of the Penance

I WAS but little interested in the legends of the remote antiquity of Lichfield, being drawn thither partly to see its beautiful cathedral, and still more, I believe, because it was the birthplace of Dr. Johnson, with whose sturdy English character I became acquainted, at a very early period of my life, through the good offices of Mr. Boswell. In truth, he seems as familiar to my recollection, and almost as vivid in his personal aspect to my mind's eye, as the kindly figure of my own grandfather. It is only a solitary child,—left much to such wild modes of culture as he chooses for himself while yet ignorant what culture means, standing on tiptoe to pull down books from no very lofty shelf, and then shutting himself up, as it were, between the leaves, going astray through the volume at his own pleasure, and comprehending it rather by his sensibilities and affections than his intellect,—that child is the only student that ever gets the sort of intimacy which I am now thinking of, with a literary personage. I do not remember, indeed, ever caring much about any of the stalwart Doctor's grandiloquent productions, except his two stern and masculine poems, "London," and "The Vanity of Human Wishes"; it was as a man, a talker, and a humorist, that I knew and loved him, appreciating many of his qualities perhaps more thoroughly than I do now, though never seeking to put my instinctive perception of his character into language.

Beyond all question, I might have had a wiser friend than he. The atmosphere in which alone he breathed was dense; his awful dread of death showed how much muddy imperfection was to be cleansed out of him, before he could be capable of spiritual existence; he meddled only with the surface of life, and never cared to penetrate further than to ploughshare depth; his very sense and sagacity were but a one-eyed clear-sightedness. I laughed at him, sometimes, standing beside his knee. And yet, considering that my native propensities were towards Fairy Land, and also how much yeast is generally mixed up with the mental sustenance of a New-Englander, it may not have been altogether amiss, in those childish and boyish days, to keep pace with this heavy-footed traveller and feed on the gross diet that he carried in his knapsack. It is wholesome food even now. And, then, how English! Many of the latent sympathies that enabled me to enjoy the Old Country so well, and that so readily amalgamated themselves with the American ideas that seemed most adverse to them, may have been derived from, or fostered and kept alive by, the great English moralist. Never was a descriptive epithet more nicely appropriate than that! Dr. Johnson's morality was as English an article as a beefsteak.

Seeking for Johnson's birthplace, I found it in St. Mary's Square, which is not so much a square as the mere widening of a street. The house is tall and thin, of three stories, with a square front and a roof rising steep and high. On a side-view, the building looks as if it had been cut in two in the midst, there being no slope of the roof on that side. A ladder slanted against the wall, and a painter was giving a livelier hue to the plaster. In a corner-room of the basement, where old Michael Johnson may be supposed to have sold books, is now what we should call a dry-goods store, or, according to the English phrase, a mercer's and haberdasher's shop. The house has a private entrance on a cross-street, the door being accessible by several much-worn stone steps, which are bordered by an iron balustrade. I set my foot on the steps and laid my hand on the balustrade, where Johnson's hand and foot must many a time have been, and ascending to the door, I knocked once, and again, and again, and got no admittance. Going round to the shop-entrance, I tried to open it, but found it as fast bolted as the gate of Paradise. It is mortifying to be so balked in one's little enthusiasms; but looking round in quest of somebody to make inquiries of, I was a good deal consoled by the sight of Dr. Johnson himself, who happened, just at that moment, to be sitting at his ease nearly in the middle of St. Mary's Square, with his face turned towards his father's house.

Of course, it being almost fourscore years since the Doctor laid aside his weary bulk of flesh, together with the ponderous melancholy that had so long weighed him down, the intelligent reader will at once comprehend that he was marble in his substance, and seated in a marble chair, on an elevated stone pedestal. In short, it was a statue, sculptured by Lucas, and placed here in 1838, at the expense of Dr. Law, the reverend chancellor of the diocese.

The figure is colossal (though perhaps not much more so than the mountainous Doctor himself) and looks down upon the spectator from its pedestal of ten or twelve feet high, with a broad and heavy benignity of aspect, very like in feature to Sir Joshua Reynolds's portrait of Johnson, but calmer and sweeter in expression. Several big books are piled up beneath his chair, and, if I mistake not, he holds a volume in his hand, thus blinking forth at the world out of his learned abstraction, owl-like, yet benevolent at heart. The statue is immensely massive, a vast ponderosity of stone, not finely spiritualized, nor indeed, fully humanized, but rather resembling a great stone-bowlder than a man. You must look with the eyes of faith and sympathy, or, possibly, you might lose the human being altogether, and find only a big stone within your mental grasp. On the pedestal are three bas-reliefs. In the first, Johnson is represented as hardly more than a baby, bestriding an old man's shoulders, resting his chin on the bald head which he embraces with his little arms, and listening earnestly to the High-Church eloquence of Dr. Sacheverell. In the second tablet, he is seen riding to school on the shoulders of two of his comrades, while another boy supports him in the rear.

The third bas-relief possesses, to my mind, a great deal of pathos, to which my appreciative faculty is probably the more alive, because I have always been profoundly impressed by the incident here commemorated, and long ago tried to tell it for the behoof of childish readers. It shows Johnson in the market-place of Uttoxeter, doing penance for an act of disobedience to his father, committed fifty years before. He stands bareheaded, a venerable figure, and a countenance extremely sad and woe-begone, with the wind and rain driving hard against him, and thus helping to suggest to the spectator the gloom of his inward state. Some market-people and children gaze awe-stricken into his face, and an aged man and woman, with clasped and uplifted hands, seem to be praying for him. These latter personages (whose introduction by the artist is none the less effective, because, in queer proximity, there are some commodities of market-day in the shape of living ducks and dead poultry) I interpreted to represent the spirits of Johnson's father and mother, lending what aid they could to lighten his half-century's burden of remorse.

I had never heard of the above-described piece of sculpture before; it appears to have no reputation as a work of art, nor am I at all positive that it deserves any. For me, however, it did as much as sculpture could, under the circumstances, even if the artist of the Libyan Sibyl had wrought it, by reviving my interest in the sturdy old Englishman, and particularly by freshening my perception of a wonderful beauty and pathetic tenderness in the incident of the penance. So, the next day, I left Lichfield for Uttoxeter, on one of the few purely sentimental pilgrimages that I ever undertook, to see the very spot where Johnson had stood. Boswell, I think, speaks of the town (its name is pronounced Yuteoxeter) as being about nine miles off from Lichfield, but the county-map would indicate a greater distance; and by rail, passing from one line to another, it is as much as eighteen miles. I have always had an idea of old Michael Johnson sending his literary merchandise by carrier's wagon, journeying to Uttoxeter afoot on market-day morning, selling books through the busy hours, and returning to Lichfield at night. This could not possibly have been the case.

Arriving at the Uttoxeter station, the first objects that I saw, with a green field or two between them and me, were the tower and gray steeple of a church, rising among red-tiled roofs and a few scattered trees. A very short walk takes you from the station up into the town. It had been my previous impression that the market-place of Uttoxeter lay immediately roundabout the church; and, if I remember the narrative aright, Johnson, or Boswell in his behalf, describes his father's book-stall as standing in the market-place, close beside the sacred edifice. It is impossible for me to say what changes may have occurred in the topography of the town, during almost a century and a half since Michael

Johnson retired from business, and ninety years, at least, since his son's penance was performed. But the church has now merely a street of ordinary width passing around it, while the market-place, though near at hand, neither forms a part of it nor is really contiguous, nor would its throng and bustle be apt to overflow their boundaries and surge against the churchyard and the old gray tower. Nevertheless, a walk of a minute or two brings a person from the centre of the market-place to the church-door; and Michael Johnson might very conveniently have located his stall and laid out his literary ware in the corner at the tower's base; better there, indeed, than in the busy centre of an agricultural market. But the picturesque arrangement and full impressiveness of the story absolutely require that Johnson shall not have done his penance in a corner, ever so little retired, but shall have been the very nucleus of the crowd,—the midmost man of the market-place,—a central image of Memory and Remorse, contrasting with and overpowering the petty materialism around him. He himself, having the force to throw vitality and truth into what persons differently constituted might reckon a mere external ceremony, and an absurd one, could not have failed to see this necessity. I am resolved, therefore, that the true site of Dr. Johnson's penance was in the middle of the market-place.

That important portion of the town is a rather spacious and irregularly shaped vacuity, surrounded by houses and shops, some of them old, with red-tiled roofs, others wearing a pretence of newness, but probably as old in their inner substance as the rest. The people of Uttoxeter seemed very idle in the warm summer-day, and were scattered in little groups along the sidewalks, leisurely chatting with one another, and often turning about to take a deliberate stare at my humble self; insomuch that I felt as if my genuine sympathy for the illustrious penitent, and my many reflections about him, must have imbued me with some of his own singularity of mien. If their great-grandfathers were such redoubtable starers in the Doctor's day, his penance was no light one.

I stepped into one of the rustic hostelries and got my dinner,—bacon and greens, some mutton-chops, juicier and more delectable than all America could serve up at the President's table, and a gooseberry pudding; a sufficient meal for six yeomen, and good enough for a prince, besides a pitcher of foaming ale, the whole at the pitiful small charge of eighteen-pence! Dr. Johnson would have forgiven me, for nobody had a heartier faith in beef and mutton than himself.

Meanwhile I found myself still haunted by a desire to get a definite result out of my visit to Uttoxeter. The hospitable inn was called the Nag's Head, and standing beside the market-place, was as likely as any other to have entertained old Michael Johnson in the days when he used to come hither to sell books. He, perhaps, had dined on bacon and greens, and drunk his ale, and smoked his pipe, in the very room where I now sat, which was a low, ancient room, certainly much older than Queen Anne's time, with a red-brick floor, and a white-washed ceiling, traversed by bare, rough beams, the whole in the rudest fashion, but extremely neat. Neither did it lack ornament, the walls being hung with colored engravings of prize oxen and other pretty prints, and the mantel-piece adorned with earthen-ware figures of shepherdesses in the Arcadian taste of long ago. Michael Johnson's eyes might have rested on that selfsame earthen image, to examine which more closely I had just crossed the brick pavement of the room. And, sitting down again, still as I sipped my ale, I glanced through the open window into the sunny market-place, and wished that I could honestly fix on one spot rather than another, as likely to have been the holy site where Johnson stood to do his penance.

How strange and stupid it is that tradition should not have marked and kept in mind the very place! How shameful (nothing less than that) that there should be no local memorial of this incident, as beautiful and touching a passage as can be cited out of any human life! No inscription of it, almost as sacred as a verse of Scripture on the wall of the church! No statue of the venerable and illustrious penitent in the market-place to throw a wholesome awe over its earthliness, its frauds and petty wrongs of which the benumbed fingers of conscience can make no record, its selfish competition of each man with his brother or his neighbor, its traffic of soul-substance for a little worldly gain! Such a statue, if the piety of the people did not raise it, might almost have been expected to grow up out of the pavement of its own accord on the spot that had been watered by the rain that dripped from Johnson's garments, mingled with his remorseful tears.

Long after my visit to Uttoxeter, I was told that there were individuals in the town who could have shown me the exact, indubitable spot where Johnson performed his penance. I was assured, moreover, that sufficient interest was felt in the subject to have induced certain local discussions as to the expediency of erecting a memorial. With all deference to my polite informant, I surmise that there is a mistake, and decline, without further and precise evidence, giving credit to either of the above statements. The inhabitants know nothing, as a matter of general interest, about the penance, and care nothing for the scene of it. If the clergyman of the parish, for example, had ever heard of it, would he not have used the theme, time and again, wherewith to work tenderly and profoundly on the souls committed to his charge? If parents were familiar with it, would they not teach it to their young ones at the fireside, both to insure reverence to their own gray hairs, and to protect the children from such unavailing regrets as Johnson bore upon his heart for fifty years? If the site were ascertained, would not the pavement thereabouts be worn with reverential foot-steps? Would not every town-born child be able to direct the pilgrim thither? While waiting at the station, before my departure, I asked a boy who stood near me,—an intelligent and gentlemanly lad, twelve or thirteen years old, whom I should take to be a clergyman's son,—I asked him if he had ever heard the story of Dr. Johnson, how he stood an hour doing penance near that church, the spire of which rose before us. The boy stared and answered,—

"No!"

"Were you born in Uttoxeter?"

"Yes."

I inquired if no circumstance such as I had mentioned was known or talked about among the inhabitants.

"No," said the boy; "not that I ever heard of."

Just think of the absurd little town, knowing nothing of the only memorable incident which ever happened within its boundaries since the old Britons built it, this sad and lovely story, which consecrates the spot (for I found it holy to my contemplation, again, as soon as it lay behind me) in the heart of a stranger from three thousand miles over the sea!

HENRY WADSWORTH LONGFELLOW (1807-1881)

To the River Charles

RIVER! that in silence windest
　Through the meadows, bright and free,
Till at length thy rest thou findest
　In the bosom of the sea!

Four long years of mingled feeling,
　Half in rest, and half in strife,
I have seen thy waters stealing
　Onward, like the stream of life.

Thou has taught me, Silent River!
　Many a lesson, deep and long;
Thou hast been a generous giver;
　I can give thee but a song.

Oft in sadness and in illness,
　I have watched thy current glide,
Till the beauty of its stillness
　Overflowed me, like a tide.

And in better hours and brighter,
　When I saw thy waters gleam,
I have felt my heart beat lighter,
　And leap onward with thy stream.

Not for this alone I love thee,
　Nor because thy waves of blue
From celestial seas above thee
　Take their own celestial hue.

Where yon shadowy woodlands hide thee,
　And thy waters disappear,
Friends I love have dwelt beside thee,
　And have made thy margin dear.

More than this;—thy name reminds me
  Of three friends, all true and tried;
And that name, like magic, binds me
  Closer, closer to thy side.

Friends my soul with joy remembers!
  How like quivering flames they start,
When I fan the living embers
  On the hearth-stone of my heart!

'Tis for this, thou Silent River!
  That my spirit leans to thee;
Thou hast been a generous giver,
  Take this idle song from me.

The Fire of Drift-Wood

WE sat within the farmhouse old,
  Whose windows, looking o'er the bay,
Gave to the sea-breeze, damp and cold,
  An easy entrance, night and day.

Not far away we saw the port,—
  The strange, old-fashioned, silent
    town,—
The lighthouse,—the dismantled fort,—
  The wooden houses, quaint and brown.

We sat and talked until the night,
  Descending, filled the little room;
Our faces faded from the sight,
  Our voices only broke the gloom.

We spake of many a vanished scene,
  Of what we once had thought and
    said,
Of what had been, and might have been,
  And who was changed, and who was
    dead.

And all that fills the hearts of friends,
  When first they feel, with secret pain,
Their lives thenceforth have separate
    ends,
  And never can be one again;

The first slight swerving of the heart,
  That words are powerless to express,
And leave it still unsaid in part,
  Or say it in too great excess.

The very tones in which we spake
  Had something strange, I could but
    mark;
The leaves of memory seemed to make
  A mournful rustling in the dark.

Oft died the words upon our lips,
  As suddenly, from out the fire
Built of the wreck of stranded ships,
  The flames would leap and then expire.

And, as their splendor flashed and
    failed,
  We thought of wrecks upon the
    main,—
Of ships dismasted, that were hailed
  And sent no answer back again.

The windows, rattling in their frames,—
  The ocean, roaring up the beach,—
The gusty blast,—the bickering flames,
  All mingled vaguely in our speech;

Until they made themselves a part
  Of fancies floating through the brain,
The long-lost ventures of the heart,
  That send no answers back again.

O flames that glowed! O hearts that
    yearned!
  They were indeed too much akin,
The drift-wood fire without that burned,
  The thoughts that burned and glowed
    within.

My Lost Youth

OFTEN I think of the beautiful town
  That is seated by the sea;
Often in thought go up and down
The pleasant streets of that dear old
    town,
  And my youth comes back to me.
    And a verse of a Lapland song
    Is haunting my memory still:
  "A boy's will is the wind's will,
And the thoughts of youth are long, long
    thoughts."

I can see the shadowy lines of its trees,
  And catch, in sudden gleams,
The sheen of the far-surrounding seas,
And islands that were the Hesperides
  Of all my boyish dreams.
    And the burden of that old song,
    It murmurs and whispers still:
    "A boy's will is the wind's will,
And the thoughts of youth are long, long
    thoughts."

I remember the black wharves and the
    slips,
  And the sea-tides tossing free;
And the Spanish sailors with bearded
  lips,
And the beauty and mystery of the
  ships,
  And the magic of the sea.
    And the voice of that wayward song
    Is singing and saying still:
    "A boy's will is the wind's will,
And the thoughts of youth are long, long
    thoughts."

I remember the bulwarks by the shore,
  And the fort upon the hill;
The sunrise gun, with its hollow roar,
The drum-beat repeated o'er and o'er,
  And the bugle wild and shrill.
    And the music of that old song
    Throbs in my memory still:
    "A boy's will is the wind's will,
And the thoughts of youth are long, long
    thoughts."

I remember the sea-fight far away,
  How it thundered o'er the tide!
And the dead captains, as they lay
In their graves, o'erlooking the tranquil
  bay
  Where they in battle died.
    And the sound of that mournful
    song
    Goes through me with a thrill:
    "A boy's will is the wind's will,
And the thoughts of youth are long, long
    thoughts."

I can see the breezy dome of groves,
  The shadows of Deering's Woods;
And the friendships old and the early
  loves
Come back with a Sabbath sound, as of
  doves
  In quiet neighborhoods.
    And the verse of that sweet old song,
    It flutters and murmurs still:
    "A boy's will is the wind's will,
And the thoughts of youth are long, long
    thoughts."

I remember the gleams and glooms that
    dart
  Across the school-boy's brain;
The song and the silence in the heart,
That in part are prophecies, and in part
  Are longings wild and vain.
    And the voice of that fitful song
    Sings on, and is never still:
    "A boy's will is the wind's will,
And the thoughts of youth are long, long
    thoughts."

There are things of which I may not
    speak;
  There are dreams that cannot die;
There are thoughts that make the strong
  heart weak,
And bring a pallor into the cheek
  And a mist before the eye.
    And the words of that fatal song
    Come over me like a chill:
    "A boy's will is the wind's will,
And the thoughts of youth are long, long
    thoughts."

Strange to me now are the forms I meet
  When I visit the dear old town;
But the native air is pure and sweet,
And the trees that o'ershadow each well-
  known street,
  As they balance up and down,
    Are singing the beautiful song,
    Are sighing and whispering still:
    "A boy's will is the wind's will,
And the thoughts of youth are long, long
    thoughts."

And Deering's Woods are fresh and fair,
  And with joy that is almost pain
My heart goes back to wander there,
And among the dreams of the days that
    were,
  I find my lost youth again.
    And the strange and beautiful song,
    The groves are repeating it still:
    "A boy's will is the wind's will,
And the thoughts of youth are long, long
  thoughts."

Paul Revere's Ride

LISTEN, my children, and you shall hear
Of the midnight ride of Paul Revere,
On the eighteenth of April, in Seventy-
  five;
Hardly a man is now alive
Who remembers that famous day and
  year.
He said to his friend, "If the British
  march
By land or sea from the town to-night,
Hang a lantern aloft in the belfry arch
Of the North Church tower as a signal
  light,—
One, if by land, and two, if by sea;
And I on the opposite shore will be,
Ready to ride and spread the alarm
Through every Middlesex village and
  farm,
For the country-folk to be up and to
  arm."

Then he said, "Good night!" and with
  muffled oar
Silently rowed to the Charlestown shore,
Just as the moon rose over the bay,
Where swinging wide at her moorings
  lay
The Somerset, British man-of-war;
A phantom ship, with each mast and
  spar
Across the moon like a prison bar,
And a huge black hulk, that was
  magnified
By its own reflection in the tide.

Meanwhile, his friend, through alley and
  street,
Wanders and watches with eager ears,
Till in silence around him he hears
The muster of men at the barrack door,
The sound of arms, and the tramp of
  feet,
And the measured tread of the grena-
  diers,
Marching down to their boats on the
  shore.

Then he climbed to the tower of the
  church,
Up the wooden stairs, with stealthy tread,
To the belfry-chamber overhead,
And startled the pigeons from their
  perch
On the sombre rafters, that round him
  made
Masses and moving shapes of shade—
Up the trembling ladder, steep and
  tall,
To the highest window in the wall,
Where he paused to listen and look down
A moment on the roofs of the town,
And the moonlight flowing over all.

Beneath, in the churchyard, lay the dead,
In their night-encampment on the hill,
Wrapped in silence so deep and still
That he could hear, like a sentinel's
  tread,
The watchful night-wind, as it went
Creeping along from tent to tent,
And seeming to whisper, "All is well!"
A moment only he feels the spell
Of the place and the hour, and the secret
  dread
Of the lonely belfry and the dead;
For suddenly all his thoughts are bent
On a shadowy something far away,
Where the river widens to meet the
  bay,—
A line of black that bends and floats
On the rising tide, like a bridge of boats.

Meanwhile, impatient to mount and ride,
Booted and spurred, with a heavy stride

On the opposite shore walked Paul
    Revere.
Now he patted his horse's side,
Now gazed at the landscape far and
    near,
Then, impetuous, stamped the earth,
And turned and tightened his saddle-
    girth;
But mostly he watched with eager search
The belfry-tower of the Old North
    Church,
As it rose above the graves on the hill,
Lonely and spectral and sombre and
    still.
And lo! as he looks, on the belfry's
    height
A glimmer, and then a gleam of light!
He springs to the saddle, the bridle he
    turns,
But lingers and gazes, till full on his
    sight
A second lamp in the belfry burns!

A hurry of hoofs in a village street,
A shape in the moonlight, a bulk in the
    dark,
And beneath, from the pebbles, in pass-
    ing, a spark
Struck out by a steed flying fearless and
    fleet;
That was all! And yet, through the
    gloom and the light,
The fate of a nation was riding that
    night;
And the spark struck out by that steed,
    in his flight,
Kindled the land into flame with its heat.

He has left the village and mounted the
    steep,
And beneath him, tranquil and broad and
    deep,
Is the Mystic, meeting the ocean tides;
And under the alders, that skirt its edge,
Now soft on the sand, now loud on the
    ledge,
Is heard the tramp of his steed as he
    rides.

It was twelve by the village clock,
When he crossed the bridge into Med-
    ford town.
He heard the crowing of the cock,
And the barking of the farmer's dog,
And felt the damp of the river fog,
That rises after the sun goes down.

It was one by the village clock,
When he galloped into Lexington.
He saw the gilded weathercock
Swim in the moonlight as he passed,
And the meeting-house windows, blank
    and bare,
Gaze at him with spectral glare,
As if they already stood aghast
At the bloody work they would look upon.

It was two by the village clock,
When he came to the bridge in Concord
    town.
He heard the bleating of the flock,
And the twitter of birds among the
    trees,
And felt the breath of the morning breeze
Blowing over the meadows brown.
And one was safe and asleep in his bed
Who at the bridge would be first to fall,
Who that day would be lying dead,
Pierced by a British musket-ball.

You know the rest. In the books you
    have read,
How the British Regulars fired and
    fled,—
How the farmers gave them ball for
    ball,
From behind each fence and farmyard
    wall,
Chasing the red-coats down the lane,
Then crossing the fields to emerge again
Under the trees at the turn of the road,
And only pausing to fire and load.

So through the night rode Paul Revere;
And so through the night went his cry of
    alarm
To every Middlesex village and farm,—
A cry of defiance and not of fear,

A voice in the darkness, a knock at the door,
And a word that shall echo for evermore!
For, borne on the night-wind of the Past,
Through all our history, to the last,
In the hour of darkness and peril and need,
The people will waken and listen to hear
The hurrying hoof-beats of that steed,
And the midnight message of Paul Revere.

The Bells of Lynn

HEARD AT NAHANT

O CURFEW of the setting sun! O Bells of Lynn!
O requiem of the dying day! O Bells of Lynn!

From the dark belfries of yon cloud-cathedral wafted,
Your sounds aerial seem to float, O Bells of Lynn!

Borne on the evening wind across the crimson twilight,
O'er land and sea they rise and fall, O Bells of Lynn!

The fisherman in his boat, far out beyond the headland,
Listens, and leisurely rows ashore, O Bells of Lynn!

Over the shining sands the wandering cattle homeward
Follow each other at your call, O Bells of Lynn!

The distant lighthouse hears, and with his flaming signal
Answers you, passing the watch-word on, O Bells of Lynn!

And down the darkening coast run the tumultuous surges,
And clap their hands, and shout to you, O Bells of Lynn!

Till from the shuddering sea, with your wild incantations,
Ye summon up the spectral moon, O Bells of Lynn!

And startled at the sight, like the weird woman of Endor,
Ye cry aloud, and then are still, O Bells of Lynn!

JOHN GREENLEAF WHITTIER
(1807-1892)

Vesta

O CHRIST of God! whose life and death
Our own have reconciled,
Most quietly, most tenderly
Take home thy star-named child!

Thy grace is in her patient eyes,
Thy words are on her tongue;
The very silence round her seems
As if the angels sung.

Her smile is as a listening child's
Who hears its mother's call;
The lilies of Thy perfect peace
About her pillow fall.

She leans from out our clinging arms
To rest herself in Thine;
Alone to Thee, dear Lord, can we
Our well-beloved resign.

O, less for her than for ourselves
We bow our heads and pray;
Her setting star, like Bethlehem's,
To Thee shall point the way!

Barbara Frietchie

UP from the meadows rich with corn,
Clear in the cool September morn,

The clustered spires of Frederick stand
Green-walled by the hills of Maryland.

Round about them orchards sweep,
Apple and peach tree fruited deep,

Fair as the garden of the Lord
To the eyes of the famished rebel horde,

On that pleasant morn of the early fall
When Lee marched over the mountain
  wall;

Over the mountains winding down,
Horse and foot, into Frederick town.

Forty flags with their silver stars,
Forty flags with their crimson bars,

Flapped in the morning wind: the sun
Of noon looked down, and saw not one.

Up rose old Barbara Frietchie then,
Bowed with her fourscore years and ten;

Bravest of all in Frederick town,
She took up the flag the men hauled
  down.

In her attic window the staff she set,
To show that one heart was loyal yet.

Up the street came the rebel tread,
Stonewall Jackson riding ahead.

Under his slouched hat left and right
He glanced; the old flag met his sight.

"Halt!"—the dust-brown ranks stood
  fast.
"Fire!"—out blazed the rifle-blast.

It shivered the window, pane and sash;
It rent the banner with seam and gash.

Quick, as it fell, from the broken staff
Dame Barbara snatched the silken scarf.

She leaned far out on the window-sill,
And shook it forth with a royal will.

"Shoot, if you must, this old gray head,
But spare your country's flag," she said.

A shade of sadness, a blush of shame,
Over the face of the leader came;

The nobler nature within him stirred
To life at that woman's deed and word;

"Who touches a hair of yon gray head
Dies like a dog! March on!" he said.

All day long through Frederick street
Sounded the tread of marching feet:

All day long that free flag tossed
Over the heads of the rebel host.

Ever its torn folds rose and fell
On the loyal winds that loved it well;

And through the hill-gaps sunset light
Shone over it with a warm good-night.

Barbara Frietchie's work is o'er,
And the Rebel rides on his raids no more.

Honor to her! and let a tear
Fall, for her sake, on Stonewall's bier.

Over Barbara Frietchie's grave,
Flag of Freedom and Union, wave!

Peace and order and beauty draw
Round thy symbol of light and law;

And ever the stars above look down
On thy stars below in Frederick town!

Skipper Ireson's Ride

OF all the rides since the birth of time,
Told in story or sung in rhyme,—
On Apuleius's Golden Ass,
Or one-eyed Calender's horse of brass,
Witch astride of a human back,
Islam's prophet on Al-Borák,—
The strangest ride that ever was sped
Was Ireson's, out from Marblehead!
  Old Floyd Ireson, for his hard heart,
  Tarred and feathered and carried in a
    cart
  By the women of Marblehead!

Body of turkey, head of owl,
Wings a-droop like a rained-on fowl,
Feathered and ruffled in every part,
Skipper Ireson stood in the cart.
Scores of women, old and young,
Strong of muscle, and glib of tongue,

Pushed and pulled up the rocky lane,
Shouting and singing the shrill refrain:
   "Here's Flud Oirson, fur his horrd
      horrt
   Torr'd an' futherr'd an' corr'd in a
      corrt
   By the women o' Morble'ead!"

Wrinkled scolds with hands on hips,
Girls in bloom of cheek and lips,
Wild-eyed, free-limbed, such as chase
Bacchus round some antique vase,
Brief of skirt, with ankles bare,
Loose of kerchief and loose of hair,
With conch-shells blowing and fish-horns'
    twang,
Over and over the Mænads sang:
   "Here's Flud Oirson, fur his horrd
      horrt,
   Torr'd an' futherr'd an' corr'd in a
      corrt
   By the women o' Morble'ead!"

Small pity for him!—He sailed away
From a leaking ship on Chaleur Bay,—
Sailed away from a sinking wreck,
With his own town's-people on her deck!
"Lay by! lay by!" they called to him.
Back he answered, "Sink or swim!
Brag of your catch of fish again!"
And off he sailed through the fog and
    rain!
   Old Floyd Ireson, for his hard heart,
   Tarred and feathered and carried in a
      cart
   By the women of Marblehead!

Fathoms deep in dark Chaleur
That wreck shall lie forevermore.
Mother and sister, wife and maid,
Looked from the rocks of Marblehead
Over the moaning and rainy sea,—
Looked for the coming that might not be!
What did the winds and the sea-birds say
Of the cruel captain who sailed away?
   Old Floyd Ireson, for his hard heart,
   Tarred and feathered and carried in a
      cart
   By the women of Marblehead!

Through the street, on either side,
Up flew windows, doors swung wide;
Sharp-tongued spinsters, old wives gray,
Treble lent the fish-horn's bray.
Sea-worn grandsires, cripple-bound,
Hulks of old sailors run aground,
Shook head, and fist, and hat, and cane,
And cracked with curses the hoarse re-
    frain:
   "Here's Flud Oirson, fur his horrd
      horrt,
   Torr'd an' futherr'd an' corr'd in a
      corrt
   By the women o' Morble'ead!"

Sweetly along the Salem road
Bloom of orchard and lilac showed.
Little the wicked skipper knew
Of the fields so green and sky so blue.
Riding there in his sorry trim,
Like an Indian idol glum and grim,
Scarcely he seemed the sound to hear
Of voices shouting, far and near:
   "Here's Flud Oirson, fur his horrd
      horrt,
   Torr'd an' futherr'd an' corr'd in a
      corrt
   By the women o' Morble'ead!"

"Hear me, neighbors!" at last he cried,—
"What to me is this noisy ride?
What is the shame that clothes the skin
To the nameless horror that lives within?
Waking or sleeping, I see a wreck,
And hear a cry from a reeling deck!
Hate me and curse me,—I only dread
The hand of God and the face of the
    dead!"
   Said old Floyd Ireson, for his hard
      heart,
   Tarred and feathered and carried in a
      cart
   By the women of Marblehead!

Then the wife of the skipper lost at sea
Said, "God has touched him! why should
    we!"
Said an old wife mourning her only son,
"Cut the rogue's tether and let him run!"

So with soft relentings and rude excuse,
Half scorn, half pity, they cut him loose,
And gave him a cloak to hide him in,
And left him alone with his shame and
      sin.
   Poor Floyd Ireson, for his hard heart,
   Tarred and feathered and carried in a
      cart
   By the women of Marblehead!

EDGAR ALLAN POE (1809-1849)

The City in the Sea

Lo! Death has reared himself a throne
In a strange city lying alone
Far down within the dim West,
Where the good and the bad and the
      worst and the best
Have gone to their eternal rest.
There shrines and palaces and towers
(Time-eaten towers that tremble not)
Resemble nothing that is ours.
Around, by lifting winds forgot,
Resignedly beneath the sky
The melancholy waters lie.

No rays from the holy heaven come down
On the long night-time of that town;
But light from out the lurid sea
Streams up the turrets silently,
Gleams up the pinnacles far and free:
Up domes, up spires, up kingly halls,
Up fanes, up Babylon-like walls,
Up shadowy long-forgotten bowers
Of sculptured ivy and stone flowers,
Up many and many a marvellous shrine
Whose wreathèd friezes intertwine
The viol, the violet, and the vine.

Resignedly beneath the sky
The melancholy waters lie.
So blend the turrets and shadows there
That all seem pendulous in air,
While from a proud tower in the town
Death looks gigantically down.

There open fanes and gaping graves
Yawn level with the luminous waves;
But not the riches there that lie
In each idol's diamond eye,—
Not the gayly-jewelled dead,
Tempt the waters from their bed;
For no ripples curl, alas,
Along that wilderness of glass;
No swellings tell that winds may be
Upon some far-off happier sea;
No heavings hint that winds have been
On seas less hideously serene!

But lo, a stir is in the air!
The wave—there is a movement there!
As if the towers had thrust aside,
In slightly sinking, the dull tide;
As if their tops had feebly given
A void within the filmy Heaven!
The waves have now a redder glow,
The hours are breathing faint and low;
And when, amid no earthly moans,
Down, down that town shall settle hence,
Hell, rising from a thousand thrones,
Shall do it reverence.

The Raven

ONCE upon a midnight dreary, while I
      pondered, weak and weary,
Over many a quaint and curious volume
      of forgotten lore,
While I nodded, nearly napping, suddenly
      there came a tapping,
As of some one gently rapping, rapping at
      my chamber door.
" 'Tis some visitor," I muttered, "tapping
      at my chamber door—
      Only this and nothing more."

Ah, distinctly I remember it was in the
      bleak December,
And each separate dying ember wrought
      its ghost upon the floor.
Eagerly I wished the morrow; vainly I
      had sought to borrow
From my books surcease of sorrow—
      sorrow for the lost Lenore,
For the rare and radiant maiden whom
      the angels name Lenore—
      Nameless *here* for evermore.

And the silken, sad, uncertain rustling of
  each purple curtain
Thrilled me—filled me with fantastic
  terrors never felt before;
So that now, to still the beating of my
  heart, I stood repeating,
" 'Tis some visitor entreating entrance at
  my chamber door—
Some late visitor entreating entrance at
  my chamber door—
    This it is and nothing more."

Presently my soul grew stronger: hesitating then no longer,
"Sir," said I, "or Madam, truly your
  forgiveness I implore;
But the fact is I was napping, and so
  gently you came rapping,
And so faintly you came tapping, tapping
  at my chamber door,
That I scarce was sure I heard you"—
  here I opened wide the door—
    Darkness there and nothing more.

Deep into that darkness peering, long I
  stood there, wondering, fearing,
Doubting, dreaming dreams no mortal
  ever dared to dream before;
But the silence was unbroken, and the
  stillness gave no token,
And the only word there spoken was the
  whispered word "Lenore!"
This I whispered, and an echo murmured
  back the word "Lenore!"
    Merely this and nothing more.

Back into the chamber turning, all my
  soul within me burning,
Soon again I heard a tapping, somewhat
  louder than before.
"Surely," said I, "surely that is something at my window lattice;
Let me see, then, what thereat is, and
  this mystery explore,—
Let my heart be still a moment and this
  mystery explore—
    'Tis the wind and nothing more."

Open here I flung the shutter, when,
  with many a flirt and flutter,
In there stepped a stately Raven of the
  saintly days of yore.
Not the least obeisance made he, not a
  minute stopped or stayed he,
But with mien of lord or lady perched
  above my chamber door—
Perched upon a bust of Pallas just above
  my chamber door—
    Perched and sat, and nothing
  more.

Then, this ebony bird beguiling my sad
  fancy into smiling
By the grave and stern decorum of the
  countenance it wore,
"Though thy crest be shorn and shaven,
  thou," I said, "art sure no craven,
Ghastly, grim, and ancient Raven, wandering from the nightly shore:
Tell me what thy lordly name is on the
  night's Plutonian shore!"
    Quoth the Raven, "Nevermore."

Much I marveled this ungainly fowl to
  hear discourse so plainly,
Though its answer little meaning, little
  relevancy bore;
For we cannot help agreeing that no
  living human being
Ever yet was blessed with seeing bird
  above his chamber door—
Bird or beast upon the sculptured bust
  above his chamber door—
    With such name as "Nevermore."

But the Raven, sitting lonely on the
  placid bust, spoke only
That one word, as if his soul in that one
  word he did outpour.
Nothing farther then he uttered, not a
  feather then he fluttered;
Till I scarcely more than muttered,
  "Other friends have flown before;
On the morrow *he* will leave me, as my
  hopes have flown before."
    Then the bird said, "Nevermore."

Startled at the stillness broken by reply
    so aptly spoken,
"Doubtless," said I, "what it utters is its
    only stock and store,
Caught from some unhappy master whom
    unmerciful Disaster
Followed fast and followed faster till his
    songs one burden bore,
Till the dirges of his hope that melan-
    choly burden bore
      Of 'Never—nevermore.' "

But the Raven still beguiling my sad
    fancy into smiling,
Straight I wheeled a cushioned seat in
    front of bird and bust and door;
Then, upon the velvet sinking, I betook
    myself to linking
Fancy unto fancy, thinking what this
    ominous bird of yore,
What this grim, ungainly, ghastly, gaunt,
    and ominous bird of yore
      Meant in croaking "Nevermore."

Thus I sat engaged in guessing, but no
    syllable expressing
To the fowl whose fiery eyes now burned
    into my bosom's core;
This and more I sat divining, with my
    head at ease reclining
On the cushion's velvet lining that the
    lamp-light gloated o'er,
But whose velvet violet lining, with the
    lamp-light gloating o'er,
      She shall press, ah, nevermore!

Then, methought, the air grew denser,
    perfumed from an unseen censer
Swung by seraphim whose footfalls
    tinkled on the tufted floor.
"Wretch!" I cried, "thy God hath lent
    thee,—by these angels he hath sent
    thee,
Respite—respite and nepenthe from thy
    memories of Lenore!
Quaff, oh quaff this kind nepenthe, and
    forget this lost Lenore!"
      Quoth the Raven, "Nevermore."

"Prophet!" said I, "thing of evil, prophet
    still, if bird or devil!
Whether Tempter sent, or whether temp-
    est tossed thee here ashore,
Desolate yet all undaunted, on this desert
    land enchanted—
On this home by horror haunted—tell me
    truly, I implore,
Is there—is there balm in Gilead?—tell
    me—tell me, I implore!"
      Quoth the Raven, "Nevermore."

"Prophet!" said I, "thing of evil, prophet
    still, if bird or devil!
By that Heaven that bends above us—by
    that God we both adore—
Tell this soul with sorrow laden if, with-
    in the distant Aidenn,
It shall clasp a sainted maiden whom the
    angels name Lenore—
Clasp a rare and radiant maiden whom
    the angels name Lenore."
      Quoth the Raven, "Nevermore."

"Be that word our sign of parting, bird
    or fiend!" I shrieked, up-starting;
"Get thee back into the tempest and the
    night's Plutonian shore!
Leave no black plume as a token of that
    lie thy soul hath spoken!
Leave my loneliness unbroken!—Quit the
    bust above my door!
Take thy beak from out my heart, and
    take thy form from off my door!"
      Quoth the Raven, "Nevermore."

And the Raven, never flitting, still is sit-
    ting, still is sitting
On the pallid bust of Pallas just above
    my chamber door;
And his eyes have all the seeming of a
    demon's that is dreaming,
And the lamp-light o'er him streaming
    throws his shadow on the floor;
And my soul from out that shadow that
    lies floating on the floor
      Shall be lifted—nevermore!

Ulalume

THE skies they were ashen and sober;
  The leaves they were crispèd and sere,
  The leaves they were withering and
    sere;
It was night in the lonesome October
  Of my most immemorial year;
It was hard by the dim lake of Auber,
  In the misty mid region of Weir:
It was down by the dank tarn of Auber,
  In the ghoul-haunted woodland of
  Weir.

Here once, through an alley Titanic
  Of cypress, I roamed with my Soul—
  Of cypress, with Psyche, my Soul.
These were days when my heart was
    volcanic
  As the scoriac rivers that roll,
  As the lavas that restlessly roll
Their sulphurous currents down Yaanek
  In the ultimate climes of the pole,
That groan as they roll down Mount
    Yaanek
  In the realms of the boreal pole.

Our talk had been serious and sober,
  But our thoughts they were palsied and
    sere,
  Our memories were treacherous and
    sere,
For we knew not the month was October,
  And we marked not the night of the
    year,
  (Ah, night of all nights in the year!)
We noted not the dim lake of Auber
  (Though once we had journeyed down
    here),
Remembered not the dank tarn of Auber
  Nor the ghoul-haunted woodland of
  Weir.

And now, as the night was senescent
  And star-dials pointed to morn,
  As the star-dials hinted of morn,
At the end of our path a liquescent
  And nebulous lustre was born,

Out of which a miraculous crescent
  Arose with a duplicate horn,
Astarte's bediamonded crescent
  Distinct with its duplicate horn.

And I said—"She is warmer than Dian:
  She rolls through an ether of sighs,
  She revels in a region of sighs:
She has seen that the tears are not dry on
    These cheeks, where the worm never
    dies,
And has come past the stars of the Lion
  To point us the path to the skies,
  To the Lethean peace of the skies:
Come up, in despite of the Lion,
  To shine on us with her bright eyes:
Come up through the lair of the Lion,
  With love in her luminous eyes."

But Psyche, uplifting her finger,
  Said—"Sadly this star I mistrust,
  Her pallor I strangely mistrust:
Oh, hasten!—oh, let us not linger!
  Oh, fly!—let us fly!—for we must."
In terror she spoke, letting sink her
  Wings until they trailed in the dust;
In agony sobbed, letting sink her
  Plumes till they trailed in the dust,
  Till they sorrowfully trailed in the
    dust.

I replied—"This is nothing but dream-
    ing:
  Let us on by this tremulous light!
  Let us bathe in this crystalline light!
Its sibyllic splendor is beaming
  With hope and in beauty to-night:
  See, it flickers up the sky through the
    night!
Ah, we safely may trust to its gleaming,
  And be sure it will lead us aright:
We safely may trust to a gleaming
  That cannot but guide us aright,
  Since it flickers up to Heaven through
    the night."

Thus I pacified Psyche and kissed her,
  And tempted her out of her gloom,
  And conquered her scruples and gloom;

And we passed to the end of the vista,
  But were stopped by the door of a
    tomb,
  By the door of a legended tomb;
And I said—"What is written, sweet
    sister,
  On the door of this legended tomb?"
  She replied—"Ulalume—Ulalume—
  'Tis the vault of thy lost Ulalume!"

Then my heart it grew ashen and sober
  As the leaves that were crispèd and
    sere,
  As the leaves that were withering and
    sere,
And I cried—"It was surely October
  On this very night of last year
  That I journeyed—I journeyed down
    here,
  That I brought a dread burden down
    here:
  On this night of all nights in the year,
  Ah, what demon has tempted me here?
Well I know, now, this dim lake of
    Auber,
  This misty mid region of Weir:
Well I know, now, this dank tarn of
    Auber,
  This ghoul-haunted woodland of
    Weir."

To Helen

HELEN, thy beauty is to me
  Like those Nicæan barks of yore
That gently, o'er a perfumed sea,
  The weary way-worn wanderer bore
  To his own native shore.

On desperate seas long wont to roam,
  Thy hyacinth hair, thy classic face,
Thy Naiad airs have brought me home
  To the glory that was Greece,
And the grandeur that was Rome.

Lo, in yon brilliant window-niche
  How statue-like I see thee stand,
  The agate lamp within thy hand,
Ah! Psyche, from the regions which
  Are holy land!

For Annie

THANK Heaven! the crisis—
  The danger is past,
And the lingering illness
  Is over at last—
And the fever called "Living"
  Is conquer'd at last.

Sadly, I know
  I am shorn of my strength,
And no muscle I move
  As I lie at full length:
But no matter—I feel
  I am better at length.

And I rest so composedly
  Now, in my bed,
That any beholder
  Might fancy me dead—
Might start at beholding me,
  Thinking me dead.

The moaning and groaning,
  The sighing and sobbing,
Are quieted now,
  With that horrible throbbing
At heart—ah, that horrible,
  Horrible throbbing!

The sickness—the nausea—
  The pitiless pain—
Have ceased, with the fever
  That madden'd my brain—
With the fever called "Living"
  That burn'd in my brain.

And O! of all tortures
  That torture the worst
Has abated—the terrible
  Torture of thirst
For the naphthaline river
  Of Passion accurst—
I have drunk of a water
  That quenches all thirst.

—Of a water that flows,
  With a lullaby sound,
From a spring but a very few
  Feet under ground—

From a cavern not very far
  Down under ground.

And ah! let it never
  Be foolishly said
That my room it is gloomy,
  And narrow my bed;
For man never slept
  In a different bed—
And, to *sleep,* you must slumber
  In just such a bed.

My tantalized spirit
  Here blandly reposes,
Forgetting, or never
  Regretting its roses—
Its old agitations
  Of myrtles and roses:

For now, while so quietly
  Lying, it fancies
A holier odour
  About it, of pansies—
A rosemary odour,
  Commingled with pansies—
With rue and the beautiful
  Puritan pansies.

And so it lies happily,
  Bathing in many
A dream of the truth
  And the beauty of Annie—
Drown'd in a bath
  Of the tresses of Annie.

She tenderly kiss'd me,
  She fondly caress'd,
And then I fell gently
  To sleep on her breast—
Deeply to sleep
  From the heaven of her breast.

When the light was extinguish'd,
  She cover'd me warm,
And she pray'd to the angels
  To keep me from harm—
To the queen of the angels
  To shield me from harm.

And I lie so composedly,
  Now, in my bed
(Knowing her love),
  That you fancy me dead—
And I rest so contentedly,
  Now, in my bed
(With her love at my breast),
  That you fancy me dead—
That you shudder to look at me,
  Thinking me dead.

But my heart it is brighter
  Than all of the many
Stars in the sky,
  For it sparkles with Annie—
It glows with the light
  Of the love of my Annie—
With the thought of the light
  Of the eyes of my Annie.

Annabel Lee

It was many and many a year ago,
  In a kingdom by the sea,
That a maiden there lived whom you
      may know
  By the name of Annabel Lee.
And this maiden she lived with no other
      thought
  Than to love and be loved by me.

I was a child and she was a child
  In this kingdom by the sea:
But we loved with a love that was more
      than love—
  I and my Annabel Lee,
With a love that the wingèd seraphs of
      heaven
  Coveted her and me.

And this was the reason that, long ago,
  In this kingdom by the sea,
A wind blew out of a cloud, chilling
  My beautiful Annabel Lee,
So that her high-born kinsmen came
  And bore her away from me,
To shut her up in a sepulchre
  In this kingdom by the sea.

The angels, not half so happy in heaven,
  Went envying her and me—
Yes! that was the reason (as all men
    know,
  In this kingdom by the sea)
That the wind came out of the cloud one
    night,
  Chilling and killing my Annabel Lee.

But our love it was stronger by far than
    the love
  Of those who were older than we—
  Of many far wiser than we—
And neither the angels in heaven above,
  Nor the demons down under the sea,

Can ever dissever my soul from the soul
  Of the beautiful Annabel Lee:

For the moon never beams without bring-
    ing me dreams
  Of the beautiful Annabel Lee;
And the stars never rise, but I feel the
    bright eyes
  Of the beautiful Annabel Lee;
And so, all the night-tide, I lie down by
    the side
Of my darling—my darling—my life and
    my bride,
  In her sepulchre there by the sea,
  In her tomb by the sounding sea.

The Masque of the Red Death

(NORTHERN ITALY)

THE "Red Death" had long devastated the country. No pestilence had ever been so fatal, or so hideous. Blood was its avatar and its seal —the redness and the horror of blood. There were sharp pains, and sudden dizziness, and then profuse bleeding at the pores, with dissolution. The scarlet stains upon the body, and especially upon the face, of the victim were the pest ban which shut him out from the aid and from the sympathy of his fellow-men. And the whole seizure, progress, and termination of the disease were the incidents of half an hour.

But the Prince Prospero was happy and dauntless and sagacious. When his dominions were half depopulated, he summoned to his presence a thousand hale and light-hearted friends from among the knights and dames of his court, and with these retired to the deep seclusion of one of his castellated abbeys. This was an extensive and magnificent structure, the creation of the Prince's own eccentric yet august taste. A strong and lofty wall girdled it in. This wall had gates of iron. The courtiers, having entered, brought furnaces and massy hammers, and welded the bolts. They resolved to leave means neither of ingress or egress to the sudden impulses of despair or of frenzy from within. The abbey was amply provisioned. With such precautions the courtiers might bid defiance to contagion. The external world could take care of itself. In the mean time it was folly to grieve, or to think. The Prince had provided all the appliances of pleasure. There were buffoons, there were improvisatori, there were ballet-dancers, there were musicians, there was Beauty, there was wine. All these and security were within. Without was the "Red Death."

It was toward the close of the fifth or sixth month of his seclusion, and while the pestilence raged most furiously abroad, that the Prince Prospero entertained his thousand friends at a masked ball of the most unusual magnificence.

It was a voluptuous scene, that masquerade. But first let me tell of the rooms in which it was held. There were seven—an imperial suite. In many palaces, however, such suites form a long and straight vista, while the folding-doors slide back nearly to the walls on either hand, so that the view of the whole extent is scarcely impeded. Here the case was very different, as might have been expected from the Prince's love of the bizarre. The apartments were so irregularly disposed that the vision embraced but little more than one at a time. There was a sharp turn at every twenty or thirty yards, and at each turn a novel effect. To the right and left, in the middle of each wall, a tall and narrow Gothic window looked out upon a closed corridor which pursued the windings of the suite. These windows were of stained glass, whose color varied in accordance with the prevailing hue of the decorations of the chamber into which it opened. That at the eastern extremity was hung, for example, in blue—and vividly blue were its windows. The second chamber was purple in its ornaments and tapestries, and here the panes were purple. The third was green throughout, and so were the casements. The fourth was furnished and lighted with orange, the fifth with white, the sixth with violet. The seventh apartment was closely shrouded in black velvet tapestries that hung all over the ceiling and down the walls, falling in heavy folds upon a carpet of the same material and hue. But, in this chamber only, the color of the windows failed to correspond with the decorations. The panes here were scarlet—a deep blood-color. Now in no one of the seven apartments was there any lamp or candelabrum, amid the profusion of golden ornaments that lay scattered to and fro or depended from the roof. There was no light of any kind emanating from lamp or candle within the suite of chambers. But in the corridors that followed the suite there stood, opposite to each window, a heavy tripod, bearing a brazier of fire, that projected its rays through the tinted glass and so glaringly illumined the room. And thus were produced a multitude of gaudy and fantastic appearances. But in the western or black chamber the effect of the firelight that streamed upon the dark hangings through the blood-tinted panes was ghastly in the extreme, and produced so wild a look upon the countenances of those who entered that

there were few of the company bold enough to set foot within its precincts at all.

It was in this apartment, also, that there stood against the western
wall a gigantic clock of ebony. Its pendulum swung to and fro with a
dull, heavy, monotonous clang; and when the minute-hand made the
circuit of the face, and the hour was to be stricken, there came from the
brazen lungs of the clock a sound which was clear and loud and deep
and exceedingly musical, but of so peculiar a note and emphasis that,
at each lapse of an hour, the musicians of the orchestra were constrained
to pause, momentarily, in their performance, to hearken to the sound;
and thus the waltzers perforce ceased their evolutions; and there was
a brief disconcert of the whole gay company; and, while the chimes of
the clock yet rang, it was observed that the giddiest grew pale, and the
more aged and sedate passed their hands over their brows as if in confused revery or meditation. But when the echoes had fully ceased, a
light laughter at once pervaded the assembly; the musicians looked at
each other and smiled as if at their own nervousness and folly, and made
whispering vows, each to the other, that the next chiming of the clock
should produce in them no similar emotion; and then, after the lapse
of sixty minutes (which embrace three thousand and six hundred seconds of the Time that flies) there came yet another chiming of the clock,
and then were the same disconcert and tremulousness and meditation as
before.

But, in spite of these things, it was a gay and magnificent reveı.
The tastes of the Prince were peculiar. He had a fine eye for colors
and effects. He disregarded the *decora* of mere fashion. His plans were
bold and fiery, and his conceptions glowed with barbaric lustre. There
are some who would have thought him mad. His followers felt that he
was not. It was necessary to hear and see and touch him to be *sure* that
he was not.

He had directed, in great part, the movable embellishments of the
seven chambers, upon occasion of this great *fête;* and it was his own
guiding taste which had given character to the masqueraders. Be sure
they were grotesque. There were much glare and glitter and piquancy
and phantasm—much of what has been since seen in *Hernani.* There
were arabesque figures with unsuited limbs and appointments. There
were delirious fancies such as the madman fashions. There was much
of the beautiful, much of the wanton, much of the bizarre, something
of the terrible, and not a little of that which might have excited disgust.
To and fro in the seven chambers there stalked, in fact, a multitude of
dreams. And these—the dreams—writhed in and about, taking hue

from the rooms, and causing the wild music of the orchestra to seem as the echo of their steps. And, anon, there strikes the ebony clock which stands in the hall of the velvet. And then, for a moment, all is still, and all is silent save the voice of the clock. The dreams are stiff-frozen as they stand. But the echoes of the chime die away—they have endured but an instant—and a light, half-subdued laughter floats after them as they depart. And now again the music swells, and the dreams live, and writhe to and fro more merrily than ever, taking hue from the many tinted windows through which stream the rays from the tripods. But to the chamber which lies most westwardly of the seven, there are now none of the maskers who venture; for the night is waning away, and there flows a ruddier light through the blood-colored panes; and the blackness of the sable drapery appalls; and to him whose foot falls upon the sable carpet, there comes from the near clock of ebony a muf-fled peal more solemnly emphatic than any which reaches *their* ears who indulge in the more remote gayeties of the other apartments.

But these other apartments were densely crowded, and in them beat feverishly the heart of life. And the revel went whirlingly on, until at length there commenced the sounding of midnight upon the clock. And then the music ceased, as I have told; and the evolutions of the waltzers were quieted; and there was an uneasy cessation of all things as before. But now there were twelve strokes to be sounded by the bell of the clock; and thus it happened, perhaps, that more of thought crept, with more of time, into the meditations of the thoughtful among those who revelled. And thus too it happened, perhaps, that before the last echoes of the last chime had utterly sunk into silence, there were many individuals in the crowd who had found leisure to become aware of the presence of a masked figure which had arrested the attention of no single individual before. And the rumor of this new presence having spread itself whisperingly around, there arose at length from the whole company a buzz, or murmur, expressive of disapprobation and surprise—then, finally, of terror, of horror, and of disgust.

In an assembly of phantasms such as I have painted, it may well be supposed that no ordinary appearance could have excited such sen-sation. In truth the masquerade license of the night was nearly unlim-ited; but the figure in question had out-Heroded Herod, and gone be-yond the bounds of even the Prince's indefinite decorum. There are chords in the hearts of the most reckless which cannot be touched with-out emotion. Even with the utterly lost, to whom life and death are equally jests, there are matters of which no jest can be made. The whole company, indeed, seemed now deeply to feel that in the costume and bearing of the stranger neither wit nor propriety existed. The figure was tall and gaunt, shrouded from head to foot in the habiliments of the grave. The mask which concealed the visage was made so nearly to resemble the countenance of a stiffened corpse that the closest scrutiny must have had difficulty in detecting the cheat. And yet all this might have been endured, if not approved, by the mad revellers around. But the mummer had gone so far as to assume the type of the Red Death. His vesture was dabbled in *blood*—and his broad brow, with all the features of the face, was besprinkled with the scarlet horror.

When the eyes of Prince Prospero fell upon this spectral image (which with a slow and solemn movement, as if more fully to sustain its *rôle,* stalked to and fro among the waltzers) he was seen to be convulsed, in the first moment, with a strong shudder either of terror or distaste; but, in the next, his brow reddened with rage.

"Who dares?" he demanded hoarsely of the courtiers who stood near him—"who dares insult us with this blasphemous mockery? Seize him and unmask him—that we may know whom we have to hang at sunrise, from the battlements!"

It was in the eastern or blue chamber in which stood the Prince Prospero as he uttered these words. They rang throughout the seven rooms loudly and clearly—for the Prince was a bold and robust man, and the music had become hushed at the waving of his hand.

It was in the blue room where stood the Prince, with a group of pale courtiers by his side. At first, as he spoke, there was a slight rushing movement of this group in the direction of the intruder, who at the moment was also near at hand, and now, with deliberate and stately step, made closer approach to the speaker. But from a certain nameless awe with which the mad assumptions of the mummer had inspired the whole party, there were found none who put forth hand to seize him; so that, unimpeded, he passed within a yard of the Prince's person; and, while the vast assembly, as if with one impulse, shrank from the centres of the rooms to the walls, he made his way uninterruptedly, but with the same solemn and measured step which had distinguished him from the first, through the blue chamber to the purple—through the purple to the green—through the green to the orange—through this again to the white—and even thence to the violet, ere a decided movement had been made to arrest him. It was then, however, that the Prince Prospero, maddening with rage and the shame of his own momentary cowardice, rushed hurriedly through the six chambers, while none followed him on account of a deadly terror that had seized upon all. He bore aloft a drawn dagger, and had approached, in rapid impetuosity, to within three or four feet of the retreating figure, when the latter, having attained the extremity of the velvet apartment, turned suddenly and confronted his pursuer. There was a sharp cry—and the dagger dropped gleaming upon the sable carpet, upon which, instantly afterwards, fell prostrate in death the Prince Prospero. Then, summoning the wild courage of despair, a throng of the revellers at once threw themselves into the black apartment, and, seizing the mummer, whose tall figure stood erect and motionless within the shadow of the ebony clock, gasped in unutterable horror at finding the grave cerements and corpse-like mask, which they handled with so violent a rudeness, untenanted by any tangible form.

And now was acknowledged the presence of the Red Death. He had come like a thief in the night. And one by one dropped the revellers in the blood-bedewed halls of their revel, and died each in the despairing posture of his fall. And the life of the ebony clock went out with that of the last of the gay. And the flames of the tripods expired. And Darkness and Decay and the Red Death held illimitable dominion over all.

The Fall of the House of Usher

> Son cœur est un luth suspendu;
> Sitôt qu'on le touche il résonne.
> BÉRANGER.

DURING the whole of a dull, dark, and soundless day in the autumn of the year, when the clouds hung oppressively low in the heavens, I had been passing alone, on horseback, through a singularly dreary tract of country; and at length found myself, as the shades of the evening drew on, within view of the melancholy House of Usher. I know not how it was—but, with the first glimpse of the building, a sense of insufferable gloom pervaded my spirit. I say insufferable; for the feeling was unrelieved by any of that half-pleasurable, because poetic, sentiment with which the mind usually receives even the sternest natural images of the desolate or terrible. I looked upon the scene before me—upon the mere house, and the simple landscape features of the domain, upon the bleak walls, upon the vacant eye-like windows, upon a few rank sedges, and upon a few white trunks of decayed trees—with an utter depression of soul which I can compare to no earthly sensation more properly than to the after-dream of the reveller upon opium: the bitter lapse into everyday life, the hideous dropping off of the veil. There was an iciness, a sinking, a sickening of the heart, an unredeemed dreariness of thought which no goading of the imagination could torture into aught of the sublime. What was it—I paused to think—what was it that so

unnerved me in the contemplation of the House of Usher? It was a
mystery all insoluble; nor could I grapple with the shadowy fancies that
crowded upon me as I pondered. I was forced to fall back upon the
unsatisfactory conclusion, that while, beyond doubt, there *are* combinations of very simple natural objects which have the power of thus affecting us, still the analysis of this power lies among considerations beyond
our depth. It was possible, I reflected, that a mere different arrangement
of the particulars of the scene, of the details of the picture, would be
sufficient to modify, or perhaps to annihilate, its capacity for sorrowful
impression; and acting upon this idea, I reined my horse to the precipitous brink of a black and lurid tarn that lay in unruffled lustre by the
dwelling, and gazed down—but with a shudder even more thrilling than
before—upon the remodelled and inverted images of the gray sedge, and
the ghastly tree-stems, and the vacant and eye-like windows.

Nevertheless, in this mansion of gloom I now proposed to myself
a sojourn of some weeks. Its proprietor, Roderick Usher, had been
one of my boon companions in boyhood; but many years had elapsed
since our last meeting. A letter, however, had lately reached me in a
distant part of the country—a letter from him—which in its wildly
importunate nature had admitted of no other than a personal reply.
The MS. gave evidence of nervous agitation. The writer spoke of acute
bodily illness, of a mental disorder which oppressed him, and of an earnest desire to see me, as his best and indeed his only personal friend,
with a view of attempting, by the cheerfulness of my society, some alle-
viation of his malady. It was the manner in which all this, and much
more, was said—it was the apparent *heart* that went with his request—
which allowed me no room for hesitation; and I accordingly obeyed
forthwith what I still considered a very singular summons.

Although as boys we had been even intimate associates, yet I really
knew little of my friend. His reserve had been always excessive and
habitual. I was aware, however, that his very ancient family had been
noted, time out of mind, for a peculiar sensibility of temperament, displaying itself, through long ages, in many works of exalted art, and
manifested of late in repeated deeds of munificent yet unobtrusive charity,
as well as in a passionate devotion to the intricacies, perhaps even more
than to the orthodox and easily recognizable beauties, of musical science.
I had learned, too, the very remarkable fact that the stem of the Usher
race, all time-honored as it was, had put forth at no period any enduring
branch; in other words, that the entire family lay in the direct line of
descent, and had always, with very trifling and very temporary variation, so lain. It was this deficiency, I considered, while running over

in thought the perfect keeping of the character of the premises with the accredited character of the people, and while speculating upon the possible influence which the one, in the long lapse of centuries, might have exercised upon the other—it was this deficiency perhaps, of collateral issue, and the consequent undeviating transmission from sire to son of the patrimony with the name, which had, at length, so identified the two as to merge the original title of the estate in the quaint and equivocal appellation of the "House of Usher"—an appellation which seemed to include, in the minds of the peasantry who used it, both the family and the family mansion.

I have said that the sole effect of my somewhat childish experiment, that of looking down within the tarn, had been to deepen the first singular impression.   There can be no doubt that the consciousness of the rapid increase of my superstition—for why should I not so term it?— served mainly to accelerate the increase itself.   Such, I have long known, is the paradoxical law of all sentiments having terror as a basis.   And it might have been for this reason only, that, when I again uplifted my eyes to the house itself, from its image in the pool, there grew in my mind a strange fancy—a fancy so ridiculous, indeed, that I but mention it to show the vivid force of the sensations which oppressed me. I had so worked upon my imagination as really to believe that about the whole mansion and domain there hung an atmosphere peculiar to themselves and their immediate vicinity: an atmosphere which had no affinity with the air of heaven, but which had reeked up from the decayed trees, and the gray wall, and the silent tarn: a pestilent and mystic vapor, dull, sluggish, faintly discernible, and leaden-hued.

Shaking off from my spirit what *must* have been a dream, I scanned more narrowly the real aspect of the building.   Its principal feature seemed to be that of an excessive antiquity.   The discoloration of ages had been great.   Minute fungi overspread the whole exterior, hanging in a fine tangled web-work from the eaves.   Yet all this was apart from any extraordinary dilapidation.   No portion of the masonry had fallen: and there appeared to be a wild inconsistency between its still perfect adaptation of parts and the crumbling condition of the individual stones. In this there was much that reminded me of the specious totality of old wood-work which has rotted for long years in some neglected vault, with no disturbance from the breath of the external air.   Beyond this indication of extensive decay, however, the fabric gave little token of instability.   Perhaps the eye of a scrutinizing observer might have discovered a barely perceptible fissure, which, extending from the roof of the building in front, made its way down the wall in a zigzag direction, until it became lost in the sullen waters of the tarn.

Noticing these things, I rode over a short causeway to the house. A servant in waiting took my horse, and I entered the Gothic archway of the hall. A valet, of stealthy step, thence conducted me, in silence, through many dark and intricate passages in my progress to the studio of his master. Much that I encountered on the way contributed, I know not how, to heighten the vague sentiments of which I have already spoken. While the objects around me—while the carvings of the ceilings, the sombre tapestries of the walls, the ebon blackness of the floors, and the phantasmagoric armorial trophies which rattled as I strode, were but matters to which, or to such as which, I had been accustomed from my infancy—while I hesitated not to acknowledge how familiar was all this—I still wondered to find how unfamiliar were the fancies which ordinary images were stirring up. On one of the staircases, I met the physician of the family. His countenance, I thought, wore a mingled expression of low cunning and perplexity. He accosted me with trepidation and passed on. The valet now threw open a door and ushered me into the presence of his master.

The room in which I found myself was very large and lofty. The windows were long, narrow, and pointed, and at so vast a distance from the black oaken floor as to be altogether inaccessible from within. Feeble gleams of encrimsoned light made their way through the trellised panes, and served to render sufficiently distinct the more prominent objects around; the eye, however, struggled in vain to reach the remoter angles of the chamber, or the recesses of the vaulted and fretted ceiling. Dark draperies hung upon the walls. The general furniture was profuse, comfortless, antique, and tattered. Many books and musical instruments lay scattered about, but failed to give any vitality to the scene. I felt that I breathed an atmosphere of sorrow. An air of stern, deep, and irredeemable gloom hung over all and pervaded all.

Upon my entrance, Usher arose from a sofa on which he had been lying at full length, and greeted me with a vivacious warmth which had much in it, I at first thought, of an overdone cordiality—of the constrained effort of the *ennuyé* man of the world. A glance, however, at his countenance, convinced me of his perfect sincerity. We sat down: and for some moments, while he spoke not, I gazed upon him with a feeling half of pity, half of awe. Surely man had never before so terribly altered, in so brief a period, as had Roderick Usher! It was with difficulty that I could bring myself to admit the identity of the wan being before me with the companion of my early boyhood. Yet the character of his face had been at all times remarkable. A cadaverousness of complexion; an eye large, liquid, and luminous beyond comparison; lips somewhat thin and very pallid, but of a surpassingly beautiful curve; a nose of a delicate Hebrew model, but with a breadth of nostril unusual in similar formations; a finely moulded chin, speaking, in its want of prominence, of a want of moral energy; hair of a more than web-like softness and tenuity; these features, with an inordinate expansion above the regions of the temple, made up altogether a countenance not easily to be forgotten. And now in the mere exaggeration of the prevailing character of these features, and of the expression they were wont to convey, lay so much of change that I doubted to whom I spoke. The now ghastly pallor of the skin, and the now miraculous lustre of the eye, above all things startled and even awed me. The silken hair, too, had been suffered to grow all unheeded, and as, in its wild gossamer texture, it floated rather than fell about the face, I could not, even with effort, connect its arabesque expression with any idea of simple humanity.

In the manner of my friend I was at once struck with an incoherence, an inconsistency; and I soon found this to arise from a series of feeble and futile struggles to overcome an habitual trepidancy, an excessive nervous agitation. For something of this nature I had indeed been prepared, no less by his letter than by reminiscences of certain boyish traits, and by conclusions deduced from his peculiar physical conformation and temperament. His action was alternately vivacious and sullen. His voice varied rapidly from a tremulous indecision (when the animal spirits seemed utterly in abeyance) to that species of energetic concision—that abrupt, weighty, unhurried, and hollow-sounding enunciation — that leaden, self-balanced and perfectly modulated guttural utterance—which may be observed in the lost drunkard, or the irreclaimable eater of opium, during the periods of his most intense excitement.

It was thus that he spoke of the object of my visit, of his earnest desire to see me, and of the solace he expected me to afford him. He entered, at some length, into what he conceived to be the nature of his malady. It was, he said, a constitutional and a family evil, and one for which he despaired to find a remedy—a mere nervous affection, he immediately added, which would undoubtedly soon pass off. It displayed itself in a host of unnatural sensations. Some of these, as he detailed them, interested and bewildered me; although, perhaps, the terms and the general manner of the narration had their weight. He suffered much from a morbid acuteness of the senses; the most insipid food was alone endurable; he could wear only garments of certain texture; the odors of all flowers were oppressive; his eyes were tortured by even a faint light; and there were but peculiar sounds, and these from stringed instruments, which did not inspire him with horror.

To an anomalous species of terror I found him a bounden slave. "I shall perish," said he, "I *must* perish in this deplorable folly. Thus, thus, and not otherwise, shall I be lost. I dread the events of the future, not in themselves, but in their results. I shudder at the thought of any, even the most trivial, incident, which may operate upon this intolerable agitation of soul. I have, indeed, no abhorrence of danger, except in its absolute effect—in terror. In this unnerved—in this pitiable condition, I feel that the period will sooner or later arrive when I must abandon life and reason together, in some struggle with the grim phantasm, FEAR."

I learned moreover at intervals, and through broken and equivocal hints, another singular feature of his mental condition. He was enchained by certain superstitious impressions in regard to the dwelling which he tenanted, and whence, for many years, he had never ventured forth—in regard to an influence whose supposititious force was conveyed in terms too shadowy here to be re-stated—an influence which some peculiarities in the mere form and substance of his family mansion, had by dint of long sufferance, he said, obtained over his spirit—an effect which the physique of the gray walls and turrets, and of the dim tarn into which they all looked down, had, at length, brought about upon the morale of his existence.

He admitted, however, although with hesitation, that much of the peculiar gloom which thus afflicted him could be traced to a more natural and far more palpable origin—to the severe and long-continued illness, indeed to the evidently approaching dissolution, of a tenderly beloved sister—his sole companion for long years, his last and only relative on earth. "Her decease," he said, with a bitterness which I can never forget, "would leave him (him the hopeless and the frail) the last of the ancient race of the Ushers." While he spoke, the lady Madeline (for so was she called) passed slowly through a remote portion of the apartment, and, without having noticed my presence, disappeared. I regarded her with an utter astonishment not unmingled with dread, and yet I found it impossible to account for such feelings. A sensation of stupor oppressed me, as my eyes followed her retreating steps. When a door, at length, closed upon her, my glance sought instinctively and eagerly the countenance of the brother; but he had buried his face in his hands, and I could only perceive that a far more than ordinary wanness had overspread the emaciated fingers through which trickled many passionate tears.

The disease of the lady Madeline had long baffled the skill of her physicians. A settled apathy, a gradual wasting away of the person, and frequent although transient affections of a partially cataleptical character, were the unusual diagnosis. Hitherto she had steadily borne up against the pressure of her malady, and had not betaken herself finally to bed; but, on the closing in of the evening of my arrival at the house, she succumbed (as her brother told me at night with inexpressible agitation) to the prostrating power of the destroyer; and I learned that the glimpse I had obtained of her person would thus probably be the last I should obtain—that the lady, at least while living, would be seen by me no more.

For several days ensuing, her name was unmentioned by either Usher or myself; and during this period I was busied in earnest endeavors to alleviate the melancholy of my friend. We painted and read together; or I listened, as if in a dream, to the wild improvisations of his speaking guitar. And thus, as a closer and still closer intimacy admitted me more unreservedly into the recesses of his spirit, the more bitterly did I perceive the futility of all attempt at cheering a mind from which darkness, as if an inherent positive quality, poured forth upon all objects of the moral and physical universe, in one unceasing radiation of gloom.

I shall ever bear about me a memory of the many solemn hours I thus spent alone with the master of the House of Usher. Yet I should fail in any attempt to convey an idea of the exact character of the studies, or of the occupations, in which he involved me, or led me the way. An excited and highly distempered ideality threw a sulphureous lustre over all. His long improvised dirges will ring forever in my ears. Among other things, I hold painfully in mind a certain singular perversion and amplification of the wild air of the last waltz of Von Weber. From the paintings over which his elaborate fancy brooded, and which grew, touch by touch, into vaguenesses at which I shuddered the more thrillingly because I shuddered knowing not why;—from these paintings (vivid as their images now are before me) I would in vain endeavor to educe more than a small portion which should lie within the compass of merely written words. By the utter simplicity, by the nakedness of his designs, he arrested and overawed attention. If ever mortal painted an idea, that mortal was Roderick Usher. For me at least, in the circumstances then surrounding me, there arose, out of the pure abstractions which the hypochondriac contrived to throw upon his canvas, an intensity of intolerable awe, no shadow of which felt I ever yet in the contemplation of the certainly glowing yet too concrete reveries of Fuseli.

One of the phantasmagoric conceptions of my friend, partaking not

THE FALL OF THE HOUSE OF USSHER

From a drawing by Albert E. Sterner

so rigidly of the spirit of abstraction, may be shadowed forth, although feebly, in words. A small picture presented the interior of an immensely long and rectangular vault or tunnel, with low walls, smooth, white, and without interruption or device. Certain accessory points of the design served well to convey the idea that this excavation lay at an exceeding depth below the surface of the earth. No outlet was observed in any portion of its vast extent, and no torch or other artificial source of light was discernible; yet a flood of intense rays rolled throughout, and bathed the whole in a ghastly and inappropriate splendor.

I have just spoken of that morbid condition of the auditory nerve which rendered all music intolerable to the sufferer, with the exception of certain effects of stringed instruments. It was, perhaps, the narrow limits to which he thus confined himself upon the guitar, which gave birth, in great measure, to the fantastic character of his performances. But the fervid *facility* of his impromptus could not be so accounted for. They must have been, and were, in the notes, as well as in the words of his wild fantasias (for he not unfrequently accompanied himself with rhymed verbal improvisations), the result of that intense mental collectedness and concentration to which I have previously alluded as observable only in particular moments of the highest artificial excitement. The words of one of these rhapsodies I have easily remembered. I was, perhaps, the more forcibly impressed with it, as he gave it, because, in the under or mystic current of its meaning, I fancied that I perceived, and for the first time, a full consciousness, on the part of Usher, of the tottering of his lofty reason upon her throne. The verses, which were entitled "The Haunted Palace," ran very nearly, if not accurately, thus:—

I

In the greenest of our valleys
　By good angels tenanted,
Once a fair and stately palace—
　Radiant palace—reared its head.
In the monarch Thought's dominion,
　It stood there;
Never seraph spread a pinion
　Over fabric half so fair.

II

Banners yellow, glorious, golden,
　On its roof did float and flow,
(This—all this—was in the olden
　Time long ago)

And every gentle air that dallied,
    In that sweet day,
Along the ramparts plumed and pallid,
    A wingèd odor went away.

III

Wanderers in that happy valley
    Through two luminous windows saw
Spirits moving musically
    To a lute's well-tunèd law,
Round about a throne where, sitting,
    Porphyrogene,
In state his glory well befitting,
    The ruler of the realm was seen.

IV

And all with pearl and ruby glowing
    Was the fair palace door,
Through which came flowing, flowing, flowing,
    And sparkling evermore,
A troop of Echoes whose sweet duty
    Was but to sing,
In voices of surpassing beauty,
    The wit and wisdom of their king.

V

But evil things, in robes of sorrow,
    Assailed the monarch's high estate;
(Ah, let us mourn, for never morrow
    Shall dawn upon him, desolate!)
And round about his home the glory
    That blushed and bloomed
Is but a dim-remembered story
    Of the old time entombed.

VI

And travellers now within that valley
    Through the red-litten windows see
Vast forms that move fantastically
    To a discordant melody;
While, like a ghastly rapid river,
    Through the pale door
A hideous throng rush out forever,
    And laugh—but smile no more.

I well remember that suggestions arising from this ballad led us
into a train of thought, wherein there became manifest an opinion of

Usher's which I mention not so much on account of its novelty, (for other men have thought thus,) as on account of the pertinacity with which he maintained it. This opinion, in its general form, was that of the sentience of all vegetable things. But in his disordered fancy the idea had assumed a more daring character, and trespassed, under certain conditions, upon the kingdom of inorganization. I lack words to express the full extent, or the earnest *abandon* of his persuasion. The belief, however, was connected (as I have previously hinted) with the gray stones of the home of his forefathers. The conditions of the sentience had been here, he imagined, fulfilled in the method of collocation of these stones—in the order of their arrangement, as well as in that of the many fungi which overspread them, and of the decayed trees which stood around—above all, in the long undisturbed endurance of this arrangement, and in its reduplication in the still waters of the tarn. Its evidence—the evidence of the sentience—was to be seen, he said (and I here started as he spoke), in the gradual yet certain condensation of an atmosphere of their own about the waters and the walls. The result was discoverable, he added, in that silent, yet importunate and terrible influence which for centuries had moulded the destinies of his family, and which made *him* what I now saw him—what he was. Such opinions need no comment, and I will make none.

Our books—the books which, for years, had formed no small portion of the mental existence of the invalid—were, as might be supposed, in strict keeping with this character of phantasm. We pored together over such works as the Ververt and Chartreuse of Gresset; the Belphegor of Machiavelli; the Heaven and Hell of Swedenborg; the Subterranean Voyage of Nicholas Klimm by Holberg; the Chiromancy of Robert Flud, of Jean D'Indaginé, and of De la Chambre; the Journey into the Blue Distance of Tieck; and the City of the Sun of Campanella. One favorite volume was a small octavo edition of the *Directorium Inquisitorum,* by the Dominican Eymeric de Gironne; and there were passages in Pomponius Mela, about the old African Satyrs and Ægipans, over which Usher would sit dreaming for hours. His chief delight, however, was found in the perusal of an exceedingly rare and curious book in quarto Gothic—the manual of a forgotten church— the *Vigiliæ Mortuorum secundum Chorum Ecclesiæ Maguntinæ.*

I could not help thinking of the wild ritual of this work, and of its probable influence upon the hypochondriac, when one evening, having informed me abruptly that the lady Madeline was no more, he stated his intention of preserving her corpse for a fortnight, (previously to its final interment,) in one of the numerous vaults within the main walls of the building. The worldly reason, however, assigned for this singular proceeding, was one which I did not feel at liberty to dispute. The brother had been led to his resolution (so he told me) by consideration of the unusual character of the malady of the deceased, of certain obtrusive and eager inquiries on the part of her medical men, and of the remote and exposed situation of the burial-ground of the family. I will not deny that when I called to mind the sinister countenance of the person whom I met upon the staircase, on the day of my arrival at the house, I had no desire to oppose what I regarded as at best but a harmless, and by no means an unnatural, precaution.

At the request of Usher, I personally aided him in the arrangements for the temporary entombment. The body having been encoffined, we two alone bore it to its rest. The vault in which we placed it (and which had been so long unopened that our torches, half smothered in its oppressive atmosphere, gave us little opportunity for investigation) was small, damp, and entirely without means of admission for light; lying, at great depth, immediately beneath that portion of the building in which was my own sleeping apartment. It had been used, apparently, in remote feudal times, for the worst purposes of a donjon-keep, and in later days as a place of deposit for powder, or some other highly combustible substance, as a portion of its floor, and the whole interior of a long archway through which we reached it, were carefully sheathed with copper. The door, of massive iron, had been, also, similarly protected. Its immense weight caused an unusually sharp grating sound, as it moved upon its hinges.

Having deposited our mournful burden upon tressels within this region of horror, we partially turned aside the yet unscrewed lid of the coffin, and looked upon the face of the tenant. A striking similitude between the brother and sister now first arrested my attention; and Usher, divining, perhaps, my thoughts, murmured out some few words from which I learned that the deceased and himself had been twins, and that sympathies of a scarcely intelligible nature had always existed between them. Our glances, however, rested not long upon the dead— for we could not regard her unawed. The disease which had thus entombed the lady in the maturity of youth, had left, as usual in all maladies of a strictly cataleptical character, the mockery of a faint blush upon the bosom and the face, and that suspiciously lingering smile upon the lip which is so terrible in death. We replaced and screwed down the lid, and, having secured the door of iron, made our way, with toil, into the scarcely less gloomy apartments of the upper portion of the house.

And now, some days of bitter grief having elapsed, an observable change came over the features of the mental disorder of my friend. His ordinary manner had vanished. His ordinary occupations were neglected or forgotten. He roamed from chamber to chamber with hurried, unequal, and objectless step. The pallor of his countenance had assumed, if possible, a more ghastly hue—but the luminousness of his eye had utterly gone out. The once occasional huskiness of his tone was heard no more; and a tremulous quaver, as if of extreme terror, habitually characterized his utterance. There were times, indeed, when I thought his unceasingly agitated mind was laboring with some oppressive secret, to divulge which he struggled for the necessary courage. At times, again, I was obliged to resolve all into the mere inexplicable vagaries of madness, for I beheld him gazing upon vacancy for long hours, in an attitude of the profoundest attention, as if listening to some imaginary sound. It was no wonder that his condition terrified—that it infected me. I felt creeping upon me, by slow yet certain degrees, the wild influences of his own fantastic yet impressive superstitions.

It was, especially, upon retiring to bed late in the night of the seventh or eighth day after the placing of the lady Madeline within the donjon, that I experienced the full power of such feelings. Sleep came not near my couch, while the hours waned and waned away. I struggled to reason off the nervousness which had dominion over me. I endeavored to believe that much, if not all, of what I felt was due to the bewildering influence of the gloomy furniture of the room—of the dark and tattered draperies which, tortured into motion by the breath of a rising tempest, swayed fitfully to and fro upon the walls, and rustled uneasily about the decorations of the bed. But my efforts were fruitless. An irrepressible tremor gradually pervaded my frame; and at length there sat upon my very heart an incubus of utterly causeless alarm. Shaking this off with a gasp and a struggle, I uplifted myself upon the pillows, and, peering earnestly within the intense darkness of the chamber, hearkened—I know not why, except that an instinctive spirit prompted me—to certain low and indefinite sounds which came, through the pauses of the storm at long intervals, I knew not whence. Overpowered by an intense sentiment of horror, unaccountable yet unendurable, I threw on my clothes with haste, (for I felt that I should sleep no more during the night,) and endeavored to arouse myself from the pitiable condition into which I had fallen, by pacing rapidly to and fro through the apartment.

I had taken but few turns in this manner, when a light step on an adjoining staircase arrested my attention. I presently recognized it as that of Usher. In an instant afterward he rapped with a gentle touch at my door, and entered, bearing a lamp. His countenance was, as usual, cadaverously wan—but, moreover, there was a species of mad hilarity in his eyes—an evidently restrained hysteria in his whole demeanor. His air appalled me—but anything was preferable to the solitude which I had so long endured, and I even welcomed his presence as a relief.

"And you have not seen it?" he said abruptly, after having stared about him for some moments in silence—"you have not then seen it?— but, stay! you shall." Thus speaking, and having carefully shaded his lamp, he hurried to one of the casements, and threw it freely open to the storm.

The impetuous fury of the entering gust nearly lifted us from our feet. It was, indeed, a tempestuous yet sternly beautiful night, and one wildly singular in its terror and its beauty. A whirlwind had apparently collected its force in our vicinity; for there were frequent and violent alterations in the direction of the wind; and the exceeding density of the clouds (which hung so low as to press upon the turrets of the house) did not prevent our perceiving the life-like velocity with which they flew careering from all points against each other, without passing away into the distance. I say that even their exceeding density did not prevent our perceiving this; yet we had no glimpse of the moon or stars, nor was there any flashing forth of the lightning. But the under surfaces of the huge masses of agitated vapor, as well as all terrestrial objects imme- diately around us, were glowing in the unnatural light of a faintly luminous and distinctly visible gaseous exhalation which hung about and enshrouded the mansion.

"You must not—you shall not behold this!" said I, shudderingly, to Usher, as I led him with a gentle violence from the window to a seat. "These appearances, which bewilder you, are merely electrical phenomena not uncommon—or it may be that they have their ghastly origin in the rank miasma of the tarn. Let us close this casement; the air is chilling and dangerous to your frame. Here is one of your favorite romances. I will read, and you shall listen;—and so we will pass away this terrible night together."

The antique volume which I had taken up was the "Mad Trist" of Sir Launcelot Canning; but I had called it a favorite of Usher's more in sad jest than in earnest; for, in truth, there is little in its uncouth and unimaginative prolixity which could have had interest for the lofty and spiritual ideality of my friend. It was, however, the only book imme- diately at hand; and I indulged a vague hope that the excitement which now agitated the hypochondriac might find relief (for the history of mental disorder is full of similar anomalies) even in the extremeness of the folly which I should read. Could I have judged, indeed, by the wild overstrained air of vivacity with which he hearkened, or apparently hearkened, to the words of the tale, I might well have congratulated myself upon the success of my design.

I had arrived at that well-known portion of the story where Ethelred, the hero of the Trist, having sought in vain for peaceable admission into the dwelling of the hermit, proceeds to make good an entrance by force. Here, it will be remembered, the words of the narrative run thus :—

"And Ethelred, who was by nature of a doughty heart, and who was now mighty withal, on account of the powerfulness of the wine which he had drunken, waited no longer to hold parley with the hermit, who, in sooth, was of an obstinate and maliceful turn, but, feeling the rain upon his shoulders, and fearing the rising of the tempest, uplifted his mace outright, and with blows made quickly room in the plankings of the door for his gauntleted hand; and now pulling therewith sturdily, he so cracked, and ripped, and tore all asunder, that the noise of the dry and hollow-sounding wood alarumed and reverberated throughout the forest."

At the termination of this sentence I started, and for a moment paused; for it appeared to me (although I at once concluded that my excited fancy had deceived me)—it appeared to me that from some very remote portion of the mansion there came, indistinctly, to my ears, what might have been, in its exact similarity of character, the echo (but a stifled and dull one certainly) of the very cracking and ripping sound which Sir Launcelot had so particularly described. It was, beyond doubt, the coincidence alone which had arrested my attention; for, amid the rattling of the sashes of the casements, and the ordinary commingled noises of the still increasing storm, the sound, in itself, had nothing, surely, which would have interested or disturbed me. I continued the story :—

"But the good champion Ethelred, now entering within the door, was sore enraged and amazed to perceive no signal of the maliceful hermit; but, in the stead thereof, a dragon of a scaly and prodigious demeanor, and of a fiery tongue, which sate in guard before a palace of gold, with a floor of silver; and upon the wall there hung a shield of shining brass with this legend enwritten—

Who entereth herein, a conqueror hath bin;
Who slayeth the dragon, the shield he shall win.

And Ethelred uplifted his mace, and struck upon the head of the dragon, which fell before him, and gave up his pesty breath, with a shriek so horrid and harsh, and withal so piercing, that Ethelred had fain to close his ears with his hands against the dreadful noise of it, the like whereof was never before heard."

Here again I paused abruptly, and now with a feeling of wild amazement; for there could be no doubt whatever that, in this instance, I did actually hear (although from what direction it proceeded I found it impossible to say) a low and apparently distant, but harsh, protracted, and most unusual screaming or grating sound—the exact counterpart of what my fancy had already conjured up for the dragon's unnatural shriek as described by the romancer.

Oppressed, as I certainly was, upon the occurrence of this second and most extraordinary coincidence, by a thousand conflicting sensations, in which wonder and extreme terror were predominant, I still retained sufficient presence of mind to avoid exciting, by any observation, the sensitive nervousness of my companion. I was by no means certain that he had noticed the sounds in question; although, assuredly, a strange alteration had during the last few minutes taken place in his demeanor. From a position fronting my own, he had gradually brought round his chair, so as to sit with his face to the door of the chamber; and thus I could but partially perceive his features, although I saw that his lips trembled as if he were murmuring inaudibly. His head had dropped upon his breast—yet I knew that he was not asleep, from the wide and rigid opening of the eye as I caught a glance of it in profile. The motion of his body, too, was at variance with this idea—for he rocked from side to side with a gentle yet constant and uniform sway. Having rapidly taken notice of all this, I resumed the narrative of Sir Launcelot, which thus proceeded:—

"And now, the champion, having escaped from the terrible fury of the dragon, bethinking himself of the brazen shield, and of the breaking up of the enchantment which was upon it, removed the carcass from out of the way before him, and approached valorously over the silver pavement of the castle to where the shield was upon the wall; which in sooth tarried not for his full coming, but fell down at his feet upon the silver floor, with a mighty great and terrible ringing sound."

No sooner had these syllables passed my lips, than—as if a shield of brass had indeed, at the moment, fallen heavily upon a floor of silver —I became aware of a distinct, hollow, metallic and clangorous, yet apparently muffled reverberation. Completely unnerved, I leaped to my feet; but the measured rocking movement of Usher was undisturbed. I rushed to the chair in which he sat. His eyes were bent fixedly before him, and throughout his whole countenance there reigned a stony rigidity. But, as I placed my hand upon his shoulder, there came a strong shudder over his whole person; a sickly smile quivered about his lips; and I saw that he spoke in a low, hurried, and gibbering murmur, as if unconscious of my presence. Bending closely over him, I at length drank in the hideous import of his words.

"Not hear it?—yes, I hear it, and *have* heard it. Long—long—long—many minutes, many hours, many days, have I heard it—yet I dared not—oh, pity me, miserable wretch that I am!—I dared not—I *dared* not speak! *We have put her living in the tomb!* Said I not that my senses were acute? I *now* tell you that I heard her first feeble movements in the hollow coffin. I heard them—many, many days ago—yet I dared not—*I dared not speak!* And now—to-night—Ethelred—ha! ha!—the breaking of the hermit's door, and the death-cry of the dragon, and the clangor of the shield!—say, rather, the rending of her coffin, and the grating of the iron hinges of her prison, and her struggles within the coppered archway of the vault! Oh, whither shall I fly? Will she not be here anon? Is she not hurrying to upbraid me for my haste? Have I not heard her footstep on the stair? Do I not distinguish that heavy and horrible beating of her heart? Madman!"—here he sprang furiously to his feet, and shrieked out his syllables, as if in the effort he were giving up his soul—*"Madman! I tell you that she now stands without the door!"*

As if in the superhuman energy of his utterance there had been found the potency of a spell, the huge antique panels to which the speaker pointed threw slowly back, upon the instant, their ponderous and ebony jaws. It was the work of the rushing gust—but then without those doors there *did* stand the lofty and enshrouded figure of the lady Madeline of Usher. There was blood upon her white robes, and the evidence of some bitter struggle upon every portion of her emaciated frame. For a moment she remained trembling and reeling to and fro upon the threshold—then, with a low moaning cry, fell heavily inward upon the person of her brother, and, in her violent and now final death-agonies, bore him to the floor a corpse, and a victim to the terrors he had anticipated.

From that chamber, and from that mansion, I fled aghast. The storm was still abroad in all its wrath as I found myself crossing the old causeway. Suddenly there shot along the path a wild light, and I turned to see whence a gleam so unusual could have issued; for the vast house and its shadows were alone behind me. The radiance was that of the full, setting, and blood-red moon, which now shone vividly through that once barely discernible fissure, of which I have before spoken as extending from the roof of the building, in a zigzag direction, to the base. While I gazed, this fissure rapidly widened—there came a fierce breath of the whirlwind—the entire orb of the satellite burst at once upon my sight—my brain reeled as I saw the mighty walls rushing asunder—there was a long tumultuous shouting sound like the voice of a thousand waters—and the deep and dank tarn at my feet closed sullenly and silently over the fragments of the *"House of Usher."*

The Gold-Bug

What ho! what ho! this fellow is dancing mad!
He hath been bitten by the Tarantula.

All in the Wrong.

MANY years ago, I contracted an intimacy with a Mr. William Legrand. He was of an ancient Huguenot family, and had once been wealthy; but a series of misfortunes had reduced him to want. To avoid the mortification consequent upon his disasters, he left New Orleans, the city of his forefathers, and took up his residence at Sullivan's Island, near Charleston, South Carolina.

This island is a very singular one. It consists of little else than the sea sand, and is about three miles long. Its breadth at no point exceeds a quarter of a mile. It is separated from the main-land by a scarcely perceptible creek, oozing its way through a wilderness of reeds and slime, a favorite resort of the marsh-hen. The vegetation, as might be supposed, is scant, or at least dwarfish. No trees of any magnitude are to be seen. Near the western extremity, where Fort Moultrie stands, and where are some miserable frame buildings, tenanted during summer by the fugitives from Charleston dust and fever, may be found, indeed, the bristly palmetto; but the whole island, with the exception of this western point, and a line of hard white beach on the seacoast, is covered with a dense undergrowth of the sweet myrtle, so much prized by the horticulturists of England. The shrub here often attains the height of fifteen or twenty feet, and forms an almost impenetrable coppice, burdening the air with its fragrance.

In the utmost recesses of this coppice, not far from the eastern or more remote end of the island, Legrand had built himself a small hut, which he occupied when I first, by mere accident, made his acquaintance. This soon ripened into friendship—for there was much in the recluse to excite interest and esteem. I found him well educated, with unusual powers of mind, but infected with misanthropy, and subject to perverse moods of alternate enthusiasm and melancholy. He had with him many books, but rarely employed them. His chief amusements were gunning and fishing, or sauntering along the beach and through the myrtles, in quest of shells or entomological specimens;—his collection of the latter might have been envied by a Swammerdamm. In these excursions he was usually accompanied by an old negro, called Jupiter, who had been manumitted before the reverses of the family, but who could be induced, neither by threats nor by promises, to abandon what he considered his right of attendance upon the footsteps of his young "Massa Will." It is not improbable that the relatives of Legrand, conceiving him to be somewhat unsettled in intellect, had contrived to instil this obstinacy into Jupiter, with a view to the supervision and guardianship of the wanderer.

The winters in the latitude of Sullivan's Island are seldom very severe, and in the fall of the year it is a rare event indeed when a fire is considered necessary. About the middle of October, 18—, there occurred, however, a day of remarkable chilliness. Just before sunset I scrambled my way through the evergreens to the hut of my friend, whom I had not visited for several weeks—my residence being at that time in Charleston, a distance of nine miles from the island, while the facilities of passage and re-passage were very far behind those of the present day. Upon reaching the hut I rapped, as was my custom, and, getting no reply, sought for the key, where I knew it was secreted, unlocked the door and went in. A fine fire was blazing upon the hearth. It was a novelty, and by no means an ungrateful one. I threw off an overcoat, took an armchair by the crackling logs, and awaited patiently the arrival of my hosts.

Soon after dark they arrived, and gave me a most cordial welcome. Jupiter, grinning from ear to ear, bustled about to prepare some marsh-hens for supper. Legrand was in one of his fits—how else shall I term them?—of enthusiasm. He had found an unknown bivalve, forming a new genus, and, more than this, he had hunted down and secured, with Jupiter's assistance, a *scarabæus* which he believed to be totally new, but in respect to which he wished to have my opinion on the morrow.

"And why not to-night?" I asked, rubbing my hands over the blaze, and wishing the whole tribe of *scarabæi* at the devil.

"Ah, if I had only known you were here!" said Legrand, "but it's so long since I saw you; and how could I foresee that you would pay me a visit this very night of all others? As I was coming home I met Lieutenant G——, from the fort, and, very foolishly, I lent him the bug; so it will be impossible for you to see it until the morning. Stay here to-night, and I will send Jup down for it at sunrise. It is the loveliest thing in creation!"

"What?—sunrise?"

"Nonsense! no!—the bug. It is of a brilliant gold color—about the size of a large hickory-nut—with two jet black spots near one extremity of the back, and another, somewhat longer, at the other. The *antennæ* are—"

"Dey ain't *no* tin in him, Massa Will, I keep a tellin' on you," here interrupted Jupiter; "de bug is a goole-bug, solid, ebery bit of him, inside and all, 'sep him wing—neber feel half so hebby a bug in my life."

"Well, suppose it is, Jup," replied Legrand, somewhat more earnestly, it seemed to me, than the case demanded, "is that any reason for your letting the birds burn? The color"—here he turned to me—"is really almost enough to warrant Jupiter's idea. You never saw a more brilliant metallic lustre than the scales emit—but of this you cannot judge till to-morrow. In the mean time I can give you some idea of the shape." Saying this, he seated himself at a small table, on which were a pen and ink, but no paper. He looked for some in a drawer, but found none.

"Never mind," said he at length, "this will answer;" and he drew from his waistcoat pocket a scrap of what I took to be very dirty foolscap, and made upon it a rough drawing with the pen. While he did this, I retained my seat by the fire, for I was still chilly. When the design was complete, he handed it to me without rising. As I received it, a low growl was heard, succeeded by a scratching at the door. Jupiter opened it, and a large Newfoundland, belonging to Legrand, rushed in, leaped upon my shoulders, and loaded me with caresses; for I had shown him much attention during previous visits. When his gambols were over, I looked at the paper, and, to speak the truth, found myself not a little puzzled at what my friend had depicted.

"Well!" I said, after contemplating it for some minutes, "this *is* a strange *scarabæus,* I must confess; new to me: never saw anything like it before—unless it was a skull, or a death's-head, which it more nearly resembles than anything else that has come under *my* observation."

"A death's-head!" echoed Legrand—"Oh—yes—well, it has something of that appearance upon paper, no doubt. The two upper black spots look like eyes, eh? and the longer one at the bottom like a mouth— and then the shape of the whole is oval."

"Perhaps so," said I; "but, Legrand, I fear you are no artist. I must wait until I see the beetle itself, if I am to form any idea of its personal appearance."

"Well, I don't know," said he, a little nettled, "I draw tolerably— *should* do it at least—have had good masters, and flatter myself that I am not quite a blockhead."

"But, my dear fellow, you are joking then," said I, "this is a very passable *skull,*—indeed, I may say that it is a very *excellent* skull, according to the vulgar notions about such specimens of physiology—and your

scarabæus must be the queerest *scarabæus* in the world if it resembles
it. Why, we may get up a very thrilling bit of superstition upon this
hint. I presume you will call the bug *scarabæus caput hominis,* or something of that kind—there are many similar titles in the Natural Histories.
But where are the *antennæ* you spoke of?"

"The *antennæ!*" said Legrand, who seemed to be getting unaccountably warm upon the subject; "I am sure you must see the *antennæ.* I
made them as distinct as they are in the original insect, and I presume
that is sufficient."

"Well, well," I said, "perhaps you have—still I don't see them;" and
I handed him the paper without additional remark, not wishing to ruffle
his temper; but I was much surprised at the turn affairs had taken; his
ill humor puzzled me—and, as for the drawing of the beetle, there were
positively *no antennæ* visible, and the whole *did* bear a very close resemblance to the ordinary cuts of a death's-head.

He received the paper very peevishly, and was about to crumple it,
apparently to throw it in the fire, when a casual glance at the design
seemed suddenly to rivet his attention. In an instant his face grew
violently red—in another as excessively pale. For some minutes he
continued to scrutinize the drawing minutely where he sat. At length
he arose, took a candle from the table, and proceeded to seat himself
upon a sea-chest in the farthest corner of the room. Here again he made
an anxious examination of the paper; turning it in all directions. He
said nothing, however, and his conduct greatly astonished me; yet I
thought it prudent not to exacerbate the growing moodiness of his temper
by any comment. Presently he took from his coat pocket a wallet, placed
the paper carefully in it, and deposited both in a writing-desk, which he
locked. He now grew more composed in his demeanor; but his original
air of enthusiasm had quite disappeared. Yet he seemed not so much
sulky as abstracted. As the evening wore away he became more and
more absorbed in revery, from which no sallies of mine could arouse
him. It had been my intention to pass the night at the hut, as I had
frequently done before, but, seeing my host in this mood, I deemed it
proper to take leave. He did not press me to remain, but, as I departed,
he shook my hand with even more than his usual cordiality.

It was about a month after this (and during the interval I had seen
nothing of Legrand) when I received a visit, at Charleston, from his
man, Jupiter. I had never seen the good old negro look so dispirited,
and I feared that some serious disaster had befallen my friend.

"Well, Jup," said I, "what is the matter now?—how is your master?"

"Why, to speak de troof, massa, him not so berry well as mought be."

"Not well! I am truly sorry to hear it. What does he complain of?"

"Dar! dat's it!—him neber plain of notin'—but him berry sick for all dat."

"*Very* sick, Jupiter!—why didn't you say so at once? Is he confined to bed?"

"No, dat he ain't!—he ain't 'fined nowhar—dat's just whar de shoe pinch—my mind is got to be berry hebby 'bout poor Massa Will."

"Jupiter, I should like to understand what it is you are talking about. You say your master is sick. Hasn't he told you what ails him?"

"Why, massa, 'tain't worf while for to git mad 'bout de matter—Massa Will say noffin' at all ain't de matter wid him—but den what make him go about looking dis here way, wid he head down and he soldiers up, and as white as a gose? And den he keep a syphon all de time—"

"Keeps a what, Jupiter?"

"Keeps a syphon wid de figgurs on de slate—de queerest figgurs I ebber did see. I'se gittin' to be skeered, I tell you. Hab for to keep mighty tight eye 'pon him noovers. Todder day he gib me slip 'fore de sun up and was gone de whole ob de blessed day. I had a big stick ready cut for to gib him d——d good beating when he did come—but I'se sich a fool dat I hadn't de heart arter all—he look so berry poorly."

"Eh!—what?—ah yes!—upon the whole I think you had better not be too severe with the poor fellow—don't flog him, Jupiter—he can't very well stand it—but can you form no idea of what has occasioned this illness, or rather this change of conduct? Has anything unpleasant happened since I saw you?"

"No, massa, dey ain't bin noffin' onpleasant *since* den—'twas '*fore* den I'm feared—'twas de berry day you was dare."

"How? what do you mean?"

"Why, massa, I mean de bug—dare now."

"The what?"

"De bug—I'm berry sartain dat Massa Will bin bit somewhere 'bout de head by dat goole-bug."

"And what cause have you, Jupiter, for such a supposition?"

"Claws enuff, massa, and mouff too. I nebber did see sich a d——d bug—he kick and he bite ebery ting what cum near him. Massa Will cotch him fuss, but had for to let him go 'gin mighty quick, I tell you—den was de time he must ha' got de bite. I didn't like de look ob de bug mouff, myself, no how, so I wouldn't take hold ob him wid my finger, but I cotch him wid a piece ob paper dat I found. I wrap him up in de paper and stuff piece ob it in he mouff—dat was de way."

"And you think, then, that your master was really bitten by the beetle, and that the bite made him sick?"

"I don't tink noffin' about it—I nose it. What make him dream 'bout de goole so much, if 'tain't 'cause he bit by de goole-bug? I'se heerd 'bout dem goole-bugs 'fore dis."

"But how do you know he dreams about gold?"

"How I know? why 'cause he talk about it in he sleep—dat's how I nose."

"Well, Jup, perhaps you are right; but to what fortunate circumstance am I to attribute the honor of a visit from you to-day?"

"What de matter, massa?"

"Did you bring any message from Mr. Legrand?"

"No, massa, I bring dis here 'pissel;" and here Jupiter handed me a note which ran thus:

"MY DEAR ——, Why have I not seen you for so long a time? I hope you have not been so foolish as to take offence at any little *brusquerie* of mine; but no, that is improbable.

"Since I saw you I have had great cause for anxiety. I have something to tell you, yet scarcely know how to tell it, or whether I should tell it at all.

"I have not been quite well for some days past, and poor old Jup annoys me, almost beyond endurance, by his well-meant attentions. Would you believe it?— he had prepared a huge stick, the other day, with which to chastise me for giving him the slip, and spending the day, *solus,* among the hills on the mainland. I verily believe that my ill looks alone saved me a flogging.

"I have made no addition to my cabinet since we met.

"If you can, in any way, make it convenient, come over with Jupiter. *Do* come. I wish to see you *to-night,* upon business of importance. I assure you that it is of the *highest* importance.
                              "Ever yours,
                                        "WILLIAM LEGRAND."

There was something in the tone of this note which gave me great uneasiness. Its whole style differed materially from that of Legrand. What could he be dreaming of? What new crotchet possessed his excitable brain? What "business of the highest importance" could *he* possibly have to transact? Jupiter's account of him boded no good. I dreaded lest the continued pressure of misfortune had, at length, fairly unsettled the reason of my friend. Without a moment's hesitation, therefore, I prepared to accompany the negro.

Upon reaching the wharf, I noticed a scythe and three spades, all apparently new, lying in the bottom of the boat in which we were to embark.

"What is the meaning of all this, Jup?" I inquired.

"Him syfe, massa, and spade."

"Very true; but what are they doing here? "

"Him de syfe and de spade what Massa Will 'sis 'pon my buying for him in de town, and de debbil's own lot of money I had to gib for 'em."

"But what, in the name of all that is mysterious, is your 'Massa Will' going to do with scythes and spades?"

"Dat's more dan I know, and debbil take me if I don't believe 'tis more dan he know, too. But it's all cum ob de bug."

Finding that no satisfaction was to be obtained of Jupiter, whose whole intellect seemed to be absorbed by "de bug," I now stepped into the boat and made sail. With a fair and strong breeze we soon ran into the little cove to the northward of Fort Moultrie, and a walk of some two miles brought us to the hut. It was about three in the afternoon when we arrived. Legrand had been awaiting us in eager expectation. He grasped my hand with a nervous *empressement,* which alarmed me and strength-ened the suspicions already entertained. His countenance was pale even to ghastliness, and his deep-set eyes glared with unnatural lustre. After some inquiries respecting his health, I asked him, not knowing what better to say, if he had yet obtained the *scarabæus* from Lieutenant G——.

"Oh, yes," he replied, coloring violently, "I got it from him the next morning. Nothing should tempt me to part with that *scarabæus.* Do you know that Jupiter is quite right about it?"

"In what way?" I asked, with a sad foreboding at heart.

"In supposing it to be a bug of *real gold.*" He said this with an air of profound seriousness, and I felt inexpressibly shocked.

"This bug is to make my fortune," he continued, with a triumphant smile, "to reinstate me in my family possessions. Is it any wonder, then, that I prize it? Since Fortune has thought fit to bestow it upon me, I have only to use it properly and I shall arrive at the gold of which it is the index. Jupiter, bring me that *scarabæus!*"

"What! de bug, massa? I'd rudder not go fer trubble dat bug— you mus' git him for your own self." Hereupon Legrand arose, with a grave and stately air, and brought me the beetle from a glass case in which it was enclosed. It was a beautiful *scarabæus,* and, at that time, unknown to naturalists—of course a great prize in a scientific point of view. There were two round, black spots near one extremity of the back, and a long one near the other. The scales were exceedingly hard and glossy, with all the appearance of burnished gold. The weight of the insect was very remarkable, and, taking all things into consideration, I could hardly blame Jupiter for his opinion respecting it; but what to make of Legrand's agreement with that opinion, I could not, for the life of me, tell.

"I sent for you," said he, in a grandiloquent tone, when I had completed my examination of the beetle, "I sent for you, that I might have your counsel and assistance in furthering the views of Fate and of the bug"—

"My dear Legrand," I cried, interrupting him, "you are certainly unwell, and had better use some little precautions. You shall go to bed, and I will remain with you a few days, until you get over this. You are feverish and—"

"Feel my pulse," said he.

I felt it, and, to say the truth, found not the slightest indication of fever.

"But you may be ill, and yet have no fever. Allow me this once to prescribe for you. In the first place, go to bed. In the next—"

"You are mistaken," he interposed, "I am as well as I can expect to be under the excitement which I suffer. If you really wish me well, you will relieve this excitement."

"And how is this to be done?"

"Very easily. Jupiter and myself are going upon an expedition into the hills, upon the mainland, and, in this expedition, we shall need the aid of some person in whom we can confide. You are the only one we can trust. Whether we succeed or fail, the excitement which you now perceive in me will be equally allayed."

"I am anxious to oblige you in any way," I replied; "but do you mean to say that this infernal beetle has any connection with your expedition into the hills?"

"It has."

"Then, Legrand, I can become a party to no such absurd proceeding."

"I am sorry—very sorry—for we shall have to try it by ourselves."

"Try it by yourselves! The man is surely mad!—but stay—how long do you propose to be absent?"

"Probably all night. We shall start immediately, and be back, at all events, by sunrise."

"And will you promise me, upon your honor, that when this freak of yours is over, and the bug business (good God!) settled to your satisfaction, you will then return home and follow my advice implicitly, as that of your physician?"

"Yes; I promise; and now let us be off, for we have no time to lose."

With a heavy heart I accompanied my friend. We started about four o'clock—Legrand, Jupiter, the dog, and myself. Jupiter had with him the scythe and spades—the whole of which he insisted upon carrying, more through fear, it seemed to me, of trusting either of the implements within reach of his master, than from any excess of industry or complaisance.　His demeanor was dogged in the extreme, and "dat d——d bug" were the sole words which escaped his lips during the journey.　For my own part, I had charge of a couple of dark lanterns, while Legrand contented himself with the *scarabæus,* which he carried attached to the end of a bit of whip-cord; twirling it to and fro, with the air of a conjurer, as he went.　When I observed this last, plain evidence of my friend's aberration of mind, I could scarcely refrain from tears.　I thought it best, however, to humor his fancy, at least for the present, or until I could adopt some more energetic measures with a chance of success.　In the meantime I endeavored, but all in vain, to sound him in regard to the object of the expedition.　Having succeeded in inducing me to accompany him, he seemed unwilling to hold conversation upon any topic of minor importance, and to all my questions vouchsafed no other reply than "we shall see!"

We crossed the creek at the head of the island by means of a skiff, and, ascending the high grounds on the shore of the mainland, proceeded in a northwesterly direction, through a tract of country excessively wild and desolate, where no trace of a human footstep was to be seen. Legrand led the way with decision; pausing only for an instant, here and there, to consult what appeared to be certain landmarks of his own contrivance upon a former occasion.

In this manner we journeyed for about two hours, and the sun was just setting when we entered a region infinitely more dreary than any yet seen.　It was a species of tableland, near the summit of an almost inaccessible hill, densely wooded from base to pinnacle, and interspersed with huge crags that appeared to lie loosely upon the soil, and in many cases were prevented from precipitating themselves into the valleys below merely by the support of the trees against which they reclined.　Deep ravines, in various directions, gave an air of still sterner solemnity to the scene.

The natural platform to which we had clambered was thickly overgrown with brambles, through which we soon discovered that it would have been impossible to force our way but for the scythe; and Jupiter, by direction of his master, proceeded to clear for us a path to the foot of an enormously tall tulip-tree, which stood, with some eight or ten oaks, upon the level, and far surpassed them all, and all other trees which I had then ever seen, in the beauty of its foliage and form, in the wide spread of its branches, and in the general majesty of its appearance.

When we reached this tree, Legrand turned to Jupiter, and asked him if he thought he could climb it. The old man seemed a little staggered by the question, and for some moments made no reply. At length he approached the huge trunk, walked slowly around it, and examined it with minute attention. When he had completed his scrutiny, he merely said:

"Yes, massa, Jup climb any tree he ebber see in he life."

"Then up with you as soon as possible, for it will soon be too dark to see what we are about."

"How far mus' go up, massa?" inquired Jupiter.

"Get up the main trunk first, and then I will tell you which way to go—and here—stop! take this beetle with you."

"De bug, Massa Will!—de goole-bug!" cried the negro, drawing back in dismay—"what for mus' tote de bug way up de tree?—d—n if I do!"

"If you're afraid, Jup, a great big negro like you, to take hold of a harmless little dead beetle, why, you can carry it up by this string— but, if you do not take it up with you in some way, I shall be under the necessity of breaking your head with this shovel."

"What de matter now, massa?" said Jup, evidently shamed into compliance; "always want fur to raise fuss wid old nigger. Was only funnin' anyhow. *Me* feered de bug! what I keer for de bug?" Here he took cautiously hold of the extreme end of the string, and, maintaining the insect as far from his person as circumstances would permit, prepared to ascend the tree.

In youth, the tulip-tree, or *Liriodendron Tulipifera,* the most magnificent of American foresters, has a trunk peculiarly smooth, and often rises to a great height without lateral branches; but, in its riper age, the bark becomes gnarled and uneven, while many short limbs make their appearance on the stem. Thus the difficulty of ascension, in the present case, lay more in semblance than in reality. Embracing the huge cylinder, as closely as possible, with his arms and knees, seizing with his hands some projections, and resting his naked toes upon others, Jupiter, after one or two narrow escapes from falling, at length wriggled himself into the first great fork, and seemed to consider the whole business as virtually accomplished. The *risk* of the achievement was, in fact, now over, although the climber was some sixty or seventy feet from the ground.

"Which way mus' go now, Massa Will?" he asked.

"Keep up the largest branch,—the one on this side," said Legrand. The negro obeyed him promptly, and apparently with but little trouble, ascending higher and higher, until no glimpse of his squat figure could be obtained through the dense foliage which enveloped it. Presently his voice was heard in a sort of halloo.

"How much fudder is got for go?"

"How high up are you?" asked Legrand.

"Ebber so fur," replied the negro; "can see de sky fru de top ob de tree."

"Never mind the sky, but attend to what I say. Look down the trunk and count the limbs below you on this side. How many limbs have you passed?"

"One, two, three, four, fibe—I done pass fibe big limbs, massa, 'pon dis side."

"Then go one limb higher."

In a few minutes the voice was heard again, announcing that the seventh limb was attained.

"Now, Jup," cried Legrand, evidently much excited, "I want you to work your way out upon that limb as far as you can. If you see anything strange, let me know."

By this time what little doubt I might have entertained of my poor friend's insanity was put finally at rest. I had no alternative but to conclude him stricken with lunacy, and I became seriously anxious about getting him home. While I was pondering upon what was best to be done, Jupiter's voice was again heard.

"'Mos' feerd for to ventur 'pon dis limb berry far—'tis dead limb putty much all de way."

"Did you say it was a *dead* limb, Jupiter?" cried Legrand in a quavering voice.

"Yes, massa, him dead as de door-nail—done up for sartain—done departed dis here life."

"What in the name of heaven shall I do?" asked Legrand, seemingly in the greatest distress.

"Do!" said I, glad of an opportunity to interpose a word, "why come home and go to bed. Come now!—that's a fine fellow. It's getting late, and, besides, you remember your promise."

"Jupiter," cried he, without heeding me in the least, "do you hear me?"

"Yes, Massa Will, hear you ebber so plain."

"Try the wood well, then, with your knife, and see if you think it *very* rotten."

"Him rotten, massa, sure 'nuff," replied the negro in a few moments, "but not so berry rotten as mought be. Mought ventur out leetle way 'pon de limb by myself, dat's true."

"By yourself!—what do you mean?"

"Why, I mean de bug. 'Tis *berry* hebby bug. S'pose I drop him down fuss, and den de limb won't break wid just de weight ob one nigger."

"You infernal scoundrel!" cried Legrand, apparently much relieved, "what do you mean by telling me such nonsense as that? As sure as you let that beetle fall, I'll break your neck. Look here, Jupiter! do you hear me?"

"Yes, massa, needn't hollo at poor nigger dat style."

"Well! now listen!—if you will venture out on the limb as far as you think safe, and not let go the beetle, I'll make you a present of a silver dollar as soon as you get down."

"I'm gwine, Massa Will—'deed I is," replied the negro very promptly —"mos' out to the eend now."

"*Out to the end!*" here fairly screamed Legrand, "do you say you are out to the end of that limb?"

"Soon be to de eend, massa,—o-o-o-o-oh! Lor-gol-a-marcy! what *is* dis here 'pon de tree?"

"Well!" cried Legrand, highly delighted, "what is it?"

"Why 'tain't noffin' but a skull—somebody bin lef' him head up de tree, and de crows done gobble ebery bit ob de meat off."

"A skull, you say!—very well!—how is it fastened to the limb?— what holds it on?"

"Sure 'nuff, massa; mus' look. Why, dis berry curous sarcumstance, 'pon my word—dare's a great big nail in de skull, what fastens ob it on to de tree."

"Well now, Jupiter, do exactly as I tell you—do you hear?"

"Yes, massa."

"Pay attention, then!—find the left eye of the skull."

"Hum! hoo! dat's good! why, dar ain't no eye lef' at all."

"Curse your stupidity! do you know your right hand from your left?"

"Yes, I nose dat—nose all 'bout dat—'tis my lef' hand what I chops de wood wid."

"To be sure! you are left-handed; and your left eye is on the same side as your left hand. Now, I suppose, you can find the left eye of the skull, or the place where the left eye has been. Have you found it?"

Here was a long pause. At length the negro asked,

"Is de lef' eye of de skull 'pon de same side as de lef' hand of de

skull, too?—'cause de skull ain't got not a bit ob hand at all—nebber
mind! I got de lef' eye now—here de lef' eye! what mus' do wid it?"

"Let the beetle drop through it, as far as the string will reach—but
be careful and not let go your hold of the string."

"All dat done, Massa Will; mighty easy ting for to put de bug fru
de hole—look out for him dar below!"

During this colloquy no portion of Jupiter's person could be seen;
but the beetle, which he had suffered to descend, was now visible at
the end of the string, and glistened, like a globe of burnished gold, in
the last rays of the setting sun, some of which still faintly illumined the
eminence upon which we stood. The *scarabæus* hung quite clear of any
branches, and, if allowed to fall, would have fallen at our feet. Legrand
immediately took the scythe, and cleared with it a circular space, three
or four yards in diameter, just beneath the insect, and, having accomplished this, ordered Jupiter to let go the string and come down from
the tree.

Driving a peg, with great nicety, into the ground, at the precise spot
where the beetle fell, my friend now produced from his pocket a tape-
measure. Fastening one end of this at that point of the trunk of the
tree which was nearest the peg, he unrolled it till it reached the peg,
and thence farther unrolled it, in the direction already established by
the two points of the tree and the peg, for the distance of fifty feet—
Jupiter clearing away the brambles with the scythe. At the spot thus
attained a second peg was driven, and about this, as a centre, a rude
circle, about four feet in diameter, described. Taking now a spade himself, and giving one to Jupiter and one to me, Legrand begged us to
set about digging as quickly as possible.

To speak the truth, I had no especial relish for such amusement at
any time, and, at that particular moment, would most willingly have
declined it; for the night was coming on, and I felt much fatigued with
the exercise already taken; but I saw no mode of escape, and was fearful
of disturbing my poor friend's equanimity by a refusal. Could I have
depended, indeed, upon Jupiter's aid, I would have had no hesitation
in attempting to get the lunatic home by force; but I was too well
assured of the old negro's disposition to hope that he would assist me,
under any circumstances, in a personal contest with his master. I made
no doubt that the latter had been infected with some of the innumerable
Southern superstitions about money buried, and that his fantasy had
received confirmation by the finding of the *scarabæus*, or, perhaps, by
Jupiter's obstinacy in maintaining it to be "a bug of real gold." A mind
disposed to lunacy would readily be led away by such suggestions, espe-

cially if chiming in with favorite preconceived ideas; and then I called
to mind the poor fellow's speech about the beetle's being "the index of
his fortune." Upon the whole, I was sadly vexed and puzzled, but at
length I concluded to make a virtue of necessity—to dig with a good
will, and thus the sooner to convince the visionary, by ocular demonstration, of the fallacy of the opinions he entertained.

The lanterns having been lit, we all fell to work with a zeal worthy
a more rational cause; and, as the glare fell upon our persons and implements, I could not help thinking how picturesque a group we composed,
and how strange and suspicious our labors must have appeared to any
interloper who, by chance, might have stumbled upon our whereabouts.

We dug very steadily for two hours. Little was said; and our chief
embarrassment lay in the yelpings of the dog, who took exceeding interest
in our proceedings. He, at length, became so obstreperous that we grew
fearful of his giving the alarm to some stragglers in the vicinity; or,
rather, this was the apprehension of Legrand; for myself, I should have
rejoiced at any interruption which might have enabled me to get the
wanderer home. The noise was, at length, very effectually silenced by
Jupiter, who, getting out of the hole with a dogged air of deliberation,
tied the brute's mouth up with one of his suspenders, and then returned,
with a grave chuckle, to his task.

When the time mentioned had expired, we had reached a depth of
five feet, and yet no signs of any treasure became manifest. A general
pause ensued, and I began to hope that the farce was at an end. Legrand,
however, although evidently much disconcerted, wiped his brow thought-
fully and recommenced. We had excavated the entire circle of four feet
diameter, and now we slightly enlarged the limit, and went to the farther
depth of two feet. Still nothing appeared. The gold-seeker, whom I
sincerely pitied, at length clambered from the pit, with the bitterest disappointment imprinted upon every feature, and proceeded, slowly and
reluctantly, to put on his coat, which he had thrown off at the beginning
of his labor. In the mean time I made no remark. Jupiter, at a signal
from his master, began to gather up his tools. This done, and the dog
having been unmuzzled, we turned in profound silence towards home.

We had taken, perhaps, a dozen steps in this direction, when, with
a loud oath, Legrand strode up to Jupiter, and seized him by the collar.
The astonished negro opened his eyes and mouth to the fullest extent,
let fall the spades, and fell upon his knees.

"You scoundrel," said Legrand, hissing out the syllables from between his clenched teeth—"you infernal black villain!—speak, I tell you!

—answer me this instant, without prevarication!—which—which is your left eye?"

"Oh, my golly, Massa Will! ain't dis here my lef' eye for sartain?" roared the terrified Jupiter, placing his hand upon his *right* organ of vision, and holding it there with a desperate pertinacity, as if in immediate dread of his master's attempt at a gouge.

"I thought so!—I knew it! hurrah!" vociferated Legrand, letting the negro go, and executing a series of curvets and caracoles, much to the astonishment of his valet, who, arising from his knees, looked mutely from his master to myself, and then from myself to his master.

"Come! we must go back," said the latter, "the game's not up yet;" and he again led the way to the tulip-tree.

"Jupiter," said he, when we reached its foot, "come here! was the skull nailed to the limb with the face outward, or with the face to the limb?"

"De face was out, massa, so dat de crows could get at de eyes good, widout any trouble."

"Well, then, was it this eye or that through which you dropped the beetle?"—here Legrand touched each of Jupiter's eyes.

"'Twas dis eye, massa—de lef' eye—jis' as you tell me," and here it was his right eye that the negro indicated.

"That will do—we must try it again."

Here my friend, about whose madness I now saw, or fancied that I saw, certain indications of method, removed the peg which marked the spot where the beetle fell, to a spot about three inches to the westward of its former position. Taking, now, the tape-measure from the nearest point of the trunk to the peg, as before, and continuing the extension in a straight line to the distance of fifty feet, a spot was indicated, removed by several yards, from the point at which we had been digging.

Around the new position a circle, somewhat larger than in the former instance, was now described, and we again set to work with the spades. I was dreadfully weary, but, scarcely understanding what had occasioned the change in my thoughts, I felt no longer any great aversion from the labor imposed. I had become most unaccountably interested—nay, even excited. Perhaps there was something, amid all the extravagant demeanor of Legrand—some air of forethought, or of deliberation—which impressed me. I dug eagerly, and now and then caught myself actually looking, with something that very much resembled expectation, for the fancied treasure, the vision of which had demented my unfortunate companion. At a period when such vagaries of thought most

fully possessed me, and when we had been at work perhaps an hour
and a half, we were again interrupted by the violent howlings of the
dog. His uneasiness, in the first instance, had been evidently but the
result of playfulness or caprice, but he now assumed a bitter and serious
tone. Upon Jupiter's again attempting to muzzle him, he made furious
resistance, and, leaping into the hole, tore up the mould frantically with
his claws. In a few seconds he had uncovered a mass of human bones,
forming two complete skeletons, intermingled with several buttons of
metal, and what appeared to be the dust of decayed woollen. One or two
strokes of a spade upturned the blade of a large Spanish knife, and,
as we dug farther, three or four loose pieces of gold and silver coin
came to light.

At sight of these the joy of Jupiter could scarcely be restrained,
but the countenance of his master wore an air of extreme disappointment. He urged us, however, to continue our exertions, and the words
were hardly uttered when I stumbled and fell forward, having caught
the toe of my boot in a large ring of iron that lay half buried in the
loose earth.

We now worked in earnest, and never did I pass ten minutes of more
intense excitement. During this interval we had fairly unearthed an
oblong chest of wood, which, from its perfect preservation and wonderful hardness, had plainly been subjected to some mineralizing process
—perhaps that of the bichloride of mercury. This box was three feet
and a half long, three feet broad, and two and a half feet deep. It was
firmly secured by bands of wrought iron, riveted, and forming a kind
of trellis-work over the whole. On each side of the chest, near the top,
were three rings of iron—six in all—by means of which a firm hold
could be obtained by six persons. Our utmost united endeavors served
only to disturb the coffer very slightly in its bed. We at once saw the
impossibility of removing so great a weight. Luckily, the sole fasten-
ings of the lid consisted of two sliding bolts. These we drew back—
trembling and panting with anxiety. In an instant, a treasure of incalculable value lay gleaming before us. As the rays of the lanterns fell
within the pit, there flashed upwards, from a confused heap of gold and
of jewels, a glow and a glare that absolutely dazzled our eyes.

I shall not pretend to describe the feelings with which I gazed.
Amazement was, of course, predominant. Legrand appeared exhausted
with excitement, and spoke very few words. Jupiter's countenance wore,
for some minutes, as deadly a pallor as it is possible, in the nature of
things, for any negro's visage to assume. He seemed stupefied—thun-
der-stricken. Presently he fell upon his knees in the pit, and, burying

his naked **arms up to** the elbows in gold, let them there remain, as **if** enjoying the luxury of a bath. At length, with a deep sigh, he exclaimed, as if in a soliloquy:

"And dis all cum ob de goole-bug! de putty goole-bug! de poor little goole-bug, what I boosed in dat sabage kind ob style! Ain't you shamed ob yourself, nigger?—answer me dat!"

It became necessary, at last, that I should arouse both master and valet to the expediency of removing the treasure. It was growing late, and it behooved us to make exertion, that we might get everything housed before daylight. It was difficult to say what should be done, and much time was spent in deliberation—so confused were the ideas of all. We finally lightened the box by removing two-thirds of its contents, when we were enabled, with some trouble, to raise it from the hole. The articles taken out were deposited among the brambles, and the dog left to guard them, with strict orders from Jupiter neither, upon any pretence, to stir from the spot, nor to open his mouth until our return. We then hurriedly made for home with the chest; reaching the hut in safety, but after excessive toil, at one o'clock in the morning. Worn out as we were, it was not in human nature to do more just now. We rested until two, and had supper; starting for the hills immediately afterwards, armed with three stout sacks, which by good luck were upon the premises. A little before four we arrived at the pit, divided the remainder of the booty, as equally as might be, among us, and, leaving the holes unfilled, again set out for the hut, at which, for the second time, we deposited our golden burdens, just as the first streaks of the dawn gleamed from over the tree-tops in the East.

We were now thoroughly broken down; but the intense excitement of the time denied us repose. After an unquiet slumber of some three or four hours' duration, we arose, as if by preconcert, to make examination of our treasure.

The chest had been full to the brim, and we spent the whole day, and the greater part of the next night, in a scrutiny of its contents. There had been nothing like order or arrangement. Everything had been heaped in promiscuously. Having assorted all with care, we found ourselves possessed of even vaster wealth than we had at first supposed. In coin there was rather more than four hundred and fifty thousand dollars; estimating the value of the pieces, as accurately as we could, by the tables of the period. There was not a particle of silver. All was gold of antique date and of great variety: French, Spanish, and German money, with a few English guineas, and some counters, of which we had never seen specimens before. There were several very large and heavy coins, so worn that we could make nothing of their inscriptions. There was no American money. The value of the jewels we found more difficulty in estimating. There were diamonds—some of them exceedingly large and fine—a hundred and ten in all, and not one of them small; eighteen rubies of remarkable brilliancy; three hundred and ten emeralds, all very beautiful; and twenty-one sapphires, with an opal. These stones had all been broken from their settings and thrown loose in the chest. The settings themselves, which we picked out from among the other gold, appeared to have been beaten up with hammers, as if to prevent identification. Besides all this, there was a vast quantity of solid gold ornaments: nearly two hundred massive finger and ear rings; rich chains —thirty of these, if I remember; eighty-three very large and heavy crucifixes; five gold censers of great value; a prodigious golden punch-bowl, ornamented with richly chased vine-leaves and Bacchanalian figures; with two sword-handles exquisitely embossed, and many other smaller articles which I cannot recollect. The weight of these valuables exceeded three hundred and fifty pounds avoirdupois; and in this estimate I have not included one hundred and ninety-seven superb gold watches; three of the number being worth each five hundred dollars, if one. Many of them were very old, and as time-keepers valueless, the works having suffered more or less from corrosion; but all were richly jewelled and in cases of great worth. We estimated the entire contents of the chest, that night, at a million and a half dollars; and, upon the subsequent disposal of the trinkets and jewels (a few being retained for our own use), it was found that we had greatly undervalued the treasure.

When, at length, we had concluded our examination, and the intense excitement of the time had in some measure subsided, Legrand, who saw that I was dying with impatience for a solution of this most extraordinary riddle, entered into a full detail of all the circumstances connected with it.

"You remember," said he, "the night when I handed you the rough sketch I had made of the *scarabæus*. You recollect also, that I became quite vexed at you for insisting that my drawing resembled a death's-head. When you first made this assertion I thought you were jesting; but afterwards I called to mind the peculiar spots on the back of the insect, and admitted to myself that your remark had some little foundation in fact. Still, the sneer at my graphic powers irritated me—for I am considered a good artist—and, therefore, when you handed me the scrap of parchment, I was about to crumple it up and throw it angrily into the fire."

"The scrap of paper, you mean," said I.

"No: it had much of the appearance of paper, and at first I supposed it to be such, but when I came to draw upon it, I discovered it, at once, to be a piece of very thin parchment. It was quite dirty, you remember. Well, as I was in the very act of crumpling it up, my glance fell upon the sketch at which you had been looking, and you may imagine my astonishment when I perceived, in fact, the figure of a death's-head just where, it seemed to me, I had made the drawing of the beetle. For a moment I was too much amazed to think with accuracy. I knew that my design was very different in detail from this—although there was a certain similarity in general outline. Presently I took a candle and, seating myself at the other end of the room, proceeded to scrutinize the parchment more closely. Upon turning it over, I saw my own sketch upon the reverse, just as I had made it. My first idea, now, was mere surprise at the really remarkable similarity of outline—at the singular coincidence involved in the fact that, unknown to me, there should have been a skull upon the other side of the parchment, immediately beneath my figure of the *scarabæus,* and that this skull, not only in outline, but in size, should so closely resemble my drawing. I say the singularity of this coincidence absolutely stupefied me for a time. This is the usual effect of such coincidences. The mind struggles to establish a connection—a sequence of cause and effect—and, being unable to do so, suffers a species of temporary paralysis. But, when I recovered from this stupor, there dawned upon me gradually a conviction which startled me even far more than the coincidence. I began distinctly, positively, to remember that there had been *no* drawing on the parchment when I made my sketch of the *scarabæus.* I became perfectly certain of this; for I recollected turning up first one side and then the other, in search of the cleanest spot. Had the skull been then there, of course I could not have failed to notice it. Here was indeed a mystery which I felt it impossible to explain; but, even at that early moment, there seemed to glimmer, faintly, within the most remote and secret chambers of my intellect, a glow-worm-like conception of that truth which last night's adventure brought to so magnificent a demonstration. I arose at once, and, putting the parchment securely away, dismissed all farther reflection until I should be alone.

"When you had gone, and when Jupiter was fast asleep, I betook myself to a more methodical investigation of the affair. In the first place I considered the manner in which the parchment had come into my possession. The spot where we discovered the *scarabæus* was on the coast of the main-land, about a mile eastward of the island, and but a short distance above high-water mark. Upon my taking hold of it, it gave me a sharp bite, which caused me to let it drop. Jupiter, with his accustomed caution, before seizing the insect, which had flown towards him, looked about him for a leaf, or something of that nature, by which to take hold of it. It was at this moment that his eyes, and mine also, fell upon the scrap of parchment, which I then supposed to be paper. It was lying half-buried in the sand, a corner sticking up. Near the spot where we found it, I observed the remnants of the hull of what appeared to have been a ship's long boat. The wreck seemed to have been there for a very great while; for the resemblance to boat timbers could scarcely be traced.

"Well, Jupiter picked up the parchment, wrapped the beetle in it, and gave it to me. Soon afterwards we turned to go home, and on the way met Lieutenant G——. I showed him the insect, and he begged me to let him take it to the fort. On my consenting, he thrust it forthwith into his waistcoat pocket, without the parchment in which it had been wrapped, and which I had continued to hold in my hand during his inspection. Perhaps he dreaded my changing my mind, and thought it best to make sure of the prize at once—you know how enthusiastic he is on all subjects connected with Natural History. At the same time, without being conscious of it, I must have deposited the parchment in my own pocket.

"You remember that when I went to the table, for the purpose of making a sketch of the beetle, I found no paper where it was usually kept. I looked in the drawer, and found none there. I searched my pockets, hoping to find an old letter, and then my hand fell upon the parchment. I thus detail the precise mode in which it came into my possession; for the circumstances impressed me with peculiar force.

"No doubt you will think me fanciful—but I had already established a kind of *connection*. I had put together two links of a great chain. There was a boat lying on a seacoast, and not far from the boat was a parchment—*not a paper*—with a skull depicted on it. You will, of course, ask 'where is the connection?' I reply that the skull, or death's-head, is the well-known emblem of the pirate. The flag of the death's-head is hoisted in all engagements.

"I have said that the scrap was parchment, and not paper. Parchment is durable—almost imperishable. Matters of little moment are rarely consigned to parchment; since, for the mere ordinary purposes of drawing or writing, it is not nearly so well adapted as paper. This reflection suggested some meaning—some relevancy—in the death's-head. I did not fail to observe, also, the *form* of the parchment. Although one of its corners had been, by some accident, destroyed, it could be seen that the original form was oblong. It was just such a slip, indeed, as might have been chosen for a memorandum—for a record of something to be long remembered and carefully preserved."

"But," I interposed, "you say that the skull was *not* upon the parch-ment when you made the drawing of the beetle. How then do you trace any connection between the boat and the skull—since this latter, accord-ing to your own admission, must have been designed (God only knows how or by whom) at some period subsequent to your sketching the *scarabæus?*"

"Ah, hereupon turns the whole mystery; although the secret, at this point, I had comparatively little difficulty in solving. My steps were sure, and could afford but a single result. I reasoned, for example, thus: When I drew the *scarabæus,* there was no skull apparent on the parch-ment. When I had completed the drawing I gave it to you, and observed you narrowly until you returned it. *You,* therefore, did not design the skull, and no one else was present to do it. Then it was not done by human agency. And nevertheless it was done.

"At this stage of my reflections I endeavored to remember, and *did* remember, with entire distinctness, every incident which occurred about the period in question. The weather was chilly (O rare and happy acci-dent!), and a fire was blazing on the hearth. I was heated with exercise and sat near the table. You, however, had drawn a chair close to the chimney. Just as I placed the parchment in your hand, and as you were in the act of inspecting it, Wolf, the Newfoundland, entered, and leaped upon your shoulders. With your left hand you caressed him and kept him off, while your right, holding the parchment, was permitted to fall listlessly between your knees, and in close proximity to the fire. At one moment I thought the blaze had caught it, and was about to caution you, but, before I could speak, you had withdrawn it, and were engaged in its examination. When I considered all these particulars, I doubted not for a moment that *heat* had been the agent in bringing to light, on the parchment, the skull which I saw designed on it. You are well aware that chemical preparations exist, and have existed time out of mind, by means of which it is possible to write on either paper or vellum, so that the characters shall become visible only when subjected to the action of fire. Zaffre, digested in *aqua regia,* and diluted with four times its weight of water, is sometimes employed; a green tint results. The regulus of cobalt, dissolved in spirit of nitre, gives a red. These colors disappear at longer or shorter intervals after the material written upon cools, but again become apparent upon the re-application of heat.

"I now scrutinized the death's-head with care. Its outer edges—

the edges of the drawing nearest the edge of the vellum—were far more *distinct* than the others. It was clear that the action of the caloric had been imperfect or unequal. I immediately kindled a fire, and subjected every portion of the parchment to a glowing heat. At first, the only effect was the strengthening of the faint lines in the skull: but, on persevering in the experiment, there became visible at the corner of the slip, diagonally opposite to the spot in which the death's-head was delineated, the figure of what I at first supposed to be a goat. A closer scrutiny, however, satisfied me that it was intended for a kid."

"Ha! ha!" said I, "to be sure I have no right to laugh at you—a million and a half of money is too serious a matter for mirth—but you are not about to establish a third link in your chain: you will not find any especial connection between your pirates and a goat; pirates, you know, have nothing to do with goats; they appertain to the farming interest."

"But I have just said that the figure was *not* that of a goat."

"Well, a kid, then—pretty much the same thing."

"Pretty much, but not altogether," said Legrand. "You may have heard of one *Captain* Kidd. I at once looked on the figure of the animal as a kind of punning or hieroglyphical signature. I say signature; because its position on the vellum suggested this idea. The death's-head at the corner diagonally opposite had, in the same manner, the air of a stamp, or seal. But I was sorely put out by the absence of all else— of the body to my imagined instrument—of the text for my context."

"I presume you expected to find a letter between the stamp and the signature."

"Something of that kind. The fact is, I felt irresistibly impressed with a presentiment of some vast good fortune impending. I can scarcely say why. Perhaps, after all, it was rather a desire than an actual belief;—but do you know that Jupiter's silly words, about the bug being of solid gold, had a remarkable effect on my fancy? And then the series of accidents and coincidences—these were so *very* extraordinary. Do you observe how mere an accident it was that these events should have occurred on the *sole* day of all the year in which it has been, or may be, sufficiently cool for fire, and that without the fire, or without the intervention of the dog at the precise moment in which he appeared, I should never have become aware of the death's-head, and so never the possessor of the treasure?"

"But proceed—I am all impatience."

"Well; you have heard, of course, the many stories current—the thousand vague rumors afloat about money buried, somewhere on the

Atlantic coast, by Kidd and his associates. These rumors must have had some foundation in fact. And that the rumors have existed so long and so continuously, could have resulted, it appeared to me, only from the circumstance of the buried treasure still *remaining* entombed. Had Kidd concealed his plunder for a time, and afterwards reclaimed it, the rumors would scarcely have reached us in their present unvarying form. You will observe that the stories told are all about money-seekers, not about money-finders. Had the pirate recovered his money, there the affair would have dropped. It seemed to me that some accident—say the loss of a memorandum indicating its locality—had deprived him of the means of recovering it, and that this accident had become known to his followers, who otherwise might never have heard that treasure had been concealed at all, and who, busying themselves in vain, because unguided, attempts to regain it, had given first birth, and then universal currency, to the reports which are now so common. Have you ever heard of any important treasure being unearthed along the coast?"

"Never."

"But that Kidd's accumulations were immense is well known. I took it for granted, therefore, that the earth still held them; and you will scarcely be surprised when I tell you that I felt a hope, nearly amounting to certainty, that the parchment so strangely found involved a lost record of the place of deposit."

"But how did you proceed?"

"I held the vellum again to the fire, after increasing the heat, but nothing appeared. I now thought it possible that the coating of dirt might have something to do with the failure; so I carefully rinsed the parchment by pouring warm water over it, and, having done this, I placed it in a tin pan, with the skull downwards, and put the pan upon a furnace of lighted charcoal. In a few minutes, the pan having become thoroughly heated, I removed the slip, and, to my inexpressible joy, found it spotted, in several places, with what appeared to be figures arranged in lines. Again I placed it in the pan, and suffered it to remain another minute. Upon taking it off, the whole was just as you see it now."

Here Legrand, having reheated the parchment, submitted it to my inspection. The following characters were rudely traced, in a red tint, between the death's-head and the goat:—

53‡‡†305))6*;4826)4‡.)4‡);806*;48†8¶60))85;;]8*:‡*8†83(88)5*†;46(;88*9
6*?;8)*‡(;485);5*†2:*‡(;4956*2(5*—4)8¶8*;4069285);)6†8)4‡‡;1(‡9;48081;8:
8‡1;48†85;4)485†528806*81(‡9;48;(88;4(‡?34;48)4‡;161;:188;‡?;

"But," said I, returning him the slip, "I am as much in the dark as ever. Were all the jewels of Golconda awaiting me on my solution of this enigma, I am quite sure that I should be unable to earn them."

"And yet," said Legrand, "the solution is by no means so difficult as you might be led to imagine from the first hasty inspection of the characters. These characters, as any one might readily guess, form a cipher—that is to say, they convey a meaning; but then, from what is known of Kidd, I could not suppose him capable of constructing any of the more abstruse cryptographs. I made up my mind, at once, that this was of a simple species—such, however, as would appear, to the crude intellect of the sailor, absolutely insoluble without the key."

"And you really solved it?"

"Readily; I have solved others of an abstruseness ten thousand times greater. Circumstances, and a certain bias of mind, have led me to take interest in such riddles, and it may well be doubted whether human ingenuity can construct an enigma of the kind which human ingenuity may not, by proper application, resolve. In fact, having once established connected and legible characters, I scarcely gave a thought to the mere difficulty of developing their import.

"In the present case—indeed in all cases of secret writing—the first question regards the *language* of the cipher; for the principles of solution, so far, especially, as the more simple ciphers are concerned, depend on, and are varied by, the genius of the particular idiom. In general, there is no alternative but experiment (directed by probabilities) of every tongue known to him who attempts the solution, until the true one be attained. But, with the cipher now before us, all difficulty is removed by the signature. The pun upon the word 'Kidd' is appreciable in no other language than the English. But for this consideration I should have begun my attempts with the Spanish and French, as the tongues in which a secret of this kind would most naturally have been written by a pirate of the Spanish main. As it was, I assumed the cryptograph to be English.

"You observe there are no divisions between the words. Had there been divisions, the task would have been comparatively easy. In such case I should have commenced with a collation and analysis of the shorter words, and, had a word of a single letter occurred, as is most likely (*a* or *I*, for example), I should have considered the solution as assured. But, there being no division, my first step was to ascertain the predominant letters, as well as the least frequent. Counting all, I constructed a table, thus:

Of the character 8 there are 33

;	"	26
4	"	19
‡)	"	16
*	"	13
5	"	12
6	"	11
†1	"	8
0	"	6
92	"	5
:3	"	4
?	"	3
¶	"	2
]—.	"	1

"Now, in English, the letter which most frequently occurs is *e*. Afterwards the succession runs thus: *a o i d h n r s t u y c f g l m w b k p q x z*. *E* predominates, however, so remarkably that an individual sentence of any length is rarely seen, in which it is not the prevailing character.

"Here, then, we have, in the very beginning, the groundwork for something more than a mere guess. The general use which may be made of the table is obvious—but, in this particular cipher, we shall only very partially require its aid. As our predominant character is 8, we will commence by assuming it as the *e* of the natural alphabet. To verify the supposition, let us observe if the 8 be seen often in couples—for *e* is doubled with great frequency in English—in such words, for example, as 'meet,' 'fleet,' 'speed,' 'seen,' 'been,' 'agree,' &c. In the present instance we see it doubled no less than five times, although the cryptograph is brief.

"Let us assume 8, then, as *e*. Now, of all *words* in the language, 'the' is the most usual; let us see, therefore, whether there are not repetitions of any three characters, in the same order of collocation, the last of them being 8. If we discover repetitions of such letters, so arranged, they will most probably represent the word 'the.' On inspection, we find no less than seven such arrangements, the characters being ;48. We may, therefore, assume that the semicolon represents *t*, that 4 represents *h*, and that 8 represents *e*—the last being now well confirmed. Thus a great step has been taken.

"But, having established a single word, we are enabled to establish a vastly important point; that is to say, several commencements and terminations of other words. Let us refer, for example, to the last instance but one, in which the combination ;48 occurs—not far from the end of the cipher. We know that the semicolon immediately ensuing is the commencement of a word, and, of the six characters succeeding this 'the,' we are cognizant of no less than five. Let us set these characters down, thus, by the letters we know them to represent, leaving a space for the unknown—

t eeth.

"Here we are enabled, at once, to discard the '*th*,' as forming no portion of the word commencing with the first *t;* since, by experiment of the entire alphabet for a letter adapted to the vacancy, we perceive that no word can be formed of which this *th* can be a part. We are thus narrowed into

t ee,

and, going through the alphabet, if necessary, as before, we arrive at the word 'tree' as the sole possible reading. We thus gain another letter, *r,* represented by (, with the words 'the tree' in juxtaposition.

"Looking beyond these words, for a short distance, we again see the combination ;48, and employ it by way of *termination* to what immediately precedes. We have thus this arrangement:

the tree ;4(‡?34 the,

or, substituting the natural letters, where known, it reads thus:

the tree thr‡?3h the.

"Now, if, in place of the unknown characters, we leave blank spaces, or substitute dots, we read thus:

the tree thr . . . h the,

when the word 'through' makes itself evident at once. But this discovery gives us three new letters, *o, u,* and *g,* represented by ‡ ? and 3.

"Looking now, narrowly, through the cipher for combinations of known characters, we find, not very far from the beginning, this arrangement,

83(88, or egree,

which, plainly, is the conclusion of the word 'degree,' and gives us another letter, *d,* represented by †

"Four letters beyond the word 'degree,' we perceive the combination
;46(;88*

"Translating the known characters, and representing the unknown by dots, as before, we read thus:

th . rtee .

an arrangement immediately suggestive of the word 'thirteen,' and again furnishing us with two new characters, *i* and *n,* represented by 6 and *.

"Referring, now, to the beginning of the cryptograph, we find the combination,

53‡‡†.

"Translating, as before, we obtain

. good,

which assures us that the first letter is *A,* and that the first two words are 'A good.'

"To avoid confusion, it is now time that we arrange our key, as far as discovered, in a tabular form. It will stand thus:

5	represents	a
†	"	d
8	"	e
3	"	g
4	"	h
6	"	i
*	"	n
‡	"	o
(	"	r
;	"	t

"We have, therefore, no less than ten of the most important letters represented, and it will be unnecessary to proceed with the details of the solution. I have said enough to convince you that ciphers of this nature are readily soluble, and to give you some insight into the rationale of their development. But be assured that the specimen before us appertains to the very simplest species of cryptograph. It now only remains to give you the full translation of the characters upon the parchment, as unriddled. Here it is:

"*'A good glass in the bishop's hostel in the devil's seat twenty one degrees and thirteen minutes northeast and by north main branch seventh limb east side shoot from the left eye of the death's-head a bee line from the tree through the shot fifty feet out.'* "

"But," said I, "the enigma seems still in as bad a condition as ever. How is it possible to extort a meaning from all this jargon about 'devil's seats,' 'death's-heads,' and 'bishop's hotels'?"

"I confess," replied Legrand, "that the matter still wears a serious aspect, when regarded with a casual glance. My first endeavor was to divide the sentence into the natural division intended by the cryptographist."

"You mean, to punctuate it?"

"Something of that kind."

"But how was it possible to effect this?"

"I reflected that it had been a *point* with the writer to run his words together without division, so as to increase the difficulty of solution. Now, a not over-acute man, in pursuing such an object, would be nearly certain to overdo the matter. When, in the course of his composition, he arrived at a break in his subject which would naturally require a pause, or a point, he would be exceedingly apt to run his characters, at this place, more than usually close together. If you will observe the MS., in the present instance, you will easily detect five such cases of unusual crowding. Acting on this hint, I made the division thus:

"'*A good glass in the Bishop's hostel in the Devil's seat—twenty-one degrees and thirteen minutes—north-east and by north—main branch seventh limb east side—shoot from the left eye of the death's head— a bee-line from the tree through the shot fifty feet out.*'"

"Even this division," said I, "leaves me still in the dark."

"It left me also in the dark," replied Legrand, "for a few days; during which I made diligent inquiry, in the neighborhood of Sullivan's Island, for any building which went by the name of the 'Bishop's Hotel;' for, of course, I dropped the obsolete word 'hostel.' Gaining no information on the subject, I was on the point of extending my sphere of search, and proceeding in a more systematic manner, when one morning it entered into my head, quite suddenly, that this 'Bishop's Hostel' might have some reference to an old family, of the name of Bessop, which, time out of mind, had held possession of an ancient manor-house, about four miles to the northward of the island. I accordingly went over to the plantation, and reinstituted my inquiries among the older negroes of the place. At length one of the most aged of the women said that she had heard of such a place as *Bessop's Castle,* and thought that she could guide me to it, but that it was not a castle, nor a tavern, but a high rock.

"I offered to pay her well for her trouble, and, after some demur, she consented to accompany me to the spot. We found it without much difficulty, when, dismissing her, I proceeded to examine the place. The 'castle' consisted of an irregular assemblage of cliffs and rocks—one of the latter being quite remarkable for its height as well as for its insulated and artificial appearance. I clambered to its apex, and then felt much at a loss as to what should be next done.

"While I was busied in reflection, my eyes fell on a narrow ledge in the eastern face of the rock, perhaps a yard below the summit upon which I stood. This ledge projected about eighteen inches, and was not more than a foot wide, while a niche in the cliff just above it gave it a rude resemblance to one of the hollow-backed chairs used by our ancestors. I made no doubt that here was the 'devil's seat' alluded to in the MS., and now I seemed to grasp the full secret of the riddle.

"The 'good glass,' I knew, could have reference to nothing but a telescope; for the word 'glass' is rarely employed in any other sense by seamen. Now here, I at once saw, was a telescope to be used, and a definite point of view, *admitting no variation,* from which to use it. Nor did I hesitate to believe that the phrases, 'twenty-one degrees and thirteen minutes,' and 'north-east and by north,' were intended as directions for the levelling of the glass. Greatly excited by these discoveries, I hurried home, procured a telescope, and returned to the rock.

"I let myself down to the ledge, and found that it was impossible to retain a seat on it unless in one particular position. This fact confirmed my preconceived idea. I proceeded to use the glass. Of course, the 'twenty-one degrees and thirteen minutes' could allude to nothing but elevation above the visible horizon, since the horizontal direction was clearly indicated by the words, 'north-east and by north.' This latter direction I at once established by means of a pocket-compass; then, pointing the glass as nearly at an angle of twenty-one degrees of elevation as I could do it by guess, I moved it cautiously up or down, until my attention was arrested by a circular rift or opening in the foliage of a large tree that overtopped its fellows in the distance. In the centre of this rift I perceived a white spot, but could not, at first, distinguish what it was. Adjusting the focus of the telescope, I again looked, and now made it out to be a human skull.

"On this discovery I was so sanguine as to consider the enigma solved; for the phrase 'main branch, seventh limb, east side,' could refer only to the position of the skull on the tree, while 'shoot from the left eye of the death's-head' admitted, also, of but one interpretation, in regard to a search for buried treasure. I perceived that the design was to drop a bullet from the left eye of the skull, and that a bee-line, or, in other words, a straight line, drawn from the nearest point of the trunk through 'the shot' (or the spot where the bullet fell), and thence extended to a distance of fifty feet, would indicate a definite point— and beneath this point I thought it at least *possible* that a deposit of value lay concealed."

"All this," I said, "is exceedingly clear, and, although ingenious, still simple and explicit. When you left the Bishop's Hotel, what then?"

"Why, having carefully taken the bearings of the tree, I turned homewards. The instant that I left 'the devil's seat,' however, the circular rift vanished; nor could I get a glimpse of it afterwards, turn as I would. What seems to me the chief ingenuity in this whole business, is the fact (for repeated experiment has convinced me it *is* a fact) that the circular opening in question is visible from no other attainable point of view than that afforded by the narrow ledge on the face of the rock.

"In this expedition to the 'Bishop's Hotel' I had been attended by Jupiter, who had no doubt observed, for some weeks past, the abstraction of my demeanor, and took especial care not to leave me alone. But on the next day, getting up very early, I contrived to give him the slip, and went into the hills in search of the tree. After much toil I found it. When I came home at night my valet proposed to give me a flogging. With the rest of the adventure I believe you are as well acquainted as myself."

"I suppose," said I, "you missed the spot, in the first attempt at digging, through Jupiter's stupidity in letting the bug fall through the right instead of through the left eye of the skull."

"Precisely. This mistake made a difference of about two inches and a half in the 'shot'—that is to say, in the position of the peg nearest the tree; and had the treasure been *beneath* the 'shot,' the error would have been of little moment; but 'the shot,' together with the nearest point of the tree, were merely two points for the establishment of a line of direction; of course the error, however trivial in the beginning, increased as we proceeded with the line, and, by the time we had gone fifty feet, threw us quite off the scent. But for my deep-seated convictions that treasure was here somewhere actually buried, we might have had all our labor in vain."

"I presume the fancy of *the skull*—of letting fall a bullet through the skull's eye—was suggested to Kidd by the piratical flag. No doubt he felt a kind of poetical consistency in recovering his money through this ominous insignium."

"Perhaps so; still, I cannot help thinking that common-sense had quite as much to do with the matter as poetical consistency. To be visible from the Devil's seat, it was necessary that the object, if small, should be *white;* and there is nothing like your human skull for retaining and even increasing its whiteness under exposure to all vicissitudes of weather."

"But your grandiloquence, and your conduct in swinging the beetle —how excessively odd! I was sure you were mad. And why did you insist on letting fall the bug, instead of a bullet, from the skull?"

"Why, to be frank, I felt somewhat annoyed by your evident suspicions touching my sanity, and so resolved to punish you quietly, in my own way, by a little bit of sober mystification. For this reason I swung the beetle, and for this reason I let it fall from the tree. An observation of yours about its great weight suggested the latter idea."

"Yes, I perceive; and now there is only one point which puzzles me. What are we to make of the skeletons found in the hole?"

"That is a question I am no more able to answer than yourself. There seems, however, only one plausible way of accounting for them— and yet it is dreadful to believe in such atrocity as my suggestion would imply. It is clear that Kidd—if Kidd indeed secreted this treasure, which I doubt not—it is clear that he must have had assistance in the labor. But, the worst of this labor concluded, he may have thought it expedient to remove all participants in his secret. Perhaps a couple of blows with a mattock were sufficient, while his coadjutors were busy in the pit; perhaps it required a dozen—who shall tell?"

ABRAHAM LINCOLN (1809-1865)

First Inaugural Address

FELLOW-CITIZENS of the United States, In compliance with a custom as old as the government itself, I appear before you to address you briefly, and to take in your presence the oath prescribed by the Constitution of the United States to be taken by the President "before he enters on the execution of his office."

I do not consider it necessary at present for me to discuss those matters of administration about which there is no special anxiety or excitement.

Apprehension seems to exist among the people of the Southern States that by the accession of a Republican administration their property and their peace and personal security are to be endangered. There has never been any reasonable cause for such apprehension. Indeed, the most ample evidence to the contrary has all the while existed and been open to their inspection. It is found in nearly all the published speeches of him who now addresses you. I do but quote from one of those speeches when I declare that "I have no purpose, directly or indirectly, to interfere with the institution of slavery in the States where it exists. I believe I have no lawful right to do so, and I have no inclination to do so." Those who nominated and elected me did so with full knowledge that I had made this and many similar declarations, and had never recanted them. And, more than this, they placed in the platform for my acceptance, and as a law to themselves and to me, the clear and emphatic resolution which I now read:—

"*Resolved,* That the maintenance inviolate of the rights of the States, and especially the right of each State to order and control its own domestic institutions according to its own judgment exclusively, is essential to that balance of power on which the perfection and endurance of our political fabric depend, and we denounce the lawless invasion by armed force of the soil of any State or Territory, no matter under what pretext, as among the gravest of crimes."

I now reiterate these sentiments; and, in doing so, I only press upon the public attention the most conclusive evidence of which the case is susceptible, that the property, peace, and security of no section are to be in any wise endangered by the now incoming administration. I add, too, that all the protection which, consistently with the Constitution and the laws, can be given, will be cheerfully given to all the States when lawfully demanded, for whatever cause—as cheerfully to one section as to another.

There is much controversy about the delivering up of fugitives from service or labor. The clause I now read is as plainly written in the Constitution as any other of its provisions:—

"No person held to service or labour in one State, under the laws thereof, escaping into another, shall in consequence of any law or regulation therein be discharged from such service or labour, but shall be delivered up on claim of the party to whom such service or labour may be due."

It is scarcely questioned that this provision was intended by those who made it for the reclaiming of what we call fugitive slaves; and the intention of the lawgiver is the law. All members of Congress swear their support to the whole Constitution—to this provision as much as to any other. To the proposition, then, that slaves whose cases come within the terms of this clause "shall be delivered up," their oaths are unanimous. Now, if they would make the effort in good temper, could they not with nearly equal unanimity frame and pass a law by means of which to keep good that unanimous oath?

There is some difference of opinion whether this clause should be enforced by national or by State authority; but surely that difference is not a very material one. If the slave is to be surrendered, it can be of but little consequence to him or to others by which authority it is done. And should any one in any case be content that his oath shall go unkept on a merely unsubstantial controversy as to how it shall be kept?

Again, in any law upon this subject, ought not all the safeguards of liberty known in civilized and humane jurisprudence to be introduced, so that a free man be not, in any case, surrendered as a slave? And might it not be well at the same time to provide by law for the enforcement of that clause in the Constitution which guarantees that "the citizen of each State shall be entitled to all privileges and immunities of citizens in the several States"?

I take the official oath to-day with no mental reservations, and with no purpose to construe the Constitution or laws by any hypercritical rules. And while I do not choose now to specify particular acts of Congress as proper to be enforced, I do suggest that it will be much safer for all, both in official and private stations, to conform to and abide by all those acts which stand unrepealed, than to violate any of them, trusting to find impunity in having them held to be unconstitutional.

It is seventy-two years since the first inauguration of a President under our National Constitution. During that period fifteen different and greatly distinguished citizens have, in succession, administered the executive branch of the government. They have conducted it through many perils, and generally with great success. Yet, with all this scope of precedent, I now enter upon the same task for the brief constitutional term of four years under great and peculiar difficulty. A disruption of the Federal Union, heretofore only menaced, is now formidably attempted.

I hold that, in contemplation of universal law and of the Constitution, the Union of these States is perpetual. Perpetuity is implied, if not expressed, in the fundamental law of all national governments. It is safe to assert that no government proper ever had a provision in its organic law for its own termination. Continue to execute all the express provisions of our National Constitution, and the Union will endure for ever—it being impossible to destroy it except by some action not provided for in the instrument itself.

Again, if the United States be not a government proper, but an association of States in the nature of contract merely, can it, as a contract, be peaceably unmade by less than all the parties who made it? One party to a contract may violate it—break it, so to speak; but does it not require all to lawfully rescind it?

Descending from these general principles, we find the proposition that in legal contemplation the Union is perpetual confirmed by the history of the Union itself. The Union is much older than the Constitution. It was formed, in fact, by the Articles of Association in 1774.

It was matured and continued by the Declaration of Independence in 1776. It was further matured, and the faith of all the then thirteen States expressly plighted and engaged that it should be perpetual, by the Articles of Confederation in 1778. And, finally, in 1787 one of the declared objects for ordaining and establishing the Constitution was "to form a more perfect Union."

But if the destruction of the Union by one or by a part only of the States be lawfully possible, the Union is less perfect than before the Constitution, having lost the vital element of perpetuity.

It follows from these views that no State upon its own mere motion can lawfully get out of the Union; that resolves and ordinances to that effect are legally void; and that acts of violence, within any State or States, against the authority of the United States, are insurrectionary or revolutionary, according to circumstances.

I therefore consider that, in view of the Constitution and the laws, the Union is unbroken; and to the extent of my ability I shall take care, as the Constitution itself expressly enjoins upon me, that the laws of the Union be faithfully executed in all the States. Doing this I deem to be only a simple duty on my part; and I shall perform it so far as practicable, unless my rightful masters, the American people, shall withhold the requisite means, or in some authoritative manner direct the contrary. I trust this will not be regarded as a menace, but only as the declared purpose of the Union that it will constitutionally defend and maintain itself.

In doing this there needs to be no bloodshed or violence; and there shall be none, unless it be forced upon the national authority. The power confided to me will be used to hold, occupy, and possess the property and places belonging to the government, and to collect the duties and imposts; but beyond what may be necessary for these objects, there will be no invasion, no using of force against or among the people anywhere. Where hostility to the United States, in any interior locality, shall be so great and universal as to prevent competent resident citizens from holding the Federal offices, there will be no attempt to force obnoxious strangers among the people for that object. While the strict legal right may exist in the government to enforce the exercise of these offices, the attempt to do so would be so irritating, and so nearly impracticable withal, that I deem it better to forego for the time the uses of such offices.

The mails, unless repelled, will continue to be furnished in all parts of the Union. So far as possible, the people everywhere shall have that sense of perfect security which is most favourable to calm thought and reflection. The course here indicated will be followed unless current events and experience shall show a modification or change to be proper, and in every case and exigency my best discretion will be exercised according to circumstances actually existing, and with a view and a hope of a peaceful solution of the national troubles and the restoration of fraternal sympathies and affections.

That there are persons in one section or another who seek to destroy the Union at all events, and are glad of any pretext to do it, I will neither affirm nor deny; but if there be such, I need address no word to them. To those, however, who really love the Union may I not speak?

Before entering upon so grave a matter as the destruction of our national fabric, with all its benefits, its memories, and its hopes, would it not be wise to ascertain precisely why we do it? Will you hazard so desperate a step while there is any possibility that any portion of the ills you fly from have no real existence? Will you, while the certain ills you fly to are greater than all the real ones you fly from—will you risk the commission of so fearful a mistake?

All profess to be content in the Union if all constitutional rights can be maintained. Is it true, then, that any right, plainly written in the Constitution, has been denied? I think not. Happily the human mind is so constituted that no party can reach to the audacity of doing this. Think, if you can, of a single instance in which a plainly written provision of the Constitution has ever been denied. If by the mere force of numbers a majority should deprive a minority of any clearly written constitutional right, it might, in a moral point of view, justify revolution —certainly would if such a right were a vital one. But such is not our case. All the vital rights of minorities and of individuals are so plainly assured to them by affirmations and negations, guaranties and pro- hibitions, in the Constitution, that controversies never arise concerning them. But no organic law can ever be framed with a provision specifically applicable to every question which may occur in practical administration. No foresight can anticipate, nor any document of reasonable length contain, express provisions for all possible questions. Shall fugitives from labor be surrendered by national or by State authority? The Constitution does not expressly say. *May* Congress prohibit slavery in the Territories? The Constitution does not expressly say. *Must* Con- gress protect slavery in the Territories? The Constitution does not ex- pressly say.

From questions of this class spring all our constitutional controversies, and we divide upon them into majorities and minorities. If the minority will not acquiesce, the majority must, or the government must cease.

There is no other alternative; for continuing the government is acquiescence on one side or the other.

If a minority in such case will secede rather than acquiesce, they make a precedent which in turn will divide and ruin them; for a minority of their own will secede from them whenever a majority refuses to be controlled by such minority. For instance, why may not any portion of a new confederacy a year or two hence arbitrarily secede again, precisely as portions of the present Union now claim to secede from it? All who cherish disunion sentiments are now being educated to the exact temper of doing this.

Is there such perfect identity of interests among the States to compose a new Union, as to produce harmony only, and prevent renewed secession?

Plainly, the central idea of secession is the essence of anarchy. A majority held in restraint by constitutional checks and limitations, and always changing easily with deliberate changes of popular opinions and sentiments, is the only true sovereign of a free people. Whoever rejects it does, of necessity, fly to anarchy or to despotism. Unanimity is impossible; the rule of a minority, as a permanent arrangement, is wholly inadmissible; so that, rejecting the majority principle, anarchy or despotism in some form is all that is left.

I do not forget the position, assumed by some, that constitutional questions are to be decided by the Supreme Court; nor do I deny that such decisions must be binding, in any case, upon the parties to a suit, as to the object of that suit, while they are also entitled to very high respect and consideration in all parallel cases by all other departments of the government. And while it is obviously possible that such decision may be erroneous in any given case, still the evil effect following it, being limited to that particular case, with the chance that it may be overruled and never become a precedent for other cases, can better be borne than could the evils of a different practice. At the same time, the candid citizen must confess that if the policy of the government, upon vital questions affecting the whole people, is to be irrevocably fixed by decisions of the Supreme Court, the instant they are made, in ordinary litigation between parties in personal actions, the people will have ceased to be their own rulers, having to that extent practically resigned their government into the hands of that eminent tribunal. Nor is there in this view any assault upon the court or the judges. It is a duty from which they may not shrink to decide cases properly brought before them, and it is no fault of theirs if others seek to turn their decisions to political purposes.

One section of our country believes slavery is right, and ought to be extended, while the other believes it is wrong, and ought not to be extended. This is the only substantial dispute. The fugitive-slave clause of the Constitution, and the law for the suppression of the foreign slave-trade, are each as well enforced, perhaps, as any law can ever be in a community where the moral sense of the people imperfectly supports the law itself. The great body of the people abide by the dry legal obligation in both cases, and a few break over in each. This, I think, cannot be perfectly cured; and it would be worse in both cases after the separation of the sections than before. The foreign slave-trade, now imperfectly suppressed, would be ultimately revived, without restrictions, in one section, while fugitive slaves, now only partially surrendered, would not be surrendered at all by the other.

Physically speaking, we cannot separate. We cannot remove our respective sections from each other, nor build an impassable wall between them. A husband and wife may be divorced, and go out of the presence and beyond the reach of each other; but the different parts of our country cannot do this. They cannot but remain face to face, and intercourse, either amicable or hostile, must continue between them. Is it possible, then, to make that intercourse more advantageous or more satisfactory after separation than before? Can aliens make treaties easier than friends can make laws? Can treaties be more faithfully enforced between aliens than laws can among friends? Suppose you go to war, you cannot fight always; and when, after much loss on both sides, and no gain on either, you cease fighting, the identical old questions as to terms of intercourse are again upon you.

This country, with its institutions, belongs to the people who inhabit it. Whenever they shall grow weary of the existing government, they can exercise their constitutional right of amending it, or their revolutionary right to dismember or overthrow it. I cannot be ignorant of the fact that many worthy and patriotic citizens are desirous of having the National Constitution amended. While I make no recommendation of amendments, I fully recognize the rightful authority of the people over the whole subject, to be exercised in either of the modes prescribed in the instrument itself; and I should, under existing circumstances, favor rather than oppose a fair opportunity being afforded to the people to act upon it. I will venture to add that to me the convention mode seems preferable, in that it allows amendments to originate with the people themselves, instead of only permitting them to take or reject propositions originated by others not especially chosen for the purpose, and which might not be precisely such as they would wish to either accept or refuse.

I understand a proposed amendment to the Constitution—which amendment, however, I have not seen—has passed Congress, to the effect that the Federal Government shall never interfere with the domestic institutions of the States, including that of persons held to service. To avoid misconstruction of what I have said, I depart from my purpose not to speak of particular amendments so far as to say that, holding such a provision to now be implied constitutional law, I have no objection to its being made express and irrevocable.

The chief magistrate derives all his authority from the people, and they have conferred none upon him to fix terms for the separation of the States. The people themselves can do this also if they choose; but the Executive, as such, has nothing to do with it. His duty is to administer the present government, as it came to his hands, and to transmit it, unimpaired by him, to his successor.

Why should there not be a patient confidence in the ultimate justice of the people? Is there any better or equal hope in the world? In our present differences, is either party without faith of being in the right? If the Almighty Ruler of Nations, with his eternal truth and justice, be on your side of the North, or on yours of the South, that truth and that justice will surely prevail by the judgment of this great tribunal of the American people.

By the frame of the government under which we live, this same people have wisely given their public servants but little power for mischief; and have, with equal wisdom, provided for the return of that little to their own hands at very short intervals. While the people retain their virtue and vigilance, no administration, by any extreme of wickedness or folly, can very seriously injure the government in the short space of four years.

My countrymen, one and all, think calmly and well upon this whole subject. Nothing valuable can be lost by taking time. If there be an object to hurry any of you in hot haste to a step which you would never take deliberately, that object will be frustrated by taking time; but no good object can be frustrated by it. Such of you as are now dissatisfied still have the old Constitution unimpaired, and, on the sensitive point, the laws of your own framing under it; while the new administration will have no immediate power, if it would, to change either. If it were admitted that you who are dissatisfied hold the right side in the dispute, there still is no single good reason for precipitate action. Intelligence, patriotism, Christianity, and a firm reliance on Him who has never yet forsaken this favored land, are still competent to adjust in the best way all our present difficulty.

In your hands, my dissatisfied fellow-countrymen, and not in mine, is the momentous issue of civil war. The government will not assail you. You can have no conflict without being yourselves the aggressors. You have no oath registered in heaven to destroy the government, while I shall have the most solemn one to "preserve, protect, and defend it."

I am loath to close. We are not enemies, but friends. We must not be enemies. Though passion may have strained, it must not break our bonds of affection. The mystic chords of memory, stretching from every battlefield and patriot grave to every living heart and hearthstone all over this broad land, will yet swell the chorus of the Union when again touched, as surely they will be, by the better angels of our nature.

Letter to Horace Greeley, August 22, 1862

I HAVE just read yours of the 19th instant, addressed to myself through the "New York Tribune."

If there be in it any statements or assumptions of fact which I may know to be erroneous, I do not now and here controvert them.

If there be in it any inferences which I may believe to be falsely drawn, I do not now and here argue against them.

If there be perceptible in it an impatient and dictatorial tone, I waive it, in deference to an old friend whose heart I have always supposed to be right.

As to the policy I "seem to be pursuing," as you say, I have not meant to leave any one in doubt. I would save the Union. I would save it in the shortest way under the Constitution.

The sooner the national authority can be restored, the nearer the Union will be,—the Union as it was.

If there be those who would not save the Union unless they could at the same time save slavery, I do not agree with them.

If there be those who would not save the Union unless they could at the same time destroy slavery, I do not agree with them.

My paramount object in this struggle is to save the Union, and not either to save or to destroy slavery.

If I could save the Union without freeing any slave, I would do it; if I could save it by freeing all the slaves, I would do it; and if I could save it by freeing some and leaving others alone, I would also do that.

What I do about slavery and the colored race, I do because I believe it helps to save the Union; and what I forbear, I forbear because I do not believe it would help to save the Union.

I shall do less whenever I shall believe that what I am doing hurts the cause; and I shall do more whenever I shall believe doing more will help the cause.

I shall try to correct errors where shown to be errors, and I shall adopt new views as fast as they shall appear to be true views.

I have here stated my purpose according to my views of official duty, and I intend no modification of my oft-expressed personal wish that all men everywhere could be free.

Letter to James C. Conkling, August 26, 1863

Your letter inviting me to attend a mass meeting of unconditional Union men, to be held at the capital of Illinois on the third day of September, has been received. It would be very agreeable to me to thus meet my old friends at my own home, but I cannot just now be absent from here so long as a visit there would require.

The meeting is to be of all those who maintain unconditional devotion to the Union; and I am sure my old political friends will thank me for tendering, as I do, the nation's gratitude to those and other noble men whom no partisan malice or partisan hope can make false to the nation's life.

There are those who are dissatisfied with me. To such I would say: You desire peace, and you blame me that we do not have it. But how can we attain it? There are but three conceivable ways. First, to suppress the rebellion by force of arms. This I am trying to do. Are you for it? If you are, so far we are agreed. If you are not for it, a second way is to give up the Union. I am against this. Are you for it? If you are, you should say so plainly. If you are not for force, nor yet for dissolution, there only remains some imaginable compromise. I do not believe any compromise embracing the maintenance of the Union is now possible. All I learn leads to a directly opposite belief. The strength of the rebellion is its military, its army. That army dominates all the country and all the people within its range. Any offer of terms made by any man or men within that range, in opposition to that army, is simply nothing for the present, because such man or men have no power whatever to enforce their side of a compromise, if one were made with them.

To illustrate: Suppose refugees from the South and peace men of the North get together in convention, and frame and proclaim a compromise embracing a restoration of the Union. In what way can that compromise be used to keep Lee's army out of Pennsylvania? Meade's army can keep Lee's out of Pennsylvania, and, I think, can ultimately drive it out of existence. But no paper compromise, to which the controllers of

Lee's army are not agreed, can at all affect that army. In an effort at such compromise we should waste time which the enemy would improve to our disadvantage; and that would be all. A compromise, to be effective, must be made either with those who control the rebel army, or with the people first liberated from the domination of that army by the success of our own army. Now, allow me to assure you that no word or intimation from that rebel army, or from any of the men controlling it, in relation to any peace compromise, has ever come to my knowledge or belief. All charges and insinuations to the contrary are deceptive and groundless. And I promise you that if any such proposition shall hereafter come, it shall not be rejected and kept a secret from you. I freely acknowledge myself the servant of the people, according to the bond of service,—the United States Constitution,—and that, as such, I am responsible to them.

But to be plain. You are dissatisfied with me about the negro. Quite likely there is a difference of opinion between you and myself upon that subject. I certainly wish that all men could be free, while I suppose you do not. Yet I have neither adopted nor proposed any measure which is not consistent with even your views, provided you are for the Union. I suggested compensated emancipation, to which you replied, you wished not to be taxed to buy negroes. But I had not asked you to be taxed to buy negroes, except in such way as to save you from greater taxation to save the Union exclusively by other means.

You dislike the Emancipation Proclamation, and perhaps would have it retracted. You say it is unconstitutional. I think differently. I think the Constitution invests its commander-in-chief with the law of war in time of war. The most that can be said—if so much—is that slaves are property. Is there, has there ever been, any question that, by the law of war, property, both of enemies and friends, may be taken when needed? And is it not needed whenever taking it helps us or hurts the enemy? Armies the world over destroy enemies' property when they cannot use it, and even destroy their own to keep it from the enemy. Civilized belligerents do all in their power to help themselves or hurt the enemy, except a few things regarded as barbarous or cruel. Among the exceptions are the massacre of vanquished foes and non-combatants, male and female.

But the proclamation, as law, either is valid or is not valid. If it is not valid, it needs no retraction. If it is valid, it cannot be retracted any more than the dead can be brought to life. Some of you profess to think its retraction would operate favorably for the Union. Why better after the retraction than before the issue? There was more than a year and a half of trial to suppress the rebellion before the proclamation issued, the last one hundred days of which passed under an explicit notice that it was coming, unless averted by those in revolt returning to their allegiance. The war has certainly progressed as favorably for us since the issue of the proclamation as before. I know, as fully as one can know the opinions of others, that some of the commanders of our armies in the field who have given us our most important successes, believe the emancipation policy and the use of colored troops constitute the heaviest blow yet dealt to the rebellion, and that at least one of these important successes could not have been achieved when it was but for the aid of black soldiers. Among the commanders holding these views are some who have never had any affinity with what is called Abolitionism or with Republican party politics, but who hold them purely as military opinions. I submit these opinions as being entitled to some weight against the objections often urged, that emancipation and arming the blacks are unwise as military measures, and were not adopted as such in good faith.

You say you will not fight to free negroes. Some of them seem willing to fight for you; but no matter. Fight you, then, exclusively to save the Union. I issued the proclamation on purpose to aid you in saving the Union. Whenever you shall have conquered all resistance to the Union, if I shall urge you to continue fighting, it will be an apt time then for you to declare you will not fight to free negroes.

I thought that in your struggle for the Union, to whatever extent the negroes should cease helping the enemy, to that extent it weakened the enemy in his resistance to you. Do you think differently? I thought that whatever negroes could be got to do as soldiers leaves just so much less for white soldiers to do in saving the Union. Does it appear otherwise to you? But negroes, like other people, act upon motives. Why should they do anything for us, if we will do nothing for them? If they stake their lives for us, they must be prompted by the strongest motive, even the promise of freedom. And the promise being made, must be kept.

The signs look better. The Father of Waters again goes unvexed to the sea. Thanks to the great Northwest for it. Nor yet wholly to them. Three hundred miles up they met New England, Empire, Keystone, and Jersey hewing their way right and left. The sunny South, too, in more colors than one, also lent a hand. On the spot, their part of the history was jotted down in black and white. The job was a great national one, and let none be banned who bore an honorable part in it. And while those who cleared the great river may well be proud, even that is not all. It is hard to say that anything has been more bravely and well done than at Antietam, Murfreesboro, Gettysburg, and on many fields of lesser note. Nor must Uncle Sam's web-feet be forgotten. At all the watery margins they have been present. Not only on the deep sea, the broad bay, and the rapid river, but also up the narrow, muddy bayou, and wherever the ground was a little damp, they have been and made their tracks. Thanks to all,—for the great Republic, for the principle it lives by and keeps alive, for man's vast future,—thanks to all.

Peace does not appear so distant as it did. I hope it will come soon, and come to stay; and so come as to be worth the keeping in all future time. It will then have been proved that among freemen there can be no successful appeal from the ballot to the bullet, and that they who take such appeal are sure to lose their case and pay the cost. And then there will be some black men who can remember that with silent tongue, and clenched teeth, and steady eye, and well-poised bayonet, they have helped mankind on to this great consummation, while I fear there will be some white ones unable to forget that with malignant heart and deceitful speech they strove to hinder it.

Still, let us not be over-sanguine of a speedy, final triumph. Let us be quite sober. Let us diligently apply the means, never doubting that a just God, in His own good time, will give us the rightful result.

Address at the Dedication of the National Cemetery at Gettysburg

FOURSCORE and seven years ago our fathers brought forth upon this continent a new nation, conceived in liberty, and dedicated to the proposition that all men are created equal.

Now we are engaged in a great civil war, testing whether that nation, or any nation so conceived and so dedicated, can long endure. We are met on a great battle-field of that war. We have come to dedicate a portion of that field as a final resting-place for those who here gave their lives that that nation might live. It is altogether fitting and proper that we should do this.

But in a larger sense we cannot dedicate, we cannot consecrate, we cannot hallow this ground. The brave men, living and dead, who struggled here, have consecrated it far above our power to add or detract. The world will little note nor long remember what we say here, but it can never forget what they did here. It is for us, the living, rather, to be dedicated here to the unfinished work which they who fought here have thus far so nobly advanced. It is rather for us to be here dedicated to the great task remaining before us; that from these honored dead we take increased devotion to that cause for which they gave the last full measure of devotion; that we here highly resolve that these dead shall not have died in vain; that this nation, under God, shall have a new birth of freedom; and that government of the people, by the people, and for the people, shall not perish from the earth.

Letter to Mrs. Bixby, of Boston, November 21, 1864

DEAR MADAM, I have been shown in the files of the War Department a statement of the Adjutant-General of Massachusetts that you are the mother of five sons who have died gloriously on the field of battle. I feel how weak and fruitless must be any words of mine which should attempt to beguile you from the grief of a loss so overwhelming. But I cannot refrain from tendering to you the consolation that may be found in the thanks of the Republic they died to save. I pray that our heavenly Father may assuage the anguish of your bereavement, and leave you only the cherished memory of the loved and lost, and the solemn pride that must be yours to have laid so costly a sacrifice upon the altar of freedom.

Yours very sincerely and respectfully,

ABRAHAM LINCOLN.

Second Inaugural Address

FELLOW-COUNTRYMEN, At this second appearance to take the oath of the Presidential office, there is less occasion for an extended address than there was at the first. Then a statement, somewhat in detail, of a course to be pursued, seemed fitting and proper. Now, at the expiration of four years, during which public declarations have been constantly called forth on every point and phase of the great contest which still absorbs the attention and engrosses the energies of the nation, little that is new could be presented. The progress of our arms, upon which all else chiefly depends, is as well known to the public as to myself; and it is, I trust, reasonably satisfactory and encouraging to all. With high hope for the future, no prediction in regard to it is ventured.

On the occasion corresponding to this four years ago, all thoughts were anxiously directed to an impending civil war. All dreaded it,— all sought to avert it. While the inaugural address was being delivered from this place, devoted altogether to saving the Union without war, in-surgent agents were in the city seeking to destroy it without war,—seeking to dissolve the Union, and divide effects, by negotiation. Both parties deprecated war; but one of them would make war rather than let the nation survive, and the other would accept war rather than let it perish. And the war came.

One-eighth of the whole population were colored slaves, not distributed generally over the Union, but localized in the southern part of it. These slaves constituted a peculiar and powerful interest. All knew that this interest was, somehow, the cause of the war. To strengthen, perpetuate, and extend this interest was the object for which the insurgents would rend the Union, even by war; while the government claimed no right to do more than to restrict the territorial enlargement of it.

Neither party expected for the war the magnitude or the duration which it has already attained. Neither anticipated that the cause of the conflict might cease with, or even before, the conflict itself should cease. Each looked for an easier triumph and a result less fundamental and astounding. Both read the same Bible, and pray to the same God; and each invokes His aid against the other. It may seem strange that any men should dare to ask a just God's assistance in wringing their bread from the sweat of other men's faces; but let us judge not, that we be not judged. The prayers of both could not be answered—that of neither has been answered fully.

The Almighty has His own purposes. "Woe unto the world because of offences! for it must needs be that offences come; but woe to that man by whom the offence cometh." If we shall suppose that American slavery is one of those offences which, in the Providence of God, must needs come, but which having continued through His appointed time, He now wills to remove, and that He gives to both North and South this terrible war, as the woe due to those by whom the offence came, shall we discern therein any departure from those divine attributes which the believers in a living God always ascribe to Him? Fondly do we hope—fervently do we pray—that this mighty scourge of war may speedily pass away. Yet, if God wills that it continue until all the wealth piled up by the bondman's two hundred and fifty years of unrequited toil shall be sunk, and until every drop of blood drawn by the lash shall be paid by another drawn with the sword, as was said three thousand years ago, so still it must be said, "The judgments of the Lord are true and righteous altogether."

With malice toward none; with charity for all; with firmness in the right, as God gives us to see the right,—let us strive on to finish the work we are in: to bind up the nation's wounds; to care for him who shall have borne the battle, and for his widow and his orphan; to do all which may achieve and cherish a just and lasting peace among ourselves, and with all nations.

OLIVER WENDELL HOLMES
(1809-1894)

The Last Leaf

I SAW him once before,
As he passed by the door,
    And again
The pavement stones resound,
As he totters o'er the ground
    With his cane.

They say that in his prime,
Ere the pruning-knife of Time
    Cut him down,
Not a better man was found
By the crier on his round
    Through the town.

But now he walks the streets,
And he looks at all he meets
    Sad and wan,
And he shakes his feeble head,
That it seems as if he said,
    "They are gone."

The mossy marbles rest
On the lips that he has pressed
    In their bloom,
And the names he loved to hear
Have been carved for many a year
    On the tomb.

My grandmamma has said—
Poor old lady, she is dead
    Long ago—
That he had a Roman nose,
And his cheek was like a rose
    In the snow.

But now his nose is thin,
And it rests upon his chin
    Like a staff,
And a crook is in his back,
And a melancholy crack
    In his laugh.

I know it is a sin
For me to sit and grin
    At him here;

But the old three-cornered hat,
And the breeches, and all that,
    Are so queer!

And if I should live to be
The last leaf upon the tree
    In the spring,
Let them smile, as I do now,
At the old, forsaken bough
    Where I cling.

The Chambered Nautilus

THIS is the ship of pearl, which, poets
        feign,
    Sails the unshadowed main,—
    The venturous bark that flings
On the sweet summer wind its purpled
        wings
In gulfs enchanted, where the Siren sings,
    And coral reefs lie bare,
Where the cold sea-maids rise to sun
        their streaming hair.

Its webs of living gauze no more unfurl;
    Wrecked is the ship of pearl!
    And every chambered cell,
Where its dim dreaming life was wont to
        dwell,
As the frail tenant shaped his growing
        shell,
    Before thee lies revealed,—
Its irised ceiling rent, its sunless crypt
        unsealed!

Year after year beheld the silent toil
    That spread his lustrous coil;
    Still, as the spiral grew,
He left the past year's dwelling for the
        new,
Stole with soft step its shining archway
        through,
    Built up its idle door,
Stretched in his last-found home, and
        knew the old no more.

Thanks for the heavenly message brought
    by thee,
    Child of the wandering sea,
    Cast from her lap, forlorn!
From thy dead lips a clearer note is born
Than ever Triton blew from wreathèd
    horn!
    While on mine ear it rings,
Through the deep caves of thought I
    hear a voice that sings:

Build thee more stately mansions, O my
    soul,
    As the swift seasons roll!
    Leave thy low-vaulted past!
Let each new temple, nobler than the last,
Shut thee from heaven with a dome more
    vast,
    Till thou at length art free,
Leaving thine outgrown shell by life's un-
    resting sea!

The Broomstick Train

Look out! Look out, boys! Clear the
    track!
The witches are here! They've all come
    back!
They hanged them high,—No use! No
    use!
What cares a witch for a hangman's
    noose?
They buried them deep, but they wouldn't
    lie still,
For cats and witches are hard to kill;
They swore they shouldn't and wouldn't
    die,—
Books said they did, but they lie! they lie!
—A couple of hundred years, or so,
They had knocked about in the world
    below,
When an Essex Deacon dropped in to
    call,
And a homesick feeling seized them all;
For he came from a place they knew full
    well,
And many a tale he had to tell.

They long to visit the haunts of men,
To see the old dwellings they knew again,
And ride on their broomsticks all around
Their wide domain of unhallowed
    ground.

In Essex county there's many a roof
Well known to him of the cloven hoof;
The small square windows are full in
    view
Which the midnight hags went sailing
    through,
On their well-trained broomsticks mount-
    ed high,
Seen like shadows against the sky;
Crossing the track of owls and bats,
Hugging before them their coal-black
    cats.

Well did they know, those gray old wives,
The sights we see in our daily drives:
Shimmer of lake and shine of sea,
Brown's bare hill with its lonely tree,
(It wasn't then as we see it now,
With one scant scalp-lock to shade its
    brow;)
Dusky nooks in the Essex woods,
Dark, dim, Dante-like solitudes,
Where the tree-toad watches the sinuous
    snake
Glide through his forests of fern and
    brake;
Ipswich River; its old stone bridge;
Far off Andover's Indian Ridge,
And many a scene where history tells
Some shadow of bygone terror dwells,—
Of "Norman's Woe" with its tale of
    dread,
Of the Screeching Woman of Marble-
    head,
(The fearful story that turns men pale:
Don't bid me tell it,—my speech would
    fail.)

Who would not, will not, if he can,
Bathe in the breezes of fair Cape Ann,—
Rest in the bowers her bays enfold,
Loved by the sachems and squaws of old?

Home where the white magnolias bloom,
Sweet with the bayberry's chaste per-
    fume,
Hugged by the woods and kissed by the
    sea!
Where is the Eden like to thee?

For that "couple of hundred years, or
    so,"
There had been no peace in the world
    below;
The witches still grumbling, "It isn't
    fair;
Come, give us a taste of the upper air!
We've had enough of your sulphur
    springs,
And the evil odor that round them clings;
We long for a drink that is cool and
    nice,—
Great buckets of water with Wenham
    ice;
We've served you well up-stairs, you
    know;
You're a good old—fellow—come, let us
    go!"

I don't feel sure of his being good,
But he happened to be in a pleasant
    mood,—
As fiends with their skins full sometimes
    are,—
(He'd been drinking with "roughs" at a
    Boston bar.)
So what does he do but up and shout
To a graybeard turnkey, "Let 'em out!"

To mind his orders was all he knew;
The gates swung open, and out they flew.
"Where are our broomsticks?" the bel-
    dams cried.
"Here are your broomsticks," an imp
    replied.
"They've been in—the place, you know—
    so long
They smell of brimstone uncommon
    strong;
But they've gained by being left alone,—
Just look, and you'll see how tall they've
    grown."

—"And where is my cat?" a vixen
    squalled.
"Yes, where are our cats?" the witches
    bawled,
And began to call them all by name:
As fast as they called the cats, they came:
There was bob-tailed Tommy and long-
    tailed Tim,
And wall-eyed Jacky and green-eyed Jim,
And splay-foot Benny and slim-legged
    Beau,
And Skinny and Squally, and Jerry and
    Joe,
And many another that came at call,—
It would take too long to count them all.
All black,—one could hardly tell which
    was which.
But every cat knew his own old witch;
And she knew hers as hers knew her,—
Ah, didn't they curl their tails and purr!

No sooner the withered hags were free
Than out they swarmed for a midnight
    spree;
I couldn't tell all they did in rhymes,
But the Essex people had dreadful times.
The Swampscott fishermen still relate
How a strange sea-monster stole their
    bait;
How their nets were tangled in loops and
    knots,
And they found dead crabs in their
    lobster-pots.
Poor Danvers grieved for her blasted
    crops,
And Wilmington mourned over mil-
    dewed hops.
A blight played havoc with Beverly
    beans,—
It was all the work of those hateful
    queans!
A dreadful panic began at "Pride's,"
Where the witches stopped in their mid-
    night rides,
And there rose strange rumors and vague
    alarms
'Mid the peaceful dwellers at Beverly
    Farms.

Now when the Boss of the Beldams
    found
That without his leave they were ramp-
    ing round,
He called,—they could hear him twenty
    miles,
From Chelsea beach to the Misery Isles;
The deafest old granny knew his tone
Without the trick of the telephone.
"Come here, you witches! Come here!"
    says he,—
"At your games of old, without asking
    me!
I'll give you a little job to do
That will keep you stirring, you godless
    crew!"

They came, of course, at their master's
    call,
The witches, the broomsticks, the cats,
    and all;
He led the hags to a railway train
The horses were trying to drag in vain.
"Now, then," says he, "you've had your
    fun,
And here are the cars you've got to run.
The driver may just unhitch his team,
We don't want horses, we don't want
    steam;

You may keep your old black cats to hug,
But the loaded train you've got to lug."

Since then on many a car you'll see
A broomstick plain as plain can be;
On every stick there's a witch astride,—
The string you see to her leg is tied.
She will do a mischief if she can,
But the string is held by a careful man,
And whenever the evil-minded witch
Would cut some caper, he gives a twitch.
As for the hag, you can't see her,
But hark! you can hear her black cat's
    purr,
And now and then, as a car goes by,
You may catch a gleam from her wicked
    eye.

Often you've looked on a rushing train,
But just what moved it was not so plain.
It couldn't be those wires above,
For they could neither pull nor shove;
Where was the motor that made it go
You couldn't guess, *but now you know.*

Remember my rhymes when you ride
    again
On the rattling rail by the broomstick
    train!

From THE AUTOCRAT OF THE BREAKFAST-TABLE

My Last Walk with the Schoolmistress

I CAN'T say just how many walks she and I had taken together
before this one. I found the effect of going out every morning was
decidedly favorable on her health. Two pleasing dimples, the places for
which were just marked when she came, played, shadowy, in her freshening cheeks when she smiled and nodded good-morning to me from
the schoolhouse-steps.

I am afraid I did the greater part of the talking. At any rate, if
I should try to report all that I said during the first-half dozen walks
we took together, I fear that I might receive a gentle hint from my
friends the publishers, that a separate volume, at my own risk and
expense, would be the proper method of bringing them before the public.

—I would have a woman as true as Death. At the first real lie which works from the heart outward, she should be tenderly chloroformed into a better world, where she can have an angel for a governess, and feed on strange fruits which will make her all over again, even to her bones and marrow.—Whether gifted with the accident of beauty or not, she should have been moulded in the rose-red clay of Love, before the breath of life made a moving mortal of her. Love-capacity is a congenital endowment; and I think, after a while, one gets to know the warm-hued natures it belongs to from the pretty pipe-clay counterfeits of them.—Proud she may be, in the sense of respecting herself; but pride, in the sense of contemning others less gifted than herself, deserves the two lowest circles of a vulgar woman's Inferno, where the punishments are Smallpox and Bankruptcy.—She who nips off the end of a brittle courtesy, as one breaks the tip of an icicle, to bestow upon those whom she ought cordially and kindly to recognize, proclaims the fact that she comes not merely of low blood, but of bad blood. Consciousness of unquestioned position makes people gracious in proper measure to all; but if a woman put on airs with her real equals, she has something about herself or her family she is ashamed of, or ought to be. Middle, and more than middle-aged people, who know family histories, generally see through it. An official of standing was rude to me once. Oh, that is the maternal grandfather,—said a wise old friend to me,—he was a boor.—Better too few words, from the woman we love, than too many: while she is silent, Nature is working for her; while she talks, she is working for herself.—Love is sparingly soluble in the words of men; therefore they speak much of it; but one syllable of woman's speech can dissolve more of it than a man's heart can hold.

—Whether I said any or all of these things to the schoolmistress, or not,—whether I stole them out of Lord Bacon,—whether I cribbed them from Balzac,—whether I dipped them from the ocean of Tupperian wisdom,—or whether I have just found them in my head, laid there by that solemn fowl, Experience (who, according to my observation, cackles oftener than she drops real live eggs), I cannot say. Wise men have said more foolish things,—and foolish men, I don't doubt, have said as wise things. Anyhow, the schoolmistress and I had pleasant walks and long talks, all of which I do not feel bound to report.

—You are a stranger to me, Ma'am.—I don't doubt you would like to know all I said to the schoolmistress.—I sha'n't do it;—I had rather get the publishers to return the money you have invested in these pages.

Besides, I have forgotten a good deal of it. I shall tell only what I like of what I remember.

—My idea was, in the first place, to search out the picturesque spots which the city affords a sight of, to those who have eyes. I know a good many, and it was a pleasure to look at them in company with my young friend. There were the shrubs and flowers in the Franklin-Place front-yards or borders: Commerce is just putting his granite foot upon them. Then there are certain small seraglio-gardens, into which one can get a peep through the crevices of high fences,—one in Myrtle Street, or at the back of it,—here and there one at the North and South ends. Then the great elms in Essex Street. Then the stately horse-chestnuts in that vacant lot in Chambers Street, which hold their out-spread hands over your head (as I said in my poem the other day), and look as if they were whispering, "May grace, mercy, and peace be with you!"—and the rest of that benediction. Nay, there are certain patches of ground, which, having lain neglected for a time, Nature, who always has her pockets full of seeds, and holes in all her pockets, has covered with hungry plebeian growths, which fight for life with each other, until some of them get broad-leaved and succulent, and you have a coarse vegetable tapestry which Raphael would not have disdained to spread over the foreground of his masterpiece. The Professor pretends that he found such a one in Charles Street, which, in its dare-devil impudence of rough-and-tumble vegetation, beat the pretty-behaved flower-beds of the Public Garden as ignominiously as a group of young tatterdemalions playing pitch-and-toss beats a row of Sunday-school-boys with their teacher at their head.

But then the Professor has one of his burrows in that region, and puts everything in high colors relating to it. That is his way about everything.—I hold any man cheap,—he said,—of whom nothing stronger can be uttered than that all his geese are swans.—How is that, Professor?—said I;—I should have set you down for one of that sort. —Sir, said he,—I am proud to say, that Nature has so far enriched me, that I cannot own so much as a *duck* without seeing in it as pretty a swan as ever swam the basin in the garden of the Luxembourg. And the Professor showed the whites of his eyes devoutly, like one returning thanks after a dinner of many courses.

I don't know anything sweeter than this leaking in of Nature through all the cracks in the walls and floors of cities. You heap up a million tons of hewn rocks on a square mile or two of earth which was green once. The trees look down from the hill-sides and ask each other, as they stand on tiptoe,—"What are these people about?" And the small herbs at their feet look up and whisper back,—"We will go and see." So the small herbs pack themselves up in the least possible bundles, and wait until the wind steals to them at night and whispers,—"Come with me." Then they go softly with it into the great city,—one to a cleft in the pavement, one to a spout on the roof, one to a seam in the marbles over a rich gentleman's bones, and one to the grave without a stone where nothing but a man is buried,—and there they grow, looking down on the generations of men from mouldy roofs, looking up from between the less-trodden pavements, looking out through iron cemetery-railings. Listen to them, when there is only a light breath stirring, and you will hear them saying to each other,—"Wait awhile!" The words run along the telegraph of those narrow green lines that border the roads leading from the city, until they reach the slope of the hills, and the trees repeat in low murmurs to each other,—"Wait awhile!" By-and-by the flow of life in the streets ebbs, and the old leafy inhabitants—the smaller tribes always in front—saunter in, one by one, very careless seemingly, but very tenacious, until they swarm so that the great stones gape from each other with the crowding of their roots, and the feldspar begins to be picked out of the granite to find them food. At last the trees take up their solemn line of march, and never rest until they have encamped in the market-place. Wait long enough and you will find an old doting oak hugging a huge worn block in its yellow underground arms; that was the corner-stone of the State-House. Oh, so patient she is, this imperturbable Nature!

—Let us cry!—

But all this has nothing to do with my walks and talks with the schoolmistress. I did not say that I would not tell you something about them. Let me alone, and I shall talk to you more than I ought to, probably. We never tell our secrets to people that pump for them.

Books we talked about, and education. It was her duty to know something of these, and of course she did. Perhaps I was somewhat more learned than she, but I found that the difference between her reading and mine was like that of a man's and a woman's dusting a library. The man flaps about with a bunch of feathers; the woman goes to work softly with a cloth. She does not raise half the dust, nor fill her own eyes and mouth with it,—but she goes into all the corners and attends to the leaves as much as to the covers. Books are the *negative* pictures of thought, and the more sensitive the mind that receives their images, the more nicely the finest lines are reproduced. A woman (of the right kind), reading after a man, follows him as

Ruth followed the reapers of Boaz, and her gleanings are often the finest of the wheat.

But it was in talking of Life that we came most nearly together. I thought I knew something about that,—that I could speak or write about it somewhat to the purpose.

To take up this fluid earthly being of ours as a sponge sucks up water,—to be steeped and soaked in its realities as a hide fills its pores lying seven years in a tan-pit,—to have winnowed every wave of it as a mill-wheel works up the stream that runs through the flume upon its float-boards,—to have curled up in the keenest spasms and flattened out in the laxest languors of this breathing-sickness, which keeps certain parcels of matter uneasy for three or four score years,—to have fought all the devils and clasped all the angels of its delirium,—and then, just at the point when the white-hot passions have cooled down to cherry-red, plunge our experience into the ice-cold stream of some human language or other, one might think would end in a rhapsody with something of spring and temper in it. All this I thought my power and province.

The schoolmistress had tried life, too. Once in a while one meets with a single soul greater than all the living pageant which passes before it. As the pale astronomer sits in his study with sunken eyes and thin fingers, and weighs Uranus or Neptune as in a balance, so there are meek, slight women who have weighed all which this planetary life can offer, and hold it like a bauble in the palm of their slender hands. This was one of them. Fortune had left her, sorrow had baptized her; the routine of labor and the loneliness of almost friendless city-life were before her. Yet, as I looked upon her tranquil face, gradually regaining a cheerfulness which was often sprightly, as she became interested in the various matters we talked about and places we visited, I saw that eye and lip and every shifting lineament were made for love,—unconscious of their sweet office as yet, and meeting the cold aspect of Duty with the natural graces which were meant for the reward of nothing less than the Great Passion.

—I never addressed one word of love to the schoolmistress in the course of these pleasant walks. It seemed to me that we talked of everything but love on that particular morning. There was, perhaps, a little more timidity and hesitancy on my part than I have commonly shown among our people at the boarding-house. In fact, I considered myself the master at the breakfast-table; but, somehow, I could not command myself just then so well as usual. The truth is, I had secured a passage to Liverpool in the steamer which was to leave at noon,—

with the condition, however, of being released in case circumstances occurred to detain me. The schoolmistress knew nothing about all this, of course, as yet.

It was on the Common that we were walking. The *mall,* or boulevard of our Common, you know, has various branches leading from it in different directions. One of these runs down from opposite Joy Street southward across the whole length of the Common to Boylston Street. We called it the long path, and were fond of it.

I felt very weak indeed (though of a tolerably robust habit) as we came opposite the head of this path on that morning. I think I tried to speak twice without making myself distinctly audible. At last I got out the question,—Will you take the long path with me?—Certainly,—said the schoolmistress,—with much pleasure.—Think,—I said, —before you answer: if you take the long path with me now, I shall interpret it that we are to part no more!—The schoolmistress stepped back with a sudden movement, as if an arrow had struck her.

One of the long granite blocks used as seats was hard by,—the one you may still see close by the Gingko-tree.—Pray, sit down,—I said.—No, no, she answered, softly,—I will walk the *long path* with you!

—The old gentleman who sits opposite met us walking, arm in arm, about the middle of the long path, and said, very charmingly,—"Good-morning, my dears!"

JOHN LOTHROP MOTLEY (1814–1877)

From The Rise of the Dutch Republic

The Abdication of Charles V.

On the twenty-fifth day of October, 1555, the estates of the Netherlands were assembled in the great hall of the palace at Brussels. They had been summoned to be the witnesses and the guarantees of the abdication which Charles V. had long before resolved upon, and which he was that day to execute. The emperor, like many potentates before and since, was fond of great political spectacles. He knew their influence upon the masses of mankind. Although plain, even to shabbiness, in his own costume, and usually attired in black, no one ever understood better than he how to arrange such exhibitions in a striking and artistic style. We have seen the theatrical and imposing manner in which he quelled the insurrection at Ghent, and nearly crushed the life forever out of that vigorous and turbulent little commonwealth. The closing scene of his long and energetic reign he had now arranged with profound study, and with an accurate knowledge of the manner in which the requisite effects were to be produced. The termination of his own career, the opening of his beloved Philip's, were to be dramatized in a manner worthy the august character of the actors, and the importance of the great stage where they played their parts. The eyes of the whole world were directed upon that day towards Brussels; for an imperial abdication was an event which had not, in the sixteenth century, been staled by custom.

The gay capital of Brabant—of that province which rejoiced in the liberal constitution known by the cheerful title of the "joyful entrance," was worthy to be the scene of the imposing show. Brussels had been a city for more than five centuries, and, at that day, numbered about one hundred thousand inhabitants. Its walls, six miles in circumference, were already two hundred years old. Unlike most Netherland cities, lying usually upon extensive plains, it was built along the sides of an abrupt promontory. A wide expanse of living verdure, cultivated gardens, shady groves, fertile corn-fields, flowed round it like a sea. The foot of the town was washed by the little river Senne, while the irregular but picturesque streets rose up the steep sides of the hill like the semicircles and stairways of an amphitheatre. Nearly in the heart of the place rose the audacious and exquisitely embroidered tower of the town-house, three hundred and sixty-six feet in height, a miracle of needlework in stone, rivalling in its intricate carving the cobweb tracery of that lace which has for centuries been synonymous with the city, and rearing itself above a façade of profusely decorated and brocaded architecture. The crest of the elevation was crowned by the towers of the old ducal palace of Brabant, with its extensive and thickly-wooded park on the left, and by the stately mansions of Orange, Egmont, Aremberg, Culemburg, and other Flemish grandees, on the right. The great forest of Soignies, dotted with monasteries and convents, swarming with every variety of game, whither the citizens made their summer pilgrimages, and where the nobles chased the wild boar and the stag, extended to within a quarter of a mile of the city walls. The population, as thrifty, as intelligent, as prosperous as that of any city in Europe, was divided into fifty-two guilds of artisans, among which the most important were the armorers, whose suits of mail would turn a musket-ball; the gardeners, upon whose gentler creations incredible sums were annually lavished; and the tapestry-workers, whose gorgeous fabrics were the wonder of the world. Seven principal churches, of which the most striking was that of St. Gudule, with its twin towers, its charming façade, and its magnificently painted windows, adorned the upper part of the city. The number seven was a magic number in Brussels, and was supposed at that epoch, during which astronomy was in its infancy and astrology in its prime, to denote the seven planets which governed all things terrestrial by their aspects and influences. Seven noble families, springing from seven ancient castles, supplied the stock from which the seven senators were selected who composed the upper council of the city. There were seven great squares, seven city gates, and upon the occasion of the present ceremony, it was observed by the lovers of wonderful coincidences, that seven crowned heads would be congregated under a single roof in the liberty-loving city.

The palace where the states-general were upon this occasion convened, had been the residence of the Dukes of Brabant since the days of John the Second, who had built it about the year 1300. It was a spacious and convenient building, but not distinguished for the beauty of its architecture. In front was a large open square, enclosed by an iron railing; in the rear an extensive and beautiful park, filled with forest trees, and containing gardens and labyrinths, fish-ponds and game preserves, fountains and promenades, racecourses and archery grounds. The main entrance to this edifice opened upon a spacious hall, connected with a beautiful and symmetrical chapel. The hall was celebrated for its size, harmonious proportions, and the richness of its decorations. It was the place where the chapters of the famous order of the Golden Fleece were held. Its walls were hung with a magnificent tapestry of Arras, representing the life and achievements of Gideon, the Midianite, and giving particular prominence to the miracle of the "fleece of wool," vouchsafed to that renowned champion, the great patron of the Knights of the Fleece. On the present occasion there were various additional embellishments of flowers and votive garlands. At the western end a spacious platform or stage, with six or seven steps, had been constructed, below which was a range of benches for the deputies of the seventeen provinces. Upon the stage itself there were rows of seats, covered with tapestry, upon the right hand and upon the left. These were respectively to accommodate the knights of the order and the guests of high distinction. In the rear of these were other benches, for the members of the three great councils. In the centre of the stage was a splendid canopy, decorated with the arms of Burgundy, beneath which were placed three gilded arm-chairs. All the seats upon the platform were vacant, but the benches below, assigned to the deputies of the provinces, were already filled. Numerous representatives from all the states but two—Gelderland and Overyssel—had already taken their places. Grave magistrates, in chain and gown, and executive officers in the splendid civic uniforms for which the Netherlands were celebrated, already filled every seat within the space allotted. The remainder of the hall was crowded with the more favored portion of the multitude which had been fortunate enough to procure admission to the exhibition. The archers and hallebardiers of the body-guard kept watch at all the doors. The theatre was filled—the audience was eager with expectation—the actors were yet to arrive. As the clock struck three, the hero of the scene appeared. Cæsar, as he was always designated in the classic language of the day, entered, leaning on the shoulder of William of Orange. They came from the chapel, and were immediately followed by Philip the Second and Queen Mary of Hungary. The Archduke Maximilian, the Duke of Savoy, and other great personages came afterwards, accompanied by a glittering throng of warriors, councillors, governors, and Knights of the Fleece.

Many individuals of existing or future historic celebrity in the Netherlands, whose names are so familiar to the student of the epoch, seemed to have been grouped, as if by premeditated design, upon this imposing platform, where the curtain was to fall forever upon the mightiest emperor since Charlemagne, and where the opening scene of the long and tremendous tragedy of Philip's reign was to be simultaneously enacted. There was the Bishop of Arras, soon to be known throughout Christendom by the more celebrated title of Cardinal Granvelle, the serene and smiling priest whose subtle influence over the destines of so many individuals then present, and over the fortunes of the whole land, was to be so extensive and so deadly. There was that flower of Flemish chivalry, the lineal descendant of ancient Frisian kings, already distinguished for his bravery in many fields, but not having yet won those two remarkable victories which were soon to make the name of Egmont like the sound of a trumpet throughout the whole country. Tall, magnificent in costume, with dark flowing hair, soft brown eye, smooth cheek, a slight moustache, and features of almost feminine delicacy; such was the gallant and ill-fated Lamoral Egmont. The Count of Horn, too, with bold, sullen face, and fan-shaped beard—a brave, honest, discontented, quarrelsome, unpopular man; those other twins in doom—the Marquis Berghen and the Lord of Montigny; the Baron Berlaymont, brave, intensely loyal, insatiably greedy for office and wages, but who, at least, never served but one party; the Duke of Arschot, who was to serve all, essay to rule all, and to betray all—a splendid seignor, magnificent in cramoisy velvet, but a poor creature, who traced his pedigree from Adam, according to the family monumental inscriptions at Louvain, but who was better known as grand-nephew of the emperor's famous tutor, Chièvres; the bold, debauched Brederode, with handsome, reckless face and turbulent demeanor; the infamous Noircarmes, whose name was to be covered with eternal execration, for aping towards his own compatriots and kindred as much of Alva's atrocities and avarice, as he was permitted to exercise; the distinguished soldiers Meghen and Aremberg—these, with many others whose deeds of arms were to become celebrated throughout Europe, were all conspicuous in the brilliant crowd. There, too, was that learned Frisian, President Viglius, crafty, plausible, adroit, eloquent

—a small, brisk man, with long yellow hair, glittering green eyes, round, tumid, rosy cheeks, and flowing beard. Foremost among the Spanish grandees, and close to Philip, stood the famous favorite, Ruy Gomez, or as he was familiarly called "Re y Gomez" (King and Gomez), a man of meridional aspect, with coal-black hair and beard, gleaming eyes, a face pallid with intense application, and slender but handsome figure; while in immediate attendance upon the emperor, was the immortal Prince of Orange.

Such were a few only of the most prominent in that gay throng, whose fortunes, in part, it will be our humble duty to narrate; how many of them passing through all this glitter to a dark and mysterious doom!—some to perish on public scaffolds, some by midnight assassination; others, more fortunate to fall on the battle-field—nearly all, sooner or later, to be laid in bloody graves!

All the company present had risen to their feet as the emperor entered. By his command, all immediately afterwards resumed their places. The benches at either end of the platform were accordingly filled with the royal and princely personages invited, with the Fleece Knights, wearing the insignia of their order, with the members of the three great councils, and with the governors. The Emperor, the King, and the Queen of Hungary, were left conspicuous in the centre of the scene. As the whole object of the ceremony was to present an impressive exhibition, it is worth our while to examine minutely the appearance of the two principal characters.

Charles the Fifth was then fifty-five years and eight months old; but he was already decrepit with premature old age. He was of about the middle height, and had been athletic and well-proportioned. Broad in the shoulders, deep in the chest, thin in the flank, very muscular in the arms and legs, he had been able to match himself with all competitors in the tourney and the ring, and to vanquish the bull with his own hand in the favorite national amusement of Spain. He had been able in the field to do the duty of captain and soldier, to endure fatigue and exposure, and every privation except fasting. These personal advantages were now departed. Crippled in hands, knees, and legs, he supported himself with difficulty upon a crutch, with the aid of an attendant's shoulder. In face he had always been extremely ugly, and time had certainly not improved his physiognomy. His hair, once of a light color, was now white with age, close-clipped and bristling; his beard was gray, coarse, and shaggy. His forehead was spacious and commanding; the eye was dark-blue, with an expression both majestic and benignant. His nose was aquiline but crooked. The lower part of his face was famous for its deformity. The under lip, a Burgundian inheritance, as faithfully transmitted as the duchy and county, was heavy and hanging; the lower jaw protruding so far beyond the upper, that it was impossible for him to bring together the few fragments of teeth which still remained, or to speak a whole sentence in an intelligible voice. Eating and talking, occupations to which he was always much addicted, were becoming daily more arduous, in consequence of this original defect, which now seemed hardly human, but rather an original deformity.

So much for the father. The son, Philip the Second, was a small, meagre man, much below the middle height, with thin legs, a narrow chest, and the shrinking, timid air of an habitual invalid. He seemed so little, upon his first visit to his aunts, the Queens Eleanor and Mary, accustomed to look upon proper men in Flanders and Germany, that he was fain to win their favor by making certain attempts in the tournament, in which his success was sufficiently problematical. "His body," says his professed panegyrist, "was but a human cage, in which, however brief and narrow, dwelt a soul to whose flight the immeasurable expanse of heaven was too contracted." The same wholesale admirer adds, that "his aspect was so reverend, that rustics who met him alone in a wood, without knowing him, bowed down with instinctive veneration." In face, he was the living image of his father, having the same broad forehead, and blue eye, with the same aquiline, but better proportioned, nose. In the lower part of the countenance, the remarkable Burgundian deformity was likewise reproduced. He had the same heavy, hanging lip, with a vast mouth, and monstrously protruding lower jaw. His complexion was fair, his hair light and thin, his beard yellow, short, and pointed. He had the aspect of a Fleming, but the loftiness of a Spaniard. His demeanor in public was still, silent, almost sepulchral. He looked habitually on the ground when he conversed, was chary of speech, embarrassed, and even suffering in manner. This was ascribed partly to a natural haughtiness which he had occasionally endeavored to overcome, and partly to habitual pains in the stomach, occasioned by his inordinate fondness for pastry.

Such was the personal appearance of the man who was about to receive into his single hand the destines of half the world; whose single will was, for the future, to shape the fortunes of every individual then present, of many millions more in Europe, America, and at the ends of the earth, and of countless millions yet unborn.

The three royal personages being seated upon chairs placed triangularly under the canopy, such of the audience as had seats provided for them, now took their places, and the proceedings commenced. Philibert de Bruxelles, a member of the privy council of the Netherlands, arose at the emperor's command, and made a long oration. He spoke of the emperor's warm affection for the provinces, as the land of his birth; of his deep regret that his broken health and failing powers, both of body and mind, compelled him to resign his sovereignty, and to seek relief for his shattered frame in a more genial climate. Cæsar's gout was then depicted in energetic language, which must have cost him a twinge as he sat there and listened to the councillor's eloquence. " 'Tis a most truculent executioner," said Philibert: "it invades the whole body, from the crown of the head to the soles of the feet, leaving nothing untouched. It contracts the nerves with intolerable anguish, it enters the bones, it freezes the marrow, it converts the lubricating fluids of the joints into chalk, it pauses not until, having exhausted and debilitated the whole body, it has rendered all its necessary instruments useless, and conquered the mind by immense torture." Engaged in mortal struggle with such an enemy, Cæsar felt himself obliged, as the councillor proceeded to inform his audience, to change the scene of the contest from the humid air of Flanders to the warmer atmosphere of Spain. He rejoiced, however, that his son was both vigorous and experienced, and that his recent marriage with the Queen of England had furnished the provinces with a most valuable alliance. He then again referred to the emperor's boundless love for his subjects, and concluded with a tremendous, but superfluous, exhortation to Philip on the necessity of maintaining the Catholic religion in its purity. After this long harangue, which has been fully reported by several historians who were present at the ceremony, the councillor proceeded to read the deed of cession, by which Philip, already sovereign of Sicily, Naples, Milan, and titular King of England, France, and Jerusalem, now received all the duchies, marquisates, earldoms, baronies, cities, towns, and castles of the Burgundian property, including, of course, the seventeen Netherlands.

As De Bruxelles finished, there was a buzz of admiration throughout the assembly, mingled with murmurs of regret, that in the present great danger upon the frontiers from the belligerent King of France and his warlike and restless nation, the provinces should be left without their ancient and puissant defender. The emperor then rose to his feet. Leaning on his crutch, he beckoned from his seat the personage upon whose arm he had leaned as he entered the hall. A tall, handsome youth of twenty-two came forward—a man whose name from that time forward, and as long as history shall endure, has been, and will be, more familiar than any other in the mouths of Netherlanders. At that day he had rather a southern than a German or Flemish appearance. He had a Spanish cast of features, dark, well chiselled, and symmetrical. His head was small and well placed upon his shoulders. His hair was dark-brown, as were also his moustache and peaked beard. His forehead was lofty, spacious, and already prematurely engraved with the anxious lines of thought. His eyes were full, brown, well opened, and expressive of profound reflection. He was dressed in the magnificent apparel for which the Netherlanders were celebrated above all other nations, and which the ceremony rendered necessary. His presence being considered indispensable at this great ceremony, he had been summoned but recently from the camp on the frontier, where, notwithstanding his youth, the Emperor had appointed him to command his army in chief against such antagonists as Admiral Coligny and the Duc de Nevers.

Thus supported upon his crutch and upon the shoulder of William of Orange, the Emperor proceeded to address the states, by the aid of a closely-written brief which he held in his hand. He reviewed rapidly the progress of events from his seventeenth year up to that day. He spoke of his nine expeditions into Germany, six to Spain, seven to Italy, four to France, ten to the Netherlands, two to England, as many to Africa, and of his eleven voyages by sea. He sketched his various wars, victories, and treaties of peace, assuring his hearers that the welfare of his subjects and the security of the Roman Catholic religion had ever been the leading objects of his life. As long as God had granted him health, he continued, only enemies could have regretted that Charles was living and reigning, but now that his strength was but vanity, and life fast ebbing away, his love for dominion, his affection for his subjects, and his regard for their interests, required his departure. Instead of a decrepit man with one foot in the grave, he presented them with a sovereign in the prime of life and the vigor of health. Turning toward Philip, he observed, that for a dying father to bequeath so magnificent an empire to his son was a deed worthy of gratitude, but that when the father thus descended to the grave before his time, and by an anticipated and living burial sought to provide for the welfare of his realms and the grandeur of his son, the benefit thus conferred was surely far greater. He added, that the debt would be paid to him and with usury, should Philip conduct himself in his administration of the province with a wise and affectionate regard to their true interests. Posterity would applaud his abdication, should his son prove worthy of his bounty; and that could only be by living in the fear of God, and by maintaining law, justice, and the Catholic religion in all their purity, as the true foundation of the realm. In conclusion, he entreated the estates, and through them the nation, to render obedience to their new prince, to maintain concord and to preserve inviolate the Catholic faith; begging them, at the same time, to pardon him all errors or offences which he might have committed towards them during his reign, and assuring them that he should unceasingly remember their obedience and affection in his every prayer to that Being to whom the remainder of his life was to be dedicated.

Such brave words as these, so many vigorous asseverations of attempted performance of duty, such fervent hopes expressed of a benign administration in behalf of the son, could not but affect the sensibilities of the audience, already excited and softened by the impressive character of the whole display. Sobs were heard throughout every portion of the hall, and tears poured profusely from every eye. The Fleece Knights on the platform and the burghers in the background were all melted with the same emotion. As for the Emperor himself, he sank almost fainting upon his chair as he concluded his address. An ashy paleness overspread his countenance, and he wept like a child. Even the icy Philip was almost softened, as he rose to perform his part in the ceremony. Dropping upon his knees before his father's feet, he reverently kissed his hand. Charles placed his hands solemnly upon his son's head, made the sign of the cross, and blessed him in the name of the Holy Trinity. Then raising him in his arms he tenderly embraced him, saying, as he did so, to the great potentates around him, that he felt a sincere compassion for the son on whose shoulders so heavy a weight had just devolved, and which only a life-long labor would enable him to support. Philip now uttered a few words expressive of his duty to his father and his affection for his people. Turning to the orders, he signified his regret that he was unable to address them either in the French or Flemish language, and was therefore obliged to ask their attention to the Bishop of Arras, who would act as his interpreter. Anthony Perrenot accordingly arose, and in smooth, fluent, and well-turned commonplaces, expressed at great length the gratitude of Philip towards his father, with his firm determination to walk in the path of duty, and to obey his father's counsels and example in the future administration of the provinces. This long address of the prelate was responded to at equal length by Jacob Maas, member of the Council of Brabant, a man of great learning, eloquence and prolixity, who had been selected to reply on behalf of the states-general, and who now, in the name of these bodies, accepted the abdication in an elegant and complimentary harangue. Queen Mary of Hungary, the "Christian widow" of Erasmus, and Regent of the Netherlands during the past twenty-five years, then rose to resign her office, making a brief address expressive of her affection for the people, her regrets at leaving them, and her hopes that all errors which she might have committed during her long administration would be forgiven her. Again the redundant Maas responded, asserting in terms of fresh compliment and elegance the uniform satisfaction of the provinces with her conduct during her whole career.

The orations and replies having now been brought to a close, the ceremony was terminated. The Emperor, leaning on the shoulders of the Prince of Orange and of the Count de Buren, slowly left the hall, followed by Philip, the Queen of Hungary, and the whole court; all in the same order in which they had entered, and by the same passage into the chapel.

It is obvious that the drama had been completely successful. It had been a scene where heroic self-sacrifice, touching confidence, ingenuous love of duty, patriotism, and paternal affection upon one side; filial reverence, with a solemn regard for public duty and the highest interests of the people on the other, were supposed to be the predominant sentiments. The happiness of the Netherlands was apparently the only object contemplated in the great transaction. All had played well their parts in the past, all hoped the best in the times which were to follow. The abdicating Emperor was looked upon as a hero and a prophet. The stage was drowned in tears. There is not the least doubt as to the genuine and universal emotion which was excited throughout the assembly. "Cæsar's oration," says Secretary Godelaevus, who was present at the ceremony, "deeply moved the nobility and gentry, many of whom burst into tears; *even* the illustrious Knights of the Fleece were melted." The historian, Pontus Heuterus, who, then twenty years of age, was likewise among the audience, attests that "most of the assembly were dissolved in tears; uttering the while such sonorous sobs that they compelled his Cæsarean Majesty and the Queen to cry with them. My own face," he adds, "was certainly quite wet." The English envoy, Sir John Mason, describing in a despatch to his government the scene which he had just witnessed, paints the same picture. "The Emperor," he said, "begged the forgiveness of his subjects if he had ever unwittingly omitted the performance of any of his duties towards them. And here," continues the envoy, "he broke into a weeping, whereunto, besides the dolefulness of the matter, I think, he was moche provoked by seeing the whole company to do the lyke before; there beyng in myne opinion not one man in the whole assemblie, stranger or another, that dewring the time of a good piece of his oration poured not out as abundantly teares, some more, some lesse. And yet he prayed them to beare with his imperfections, proceeding of his sickly age, and of the mentioning of so tender a matter as the departing from such a sort of dere and loving subjects."

And yet what was the Emperor Charles to the inhabitants of the Netherlands that they should weep for him? His conduct towards them during his whole career had been one of unmitigated oppression. What to them were all these forty voyages by sea and land, these journeyings back and forth from Friesland to Tunis, from Madrid to Vienna. What was it to them that the imperial shuttle was thus industriously flying to and fro? The fabric wrought was but the daily growing grandeur and splendor of his imperial house; the looms were kept moving at the expense of their hardly-earned treasure, and the woof was often dyed red in the blood of his bravest subjects. The interests of the Netherlands had never been even a secondary consideration with their master. He had fulfilled no duty towards them, he had committed the gravest crimes against them. He had regarded them merely as a treasury upon which to draw; while the sums which he extorted were spent upon ceaseless and senseless wars, which were of no more interest

to them than if they had been waged in another planet. Of five millions of
gold annually, which he derived from all his realms, two millions came from
these industrious and opulent provinces, while but a half million came from
Spain and another half from the Indies. The mines of wealth which had
been opened by the hand of industry in that slender territory of ancient
morass and thicket, contributed four times as much income to the imperial
exchequer as all the boasted wealth of Mexico and Peru. Yet the artisans,
the farmers and the merchants, by whom these riches were produced, were
consulted about as much in the expenditure of the imposts upon their industry as were the savages of America as to the distribution of the mineral
treasures of their soil. The rivalry of the houses of Habsburg and Valois,
this was the absorbing theme, during the greater part of the reign which had
just been so dramatically terminated. To gain the empire over Francis, to
leave to Don Philip a richer heritage than the Dauphin could expect, were
the great motives of the unparalleled energy displayed by Charles during the
longer and the more successful portion of his career. To crush the Reformation throughout his dominions, was his occupation afterward till he abandoned the field in despair. It was certainly not desirable for the Netherlanders that they should be thus controlled by a man who forced them to
contribute so largely to the success of schemes, some of which were at best
indifferent, and others entirely odious to them. They paid 1,200,000 crowns
a year regularly; they paid in five years an extraordinary subsidy of eight
millions of ducats, and the States were roundly rebuked by the courtly representatives of their despot, if they presumed to inquire into the objects of the
appropriations, or to express an interest in their judicious administration.
Yet it may be supposed to have been a matter of indifference to them whether
Francis or Charles had won the day at Pavia, and it certainly was not a
cause of triumph to the daily increasing thousands of religious reformers in
Holland and Flanders that their brethren had been crushed by the Emperor
at Mühlberg. But it was not alone that he drained their treasure, and
hampered their industry. He was in constant conflict with their ancient and
dearly-bought political liberties. Like his ancestor Charles the Bold, he was
desirous of constructing a kingdom out of the provinces. He was disposed
to place all their separate and individual charters on a procrustean bed, and
shape them all into uniformity simply by reducing the whole to a nullity. The
difficulties in the way, the stout opposition offered by burghers, whose fathers
had gained these charters with their blood, and his want of leisure during the
vast labors which devolved upon him as the autocrat of so large a portion of
the world, caused him to defer indefinitely the execution of his plan. He
found time only to crush some of the foremost of the liberal institutions of
the provinces, in detail. He found the city of Tournay a happy, thriving,

self-governed little republic in all its local affairs; he destroyed its liberties, without a tolerable pretext, and reduced it to the condition of a Spanish or Italian provincial town. His memorable chastisement of Ghent for having dared to assert its ancient rights of self-taxation, is sufficiently known to the world, and has been already narrated at length. Many other instances might be adduced, if it were not a superfluous task, to prove that Charles was not only a political despot, but most arbitrary and cruel in the exercise of his despotism.

But if his sins against the Netherlands had been only those of financial and political oppression, it would be at least conceivable, although certainly not commendable, that the inhabitants should have regretted his departure. But there are far darker crimes for which he stands arraigned at the bar of history, and it is indeed strange that the man who had committed them should have been permitted to speak his farewell amid blended plaudits and tears. His hand planted the inquisition in the Netherlands. Before his day it is idle to say that the diabolical institution never had a place there. The isolated cases in which inquisitors had exercised functions proved the absence and not the presence of the system, and will be discussed in a later chapter. Charles introduced and organized a papal inquisition, side by side with those terrible "placards" of his invention, which constituted a masked inquisition even more cruel than that of Spain. The execution of the system was never permitted to languish. The number of Netherlanders who were burned, strangled, beheaded, or buried alive, in obedience to his edicts, and for the offences of reading the Scriptures, of looking askance at a graven image, or of ridiculing the actual presence of the body and blood of Christ in a wafer, have been placed as high as one hundred thousand by distinguished authorities, and have never been put at a lower mark than fifty thousand. The Venetian envoy Navigero placed the number of victims in the provinces of Holland and Friesland alone at thirty thousand, and this in 1546, ten years before the abdication, and five before the promulgation of the hideous edict of 1550!

The edicts and the inquisition were the gift of Charles to the Netherlands, in return for their wasted treasure and their constant obedience. For this, his name deserves to be handed down to eternal infamy, not only throughout the Netherlands, but in every land where a single heart beats for political or religious freedom. To eradicate these institutions after they had been watered and watched by the care of his successor, was the work of an eighty years' war, in the course of which millions of lives were sacrificed. Yet the abdicating Emperor had summoned his faithful estates around him, and stood up before them in his imperial robes for the last time, to tell them of the affectionate regard which he had always borne them, and to mingle his tears with theirs.

Could a single phantom have risen from one of the many thousand graves where human beings had been thrust alive by his decree, perhaps there might have been an answer to the question propounded by the Emperor amid all that piteous weeping. Perhaps it might have told the man who asked his hearers to be forgiven if he had ever unwittingly offended them, that there was a world where it was deemed an offence to torture, strangle, burn, and drown one's innocent fellow-creatures. The usual but trifling excuse for such enormities can not be pleaded for the Emperor. Charles was no fanatic. The man whose armies sacked Rome, who laid his sacrilegious hands on Christ's vicegerent, and kept the infallible head of the Church a prisoner to serve his own political ends, was *then* no bigot. He believed in nothing, save that when the course of his imperial will was impeded, and the interests of his imperial house in jeopardy, pontiffs were to succumb as well as anabaptists. It was the political heresy which lurked in the restiveness of the religious reformers under dogma, tradition, and supernatural sanction to temporal power, which he was disposed to combat to the death. He was too shrewd a politician not to recognize the connection between aspirations for religious and for political freedom. His hand was ever ready to crush both heresies in one. Had he been a true son of the Church, a faithful champion of her infallibility, he would not have submitted to the peace of Passau, so long as he could bring a soldier to the field. Yet he acquiesced in the Reformation for Germany, while the fires for burning the reformers were ever blazing in the Netherlands, where it was death even to allude to the existence of the peace of Passau. Nor did he acquiesce only from compulsion, for long before his memorable defeat by Maurice, he had permitted the German troops, with whose services he could not dispense, regularly to attend Protestant worship performed by their own Protestant chaplains. Lutheran preachers marched from city to city of the Netherlands under the imperial banner, while the subjects of those patrimonial provinces were daily suffering on the scaffold for their nonconformity. The influence of this garrison-preaching upon the progress of the Reformation in the Netherlands is well-known. Charles hated Lutherans, but he required soldiers, and he thus helped by his own policy to disseminate what, had he been the fanatic which he perhaps became in retirement, he would have sacrificed his life to crush. It is quite true that the growing Calvinism of the provinces was more dangerous both religiously and politically, than the Protestantism of the German princes, which had not yet been formally pronounced heresy, but it is thus the more evident that it was political rather than religious heterodoxy which the despot wished to suppress.

No man, however, could have been more observant of religious rites. He heard mass daily. He listened to a sermon every Sunday and holiday. He confessed and received the sacrament four times a year. He was sometimes to be seen in his tent at midnight, on his knees before a crucifix with eyes and hands uplifted. He ate no meat in Lent, and used extraordinary diligence to discover and to punish any man, whether courtier or plebian, who failed to fast during the whole forty days. He was too good a politician not to know the value of broad phylacteries and long prayers. He was too nice an observer of human nature not to know how easily mint and cummin could still outweigh the "weightier matters of law, judgment, mercy and faith;" as if the founder of the religion which he professed, and to maintain which he had established the inquisition and the edicts, had never cried woe upon the Pharisees. Yet there is no doubt that the Emperor was at times almost popular in the Netherlands, and that he was never as odious as his successor. There were some deep reasons for this, and some superficial ones; among others, a singularly fortunate manner. He spoke German, Spanish, Italian, French, and Flemish, and could assume the characteristics of each country as easily as he could use its language. He could be stately with Spaniards, familiar with Flemings, witty with Italians. He could strike down a bull in the ring like a matador at Madrid, or win the prize in the tourney like a knight of old; he could ride at the ring with the Flemish nobles, hit the popinjay with his crossbow among Antwerp artisans, or drink beer and exchange rude jests with the boors of Brabant. For virtues such as these, his grave crimes against God and man, against religion and chartered and solemnly-sworn rights have been palliated, as if oppression became more tolerable because the oppressor was an accomplished linguist and a good marksman.

But the great reason for his popularity no doubt lay in his military genius. Charles was inferior to no general of his age. "When he was born into the world," said Alva, "he was born a soldier," and the Emperor confirmed the statement and reciprocated the compliment, when he declared that "the three first captains of the age were himself first, and then the Duke of Alva and Constable Montmorency." It is quite true that all his officers were not of the same opinion, and many were too apt to complain that his constant presence in the field did more harm than good, and "that his Majesty would do much better to stay at home." There is, however, no doubt that he was both a good soldier and a good general. He was constitutionally fearless, and he possessed great energy and endurance. He was ever the first to arm when a battle was to be fought, and the last to take off his harness. He commanded in person and in chief, even when surrounded by veterans and crippled by the gout. He was calm in great reverses. It was said that he was never known to change color except upon two occasions: after the fatal destruction of his fleet at Algiers, and in the memorable flight from Innspruck. He was of a phlegmatic, stoical temperament, until shattered by age and disease; a man without a sentiment and without a tear. It was said by Spaniards that he was never seen to weep, even at the death of his nearest relatives and friends, except on the solitary occasion of the departure of Don Ferrante Gonzaga from court. Such a temperament was invaluable in the stormy career to which he had devoted his life. He was essentially a man of action, a military chieftain. "Pray only for my health and my life," he was accustomed to say to the young officers who came to him from every part of his dominions to serve under his banners, "for so long as I have these I will never leave you idle; at least in France. I love peace no better than the rest of you. I was born and bred to arms, and must of necessity keep on my harness till I can bear it no longer." The restless energy and the magnificent tranquillity of his character made him a hero among princes, an idol with his officers, a popular favorite everywhere. The promptness with which, at much personal hazard, he descended like a thunderbolt in the midst of the Ghent insurrection; the juvenile ardor with which the almost bedridden man arose from his sick-bed to smite the Protestants at Mühlberg; the grim stoicism with which he saw sixty thousand of his own soldiers perish in the wintry siege of Metz; all ensured him a large measure of that applause which ever follows military distinction, especially when the man who achieves it happens to wear a crown. He combined the personal prowess of a knight of old with the more modern accomplishments of a scientific tactician. He could. charge the enemy in person like the most brilliant cavalry officer, and he thoroughly understood the arrangements of a campaign, the marshalling and victualling of troops, and the whole art of setting and maintaining an army in the field.

Yet, though brave and warlike as the most chivalrous of his ancestors, Gothic, Burgundian, or Suabian, he was entirely without chivalry. Fanaticism for the faith, protection for the oppressed, fidelity to friend and foe, knightly loyalty to a cause deemed sacred, the sacrifice of personal interests to great ideas, generosity of hand and heart; all those qualities which unite with courage and constancy to make up the ideal chevalier, Charles not only lacked but despised. He trampled on the weak antagonist, whether burgher or petty potentate. He was false as water. He inveigled his foes who trusted to imperial promises, by arts unworthy an emperor or a gentleman. He led about the unfortunate John Frederic of Saxony, in his own language, "like a bear in a chain," ready to be slipped upon Maurice should "the boy" prove ungrateful. He connived at the famous forgery of the prelate of Arras, to which the Landgrave Philip owed his long imprisonment; a villany worse than many for which humbler rogues have suffered by thousands upon the gallows. The contemporary world knew well the history of his frauds, on scale both colossal and minute, and called him familiarly "Charles qui triche."

The absolute master of realms on which the sun perpetually shone, he was not only greedy for additional dominion, but he was avaricious in small matters, and hated to part with a hundred dollars. To the soldier who brought him the sword and gauntlets of Francis the First, he gave a hundred crowns, when ten thousand would have been less than the customary present; so that the man left his presence full of desperation. The three soldiers who swam the Elbe, with their swords in their mouths, to bring him the boats with which he passed to the victory of Mühlberg, received from his imperial bounty a doublet, a pair of stockings, and four crowns apiece. His courtiers and ministers complained bitterly of his habitual niggardliness, and were fain to eke out their slender salaries by accepting bribes from every hand rich enough to bestow them. In truth Charles was more than any thing else a politician, notwithstanding his signal abilities as a soldier. If to have founded institutions which could last, be the test of statesmanship, he was even a statesman; for many of his institutions have resisted the pressure of three centuries. But those of Charlemange fell as soon as his hand was cold, while the works of many ordinary legislators have attained to a perpetuity denied to the statutes of Solon or Lycurgus. Durability is not the test of merit in human institutions. Tried by the only touchstone applicable to governments, their capacity to insure the highest welfare of the governed, we shall not find his polity deserving of much admiration. It is not merely that he was a despot by birth and inclination, nor that he naturally substituted as far as was practicable, the despotic for the republican element, wherever his hand can be traced. There may be possible good in despotisms as there is often much tyranny in democracy. Tried however according to the standard by which all governments may be measured, those laws of truth and divine justice which all Christian nations recognize, and which are perpetual, whether recognized or not, we shall find little to venerate in the life work of the Emperor. The interests of his family, the security of his dynasty, these were his end and aim. The happiness or the progress of his people never furnished even the indirect motives of his conduct, and the result was a baffled policy and a crippled and bankrupt empire at last.

He knew men, especially he knew their weaknesses, and he knew how to turn them to account. He knew how much they would bear, and that little grievances would sometimes inflame more than vast and deliberate injustice. Therefore he employed natives mainly in the subordinate offices of his various states, and he repeatedly warned his successor that the haughtiness of Spaniards and the incompatibility of their character with the Flemish, would be productive of great difficulties and dangers. It was his opinion that men might be tyrannized more intelligently by their own kindred, and in this perhaps he was right. He was indefatigable in the discharge of business, and if it were possible that half a world could be administered as if it were the private property of an individual, the task would have been perhaps as well accomplished by Charles as by any man. He had not the absurdity of supposing it possible for him to attend to the details of every individual affair in every one of his realms; and he therefore intrusted the stewardship of all specialities to his various ministers and agents. It was his business to know men and to deal with affairs on a large scale, and in this he certainly was superior to his successor. His correspondence was mainly in the hands of Granvelle the elder, who analyzed letters received, and frequently wrote all but the signatures of the answers. The same minister usually possessed the imperial ear, and farmed it out for his own benefit. In all this there was of course room for vast deception, but the Emperor was quite aware of what was going on, and took a philosophic view of the matter as an inevitable part of his system. Granvelle grew enormously rich under his eye by trading on the imperial favor and sparing his majesty much trouble. Charles saw it all, ridiculed his peculations, but called him his "bed of down." His knowledge of human nature was however derived from a contemplation mainly of its weaknesses, and was therefore one-sided. He was often deceived, and made many a fatal blunder, shrewd politician though he was. He involved himself often in enterprises which could not be honorable or profitable, and which inflicted damage on his greatest interests. He often offended men who might have been useful friends, and converted allies into enemies. "His Majesty," said a keen observer who knew him well, "has not in his career shown the prudence which was necessary to him. He has often offended those whose love he might have conciliated, converted friends into enemies, and let those perish who were his most faithful partisans." Thus it must be acknowledged that even his boasted knowledge of human nature and his power of dealing with men was rather superficial and empirical than the real gift of genius.

His personal habits during the greater part of his life were those of an indefatigable soldier. He could remain in the saddle day and night, and endure every hardship but hunger. He was addicted to vulgar and miscellaneous incontinence. He was an enormous eater. He breakfasted at five, on a fowl seethed in milk and dressed with sugar and spices. After this he went to sleep again. He dined at twelve, partaking always of twenty dishes. He supped twice; at first, soon after vespers, and the second time at midnight or one o'clock, which meal was, perhaps, the most solid of the four. After meat he ate a great quantity of pastry and sweetmeats, and he irrigated every repast by vast draughts of beer and wine. His stomach, originally a wonderful one, succumbed after forty years of such labors. His taste, but not his appetite began to fail, and he complained to his major domo, that all his food was insipid. The reply is, perhaps, among the most celebrated of facetiæ. The cook could do nothing more unless he served his Majesty a pasty of watches. The allusion to the Emperor's passion for horology was received with great applause. Charles "laughed longer than he was ever known to laugh before, and all the courtiers (of course) laughed as long as his Majesty." The success of so sorry a jest would lead one to suppose that the fooling was less admirable at the imperial court than some of the recorded quips of Tribaulet would lead us to suppose.

The transfer of the other crowns and dignitaries to Philip, was accomplished a month afterwards, in a quiet manner. Spain, Sicily, the Balearic Islands, America, and other portions of the globe, were made over without more display than an ordinary *donatio inter vivos*. The Empire occasioned some difficulty. It had been already signified to Ferdinand, that his brother was to resign the imperial crown in his favor, and the symbols of sovereignty were accordingly transmitted to him by the hands of William of Orange. A deputation, moreover, of which that nobleman, Vice-Chancellor Seld, and Dr. Wolfgang Haller were the chiefs, was despatched to signify to the electors of the Empire the step which had been thus resolved upon. A delay of more than two years, however, intervened, occasioned partly by the deaths of three electors, partly by the war which so soon broke out in Europe, before the matter was formally acted upon. In February, 1553, however, the electors, having been assembled in Frankfort, received the abdication of Charles, and proceeded to the election of Ferdinand. That Emperor was crowned in March, and immediately despatched a legation to the Pope to apprize him of the fact. Nothing was less expected than any opposition on the part of the pontiff. The querulous dotard, however, who then sat in St. Peter's chair, hated Charles and all his race. He accordingly denied the validity of the whole transaction, without sanction previously obtained from the Pope, to whom all crowns belonged. Ferdinand, after listening, through his envoys, to much ridiculous dogmatism on the part of the Pope, at last withdrew from the discussion, with a formal protest, and was first recognized by Caraffa's successor, Pius IV.

Charles had not deferred his retirement till the end of these disputes. He occupied a private house in Brussels, near the gate of Louvain, until August of the year 1556. On the 27th of that month, he addressed a letter from Ghent to John of Osnabruck, president of the Chamber of Spiers, stating his abdication in favor of Ferdinand, and requesting that in the interim the same obedience might be rendered to Ferdinand, as could have been yielded to himself. Ten days later, he addressed a letter to the estates of the Empire, stating the same fact; and on the 17th September, 1556, he set sail from Zeland for Spain. These delays and difficulties occasioned some misconceptions. Many persons who did not admire an abdication, which others, on the contrary, esteemed as an act of unexampled magnanimity, stoutly denied that it was the intention of Charles to renounce the Empire. The Venetian envoy informed his government that Ferdinand was only to be lieutenant for Charles, under strict limitations, and that the Emperor was to resume the government so soon as his health would allow. The Bishop of Arras and Don Juan de Manrique had both assured him, he said, that Charles would not, on any account, definitely abdicate. Manrique even asserted that it was a mere farce to believe in any such intention. The Emperor ought to remain to protect his son, by the resources of the Empire, against France, the Turks, and the heretics. His very shadow was terrible to the Lutherans, and his form might be expected to rise again in stern reality from its temporary grave. Time has shown the falsity of all these imaginings, but views thus maintained by those in the best condition to know the truth, prove how difficult it was for men to believe in a transaction which was then so extraordinary, and how little consonant it was in their eyes with true propriety. It was necessary to ascend to the times of Diocletian, to find an example of a similar abdication of empire, on so deliberate and extensive a scale, and the great English historian of the Roman Empire has compared the two acts with each other. But there seems a vast difference between the cases. Both emperors were distinguished soldiers; both were merciless persecutors of defenceless Christians; both exchanged unbounded empire for absolute seclusion. But Diocletian was born in the lowest abyss of human degradation—the slave and the son of a slave. For such a man, after having reached the highest pinnacle of human greatness, voluntarily to descend from power, seems an act of far greater magnanimity than the retreat of Charles. Born in the purple, having exercised unlimited authority from his boyhood, and having worn from his cradle so many crowns and coronets, the German Emperor might well be supposed to have learned to estimate them at their proper value. Contemporary minds were busy, however, to discover the hidden motives which could have influenced him, and the world, even yet, has hardly ceased to wonder. Yet it would have been more wonderful, considering the Emperor's character, had he remained. The end had not crowned the work; it not unreasonably discrowned the workman. The earlier, and indeed the greater part of his career had been one unbroken procession of triumphs. The cherished dream of his grandfather, and of his own youth, to add the Pope's triple crown to the rest of the hereditary possessions of his family, he had indeed been obliged to resign. He had too much practical Flemish sense to indulge long in chimeras, but he had achieved the Empire over formidable rivals, and he had successively not only conquered, but captured almost every potentate who had arrayed himself in arms against him. Clement and Francis, the Dukes and Landgraves of Cleves, Hesse, Saxony, and Brunswick, he had bound to his chariot wheels; forcing many to eat the bread of humiliation and captivity, during long and weary years. But the concluding portion of his reign had reversed all its previous glories. His whole career had been a failure. He had been defeated, after all, in most of his projects. He had humbled Francis, but Henry had most signally avenged his father. He had trampled upon Philip of Hesse and Frederic of Saxony, but it had been reserved for one of that German race, which he characterized as "dreamy, drunken, and incapable of intrigue," to outwit the man who had outwitted all the world, and to drive before him, in ignominious flight, the conqueror of the nations. The German lad who had learned both war and dissimulation in the court and camp of him who was so profound a master of both arts, was destined to eclipse his teacher on the most august theatre of Christendom. Absorbed at Innspruck with the deliberations of the Trent Council, Charles had not heeded the distant mutterings of the tempest which was gathering around him. While he was preparing to crush, forever, the Protestant Church, with the arms which a bench of bishops were forging, lo! the rapid and desperate Maurice, with long red beard streaming like a meteor in the wind, dashing through the mountain passes, at the head of his lancers—arguments more convincing than all the dogmas of Granvelle! Disguised as an old woman, the Emperor had attempted on the 6th April, to escape in a peasant's wagon, from Innspruck into Flanders. Saved for the time by the mediation of Ferdinand, he had, a few weeks later, after his troops had been defeated by Maurice, at Füssen, again fled at midnight of the 22nd May, almost unattended, sick in body and soul, in the midst of thunder, lightning, and rain, along the difficult Alpine passes from Innspruck into Carinthia. His pupil had permitted his escape, only because in his own language, "for such a bird he had no convenient cage." The imprisoned princes now owed their liberation, not to the Emperor's clemency, but to his panic. The peace of Passau, in the following August, crushed the whole fabric of the Emperor's toil, and laid the foundation of the Protestant Church. He had smitten the Protestants at Mühlberg for the last time. On the other hand, the man who had dealt with Rome, as if the Pope, not he, had been the vassal, was compelled to witness, before he departed, the insolence of a pontiff who took a special pride in insulting and humbling his house, and trampling upon the pride of Charles, Philip and Ferdinand. In France too, the disastrous siege of Metz had taught him that in the imperial zodiac the fatal sign of Cancer had been reached. The figure of a crab, with the words "plus citra," instead of his proud motto of "plus ultra," scrawled on the walls where he had resided during that dismal epoch, avenged more deeply, perhaps, than the jester thought, the previous misfortunes of France. The Grand Turk, too, Solyman the Magnificent, possessed most of Hungary, and held at that moment a fleet ready to sail against Naples, in co-operation with the Pope and France. Thus the Infidel, the Protestant, and the Holy Church were all combined together to crush him. Towards all the great powers of the earth, he stood not in the attitude of a conqueror, but of a disappointed, baffled, defeated potentate. Moreover, he had been foiled long before in his earnest attempts to secure the imperial throne for Philip. Ferdinand and Maximilian had both stoutly resisted his arguments and his blandishments. The father had represented the slender patrimony of their branch of the family, compared with the enormous heritage of Philip; who, being after all, but a man, and endowed with finite powers, might sink under so great a pressure of empire as his father wished to provide for him. Maximilian also, assured his uncle that he had as good an appetite for the crown as Philip, and could digest the dignity quite as easily. The son, too, for whom the Emperor was thus solicitous, had already, before the abdication, repaid his affection with ingratitude. He had turned out all his father's old officials in Milan, and had refused to visit him at Brussels, till assured as to the amount of ceremonial respect which the new-made king was to receive at the hands of his father.

Had the Emperor continued to live and reign, he would have found himself likewise engaged in mortal combat with that great religious movement in the Netherlands, which he would not have been able many years longer to suppress, and which he left as a legacy of blood and fire to his successor. Born in the same year with his century, Charles was a decrepit, exhausted man at fifty-five, while that glorious age, in which humanity was to burst forever the cerements in which it had so long been buried, was but awakening to a consciousness of its strength.

Disappointed in his schemes, broken in his fortunes, with income anticipated, estates mortgaged, all his affairs in confusion; failing in mental powers, and with a constitution hopelessly shattered; it was time for him to retire. He showed his keenness in recognizing the fact that neither his power nor his glory would be increased, should he lag superfluous on the stage where mortification instead of applause was likely to be his portion. His frame was indeed but a wreck. Forty years of unexampled gluttony had done their work. He was a victim to gout, asthma, dyspepsia, gravel. He was crippled in the neck, arms, knees, and hands. He was troubled with chronic cutaneous eruptions. His appetite remained, while his stomach, unable longer to perform the task still imposed upon it, occasioned him constant suffering. Physiologists, who know how important a part this organ plays in the affairs of life, will perhaps see in this physical condition of the Emperor a sufficient explanation, if explanation were required, of his descent from the throne. Moreover, it is well known that the resolution to abdicate before his death had been long a settled scheme with him. It had been formally agreed between himself and the Empress that they should separate at the approach of old age, and pass the remainder of their lives in a convent and a monastery. He had, when comparatively a young man, been struck by the reply made to him by an aged officer, whose reasons he had asked for, earnestly soliciting permission to retire from the imperial service. It was, said the veteran, that he might put a little space of religious contemplation between the active portion of his life and the grave.

A similar determination, deferred from time to time, Charles had now carried into execution. While he still lingered in Brussels, after his abdication, a comet appeared, to warn him to the fulfilment of his purpose. From first to last, comets and other heavenly bodies were much connected with his evolutions and arrangements. There was no mistaking the motives with which this luminary had presented itself. The Emperor knew very well, says a contemporary German chronicler, that it portended pestilence and war, together with the approaching death of mighty princes. "My fates call out," he cried, and forthwith applied himself to hasten the preparations for his departure.

The romantic picture of his philosophical retirement at Juste, painted originally by Sandoval and Siguenza, reproduced by the fascinating pencil of Strada, and imitated in frequent succession by authors of every age and country, is unfortunately but a sketch of fancy. The investigations of modern writers have entirely thrown down the scaffolding on which the airy fabric, so delightful to poets and moralists, reposed. The departing Emperor stands no longer in a transparency robed in shining garments. His transfiguration is at an end. Every action, almost every moment of his retirement, accurately chronicled by those who shared his solitude, have been placed before our eyes, in the most felicitous manner, by able and brilliant writers. The Emperor, shorn of the philosophical robe in which he had been conventionally arrayed for three centuries, shivers now in the cold air of reality.

So far from his having immersed himself in profound and pious contemplation, below the current of the world's events, his thoughts, on the contrary, never were for a moment diverted from the political surface of the times. He read nothing but despatches; he wrote or dictated interminable ones in reply, as dull and prolix as any which ever came from his pen. He manifested a succession of emotions at the course of contemporary affairs, as intense and as varied, as if the world still rested in his palm. He was, in truth, essentially a man of action. He had neither the taste nor talents which make a man great in retirement. Not a lofty thought, not a generous sentiment, not a profound or acute suggestion in his retreat has been recorded from his lips. The epigrams which had been invented for him by fabulists have been all taken away, and nothing has been substituted, save a few dull jests exchanged with stupid friars. So far from having entertained and even expressed that sentiment of religious toleration for which he was said to have been condemned as a heretic by the inquisition, and for which Philip was ridiculously reported to have ordered his father's body to be burned, and his ashes scattered to the winds, he became in retreat the bigot effectually, which during his reign he had only been conventionally. Bitter regrets that he should have kept his word to Luther, as if he had not broken faith enough to reflect upon in his retirement; stern self-reproach for omitting to put to death, while he had him in his power, the man who had caused all the mischief of the age; fierce instructions thundered from his retreat to the inquisitors to hasten the execution of all heretics,—including particularly his ancient friends, preachers and almoners, Cazalla and Constantine de Fuente; furious exhortations to Philip—as if Philip needed a prompter in such a work—that he should set himself to "cutting out the root of heresy with rigor and rude chastisement;"—such explosions of savage bigotry as these, alternating with exhibitions of revolting gluttony, with surfeits of sardine omelettes, Estramadura sausages, eel pies, pickled partridges, fat capons, quince syrups, iced beer, and flagons of Rhenish, relieved by copious draughts of senna and rhubarb, to which his horror-stricken doctor doomed him as he ate—compose a spectacle less attractive to the imagination than the ancient portrait of the cloistered Charles. Unfortunately it is the one which was painted from life.

HENRY DAVID THOREAU (1817-1862)

From WALDEN OR, LIFE IN THE WOODS

I Went to the Woods

I WENT to the woods because I wished to live deliberately, to front only the essential facts of life, and see if I could not learn what it had to teach, and not, when I came to die, discover that I had not lived. I did not wish to live what was not life, living is so dear; nor did I wish to practice resignation, unless it was quite necessary. I wanted to live deep and suck out all the marrow of life, to live so sturdily and Spartan-like as to put to rout all that was not life, to cut a broad swath and shave close, to drive life into a corner, and reduce it to its lowest terms, and, if it proved to be mean, why then to get the whole and genuine meanness of it, and publish its meanness to the world; or if it were sublime, to know it by experience, and be able to give a true account of it in my next excursion. For most men, it appears to me, are in a strange uncertainty about it, whether it is of the devil or of God, and have *somewhat hastily* concluded that it is the chief end of man here to "glorify God and enjoy him forever."

Still we live meanly, like ants; though the fable tells us that we were long ago changed into men; like pygmies we fight with cranes; it is error upon error, and clout upon clout, and our best virtue has for its occasion a superfluous and evitable wretchedness. Our life is frittered away by detail. An honest man has hardly need to count more than his ten fingers, or in extreme cases he may add his ten toes, and lump the rest. Simplicity, simplicity, simplicity! I say, let your affairs be as two or three, and not a hundred or a thousand; instead of a million count half a dozen, and keep your accounts on your thumb nail. In the midst of this chopping sea of civilized life, such are the clouds and storms and quicksands and thousand-and-one items to be allowed for, that a man has to live, if he would not founder and go to the bottom and not make his port at all, by dead reckoning, and he must be a great calculator indeed who succeeds. Simplify, simplify. Instead of three meals a day, if it be necessary eat but one; instead of a hundred dishes, five; and reduce other things in proportion. Our life is like a German Confederacy, made up of petty states, with its boundary forever fluctuating, so that even a German cannot tell you how it is bounded at any moment. The nation itself, with all its so-called internal improvements, which, by the way are all external and superficial, is just such an unwieldy and overgrown establishment, cluttered with furniture and tripped up by its own traps, ruined by luxury and heedless expense, by want of calculation and a worthy aim, as the million households in the land; and the only cure for it as for them is in a rigid economy, a stern and more than Spartan simplicity of life and elevation of purpose. It lives too fast. Men think that it is essential that the *Nation* have commerce, and export ice, and talk through a telegraph, and ride thirty miles an hour, without a doubt, whether *they* do or not; but whether we should live like baboons or like men, is a little uncertain. If we do not get out sleepers, and forge rails, and devote days and nights to the work, but go to tinkering upon our *lives* to improve *them,* who will build railroads? And if railroads are not built, how shall we get to heaven in season? But if we stay at home and mind our business, who will want railroads? We do not ride on the railroad; it rides upon us. Did you ever think what those sleepers are that underlie the railroad? Each one is a man, an Irishman, or a Yankee man. The rails are laid on them, and they are covered with sand, and the cars run smoothly over them. They are sound sleepers, I assure you. And every few years a new lot is laid down and run over; so that, if some have the pleasure of riding on a rail, others have the misfortune to be ridden upon. And when they run over a man that is walking in his sleep, a supernumerary sleeper in the wrong position, and wake him up, they suddenly stop the cars, and make a hue and cry about it, as if this were an exception. I am glad to know that it takes a gang of men for every five miles to keep the sleepers down and level in their beds as it is, for this is a sign that they may sometime get up again.

Why should we live with such hurry and waste of life? We are determined to be starved before we are hungry. Men say that a stitch in time saves nine, and so they take a thousand stitches to-day to save nine to-morrow. As for *work,* we haven't any of any consequence. We have the Saint Vitus' dance, and cannot possibly keep our heads still. If I should only give a few pulls at the parish bell-rope, as for a fire, that is, without setting the bell, there is hardly a man on his farm in the outskirts of Concord, notwithstanding that press of engagements which was his excuse so many times this morning, nor a boy, nor a woman, I might almost say, but would forsake all and follow that sound, not mainly to save property from the flames, but, if we will confess the truth, much more to see it burn, since burn it must, and we, be it known, did not set it on fire,—or to see it put out, and have a hand in it, if that is done as handsomely; yes, even if it were the parish church itself. Hardly a man takes a half hour's nap after dinner, but when he wakes he holds up his head and asks, "What's the news?" as if the rest of mankind had stood his sentinels. Some give directions to be waked every half hour, doubtless for no other purpose; and then, to pay for it, they tell what they have dreamed. After a night's sleep the news is as indispensable as the breakfast. "Pray tell me anything new that has happened to a man anywhere on this globe,"—and he reads it over his coffee and rolls, that a man has had his eyes gouged out this morning on the Wachito River; never dreaming the while that he lives in the dark unfathomed mammoth cave of this world, and has but the rudiment of an eye himself.

JAMES RUSSELL LOWELL
(1819-1891)

The Courtin'

God makes sech nights, all white an' still
　Fur 'z you can look or listen;
Moonshine an' snow on field an' hill,
　All silence an' all glisten.

Zekle crep' up quite unbeknown
　An' peeked in thru the winder;
An' there sot Huldy all alone,
　'Ith no one nigh to hinder.

A fireplace filled the room's one side
　With half a cord o' wood in—
There warn't no stoves (tell comfort
　　died)
　To bake ye to a puddin'.

The wa'nut logs shot sparkles out
　Towards the pootiest, bless her,
An' leetle flames danced all about
　The chiny on the dresser.

Agin the chimbley crook-necks hung,
　An' in amongst 'em rusted
The ole queen's-arm thet gran'ther
　　Young
　Fetched back from Concord busted.

The very room, coz she was in,
　Seemed warm from floor to ceilin',
An' she looked full ez rosy agin
　Ez the apples she was peelin'.

'Twas kin' o' kingdom-come to look
　On sech a blessed cretur;
A dogrose blushin' to a brook
　Ain't modester nor sweeter.

He was six foot o' man, A 1,
　Clean grit an' human natur';
None couldn't quicker pitch a ton
　Nor dror a furrer straighter.

He'd sparked it with full twenty gals,
　He'd squired 'em, danced 'em, druv
　　'em,
Fust this one, an' then thet, by spells—
　All is, he couldn't love 'em.

But long o' her his veins 'ould run
　All crinkly like curled maple;
The side she breshed felt full o' sun
　Ez a south slope in Ap'il.

She thought no v'ice hed sech a swing
　Ez hisn in the choir;
My! when he made Ole Hunderd ring,
　She *knowed* the Lord was nigher.

An' she'd blush scarlit, right in prayer,
　When her new meetin'-bunnet
Felt somehow thru its crown a pair
　O' blue eyes sot upon it.

Thet night, I tell ye, she looked some!
　She seemed to've gut a new soul,
For she felt sartin-sure he'd come,
　Down to her very shoe-sole.

THE COURTIN'

From a painting by W. L. Taylor

She heered a foot, an' knowed it tu,
 A-raspin' on the scraper,—
All ways to once her feelin's flew
 Like sparks in burnt-up paper.

He kin' o' l'itered on the mat,
 Some doubtful o' the sekle;
His heart kep' goin' pity-pat,
 But hern went pity-Zekle.

An' yit she gin her cheer a jerk
 Ez though she wished him furder,
An' on her apples kep' to work,
 Parin' away like murder.

"You want to see my Pa, I s'pose?"
 "Wal—no—I come designin'"—
"To see my Ma? She's sprinklin' clo'es
 Again to-morrer's i'nin'."

To say why gals acts so or so,
 Or don't, 'ould be presumin';
Mebby to mean yes an' say no
 Comes nateral to women.

He stood a spell on one foot fust,
 Then stood a spell on t'other,
An' on which one he felt the wust
 He couldn't ha' told ye nuther.

Says he, "I'd better call agin";
 Says she, "Think likely, Mister"—
Thet last word pricked him like a pin,
 An'—wal he up an' kist her.

When Ma bimeby upon 'em slips,
 Huldy sot pale ez ashes,
All kin' o' smily roun' the lips
 An' teary roun' the lashes.

Fur she was jes' the quiet kind
 Whose naturs never vary,
Like streams that keep a summer mind
 Snow-hid in Jenooary.

The blood clost roun' her heart felt glued
 Too tight for all expressin',
Tell mother see how matters stood
 An' gin 'em both her blessin'.

Then her red come back like the tide
 Down to the Bay o' Fundy;
An' all I know is they was cried
 In meetin' come nex' Sunday.

Ode Recited at the Harvard Commemoration

I

WEAK-WINGED is song,
 Nor aims at that clear-ethered height
 Whither the brave deed climbs for
 light:
 We seem to do them wrong,
Bringing our robin's-leaf to deck their
 hearse
Who in warm life-blood wrote their no-
 bler verse,
Our trivial song to honor those who come
With ears attuned to strenuous trump
 and drum,
And shaped in squadron-strophes their
 desire,
Live battle-odes whose lines were steel
 and fire:
 Yet sometimes feathered words are
 strong,
A gracious memory to buoy up and save
From Lethe's dreamless ooze, the com-
 mon grave
 Of the unventurous throng.

II

To-day our Reverend Mother welcomes
 back
 Her wisest Scholars, those who under-
 stood
The deeper teaching of her mystic tome,
 And offered their fresh lives to make it
 good:
 No lore of Greece or Rome,
No science peddling with the names of
 things,
Or reading stars to find inglorious fates,
 Can lift our life with wings
Far from Death's idle gulf that for the
 many waits,
 And lengthen out our dates
With that clear fame whose memory
 sings
In manly hearts to come, and nerves them
 and dilates:

Nor such thy teaching, Mother of us all!
  Not such the trumpet-call
  Of thy diviner mood,
  That could thy sons entice
From happy homes and toils, the fruitful
    nest
Of those half-virtues which the world
    calls best,
  Into War's tumult rude;
  But rather far that stern device
The sponsors chose that round thy cradle
    stood
  In the dim, unventured wood,
  The VERITAS that lurks beneath
  The letter's unprolific sheath,
  Life of whate'er makes life worth liv-
    ing,
Seed-grain of high emprise, immortal
    food,
  One heavenly thing whereof earth hath
    the giving.

III

Many loved Truth, and lavished life's
    best oil
Amid the dust of books to find her,
Content at last, for guerdon of their toil,
  With the cast mantle she hath left be-
    hind her.
  Many in sad faith sought for her,
  Many with crossed hands sighed for
    her;
  But these, our brothers, fought for
    her,
  At life's dear peril wrought for her,
  So loved her that they died for her,
  Tasting the raptured fleetness
  Of her divine completeness:
  Their higher instinct knew
Those love her best who to themselves
    are true,
And what they dare to dream of, dare
    to do;
  They followed her and found her
  Where all may hope to find,
Not in the ashes of the burnt-out mind,
But beautiful, with danger's sweetness
    round her.

Where faith made whole with deed
Breathes its awakening breath
Into the lifeless creed,
They saw her plumed and mailed,
With sweet, stern face unveiled,
And all-repaying eyes, look proud on
    them in death.

IV

Our slender life runs rippling by, and
    glides
  Into the silent hollow of the past;
  What is there that abides
  To make the next age better for the
    last?
  Is earth too poor to give us
Something to live for here that shall
    outlive us?
  Some more substantial boon
Than such as flows and ebbs with For-
    tune's fickle moon?
  The little that we see
  From doubt is never free;
  The little that we do
  Is but half-nobly true;
  With our laborious hiving
What men call treasure, and the gods call
    dross,
  Life seems a jest of Fate's contriving,
  Only secure in every one's conniving,
A long account of nothings paid with
    loss,
Where we poor puppets, jerked by unseen
    wires,
  After our little hour of strut and rave,
With all our pasteboard passions and de-
    sires,
  Loves, hates, ambitions, and immortal
    fires,
  Are tossed pell-mell together in the
    grave.
  But stay! no age was e'er degenerate,
  Unless men held it at too cheap a rate,
  For in our likeness still we shape our
    fate.
  Ah, there is something here
  Unfathomed by the cynic's sneer,

Something that gives our feeble light
A high immunity from Night,
Something that leaps life's narrow bars
To claim its birthright with the hosts of
    heaven;
A seed of sunshine that can leaven
Our earthy dulness with the beams of
    stars,
    And glorify our clay
With light from fountains elder than the
    Day;
A conscience more divine than we,
A gladness fed with secret tears,
A vexing, forward-reaching sense
Of some more noble permanence;
    A light across the sea,
Which haunts the soul and will not let
    it be,
Still beaconing from the heights of un-
    degenerate years.

V

Whither leads the path
To ampler fates that leads?
Not down through flowery meads,
    To reap an aftermath
Of youth's vainglorious weeds;
But up the steep, amid the wrath
And shock of deadly hostile creeds,
Where the world's best hope and
    stay
By battle's flashes gropes a desperate
    way,
And every turf the fierce foot clings to
    bleeds.
    Peace hath her not ignoble wreath,
    Ere yet the sharp, decisive word
Light the black lips of cannon, and the
    sword
    Dreams in its easeful sheath;
But some day the live coal behind the
    thought,
    Whether from Baäl's stone obscene,
    Or from the shrine serene
    Of God's pure altar brought,
Bursts up in flame; the war of tongue
and pen

Learns with what deadly purpose it was
    fraught,
And, helpless in the fiery passion caught,
Shakes all the pillared state with shock of
    men:
Some day the soft Ideal that we wooed
Confronts us fiercely, foe-beset, pursued,
And cries reproachful: "Was it, then, my
    praise,
And not myself was loved? Prove now
    thy truth;
I claim of thee the promise of thy youth;
Give me thy life, or cower in empty
    phrase,
The victim of thy genius, not its mate!"
    Life may be given in many ways,
    And loyalty to Truth be sealed
As bravely in the closet as the field,
    So bountiful is Fate;
    But then to stand beside her,
    When craven churls deride her,
To front a lie in arms and not to yield,
    This shows, methinks, God's plan
    And measure of a stalwart man,
    Limbed like the old heroic breeds,
    Who stands self-poised on manhood's
    solid earth,
    Not forced to frame excuses for his
    birth,
Fed from within with all the strength he
    needs.

VI

Such was he, our Martyr-Chief,
    Whom late the Nation he had led,
    With ashes on her head,
Wept with the passion of an angry grief:
Forgive me, if from present things I turn
To speak what in my heart will beat and
    burn,
And hang my wreath on his world-hon-
    ored urn.
    Nature, they say, doth dote,
    And cannot make a man
    Save on some worn-out plan,
    Repeating us by rote:
For him her Old-World moulds aside
    she threw,

And, choosing sweet clay from the breast
Of the unexhausted West,
With stuff untainted shaped a hero new,
Wise, steadfast in the strength of God, and true.
How beautiful to see
Once more a shepherd of mankind indeed,
Who loved his charge, but never loved to lead;
One whose meek flock the people joyed to be,
Not lured by any cheat of birth,
But by his clear-grained human worth,
And brave old wisdom of sincerity!
They knew that outward grace is dust;
They could not choose but trust
In that sure-footed mind's unfaltering skill,
And supple-tempered will
That bent like perfect steel to spring again and thrust.
His was no lonely mountain-peak of mind,
Thrusting to thin air o'er our cloudy bars,
A sea-mark now, now lost in vapors blind;
Broad prairie rather, genial, level-lined,
Fruitful and friendly for all humankind,
Yet also nigh to heaven and loved of loftiest stars.
Nothing of Europe here,
Or, then, of Europe fronting morn-ward still,
Ere any names of Serf and Peer
Could Nature's equal scheme deface
And thwart her genial will;
Here was a type of the true elder race,
And one of Plutarch's men talked with us face to face.
I praise him not; it were too late;
And some innative weakness there must be
In him who condescends to victory

Such as the Present gives, and cannot wait,
Safe in himself as in a fate.
So always firmly he:
He knew to bide his time,
And can his fame abide,
Still patient in his simple faith sublime,
Till the wise years decide.
Great captains, with their guns and drums,
Disturb our judgment for the hour,
But at last silence comes;
These all are gone, and, standing like a tower,
Our children shall behold his fame,
The kindly-earnest, brave, foreseeing man,
Sagacious, patient, dreading praise, not blame,
New birth of our new soil, the first American.

VII

Long as man's hope insatiate can discern
Or only guess some more inspiring goal
Outside of Self, enduring as the pole,
Along whose course the flying axles burn
Of spirits bravely-pitched, earth's manlier brood;
Long as below we cannot find
The meed that stills the inexorable mind;
So long this faith to some ideal Good,
Under whatever mortal name it masks,
Freedom, Law, Country, this ethereal mood
That thanks the Fates for their severer tasks,
Feeling its challenged pulses leap,
While others skulk in subterfuges cheap,
And, set in Danger's van, has all the boon it asks,
Shall win man's praise and woman's love,
Shall be a wisdom that we set above

All other skills and gifts to culture dear,
A virtue round whose forehead we en-
wreathe
Laurels that with a living passion
breathe
When other crowns grow, while we twine
them, sear.
What brings us thronging these high
rites to pay,
And seal these hours the noblest of our
year,
Save that our brothers found this better way?

VIII

We sit here in the Promised Land
That flows with Freedom's honey and
milk;
But 'twas they won it, sword in hand,
Making the nettle danger soft for us as
silk.
We welcome back our bravest and our
best;—
Ah me! not all! some come not with
the rest,
Who went forth brave and bright as any
here!
I strive to mix some gladness with my
strain,
But the sad strings complain,
And will not please the ear:
I sweep them for a pæan, but they wane
Again and yet again
Into a dirge, and die away in pain.
In these brave ranks I only see the gaps,
Thinking of dear ones whom the dumb
turf wraps,
Dark to the triumph which they died to
gain:
Fitlier may others greet the living,
For me the past is unforgiving;
I with uncovered head
Salute the sacred dead,
Who went, and who return not.—Say
not so!
'Tis not the grapes of Canaan that
repay,
But the high faith that failed not by
the way;

Virtue treads paths that end not in the
grave;
No bar of endless night exiles the brave;
And to the saner mind
We rather seem the dead that stayed be-
hind.
Blow, trumpets, all your exultations
blow!
For never shall their aureoled presence
lack:
I see them muster in a gleaming row,
With ever-youthful brows that nobler
show;
We find in our dull road their shining
track;
In every nobler mood
We feel the orient of their spirit glow,
Part of our life's unalterable good,
Of all our saintlier aspiration;
They come transfigured back,
Secure from change in their high-hearted
ways,
Beautiful evermore, and with the rays
Of morn on their white Shields of Ex-
pectation!

IX

But is there hope to save
Even this ethereal essence from the
grave?
What ever 'scaped Oblivion's subtle
wrong
Save a few clarion names, or golden
threads of song?
Before my musing eye
The mighty ones of old sweep by,
Disvoicèd now and insubstantial things,
As noisy once as we; poor ghosts of
kings,
Shadows of empire wholly gone to
dust,
And many races, nameless long ago,
To darkness driven by that imperious
gust
Of ever-rushing Time that here doth
blow:
O visionary world, condition strange,
Where naught abiding is but only
Change,

Where the deep-bolted stars themselves
  still shift and range!
  Shall we to more continuance make
  pretence?
Renown builds tombs; a life-estate is
  Wit;
    And, bit by bit,
The cunning years steal all from us but
  woe:
  Leaves are we, whose decays no har-
    vest sow.
  But, when we vanish hence,
  Shall they lie forceless in the dark be-
  low,
  Save to make green their little length
    of sods,
  Or deepen pansies for a year or two,
  Who now to us are shining-sweet as
    gods?
  Was dying all they had the skill to do?
  That were not fruitless: but the Soul
    resents
  Such short-lived service, as if blind
    events
  Ruled without her, or earth could so
    endure;
  She claims a more divine investiture
  Of longer tenure than Fame's airy
    rents;
  Whate'er she touches doth her nature
    share;
  Her inspiration haunts the ennobled
    air,
  Gives eyes to mountains blind,
  Ears to the deaf earth, voices to the
    wind,
  And her clear trump sings succor
    everywhere
  By lonely bivouacs to the wakeful
    mind;
  For soul inherits all that soul could
    dare:
  Yea, Manhood hath a wider span
And larger privilege of life than man.
The single deed, the private sacrifice,
So radiant now through proudly-hidden
  tears,
Is covered up ere long from mortal
  eyes

With thoughtless drift of the deciduous
  years;
But that high privilege that makes all
  men peers,
That leap of heart whereby a people
  rise
  Up to a noble anger's height,
And, flamed on by the Fates, not shrink,
  but grow more bright,
  That swift validity in noble veins,
  Of choosing danger and disdaining
    shame,
  Of being set on flame
By the pure fire that flies all contact
  base,
But wraps its chosen with angelic might,
  These are imperishable gains,
  Sure as the sun, medicinal as light,
  These hold great futures in their lusty
  reins
And certify to earth a new imperial race.

X

  Who now shall sneer?
  Who dare again to say we trace
  Our lines to a plebeian race?
  Roundhead and Cavalier!
Dumb are those names erewhile in battle
  loud;
Dream-footed as the shadow of a cloud,
  They flit across the ear:
That is best blood that hath most iron
  in't,
To edge resolve with, pouring without
  stint
  For what makes manhood dear.
  Tell us not of Plantagenets,
Hapsburgs, and Guelfs, whose thin
  bloods crawl
Down from some victor in a border-
  brawl!
  How poor their outworn coronets,
Matched with one leaf of that plain civic
  wreath
Our brave for honor's blazon shall be-
  queath,
  Through whose desert a rescued
  Nation sets

Her heel on treason, and the trumpet
  hears
Shout victory, tingling Europe's sullen
  ears
  With vain resentments and more vain
    regrets!

XI

Not in anger, not in pride,
Pure from passion's mixture rude,
Ever to base earth allied,
But with far-heard gratitude,
Still with heart and voice renewed,
To heroes living and dear martyrs
  dead,
The strain should close that consecrates
  our brave.
  Lift the heart and lift the head!
  Lofty be its mood and grave,
  Not without a martial ring,
  Not without a prouder tread
  And a peal of exultation:
  Little right has he to sing
  Through whose heart in such an
    hour
  Beats no march of conscious power,
  Sweeps no tumult of elation!
  'Tis no Man we celebrate,
  By his country's victories great,
A hero half, and half the whim of
  Fate,
  But the pith and marrow of a
    Nation
  Drawing force from all her men,
  Highest, humblest, weakest, all,
  For her time of need, and then
  Pulsing it again through them,
Till the basest can no longer cower,
Feeling his soul spring up divinely tall,
Touched but in passing by her mantle-
  hem.
Come back, then, noble pride, for 'tis her
  dower!
  How could poet ever tower,
  If his passions, hopes, and fears,
  If his triumphs and his tears,
  Kept not measure with his people?
Boom, cannon, boom to all the winds and
  waves!

Clash out, glad bells, from every rocking
  steeple!
Banners, advance with triumph, bend
  your staves!
  And from every mountain-peak
  Let beacon-fire to answering beacon
    speak,
  Katahdin tell Monadnock, Whiteface
    he,
  And so leap on in light from sea to
    sea,
    Till the glad news be sent
    Across a kindling continent,
Making earth feel more firm and air
  breathe braver:
"Be proud! for she is saved, and all have
  helped to save her!
  She that lifts up the manhood of the
    poor,
  She of the open soul and open door,
  With room about her hearth for all
    mankind!
  The fire is dreadful in her eyes no
    more;
  From her bold front the helm she doth
    unbind,
  Sends all her handmaid armies back to
    spin,
  And bids her navies, that so lately
    hurled
  Their crashing battle, hold their thun-
    ders in,
Swimming like birds of calm along the
  unharmful shore.
  No challenge sends she to the elder
    world,
  That looked askance and hated; a light
    scorn
  Plays o'er her mouth, as round her
    mighty knees
  She calls her children back, and waits
    the morn
Of nobler day, enthroned between her
  subject seas."

XII

Bow down, dear Land, for thou hast
  found release!
  Thy God, in these distempered days,

Hath taught thee the sure wisdom of
His ways,
And through thine enemies hath wrought
thy peace!
Bow down in prayer and praise!
No poorest in thy borders but may
now
Lift to the juster skies a man's enfran-
chised brow.
O Beautiful! my Country! ours once
more!
Smoothing thy gold of war-dishevelled
hair
O'er such sweet brows as never other
wore,
And letting thy set lips,
Freed from wrath's pale eclipse,
The rosy edges of their smile lay bare,
What words divine of lover or of poet
Could tell our love and make thee know
it,
Among the Nations bright beyond com-
pare?
What were our lives without thee?
What all our lives to save thee?
We reck not what we gave thee;
We will not dare to doubt thee,
But ask whatever else, and we will dare!

WALT WHITMAN (1819-1892)

Song of the Open Road

I

AFOOT and light-hearted, I take to the
open road,
Healthy, free, the world before me,
The long brown path before me, leading
wherever I choose.

Henceforth I ask not good-fortune—I
myself am good-fortune;
Henceforth I whimper no more, postpone
no more, need nothing,
Strong and content, I travel the open
road.

The earth—that is sufficient;
I do not want the constellations any
nearer;
I know they are very well where they
are;
I know they suffice for those who belong
to them.

(Still here I carry my old delicious burdens;
I carry them, men and women—I carry
them with me wherever I go;
I swear it is impossible for me to get rid
of them;
I am fill'd with them, and I will fill them
in return.)

2

You road I enter upon and look around!
I believe you are not all that is here;
I believe that much unseen is also here.

Here the profound lesson of reception,
neither preference nor denial;
The black with his woolly head, the felon,
the diseas'd, the illiterate person, are
not denied;
The birth, the hasting after the physician,
the beggar's tramp, the drunkard's
stagger, the laughing party of me-
chanics,

The escaped youth, the rich person's carriage, the fop, the eloping couple,
The early market-man, the hearse, the
moving of furniture into the town,
the return back from the town,
They pass—I also pass—anything passes
—none can be interdicted;
None but are accepted—none but are
dear to me.

3

You air that serves me with breath to
speak!
You objects that call from diffusion my
meanings, and give them shape!
You light that wraps me and all things
in delicate equable showers!
You paths worn in the irregular hollows
by the roadsides!
I think you are latent with unseen exist-
ences—you are so dear to me.

You flagg'd walks of the cities! you strong curbs at the edges!

You ferries! you planks and posts of wharves! you timber-lined sides! you distant ships!

You rows of houses! you window-pierced façades! you roofs!

You porches and entrances! you copings and iron guards!

You windows whose transparent shells might expose so much!

You doors and ascending steps! you arches!

You gray stones of interminable pavements! you trodden crossings!

From all that has been near you, I believe you have imparted to yourselves, and now would impart the same secretly to me;

From the living and the dead I think you have peopled your impassive surfaces, and the spirits thereof would be evident and amicable with me.

4

The earth expanding right hand and left hand,

The picture alive, every part in its best light,

The music falling in where it is wanted, and stopping where it is not wanted,

The cheerful voice of the public road— the gay fresh sentiment of the road.

O highway I travel! O public road! do you say to me, *Do not leave me?*

Do you say, *Venture not? If you leave me, you are lost?*

Do you say, *I am already prepared—I am well-beaten and undenied—adhere to me?*

O public road! I say back, I am not afraid to leave you—yet I love you;

You express me better than I can express myself;

You shall be more to me than my poem.

I think heroic deeds were all conceiv'd in the open air, and all great poems also;

I think I could stop here myself, and do miracles;

(My judgments, thoughts, I henceforth try by the open air, the road;)

I think whatever I shall meet on the road I shall like, and whoever beholds me shall like me;

I think whoever I see must be happy.

5

From this hour, freedom!

From this hour I ordain myself loos'd of limits and imaginary lines,

Going where I list, my own master, total and absolute,

Listening to others, and considering well what they say,

Pausing, searching, receiving, contemplating,

Gently, but with undeniable will, divesting myself of the holds that would hold me.

I inhale great draughts of space;

The east and the west are mine, and the north and the south are mine.

I am larger, better than I thought;

I did not know I held so much goodness.

All seems beautiful to me;

I can repeat over to men and women, You have done such good to me, I would do the same to you.

I will recruit for myself and you as I go;

I will scatter myself among men and women as I go;

I will toss the new gladness and roughness among them;

Whoever denies me, it shall not trouble me;

Whoever accepts me, he or she shall be blessed, and shall bless me.

6

Now if a thousand perfect men were to appear, it would not amaze me;

Now if a thousand beautiful forms of women appear'd, it would not astonish me.

Now I see the secret of the making of the best persons,

It is to grow in the open air, and to eat and sleep with the earth.

Here a great personal deed has room;

A great deed seizes upon the hearts of
the whole race of men,
Its effusion of strength and will over-
whelms law, and mocks all authority
and all argument against it.

Here is the test of wisdom;
Wisdom is not finally tested in schools;
Wisdom cannot be pass'd from one having it, to another not having it;
Wisdom is of the Soul, is not susceptible
of proof, is its own proof,
Applies to all stages and objects and
qualities, and is content,
Is the certainty of the reality and immortality of things, and the excellence of
things;
Something there is in the float of the
sight of things that provokes it out
of the Soul.

Now I reëxamine philosophies and religions,
They may prove well in lecture-rooms,
yet not prove at all under the spacious clouds, and along the landscape
and flowing currents.
Here is realization;
Here is a man tallied—he realizes here
what he has in him;
The past, the future, majesty, love—if
they are vacant of you, you are
vacant of them.
Only the kernel of every object nourishes;
Where is he who tears off the husks for
you and me?
Where is he that undoes stratagems and
envelopes for you and me?

Here is adhesiveness—it is not previously
fashion'd—it is apropos;
Do you know what it is, as you pass, to
be loved by strangers?
Do you know the talk of those turning
eye-balls?

7

Here is the efflux of the Soul;
The efflux of the Soul comes from within, through embower'd gates, ever
provoking questions:
These yearnings, why are they? These
thoughts in the darkness, why are
they?

Why are there men and women that
while they are nigh me, the sun-light
expands my blood?
Why, when they leave me, do my pen-
nants of joy sink flat and lank?
Why are there trees I never walk under,
but large and melodious thoughts descend upon me?
(I think they hang there winter and
summer on those trees, and always
drop fruit as I pass;)
What is it I interchange so suddenly with
strangers?
What with some driver, as I ride on the
seat by his side?
What with some fisherman, drawing his
seine by the shore, as I walk by,
and pause?
What gives me to be free to a woman's
or man's good-will? What gives
them to be free to mine?

8

The efflux of the Soul is happiness—here
is happiness;
I think it pervades the open air, waiting
at all times;
Now it flows unto us—we are rightly
charged.
Here rises the fluid and attaching character;
The fluid and attaching character is the
freshness and sweetness of man and
woman;
(The herbs of the morning sprout no
fresher and sweeter every day out of
the roots of themselves, than it
sprouts fresh and sweet continually
out of itself.)

Toward the fluid and attaching character
exudes the sweat of the love of
young and old;
From it falls distill'd the charm that
mocks beauty and attainments;
Toward it heaves the shuddering longing
ache of contact.

9

Allons! whoever you are, come travel
with me!
Travelling with me, you find what never
tires.

The earth never tires;
The earth is rude, silent, incomprehensible at first—Nature is rude and
incomprehensible at first;
Be not discouraged—keep on—there are
divine things, well envelop'd;
I swear to you there are divine things
more beautiful than words can tell.

Allons! we must not stop here!
However sweet these laid-up stores—
however convenient this dwelling we
cannot remain here;
However shelter'd this port, and however
calm these waters, we must not
anchor here;
However welcome the hospitality that
surrounds us, we are permitted to
receive it but a little while.

10

Allons! the inducements shall be greater;
We will sail pathless and wild seas;
We will go where winds blow, waves dash,
and the Yankee clipper speeds by
under full sail.

Allons! with power, liberty, the earth,
the elements!
Health, defiance, gayety, self-esteem,
curiosity;
Allons! from all formules!
From your formules, O bat-eyed and ma-
terialistic priests!
The stale cadaver blocks up the passage
—the burial waits no longer.

Allons! yet take warning!
He travelling with me needs the best
blood, thews, endurance;
None may come to the trial, till he or she
brings courage and health.
Come not here if you have already spent
the best of yourself;
Only those may come, who come in sweet
and determin'd bodies;
No diseas'd person—no rum-drinker or
venereal taint is permitted here.

I and mine do not convince by arguments,
similes, rhymes;
We convince by our presence.

11

Listen! I will be honest with you;

I do not offer the old smooth prizes, but
offer rough new prizes;
These are the days that must happen to
you:
You shall not heap up what is call'd
riches,
You shall scatter with lavish hand all
that you earn or achieve,
You but arrive at the city to which you
were destin'd—you hardly settle
yourself to satisfaction, before you
are call'd by an irresistible call to
depart,
You shall be treated to the ironical smiles
and mockings of those who remain
behind you;
What beckonings of love you receive, you
shall only answer with passionate
kisses of parting,
You shall not allow the hold of those
who spread their reach'd hands
toward you.

12

Allons! after the GREAT COMPANIONS!
and to belong to them!
They too are on the road! they are the
swift and majestic men! they are the
greatest women.
Over that which hinder'd them—over
that which retarded—passing impedi-
ments large or small,
Committers of crimes, committers of
many beautiful virtues.
Enjoyers of calms of seas, and storms of
seas,
Sailors of many a ship, walkers of many
a mile of land,
Habitués of many distant countries,
habitués of far-distant dwellings,
Trusters of men and women, observers
of cities, solitary toilers,
Pausers and contemplators of tufts, blossoms, shells of the shore,
Dancers at wedding-dances, kissers of
brides, tender helpers of children,
bearers of children,
Soldiers of revolts, standers by gaping
graves, lowerers down of coffins,
Journeyers over consecutive seasons, over
the years—the curious years, each
emerging from that which preceded
it,

Journeyers as with companions, namely,
their own diverse phases,
Forth-steppers from the latent unrealized
baby-days,
Journeyers gayly with their own youth—
Journeyers with their bearded and
well-grain'd manhood,
Journeyers with their womanhood, ample,
unsurpass'd, content,
Journeyers with their own sublime old
age of manhood or womanhood,
Old age, calm, expanded, broad with the
haughty breadth of the universe,
Old age, flowing free with the delicious
near-by freedom of death.

13

Allons! to that which is endless, as it was
beginningless,
To undergo much, tramps of days, rests
of nights,
To merge all in the travel they tend to,
and the days and nights they tend to,
Again to merge them in the start of
superior journeys;
To see nothing anywhere but what you
may reach it and pass it,
To conceive no time, however distant, but
what you may reach it and pass it,
To look up or down no road but it
stretches and waits for you—however long, but it stretches and waits
for you;
To see no being, not God's or any, but
you also go thither,
To see no possession but you may possess
it—enjoying all without labor or
purchase—abstracting the feast, yet
not abstracting one particle of it;
To take the best of the farmer's farm and
the rich man's elegant villa, and the
chaste blessings of the well-married
couple, and the fruits of orchards
and flowers of gardens,
To take to your use out of the compact
cities as you pass through,
To carry buildings and streets with you
afterward wherever you go,
To gather the minds of men out of their
brains as you encounter them—to
gather the love out of their hearts,
To take your lovers on the road with you,
for all that you leave them behind you,

To know the universe itself as a road—
as many roads—as roads to travelling souls.

14

The Soul travels;
The body does not travel as much as the
soul;
The body has just as great a work as the
soul, and parts away at last for the
journeys of the soul.

All parts away for the progress of souls;
All religion, all solid things, arts, governments,—all that was or is apparent upon this globe or any globe,
falls into niches and corners before
the procession of Souls along the
grand roads of the universe.

Of the progress of the souls of men and
women along the grand roads of the
universe, all other progress is the
needed emblem and sustenance.

Forever alive, forever forward,
Stately, solemn, sad, withdrawn, baffled,
mad, turbulent, feeble, dissatisfied,
Desperate, proud, fond, sick, accepted by
men, rejected by men,
They go! they go! I know that they go,
but I know not where they go;
But I know that they go toward the best
—toward something great.

15

Allons! whoever you are! come forth!
You must not stay sleeping and dallying
there in the house, though you built
it, or though it has been built for
you.
Allons! out of the dark confinement!
It is useless to protest—I know all, and
expose it.

Behold, through you as bad as the rest,
Through the laughter, dancing, dining,
supping, of people,
Inside the dresses and ornaments, inside
of those wash'd and trimm'd faces,
Behold a secret silent loathing and despair.

No husband, no wife, no friend, trusted
to hear the confession;

Another self, a duplicate of every one, skulking and hiding it goes,

Formless and wordless through the streets of the cities, polite and bland in the parlors,

In the cars of rail-roads, in steamboats, in the public assembly,

Home to the houses of men and women, at the table, in the bed-room, everywhere,

Smartly attired, countenance smiling, form upright, death under the breast-bones, hell under the skull-bones,

Under the broadcloth and gloves, under the ribbons and artificial flowers,

Keeping fair with the customs, speaking not a syllable of itself,

Speaking of anything else, but never of itself.

16

Allons! through struggles and wars!
The goal that was named cannot be countermanded.

Have the past struggles succeeded?
What has succeeded? yourself? your nation? nature?

Now understand me well—It is provided in the essence of things, that from any fruition of success, no matter what, shall come forth something to make a greater struggle necessary.

My call is the call of battle—I nourish active rebellion;

He going with me must go well arm'd;

He going with me goes often with spare diet, poverty, angry enemies, desertions.

17

Allons! the road is before us!
It is safe—I have tried it—my own feet have tried it well.

Allons! be not detain'd!

Let the paper remain on the desk unwritten, and the book on the shelf unopen'd!

Let the tools remain in the workshop! let the money remain unearn'd!

Let the school stand! mind not the cry of the teacher!

Let the preacher preach in his pulpit! let the lawyer plead in the court, and the judge expound the law.

Mon enfant! I give you my hand!

I give you my love, more precious than money,

I give you myself, before preaching or law;

Will you give me yourself? will you come travel with me?

Shall we stick by each other as long as we live?

Beat! Beat! Drums!

1

BEAT! beat! drums!—Blow! bugles! blow!

Through the windows—through doors—burst like a ruthless force,

Into the solemn church, and scatter the congregation;

Into the school where the scholar is studying;

Leave not the bridegroom quiet—no happiness must he have now with his bride;

Nor the peaceful farmer any peace, plowing his field or gathering his grain;

So fierce you whirr and proud, you drums —so shrill you bugles blow.

2

Beat! beat! drums!—Blow! bugles! blow!

Over the traffic of cities—over the rumble of wheels in the streets:

Are beds prepared for sleepers at night in the houses? No sleepers must sleep in those beds;

No bargainer's bargains by day—no brokers or speculators—Would they continue?

Would the talkers be talking? would the singer attempt to sing?

Would the lawyer rise in the court to state his case before the judge?

Then rattle quicker, heavier drums—you bugles wilder blow.

3

Beat! beat! drums!—Blow! bugles! blow!

Make no parley—stop for no expostula-
tion;
Mind not the timid—mind not the weeper
or prayer;
Mind not the old man beseeching the
young man;
Let not the child's voice be heard, nor the
mother's entreaties;
Make even the trestles to shake the dead,
where they lie awaiting the hearses,
So strong you thump, O terrible drums—
so loud you bugles blow.

A March in the Ranks Hard-Prest

A MARCH in the ranks hard-prest, and the
road unknown;
A route through a heavy wood, with
muffled steps in the darkness;
Our army foil'd with loss severe, and the
sullen remnant retreating;
Till after midnight glimmer upon us, the
lights of a dim-lighted building;
We come to an open space in the woods,
and halt by the dim-lighted building;
'Tis a large old church at the crossing
roads—'tis now an impromptu hospital;
—Entering but for a minute, I see a sight
beyond all the pictures and poems
ever made:
Shadows of deepest, deepest black, just
lit by moving candles and lamps,
And by one great pitchy torch, stationary,
with wild red flame, and clouds of
smoke;
By these crowds, groups of forms, vaguely
I see, on the floor, some in the pews
laid down;
At my feet more distinctly, a soldier, a
mere lad, in danger of bleeding to
death, (he is shot in the abdomen;)
I staunch the blood temporarily, (the
youngster's face is white as a lily;)
Then before I depart I sweep my eyes
o'er the scene, fain to absorb it all;
Faces, varieties, postures beyond description, most in obscurity, some of them
dead;
Surgeons operating, attendants holding
lights, the smell of ether, the odor of
blood;

The crowd, O the crowd of the bloody
forms of soldiers—the yard outside
also fill'd;
Some on the bare ground, some on planks
or stretchers, some in the death-
spasm sweating;
An occasional scream or cry, the doctor's
shouted orders or calls;
The glisten of the little steel instruments
catching the glint of the torches;
These I resume as I chant—I see again
the forms, I smell the odor;
Then hear outside the orders given, *Fall
in, my men, Fall in;*
But first I bend to the dying lad—his
eyes open—a half-smile gives he me;
Then the eyes close, calmly close, and I
speed forth to the darkness,
Resuming, marching, ever in darkness
marching, on in the ranks,
The unknown road still marching.

When Lilacs Last in the Door-Yard Bloom'd

I

WHEN lilacs last in the door-yard bloom'd,
And the great star early droop'd in the
western sky in the night,
I mourn'd—and yet shall mourn with
ever-returning spring.

O ever-returning spring! trinity sure to
me you bring;
Lilac blooming perennial, and drooping
star in the west,
And thought of him I love.

2

O powerful, western, fallen star!
O shades of night! O moody, tearful
night!
O great star disappear'd! O the black
murk that hides the star!
O cruel hands that hold me powerless!
O helpless soul of me!
O harsh surrounding cloud, that will not
free my soul!

3

In the door-yard fronting an old farm-
house, near the whitewash'd palings,
Stands the lilac bush, tall-growing, with
heart-shaped leaves of rich green,

With many a pointed blossom, rising,
delicate, with the perfume strong I
love,
With every leaf a miracle . . . and from
this bush in the door-yard,
With delicate-color'd blossoms, and heart-
shaped leaves of rich green,
A sprig, with its flower, I break.

4

In the swamp, in secluded recesses,
A shy and hidden bird is warbling a song.
Solitary, the thrush,
The hermit, withdrawn to himself, avoid-
ing the settlements,
Sings by himself a song.
Song of the bleeding throat!
Death's outlet song of life—(for well,
dear brother, I know
If thou wast not gifted to sing, thou
would'st surely die.)

5

Over the breast of the spring, the land,
amid cities,
Amid lanes, and through old woods,
(where lately the violets peep'd from
the ground, spotting the gray débris;)
Amid the grass in the fields each side of
the lanes—passing the endless grass;
Passing the yellow-spear'd wheat, every
grain from its shroud in the dark-
brown fields uprising;
Passing the apple-tree blows of white and
pink in the orchards;
Carrying a corpse to where it shall rest
in the grave,
Night and day journeys a coffin.

6

Coffin that passes through lanes and
streets,
Through day and night, with the great
cloud darkening the land,
With the pomp of the inloop'd flags, with
the cities draped in black,
With the show of the States themselves,
as of crape-veil'd women, standing,
With processions long and winding, and
the flambeaus of the night,
With the countless torches lit—with the
silent sea of faces, and the unbared
heads,

With the waiting depot, the arriving
coffin, and the sombre faces,
With dirges through the night, with the
thousand voices rising strong and
solemn;
With all the mournful voices of the
dirges, pour'd around the coffin,
The dim-lit churches and the shuddering
organs—Where amid these you journey,
With the tolling, tolling bells' perpetual
clang;
Here! coffin that slowly passes,
I give you my sprig of lilac.

7

(Nor for you, for one, alone;
Blossoms and branches green to coffins
all I bring:
For fresh as the morning—thus would I
carol a song for you, O sane and
sacred death.

All over bouquets of roses,
O death! I cover you over with roses
and early lilies;
But mostly and now the lilac that blooms
the first,
Copious, I break, I break the sprigs from
the bushes;
With loaded arms I come, pouring for
you,
For you, and the coffins all of you, O
death.)

8

O western orb, sailing the heaven!
Now I know what you must have meant,
as a month since we walk'd,
As we walk'd up and down in the dark
blue so mystic,
As we walk'd in silence the transparent
shadowy night,
As I saw you had something to tell, as
you bent to me night after night,
As you droop'd from the sky low down,
as if to my side, (while the other
stars all look'd on;)
As we wander'd together the solemn
night, (for something, I know not
what, kept me from sleep;)
As the night advanced, and I saw on the
rim of the west, ere you went, how
full you were of woe;

As I stood on the rising ground in the
    breeze, in the cold transparent night,
As I watch'd where you pass'd and was
    lost in the netherward black of the
    night,
As my soul, in its trouble, dissatisfied,
    sank, as where you, sad orb,
Concluded, dropt in the night, and was
    gone.

9

Sing on, there in the swamp!
O singer bashful and tender! I hear
    your notes—I hear your call;
I hear—I come presently—I understand
    you;
But a moment I linger—for the lustrous
    star has detain'd me;
The star, my departing comrade, holds
    and detains me.

10

O how shall I warble myself for the dead
    one there I loved?
And how shall I deck my song for the
    large sweet soul that has gone?
And what shall my perfume be, for the
    grave of him I love?

Sea-winds, blown from east and west,
Blown from the eastern sea, and blown
    from the western sea, till there on
    the prairies meeting:
These, and with these, and the breath of
    my chant,
I perfume the grave of him I love.

11

O what shall I hang on the chamber
    walls?
And what shall the pictures be that I
    hang on the walls,
To adorn the burial-house of him I love?
Pictures of growing spring, and farms,
    and homes,
With the Fourth-month eve at sundown,
    and the gray smoke lucid and bright,
With floods of the yellow gold of the
    gorgeous, indolent, sinking sun, burn-
    ing, expanding the air;
With the fresh sweet herbage under foot,
    and the pale green leaves of the trees
    prolific;

In the distance the flowing glaze, the
    breast of the river, with a wind-
    dapple here and there;
With ranging hills on the banks, with
    many a line against the sky, and
    shadows;
And the city at hand, with dwellings so
    dense, and stacks of chimneys,
And all the scenes of life, and the work-
    shops, and the workmen homeward
    returning.

12

Lo! body and soul! this land!
Mighty Manhattan, with spires, and the
    sparkling and hurrying tides, and the
    ships;
The varied and ample land—the South
    and the North in the light—Ohio's
    shores, and flashing Missouri,
And ever the far-spreading prairies,
    cover'd with grass and corn.

Lo! the most excellent sun, so calm and
    haughty;
The violet and purple morn, with just-
    felt breezes;
The gentle-soft-born, measureless light;
The miracle, spreading, bathing all—the
    fulfill'd noon;
The coming eve, delicious—the welcome
    night, and the stars,
Over my cities shining all, enveloping
    man and land.

13

Sing on! sing on, you gray-brown bird!
Sing from the swamps, the recesses—
    pour your chant from the bushes;
Limitless out of the dusk, out of the
    cedars and pines.

Sing on, dearest brother—warble your
    reedy song;
Loud human song, with voice of utter-
    most woe.

O liquid, and free, and tender!
O wild and loose to my soul! O won-
    drous singer!
You only I hear . . . yet the star holds
    me, (but will soon depart;)
Yet the lilac, with mastering odor, holds
    me.

14

Now while I sat in the day, and look'd
forth,
In the close of the day, with its light, and
the fields of spring, and the farmer
preparing his crops,
In the large unconscious scenery of my
land, with its lakes and forests,
In the heavenly aerial beauty, (after the
perturb'd winds, and the storms;)
Under the arching heavens of the afternoon swift passing, and the voices of
children and women,
The many-moving sea-tides,—and I saw
the ships how they sailed,
And the summer approaching with richness, and the fields all busy with
labor,
And the infinite separate houses, how they
all went on, each with its meals and
minutia of daily usages;
And the streets, how their throbbings
throbb'd, and the cities pent—lo!
then and there,
Falling upon them all, and among them
all, enveloping me with the rest,
Appear'd the cloud, appear'd the long
black trail;
And I knew Death, its thought, and the
sacred knowledge of death.

15

Then with the knowledge of death as
walking one side of me,
And the thought of death close-walking
the other side of me,
And I in the middle, as with companions,
and as holding the hands of companions,
I fled forth to the hiding receiving night,
that talks not,
Down to the shores of the water, the
path by the swamp in the dimness,
To the solemn shadowy cedars, and
ghostly pines so still.

And the singer so shy to the rest receiv'd
me;
The gray-brown bird I know, receiv'd us
comrades three;
And he sang what seem'd the carol of
death, and a verse for him I love.

From deep secluded recesses,
From the fragrant cedars, and the
ghostly pines so still,
Came the carol of the bird.

And the charm of the carol rapt me,
As I held, as if by their hands, my comrades in the night;
And the voice of my spirit tallied the song
of the bird.

DEATH CAROL

16

Come, lovely and soothing Death,
Undulate round the world, serenely arriving,
arriving,
In the day, in the night, to all, to each,
Sooner or later, delicate Death.

Prais'd be the fathomless universe,
For life and joy, and for objects and knowl-
edge curious;
And for love, sweet love—But praise!
praise! praise!
For the sure-enwinding arms of cool-
enfolding Death.

Dark Mother, always gliding near, with
soft feet,
Have none chanted for thee a chant of
fullest welcome?
Then I chant it for thee—I glorify thee
above all;
I bring thee a song that when thou must in-
deed come, come unfalteringly.

Approach, strong Deliveress!
When it is so—when thou hast taken them,
I joyously sing the dead,
Lost in the loving, floating ocean of thee,
Laved in the flood of thy bliss, O Death.

From me to thee glad serenades,
Dances for thee I propose, saluting thee—
adornments and feastings for thee;
And the sights of the open landscape, and
the high-spread sky, are fitting,
And life and the fields, and the huge and
thoughtful night.

The night, in silence, under many a star;
The ocean shore, and the husky whispering
wave, whose voice I know;

And the soul turning to thee, O vast and well-veil'd Death,
And the body gratefully nestling close to thee.

Over the tree-tops I float thee a song!
Over the rising and sinking waves—over the myriad fields, and the prairies wide;
Over the dense-pack'd cities all, and the teeming wharves and ways,
I float this carol with joy, with joy to thee, O Death!

17

To the tally of my soul,
Loud and strong kept up the gray-brown bird,
With pure, deliberate notes, spreading, filling the night.

Loud in the pines and cedars dim,
Clear in the freshness moist, and the swamp-perfume;
And I with my comrades there in the night.

While my sight that was bound in my eyes unclosed,
As to long panoramas of visions.

18

I saw askant the armies;
And I saw, as in noiseless dreams, hundreds of battle-flags;
Borne through the smoke of the battles, and pierc'd with missiles, I saw them,
And carried hither and yon through the smoke, and torn and bloody;
And at last but a few shreds left on the staffs, (and all in silence,)
And the staffs all splinter'd and broken.

I saw battle-corpses, myriads of them,
And the white skeletons of young men—I saw them;
I saw the debris and debris of all the dead soldiers of the war;
But I saw they were not as was thought;
They themselves were fully at rest—they suffer'd not;
The living remain'd and suffer'd—the mother suffer'd,
And the wife and the child, and the musing comrade suffer'd,
And the armies that remain'd suffer'd.

19

Passing the visions, passing the night;
Passing, unloosing the hold of my comrades' hands;
Passing the song of the hermit bird, and the tallying song of my soul,
(Victorious song, death's outlet song, yet varying, ever-altering song,
As low and wailing, yet clear the notes, rising and falling, flooding the night,
Sadly sinking and fainting, as warning and warning, and yet again bursting with joy,
Covering the earth, and filling the spread of the heaven,
As that powerful psalm in the night I heard from recesses,
Passing, I leave thee, lilac with heart-shaped leaves;
I leave thee there in the door-yard, blooming, returning with spring.
I cease from my song for thee;
From my gaze on thee in the west, fronting the west, communing with thee,
O comrade lustrous, with silver face in the night.

20

Yet each I keep, and all, retrievements out of the night;
The song, the wondrous chant of the gray-brown bird,
And the tallying chant, the echo arous'd in my soul,
With the lustrous and drooping star, with the countenance full of woe,
With the lilac tall, and its blossoms of mastering odor;
With the holders holding my hand, nearing the call of the bird,
Comrades mine, and I in the midst, and their memory ever I keep—for the dead I loved so well;
For the sweetest, wisest soul of all my days and lands . . . and this for his dear sake;
Lilac and star and bird, twined with the chant of my soul,
There in the fragrant pines, and the cedars dusk and dim.

HERMAN MELVILLE (1819-1891)

From MOBY DICK; OR, THE WHITE WHALE

Captain Ahab, of the *Pequod,* cherished madly the one purpose in life or death of killing Moby Dick, the great white whale that, on a previous voyage, had taken off his leg. The *Pequod* sailed from Nantucket on the longest of voyages, round the Horn into the Pacific, to the Japanese whaling grounds and the South Seas. Captain Ahab swore the three mates, the three harpooners, and the crew to vengeance on Moby Dick. The killing of other whales did not in the least divert him from his maniacal purpose. Thoughts of home and of his young wife Mary and his boy, the child of his old age, could not deter him. Reports from other vessels of encounters with Moby Dick, and of the deaths thereby, only made him abandon sleep and remain on deck both night and day, driving the *Pequod* on in the hope of meeting the white monster. Fateful omens portended misfortune. A sea-hawk carried off his hat as he hung in a basket raised aloft, to scan the sea. Fedallah, a mysterious unsleeping Parsee of the crew, foretold that he should die, after the Parsee went and was seen again; but that neither hearse nor coffin could be his; that ere he could die two hearses must verily be seen by him on the sea, the first not made by mortal hands, and the visible wood of the last one grown in America; and that hemp alone could kill him. At last he sighted Moby Dick. The golden doubloon that had hung on the mast as a reward to the man who first saw the white whale was his own; but he left it where it was, for on that day Moby Dick destroyed with his jaws the small boat in which Captain Ahab set forth to harpoon him, and escaped, without harming the two other boats that had been lowered.

"Men," said Ahab, when he was brought back on board, "this gold is mine, for I earned it; but I shall let it abide here till the White Whale is dead; and then, whosoever of ye first raises him, upon the day he shall be killed, this gold is that man's; and if on that day I shall again raise him, then, ten times its sum shall be divided among all of ye!" With the sagacity of forty years' experience, Ahab drove his ship on in the wake of the whale through the night, and presently in the morning the lookouts at the mast-heads shouted "There she blows!—she blows!—she blows!—right ahead!" But the men in their headlong eagerness had mistaken some other thing for the whale-spout; for hardly had Ahab been raised again in his basket when "the triumphant halloo of thirty buckskin lungs was heard, as—much nearer to the ship than the place of the imaginary jet, less than a mile ahead—Moby Dick bodily burst into view! . . . 'There she breaches! there she breaches!' was the cry, as in his immeasurable bravadoes the White Whale tossed himself salmon-like to Heaven." This time from all three of the lowered boats irons went into Moby Dick; but he wrecked all three, and then dived down. The *Pequod* picked up her men—all but the Parsee—and the chase went on, through the second night.

The Chase—Third Day

THE morning of the third day dawned fair and fresh, and once more the solitary night-man at the fore-masthead was relieved by crowds of the daylight lookouts, who dotted every mast and almost every spar.

"D'ye see him?" cried Ahab; but the whale was not yet in sight.

"In his infallible wake, though; but follow that wake, that's all. Helm there; steady, as thou goest, and hast been going. What a lovely day again! were it a new-made world, and made for a summer-house to the angels, and this morning the first of its throwing open to them, a fairer day could not dawn upon that world. Here's food for thought, had Ahab time to think, but Ahab never thinks; he only feels, feels, feels, *that's* tingling enough for mortal man! to think's audacity. God only has that right and privilege. Thinking is, or ought to be, a coolness and a calmness; and our poor hearts throb, and our poor brains beat too much for that. And yet, I've sometimes thought my brain was very calm—frozen calm, this old skull cracks so, like a glass in which the contents turn to ice, and shiver it. And still this hair is growing now; this moment growing, and heat must breed it; but no, it's like that sort of common grass that will grow anywhere, between the earthly clefts of Greenland ice or in Vesuvius lava. How the wild winds blow it; they whip it about me as the torn shreds of split sails lash the tossed ship they cling to. A vile wind that has no doubt blown ere this through prison corridors and cells, and wards of hospitals, and ventilated them, and now comes blowing hither as innocent as fleeces. Out upon it!— it's tainted. Were I the wind, I'd blow no more on such a wicked, miserable world. I'd crawl somewhere to a cave, and slink there. And yet, 'tis a noble and heroic thing, the wind! who ever conquered it? In every fight it has the last and bitterest blow. Run tilting at it, and you but run through it. Ha! a coward wind that strikes stark naked men, but will not stand to receive a single blow. Even Ahab is a braver thing—a nobler thing than *that*. Would now the wind but had a body; but all the things that most exasperate and outrage mortal man, all these things are bodiless, but only bodiless as objects, not as agents. There's a most special, a most cunning, oh, a most malicious difference! And yet, I say again, and swear it now, that there's something all glorious and gracious in the wind. These warm Trade Winds, at least, that in the clear heavens blow straight on, in strong and steadfast, vigorous mildness; and veer not from their mark, however the baser currents of the sea may turn and tack, and mightiest Mississippis of the land shift and swerve about, uncertain where to go at last. And by the eternal Poles! these same Trades that so directly blow my good ship on; these Trades, or something like them—something so unchangeable, and full as strong, blow my keeled soul along! To it! Aloft there! What d'ye see?"

"Nothing, sir."

"Nothing! and noon at hand! The doubloon goes a-begging! See the sun! Aye, aye, it must be so. I've oversailed him. How, got the start? Aye, he's chasing *me* now; not I, *him*—that's bad; I might have known it, too. Fool! the lines—the harpoons he's towing. Aye,

aye, I have run him by last night. About! about! Come down, all of ye, but the regular lookouts! Man the braces!"

Steering as she had done, the wind had been somewhat on the *Pequod's* quarter, so that now being pointed in the reverse direction, the braced ship sailed hard upon the breeze as she rechurned the cream in her own white wake.

"Against the wind he now steers for the open jaw," murmured Starbuck to himself, as he coiled the new-hauled main-brace upon the rail. "God keep us, but already my bones feel damp within me, and from the inside wet my flesh. I misdoubt me that I disobey my God in obeying him!"

"Stand by to sway me up!" cried Ahab, advancing to the hempen basket. "We should meet him soon."

"Aye, aye, sir," and straightway Starbuck did Ahab's bidding, and once more Ahab swung on high.

A whole hour now passed; gold-beaten out to ages. Time itself now held long breaths with keen suspense. But at last, some three points off the weather-bow, Ahab descried the spout again, and instantly from the three mastheads three shrieks went up as if the tongues of fire had voiced it.

"Forehead to forehead I meet thee, this third time, Moby Dick! On deck there!—brace sharper up; crowd her into the wind's eye. He's too far off to lower yet, Mr. Starbuck. The sails shake! Stand over that helmsman with a topmaul! So, so; he travels fast, and I must down. But let me have one more good round look aloft here at the sea; there's time for that. An old, old sight, and yet somehow so young; aye, and not changed a wink since I first saw it, a boy, from the sand-hills of Nantucket! The same!—the same!—the same to Noah as to me. There's a soft shower to leeward. Such lovely leewardings! They must lead somewhere—to something else than common land, more palmy than the palms. Leeward! the white whale goes that way; look to windward, then; the better if the bitterer quarter. But good-bye, good-bye, old masthead! What's this?—green? aye, tiny mosses in these warped cracks. No such green weather stains on Ahab's head! There's the difference now between man's old age and matter's. But aye, old mast, we both grow old together; sound in our hulls, though, are we not, my ship? Aye, minus a leg, that's all. By heaven! this dead wood has the better of my live flesh every way. I can't compare with it; and I've known some ships made of dead trees outlast the lives of men made of the most vital stuff of vital fathers. What's that he said? he should still go before me, my pilot; and yet to be seen again? But where?

Shall I have eyes at the bottom of the sea, supposing I descend those endless stairs? and all night I've been sailing from him, wherever he did sink to. Aye, aye, like many more thou told'st direful truth as touching thyself, O Parsee; but, Ahab, there thy shot fell short. Goodbye, masthead—keep a good eye upon the whale, the while I'm gone. We'll talk to-morrow, nay, to-night, when the white whale lies down there, tied by head and tail."

He gave the word; and still gazing round him, was steadily lowered through the cloven blue air to the deck.

In due time the boats were lowered; but as standing in his shallop's stern, Ahab just hovered upon the point of the descent, he waved to the mate,—who held one of the tackle-ropes on deck—and bade him pause.

"Starbuck!"

"Sir?"

"For the third time my soul's ship starts upon this voyage, Starbuck."

"Aye, sir, thou wilt have it so."

"Some ships sail from their ports, and ever afterwards are missing, Starbuck!"

"Truth, sir: saddest truth."

"Some men die at ebb tide; some at low water; some at the full of the flood;—and I feel now like a billow that's all one crested comb, Starbuck. I am old;—shake hands with me, man."

Their hands met; their eyes fastened; Starbuck's tears the glue.

"Oh, my captain, my captain!—noble heart—go not—go not!—see, it's a brave man that weeps; how great the agony of the persuasion then!"

"Lower away!"—cried Ahab, tossing the mate's arm from him. "Stand by the crew!"

In an instant the boat was pulling round close under the stern.

"The sharks! the sharks!" cried a voice from the low cabin-window there; "O master, my master, come back!"

But Ahab heard nothing; for his own voice was high-lifted then; and the boat leaped on.

Yet the voice spake true; for scarce had he pushed from the ship, when numbers of sharks, seemingly rising from out the dark waters beneath the hull, maliciously snapped at the blades of the oars, every time they dipped in the water; and in this way accompanied the boat with their bites. It is a thing not uncommonly happening to the whaleboats in those swarming seas; the sharks at times apparently following them in the same prescient way that vultures hover over the banners of marching regiments in the east. But these were the first sharks that had been observed by the *Pequod* since the White Whale had been first descried; and whether it was that Ahab's crew were all such tiger-yellow barbarians, and therefore their flesh more musky to the senses of the sharks—a matter sometimes well known to affect them,—however it was, they seemed to follow that one boat without molesting the others.

"Heart of wrought steel!" murmured Starbuck, gazing over the side, and following with his eyes the receding boat—"canst thou yet ring boldly to that sight?—lowering thy keel among ravening sharks, and followed by them, open-mouthed, to the chase; and this the critical third day?—For when three days flow together in one continuous intense pursuit; be sure the first is the morning, the second the noon, and the third the evening and the end of that thing—be that end what it may. Oh! my God! what is this that shoots through me, and leaves me so deadly calm, yet expectant,—fixed at the top of a shudder! Future things swim before me, as in empty outlines and skeletons; all the past is somehow grown dim. Mary, girl! thou fadest in pale glories behind me; boy! I seem to see but thy eyes grown wondrous blue. Strangest problems of life seem clearing; but clouds sweep between—Is my journey's end coming? My legs feel faint; like his who has footed it all day. Feel thy heart,—beats it yet?—Stir thyself, Starbuck!—stave it off—move, move! speak aloud!—Masthead there! See ye my boy's hand on the hill?—Crazed;—aloft there!—keep thy keenest eye upon the boats:—mark well the whale!—Ho! again!—drive off that hawk! see! he pecks—he tears the vane"—pointing to the red flag flying at the maintruck—"Ha! he soars away with it!—Where's the old man now? sees't thou that sight, oh Ahab!—shudder, shudder!"

The boats had not gone very far, when by a signal from the mastheads—a downward pointed arm, Ahab knew that the whale had sounded; but intending to be near him at the next rising, he held on his way a little sideways from the vessel; the becharmed crew maintaining the profoundest silence, as the head-beat waves hammered and hammered against the opposing bow.

"Drive, drive in your nails, oh ye waves! to their uttermost heads drive them in! ye but strike a thing without a lid; and no coffin and no hearse can be mine:—and hemp only can kill me! Ha! ha!"

Suddenly the waters around them slowly swelled in broad circles; then quickly upheaved, as if sideways sliding from a submerged berg of ice, swiftly rising to the surface. A low rumbling sound was heard; a subterraneous hum; and then all held their breaths; as bedraggled with trailing ropes, and harpoons, and lances, a vast form shot lengthwise, but obliquely from the sea. Shrouded in a thin drooping veil of mist, it hovered for a moment in the rainbowed air; and then fell swamping back into the deep. Crushed thirty feet upwards, the waters flashed for an instant like heaps of fountains, then brokenly sank in a shower of flakes, leaving the circling surface creamed like new milk round the marble trunk of the whale.

"Give way!" cried Ahab to the oarsmen, and the boats darted forward to the attack; but maddened by yesterday's fresh irons that corroded in him, Moby Dick seemed combinedly possessed by all the angels that fell from heaven. The wide tiers of welded tendons overspreading his broad white forehead, beneath the transparent skin, looked knitted together; as head on, he came churning his tail among the boats; and once more flailed them apart; spilling out the irons and lances from the two mates' boats, and dashing in one side of the upper part of their bows, but leaving Ahab's almost without a scar.

While Daggoo and Queequeg were stopping the strained planks; and as the whale swimming out from them, turned, and showed one entire flank as he shot by them again; at that moment a quick cry went up. Lashed round and round to the fish's back; pinioned in the turns upon turns in which, during the past night, the whale had reeled the involutions of the lines around him, the half torn body of the Parsee was seen; his sable raiment frayed to shreds; his distended eyes turned full upon old Ahab.

The harpoon dropped from his hand.

"Befooled, befooled!"—drawing in a long lean breath—"Aye, Parsee! I see thee again.—Aye, and thou goest before; and this, *this* then is the hearse that thou didst promise. But I hold thee to the last letter of thy word. Where is the second hearse? Away, mates, to the ship! those boats are useless now; repair them if ye can in time, and return to me; if not, Ahab is enough to die—Down, men! the first thing that but offers to jump from this boat I stand in, that thing I harpoon. Ye are not other men, but my arms and my legs; and so obey me.—Where's the whale? gone down again?"

But he looked too nigh the boat; for as if bent upon escaping with the corpse he bore, and as if the particular place of the last encounter had been but a stage in his leeward voyage, Moby Dick was now again steadily swimming forward; and had almost passed the ship,—which thus far had been sailing in the contrary direction to him, though for the present her headway had been stopped. He seemed swimming with his utmost velocity, and now only intent upon pursuing his own straight path in the sea.

"Oh! Ahab," cried Starbuck, "not too late is it, even now, the third day, to desist. See! Moby Dick seeks thee not. It is thou, thou, that madly seekest him!"

Setting sail to the rising wind, the lonely boat was swiftly impelled to leeward, by both oars and canvas. And at last when Ahab was sliding by the vessel, so near as plainly to distinguish Starbuck's face as he leaned over the rail, he hailed him to turn the vessel about, and follow him, not too swiftly, at a judicious interval. Glancing upwards, he saw Tashtego, Queequeg, and Daggoo, eagerly mounting to the three mast-heads; while the oarsmen were rocking in the two staved boats which had just been hoisted to the side, and were busily at work in repairing them. One after the other, through the port-holes, as he sped, he also caught flying glimpses of Stubb and Flask, busying themselves on deck among bundles of new irons and lances. As he saw all this; as he heard the hammers in the broken boats; far other hammers seemed driving a nail into his heart. But he rallied. And now marking that the vane or flag was gone from the main masthead, he shouted to Tashtego, who had just gained that perch, to descend again for another flag, and a hammer and nails, and so nail it to the mast.

Whether fagged by the three days' running chase, and the resistance to his swimming in the knotted hamper he bore; or whether it was some latent deceitfulness and malice in him: whichever was true, the White Whale's way now began to abate, as it seemed, from the boat so rapidly nearing him once more; though indeed the whale's last start had not been so long a one as before. And still as Ahab glided over the waves the unpitying sharks accompanied him; and so pertinaciously stuck to the boat; and so continually bit at the plying oars, that the blades became jagged and crunched, and left small splinters in the sea, at almost every dip.

"Heed them not! those teeth but give new rowlocks to your oars. Pull on! 'tis the better rest, the shark's jaw than the yielding water."

"But at every bite, sir, the thin blades grow smaller and smaller!"

"They will last long enough! pull on!—But who can tell"—he muttered—"whether these sharks swim to feast on a whale or on Ahab? —But pull on! Aye, all alive, now—we near him. The helm! take the helm; let me pass,"—and so saying, two of the oarsmen helped him forward to the bows of the still flying boat.

At length as the craft was cast to one side, and ran ranging along with the White Whale's flank, he seemed strangely oblivious of its advance—as the whale sometimes will—and Ahab was fairly within the smoky mountain mist, which, thrown off from the whale's spout, curled round his great, Monadnock hump. He was even thus close to him; when, with body arched back, and both arms lengthwise high-lifted to the poise, he darted his fierce iron, and his far fiercer curse into the hated whale. As both steel and curse sank to the socket, as if sucked into a morass, Moby Dick sideways writhed; spasmodically rolled his nigh flank against the bow, and, without staving a hole in it, so suddenly canted the boat over, that had it not been for the elevated part of the gunwale to which he then clung, Ahab would once more have been tossed into the sea. As it was, three of the oarsmen—who foreknew not the precise instant of the dart, and were therefore unpre-pared for its effects—these were flung out; but so fell, that, in an instant two of them clutched the gunwale again, and rising to its level on a combing wave, hurled themselves bodily inboard again; the third man helplessly drooping astern, but still afloat and swimming.

Almost simultaneously, with a mighty volition of ungraduated, in-stantaneous swiftness, the White Whale darted through the weltering sea. But when Ahab cried out to the steersman to take new turns with the line, and hold it so; and commanded the crew to turn round on their seats, and tow the boat up to the mark; the moment the treacherous line felt that double strain and tug, it snapped in the empty air!

"What breaks in me? Some sinew cracks!—'tis whole again; oars! oars! Burst in upon him!"

Hearing the tremendous rush of the sea-crashing boat, the whale wheeled round to present his blank forehead at bay; but in that evolu-tion, catching sight of the nearing black hull of the ship; seemingly see-ing in it the source of all his persecutions; bethinking it—it may be—a larger and nobler foe; of a sudden, he bore down upon its advancing prow, smiting his jaws amid fiery showers of foam.

Ahab staggered; his hand smote his forehead. "I grow blind; hands! stretch out before me that I may yet grope my way. Is't nigh?"

"The whale! The ship!" cried the cringing oarsmen.

"Oars! oars! Slope downwards to thy depths, O sea, that ere it be for ever too late, Ahab may slide this last, last time upon his mark! I see: the ship! the ship! Dash on, my men! Will ye not save my ship?"

But as the oarsmen violently forced their boat through the sledge-hammering seas, the before whale-smitten bow-ends of two planks burst through, and in an instant almost, the temporarily disabled boat lay nearly level with the waves; its half-wading, splashing crew trying hard to stop the gap and bale out the pouring water.

Meantime, for that one beholding instant, Tashtego's masthead hammer remained suspended in his hand; and the red flag, half-wrapping him as with a plaid, then streamed itself straight out from him, as his own forward-flowing heart; while Starbuck and Stubb, standing upon the bowsprit beneath, caught sight of the down-coming monster just as soon as he.

"The whale, the whale! Up helm, up helm! Oh, all ye sweet powers of air, now hug me close! Let not Starbuck die, if die he must, in a woman's fainting fit. Up helm, I say—ye fools, the jaw! the jaw! Is this the end of all my bursting prayers? all my life-long fidelities? Oh, Ahab, Ahab, lo, thy work. Steady! helmsman, steady. Nay, nay! Up helm again! He turns to meet us! Oh, his unappeasable brow drives on towards one, whose duty tells him he cannot depart. My God, stand by me now!

"Stand not by me, but stand under me, whoever you are that will now help Stubb; for Stubb, too, sticks here. I grin at thee, thou grinning whale! Whoever helped Stubb, or kept Stubb awake, but Stubb's own unwinking eye? And now poor Stubb goes to bed upon a mattress that is all too soft; would it were stuffed with brushwood! I grin at thee, thou grinning whale! Look ye, sun, moon and stars! I call ye assassins of as good a fellow as ever spouted up his ghost. For all that, I would yet ring glasses with ye, would ye but hand the cup! Oh, oh, oh, oh! thou grinning whale, but there'll be plenty of gulping soon! Why fly ye not, O Ahab? For me, off shoes and jacket to it, let Stubb die in his drawers! A most mouldy and over-salted death, though;—cherries! cherries! cherries! Oh, Flask, for one red cherry ere we die!"

"Cherries? I only wish that we were where they grow. Oh, Stubb, I hope my poor mother's drawn my part-pay ere this; if not, few coppers will come to her now, for the voyage is up."

From the ship's bows, nearly all the seamen now hung inactive; hammers, bits of plank, lances, and harpoons, mechanically retained in their hands, just as they had darted from their various employments; all their enchanted eyes intent upon the whale, which from side to side strangely vibrating his predestinating head, sent a broad band of overspreading semicircular foam before him as he rushed. Retribution, swift vengeance, eternal malice were in his whole aspect, and spite of all that mortal man could do, the solid white buttress of his forehead smote the ship's starboard bow, till men and timbers reeled. Some fell flat upon their faces. Like dislodged trucks, the heads of the harpooneers aloft shook on their bull-like necks. Through the breach, they heard the waters pour, as mountain torrents down a flume.

"The ship! The hearse!—the second hearse!" cried Ahab from the boat; "its wood could only be American!"

Diving beneath the settling ship, the Whale ran quivering along its keel; but turning under water, swiftly shot to the surface again, far off the other bow, but within a few yards of Ahab's boat, where, for a time, he lay quiescent.

"I turn my body from the sun. What ho, Tashtego! let me hear thy hammer. Oh! ye three unsurrendered spires of mine; thou uncracked keel; and only god-bullied hull; thou firm deck, and haughty helm, and Pole-pointed prow,—death-glorious ship! must ye then perish, and without me? Am I cut off from the last fond pride of the meanest shipwrecked captains? Oh, lonely death on lonely life! Oh, now I feel my topmost greatness lies in my topmost grief. Ho, ho! from all your furthest bounds, pour ye now in, ye bold billows of my whole foregone life, and top this one piled comber of my death! Towards thee I roll, thou all-destroying but unconquering whale; to the last I grapple with thee; from hell's heart I stab at thee; for hate's sake I spit my last breath at thee. Sink all coffins and all hearses to one common pool! and since neither can be mine let me then tow to pieces, while still chasing thee, though tied to thee, thou damned whale! *Thus,* I give up the spear!"

The harpoon was darted; the stricken whale flew forward! with igniting velocity the line ran through the groove; ran foul. Ahab stooped to clear it; he did clear it; but the flying turn caught him round the neck, and voicelessly as Turkish mutes bowstring their victim, he was shot out of the boat, ere the crew knew he was gone. Next instant, the heavy eyesplice in the rope's final end flew out of the stark-empty tub, knocked down an oarsman, and smiting the sea, disappeared in its depths.

For an instant, the tranced boat's crew stood still; then turned. "The ship? Great God, where is the ship?" Soon they through dim, bewildering mediums saw her sidelong fading phantom, as in the gaseous Fata Morgana; only the uppermost masts out of water; while fixed by infatuation, or fidelity, or fate, to their once lofty perches, the pagan harpooneers still maintained their sinking lookouts on the sea. And now, concentric circles seized the lone boat itself, and all its crew, and each floating oar, and every lance-pole, and spinning, animate and inanimate, all round and round in one vortex, carried the smallest chip of the *Pequod* out of sight.

But as the last whelmings intermixingly poured themselves over the sunken head of the Indian at the mainmast, leaving a few inches of the erect spar yet visible, together with long streaming yards of the flag, which calmly undulated, with ironical coincidings, over the destroying billows they almost touched;—at that instant, a red arm and a hammer hovered backwardly uplifted in the open air, in the act of nailing the flag faster and yet faster to the subsiding spar. A sky-hawk that tauntingly had followed the main-truck downwards from its natural home among the stars, pecking at the flag, and incommoding Tashtego there; this bird now chanced to intercept its broad fluttering wing between the hammer and the wood; and simultaneously feeling that ethereal thrill, the submerged savage beneath, in his death-gasp, kept his hammer frozen there; and so the bird of heaven, with unearthly shrieks, and his imperial beak thrust upwards, and his whole captive form folded in the flag of Ahab, went down with his ship, which, like Satan, would not sink to hell till she had dragged a living part of heaven along with her, and helmeted herself with it.

Now small fowls flew screaming over the yet yawning gulf; a sullen white surf beat against its steep sides; then all collapsed, and the great shroud of the sea rolled on as it rolled five thousand years ago.

EPILOGUE

"And I only am escaped alone to tell thee."—Job.

THE drama's done. Why then here does anyone step forth?—Because one did survive the wreck.

It so chanced, that after the Parsee's disappearance, I was he whom the Fates ordained to take the place of Ahab's bowsman, when that bowsman assumed the vacant post; the same, who, when on the last day the three men were tossed from out the rocky boat, was dropped astern. So, floating on the margin of the ensuing scene, and in full sight of it, when the half-spent suction of the sunk ship reached me, I was then, but slowly, drawn towards the closing vortex. When I reached it, it had subsided to a creamy pool. Round and round, then, and ever contracting towards the button-like black bubble at the axis of that slowly wheeling circle, like another Ixion I did revolve. Till, gaining that vital centre, the black bubble upward burst; and now, liberated by reason of its cunning spring, and, owing to its great buoyancy, rising with great force, the coffin life-buoy shot lengthwise from the sea, fell over, and floated by my side. Buoyed up by that coffin, for almost one whole day and night, I floated on a soft and dirge-like main. The unharming sharks, they glided by as if with padlocks on their mouths; the savage sea-hawks sailed with sheathed beaks. On the second day, a sail drew near, nearer, and picked me up at last. It was the devious-cruising *Rachel,* that in her retracing search after her missing children, only found another orphan.

EDWARD EVERETT HALE (1822-1909)

My Double, and How He Undid Me

It is not often that I trouble the readers of the *Atlantic Monthly.* I should not trouble them now, but for the importunities of my wife, who "feels to insist" that a duty to society is unfulfilled till I have told why I had to have a double, and how he undid me. She is sure, she says, that intelligent persons cannot understand that pressure upon public servants which alone drives any man into the employment of a double. And while I fear she thinks, at the bottom of her heart, that my fortunes will never be made, she has a faint hope that, as another Rasselas, I may teach a lesson to future publics, from which they may profit, though we die. Owing to the behavior of my double, or, if you please, to that public pressure which compelled me to employ him, I have plenty of leisure to write this communication.

I am, or rather was, a minister of the Sandemanian connection. I was settled in the active, wide-awake town of Naguadavick, on one of the finest water-powers in Maine. We used to call it a western town in the heart of the civilization of New England. A charming place it was and is. A spirited, brave young parish had I; and it seemed as if we might have all "the joy of eventful living" to our heart's content.

Alas! how little we knew on the day of my ordination, and in those halcyon moments of our first housekeeping. To be the confidential friend in a hundred families in the town,—cutting the social trifle, as my friend Haliburton says, "from the top of the whipped syllabub to the bottom of the sponge-cake, which is the foundation,"—to keep abreast of the thought of the age in one's study, and to do one's best on Sunday to interweave that thought with the active life of an active town, and to inspirit both and make both infinite by glimpses of the Eternal Glory, seemed such an exquisite forelook into one's life! Enough to do, and all so real and so grand! If this vision could only have lasted!

The truth is, that this vision was not in itself a delusion, nor, indeed, half bright enough. If one could only have been left to do his own business, the vision would have accomplished itself and brought out new paraheliacal visions, each as bright as the original. The misery was and is, as we found out, I and Polly, before long, that besides the vision, and besides the usual human and finite failures in life (such as breaking the old pitcher that came over in the *Mayflower,* and putting into the fire the alpenstock with which her father climbed Mont Blanc)—besides these, I say (imitating the style of *Robinson Crusoe*), there were pitchforked in on us a great rowen-heap of humbugs, handed down from some unknown seed-time, in which we were expected, and I chiefly, to fulfil certain public functions before the community, of the character of those fulfilled by the third row of supernumeraries who stand behind the Sepoys in the spectacle of the "Cataract of the Ganges." They were the duties, in a word, which one performs as member of one or another social class or subdivision, wholly distinct from what one does as A. by himself A. What invisible power put these functions on me it would be very hard to tell. But such power there was and is. And I had not been at work a year before I found I was living two lives, one real and one merely functional,—for two sets of people, one my parish, whom I loved, and the other a vague public, for whom I did not care two straws. All this was in a vague notion, which everybody had and has, that this second life would eventually bring out some great results, unknown at present, to somebody somewhere.

Crazed by this duality of life, I first read Dr. Wigan on the *Duality of the Brain,* hoping that I could train one side of my head to do these outside jobs, and the other to do my intimate and real duties. For Richard Greenough once told me, that, in studying for the statue of Franklin, he found that the left side of the great man's face was philosophic and reflective, and the right side funny and smiling. If you will go and look at the bronze statue you will find he has repeated this observation there for posterity. The eastern profile is the portrait of the statesman Franklin, the western of poor Richard. But Dr. Wigan does not go into these niceties of this subject, and I failed. It was then that, on my wife's suggestion, I resolved to look out for a double.

I was, at first, singularly successful. We happened to be recreating at Stafford Springs that summer. We rode out one day, for one of the relaxations of that watering-place, to the great Monson Poorhouse. We were passing through one of the large halls, when my destiny was fulfilled! I saw my man!

He was not shaven. He had on no spectacles. He was dressed in a green baize roundabout and faded blue overalls, worn sadly at the knee. But I saw at once that he was of my height, five feet four and a half. He had black hair, worn off by his hat. So have and have not I. He stooped in walking. So do I. His hands were large, and mine. And—choicest gift of Fate in all—he had, not "a strawberry mark on his left arm," but a cut from a juvenile brickbat over his right eye, slightly affecting the play of that eyebrow. Reader, so have I! My fate was sealed!

A word with Mr. Holley, one of the inspectors, settled the whole thing. It proved that this Dennis Shea was a harmless, amiable fellow, of the class known as shiftless, who had sealed his fate by marrying a dumb wife, who was at that moment ironing in the laundry. Before I left Stafford I had hired both for five years. We had applied to Judge Pynchon, then the probate judge at Springfield, to change the name of Dennis Shea to Frederic Ingham. We had explained to the Judge what was the precise truth, than an eccentric gentleman wished to adopt Dennis, under this new name, into his family. It never occurred to him that Dennis might be more than fourteen years old. And thus, to shorten this preface, when we returned at night to my parsonage at Naguadavick, there entered Mrs. Ingham, her new dumb laundress, myself, who am Mr. Frederic Ingham, and my double, who was Mr. Frederic Ingham by as good right as I.

Oh, the fun we had the next morning in shaving his beard to my pattern, cutting his hair to match mine, and teaching him how to wear and how to take off gold-bowed spectacles! Really, they were electroplate, and the glass was plain (for the poor fellow's eyes were excellent). Then in four successive afternoons I taught him four speeches. I had found these would be quite enough for the supernumerary-Sepoy line of life, and it was well for me they were; for though he was goodnatured, he was very shiftless, and it was, as our national proverb says, "like pulling teeth" to teach him. But at the end of the next week he could say, with quite my easy and frisky air,—

1. "Very well, thank you. And you?" This for an answer to casual salutations.

2. "I am very glad you liked it."

3. "There has been so much said, and, on the whole, so well said, that I will not occupy the time."

4. "I agree, in general, with my friend the other side of the room."

At first I had a feeling that I was going to be at great cost for clothing him. But it proved, of course, at once, that, whenever he was out, I should be at home. And I went, during the bright period of his success, to so few of those awful pageants which require a black dress-coat and what the ungodly call, after Mr. Dickens, a white choker, that in the happy retreat of my own dressing-gowns and jackets my days went by as happily and cheaply as those of another Thalaba. And Polly declares there was never a year when the tailoring cost so little. He lived (Dennis, not Thalaba) in his wife's room over the kitchen. He had orders never to show himself at that window. When he appeared in the front of the house I retired to my sanctissimum and my dressing-gown. In short, the Dutchman and his wife, in the old weather-box, had not less to do with each other than he and I. He made the furnace-fire and split the wood before daylight; then he went to sleep again, and slept late; then came for orders, with a red silk bandanna tied round his head, with his overalls on, and his dresscoat and spectacles off. If we happened to be interrupted, no one guessed that he was Frederic Ingham as well as I; and, in the neighborhood, there grew up an impression that the minister's Irishman worked daytimes in the factory village at New Coventry. After I had given him his orders, I never saw him till the next day.

I launched him by sending him to a meeting of the Enlightenment Board. The Enlightenment Board consists of seventy-four members, of whom sixty-seven are necessary to form a quorum. One becomes a member under the regulations laid down in old Judge Dudley's will. I became one by being ordained pastor of a church in Naguadavick. You see you cannot help yourself if you would. At this particular time we had had four successive meetings, averaging four hours each,— wholly occupied in whipping in a quorum. At the first only eleven men were present; at the next, by force of three circulars, twenty-seven; at the third, thanks to two days' canvassing by Auchmuty and myself, begging men to come, we had sixty. Half the others were in Europe. But without a quorum we could do nothing. All the rest of us waited grimly for our four hours, and adjourned without any action. At the fourth meeting we had flagged, and only got fifty-nine together. But on the first appearance of my double—whom I sent on this fatal Monday to the fifth meeting—he was the *sixty-seventh* man who entered the room. He was greeted with a storm of applause! The poor fellow had missed his way—read the street signs ill through his spectacles (very ill, in fact, without them)—and had not dared to inquire. He entered the room, finding the president and secretary holding to their chairs two judges of the Supreme Court, who were also members *ex officio* and were begging leave to go away. On his entrance all was changed. *Presto,* the by-laws were amended, and the western property was given away. Nobody stopped to converse with him. He voted, as I had charged him to do, in every instance, with the minority. I won new laurels as a man of sense, though a little unpunctual—and Dennis, *alias* Ingham, returned to the parsonage, astonished to see with how little wisdom the world is governed. He cut a few of my parishioners in the street; but he had his glasses off, and I am known to be near-sighted. Eventually he recognized them more readily than I.

I "set him again" at the exhibition of the New Coventry Academy; and here he undertook a "speaking part"—as, in my boyish, worldly days, I remember the bills used to say of Mlle. Celeste. We are all trustees of the New Coventry Academy; and there has lately been "a good deal of feeling" because the Sandemanians are leaning toward Free-Will, and that we have, therefore, neglected these semi-annual exhibitions, while there is no doubt that Auchmuty last year went to Commencement at Waterville. Now the head master at New Coventry is a real good fellow, who knows a Sanskrit root when he sees it, and often cracks etymologies with me; so that, in strictness, I ought to go to their exhibitions. But think, reader, of sitting through three long July days in that Academy chapel, following the programme from

TUESDAY MORNING. *English Composition.* "SUNRISE." Miss Jones.

round to—

Trio on Three Pianos. Duel from the Opera of "Midshipman Easy." *Marryat.*

coming in at nine, Thursday evening! Think of this, reader, for men who know the world is trying to go backward, and who would give their lives if they could help it on! Well! The double had succeeded so well at the Board, that I sent him to the Academy. (Shade of Plato, pardon!) He arrived early on Tuesday, when, indeed, few but mothers and clergymen are generally expected, and returned in the evening to us, covered with honors. He had dined at the right hand of the chairman, and he spoke in high terms of the repast. The chairman had expressed his interest in the French conversation. "I am very glad you liked it," said Dennis; and the poor chairman, abashed, supposed the accent had been wrong. At the end of the day the gentlemen present had been called upon for speeches—the Rev. Frederic Ingham first, as it happened; upon which Dennis had risen, and had said: "There has been so much said, and, on the whole, so well said, that I will not occupy the time." The girls were delighted, because Dr. Dabney, the year before, had given them at this occasion a scolding on impropriety of behavior at lyceum lectures. They all declared Mr. Ingham was a love—and *so* handsome! (Dennis is good looking.) Three of them, with arms behind the others' waists, followed him up to the wagon he rode home in; and a little girl with a blue sash had been sent to give him a rosebud. After this *début* in speaking, he went to the exhibition for two days more, to the mutual satisfaction of all concerned. Indeed, Polly reported that he had pronounced the trustees' dinners of a higher grade than those of the parsonage. When the next term began I found six of the Academy girls had obtained permission to come across the river to attend our church. But this arrangement did not long continue.

After this he went to several Commencements for me, and ate the dinners provided. He sat through three of our Quarterly Conventions for me—always voting judiciously, by the simple rule mentioned above, of siding with the minority. And I, meanwhile, who had before been losing caste among my friends, as holding myself aloof from the associations of the body, began to rise in everybody's favor. "Ingham's a good fellow, always on hand;" "never talks much, but does the right thing at the right time;" "is not as unpunctual as he used to be— he comes early, and sits through to the end." "He has got over his old talkative habit, too. I spoke to a friend of his about it once; and I think Ingham took it kindly," etc., etc.

This voting power of Dennis was particularly valuable at the quarterly meetings of the proprietors of the Naguadavick Ferry. My wife inherited from her father some shares in that enterprise, which is not yet fully developed, though it doubtless will become a very valuable property. The law of Maine then forbade stockholders to appear by proxy at such meetings. Polly disliked to go, not being, in fact, a "hens'-rights hen," transferred her stock to me. I, after going once, disliked it more than she. But Dennis went to the next meeting, and liked it very much. He said the armchairs were good, the collation good, and the free rides to stockholders pleasant. He was a little frightened when they first took him upon one of the ferry-boats, but after two or three quarterly meetings he became quite brave.

Thus far I never had any difficulty with him. Indeed, being, as I implied, of that type which is called shiftless, he was only too happy to be told daily what to do, and to be charged not to be forthputting or in any way original in his discharge of that duty. He learned, however, to discriminate between the lines of his life, and very much preferred these stockholders' meetings and trustees' dinners and Commencement collations to another set of occasions, from which he used to beg off most piteously. Our excellent brother, Dr. Fillmore, had taken a notion at this time that our Sandemanian churches needed more expression of mutual sympathy. He insisted upon it that we were remiss. He said that if the bishop came to preach at Naguadavick all the Episcopal clergy of the neighborhood were present; if Dr. Pond

came, all the Congregational clergymen turned out to hear him; if
Dr. Nichols, all the Unitarians; and he thought we owed it to each
other, that, whenever there was an occasional service at a Sandemanian
church, the other brethren should all, if possible, attend. "It looked
well," if nothing more. Now this really meant that I had not been to
hear one of Dr. Fillmore's lectures on the Ethnology of Religion. He
forgot that he did not hear one of my course on the "Sandemanianism
of Anselm." But I felt badly when he said it; and afterwards I always
made Dennis go to hear all the brethren preach, when I was not
preaching myself. This was what he took exceptions to—the only
thing, as I said, which he ever did except to. Now came the advantage of his long morning nap, and of the green tea with which Polly
supplied the kitchen. But he would plead, so humbly, to be let off,
only from one or two! I never excepted him, however. I knew the
lectures were of value, and I thought it best he should be able to keep
the connection.

Polly is more rash than I am, as the reader has observed in the
outset of this memoir. She risked Dennis one night under the eyes of
her own sex. Governor Gorges had always been very kind to us, and,
when he gave his great annual party to the town, asked us. I confess
I hated to go. I was deep in the new volume of Pfeiffer's "Mystics,"
which Haliburton had just sent me from Boston. "But how rude,"
said Polly, "not to return the Governor's civility and Mrs. Gorges',
when they will be sure to ask why you are away!" Still I demurred,
and at last she, with the wit of Eve and of Semiramis conjoined, let
me off by saying that if I would go in with her, and sustain the initial
conversations with the Governor and ladies staying there, we would
risk Dennis for the rest of the evening. And that was just what we
did. She took Dennis in training all that afternoon, instructed him in
fashionable conversation, cautioned him against the temptations of the
supper-table—and at nine in the evening he drove us all down in the
carryall. I made the grand star *entrée* with Polly and the pretty
Walton girls, who were staying with us. We had put Dennis into a
great rough top-coat, without his glasses; and the girls never dreamed,
in the darkness, of looking at him. He sat in the carriage, at the door,
while we entered. I did the agreeable to Mrs. Gorges, was introduced
to her niece, Miss Fernanda; I complimented Judge Jeffries on his
decision in the great case of D'Aulnay *vs.* Laconia Mining Company;
I stepped into the dressing-room for a moment, stepped out for another, walked home after a nod with Dennis and tying the horse to

a pump;—and while I walked home, Mr. Frederic Ingham, my double, stepped in through the library into the Gorges' grand saloon.

Oh! Polly died of laughing as she told me of it at midnight! And even here, where I have to teach my hands to hew the beech for stakes to fence our cave, she dies of laughing as she recalls it, and says that single occasion was worth all we have paid for it. Gallant Eve that she is! She joined Dennis at the library-door, and in an instant presented him to Dr. Ochterlong, from Baltimore, who was on a visit in town, and was talking with her as Dennis came in. "Mr. Ingham would like to hear what you were telling us about your success among the German population." And Dennis bowed and said, in spite of a scowl from Polly, "I'm very glad you liked it." But Dr. Ochterlong did not observe, and plunged into the tide of explanation; Dennis listening like a prime minister, and bowing like a mandarin, which is, I suppose, the same thing. Polly declared it was just like Haliburton's Latin conversation with the Hungarian minister, of which he is very fond of telling. *"Quæne sit historia Reformationis in Ungaria?"* quoth Haliburton, after some thought. And his confrère replied gallantly, *"In seculo decimo tertio,"* etc., etc., etc.; and from *decimo tertio* to the nineteenth century and a half lasted till the oysters came. So was it that before Dr. Ochterlong came to the "success," or near it, Governor Gorges came to Dennis, and asked him to hand Mrs. Jeffries down to supper, a request which he heard with great joy.

Polly was skipping round the room, I guess, gay as a lark. Auchmuty came to her "in pity for poor Ingham," who was so bored by the stupid pundit; and Auchmuty could not understand why I stood so long. But when Dennis took Mrs. Jeffries down, Polly could not resist standing near them. He was a little flustered, till the sight of the eatables and drinkables gave him the same Mercian courage which it gave Diggory. A little excited then, he attempted one or two of his speeches to the judge's lady. But little he knew how hard it was to get in even a *promptu* there edgewise. "Very well, I thank you," said he, after the eating elements were adjusted; "and you?" And then did not he have to hear about the mumps, and the measles, and arnica, and belladonna, and camomile-flower, and dodecatheon, till she changed oysters for salad; and then about the old practice and the new, and what her sister said, and what her sister's friend said, and what the physician to her sister's friend said, and then what was said by the brother of the sister of the physician of the friend of her sister, exactly as if it had been in Ollendorff? There was a moment's pause, as she declined champagne. "I am very glad you liked it," said Dennis again, which he never should have said but to one who complimented a sermon. "Oh! you are so sharp, Mr. Ingham! No! I never drink any wine at all, except sometimes in summer a little currant shrub, from our own currants, you know. My own mother, that is, I call her my own mother, because, you know, I do not remember," etc., etc., etc.; till they came to the candied orange at the end of the feast, when Dennis, rather confused, thought he must say something, and tried No. 4,—"I agree, in general, with my friend the other side of the room,"—which he never should have said but at a public meeting. But Mrs. Jeffries, who never listens expecting to understand, caught him up instantly with "Well, I'm sure my husband returns the compliment; he always agrees with you, though we do worship with the Methodists; but you know, Mr. Ingham," etc., etc., etc., till the move upstairs; and as Dennis led her through the hall, he was scarcely understood by any but Polly, as he said, "There has been so much said, and, on the whole, so well said, that I will not occupy the time."

His great resource the rest of the evening was standing in the library, carrying on animated conversations with one and another in much the same way. Polly had initiated him in the mysteries of a discovery of mine, that it is not necessary to finish your sentences in a crowd, but by a sort of mumble, omitting sibilants and dentals. This, indeed, if your words fail you, answers even in public extempore speech, but better where other talking is going on. Thus: "We misssed you at the Natural History Society, Ingham." Ingham replied, "I am very gligloglum, that is, that you were mmmmm." By gradually dropping the voice, the interlocutor is compelled to supply the answer. "Mrs. Ingham, I hope your friend Augusta is better." Augusta has not been ill. Polly cannot think of explaining, however, and answers, "Thank you, ma'am; she is very rearason wewahwewoh," in lower and lower tones. And Mrs. Throckmorton, who forgot the subject of which she spoke as soon as she asked the question, is quite satisfied. Dennis could see into the cardroom, and came to Polly to ask if he might not go and play all-fours. But, of course, she sternly refused. At midnight they came home delighted—Polly, as I said, wild to tell me the story of the victory; only both the pretty Walton girls said, "Cousin Frederic, you did not come near me all the evening."

We always called him Dennis at home, for convenience, though his real name was Frederic Ingham, as I have explained. When the election day came round, however, I found that by some accident there was only one Frederic Ingham's name on the voting list; and as I was quite busy that day in writing some foreign letters to Halle, I thought I would forego my privilege of suffrage, and stay quietly at home, telling Dennis that he might use the record on the voting-list, and vote. I gave him a ticket, which I told him he might use if he liked to. That was that very sharp election in Maine which the readers of the *Atlantic* so well remember, and it had been intimated in public that the ministers would do well not to appear at the polls. Of course, after that, we had to appear by self or proxy. Still, Naguadavick was not then a city, and this standing in a double queue at town-meeting several hours to vote was a bore of the first water; and so when I found that there was but one Frederic Ingham on the list, and that one of us must give up, I stayed at home and finished the letters (which, indeed, procured for Fothergill his coveted appointment of Professor of Astronomy at Leavenworth), and I gave Dennis, as we called him, the chance. Something in the matter gave a good deal of popularity to the Frederic Ingham name; and at the adjourned election, next week, Frederic Ingham was chosen to the legislature. Whether this was I or Dennis I never really knew. My friends seemed to think it was I; but I felt that as Dennis had done the popular thing, he was entitled to the honor: so I sent him to Augusta when the time came, and he took the oaths. And a very valuable member he made. They appointed him on the Committee on Parishes; but I wrote a letter for him, resigning, on the ground that he took an interest in our claim to the stumpage in the minister's sixteenths of Gore A, next to No. 7, in the 10th Range. He never made any speeches, and always voted with the minority, which was what he was sent to do. He made me and himself a great many good friends, some of whom I did not afterwards recognize as quickly as Dennis did my parishioners. On one or two occasions, when there was wood to saw at home, I kept him at home; but I took those occasions to go to Augusta myself. Finding myself often in his vacant seat at these times, I watched the proceedings with a great deal of care; and once was so much excited that I delivered my somewhat celebrated speech on the Central School-District question, a speech of which the *State of Maine* printed some extra copies. I believe there is no formal rule permitting strangers to speak; but no one objected.

Dennis himself, as I said, never spoke at all. But our experience this session led me to think that if, by some such "general understanding" as the reports speak of in legislation daily, every member of Congress might leave a double to sit through those deadly sessions and answer to roll-calls and do the legitimate party-voting, which appears stereotyped in the regular list of Ash, Bocock, Black, etc., we should gain decidedly in working-power. As things stand, the saddest state prison I ever visit is that Representatives' Chamber in Washington. If a man leaves for an hour, twenty "correspondents" may be howling, "Where was Mr. Prendergast when the Oregon bill passed?" And if poor Prendergast stays there! Certainly the worst use you can make of a man is to put him in prison!

I know, indeed, that public men of the highest rank have resorted to this expedient long ago. Dumas' novel of the "Iron Mask" turns on the brutal imprisonment of Louis the Fourteenth's double. There seems little doubt, in our own history, that it was the real General Pierce who shed tears when the delegate from Lawrence explained to him the sufferings of the people there, and only General Pierce's double who had given the orders for the assault on that town, which was invaded the next day. My charming friend, George Withers, has, I am almost sure, a double, who preaches his afternoon sermons for him. This is the reason that the theology often varies so from that of the forenoon. But the double is almost as charming as the original. Some of the most well-defined men, who stand out most prominently on the background of history, are in this way stereoscopic men, who owe their distinct relief to the slight differences between the doubles. All this I know. My present suggestion is simply the great extension of the system, so that all public machine work may be done by it.

But I see I loiter on my story, which is rushing to the plunge. Let me stop an instant more, however, to recall, were it only to myself, that charming year while all was yet well. After the double had become a matter of course, for nearly twelve months before he undid me, what a year it was! Full of active life, full of happy love, of the hardest work, of the sweetest sleep, and the fulfilment of so many of the fresh aspirations and dreams of boyhood! Dennis went to every school-committee meeting, and sat through all those late wranglings which used to keep me up till midnight and awake till morning. He attended all the lectures to which foreign exiles sent me tickets, begging me to come for the love of Heaven and of Bohemia. He accepted and used all the tickets for charity concerts which were sent to me. He appeared everywhere where it was specially desirable that "our denomination," or "our party," or "our class," or "our family," or "our street," or "our town," or "our country," or "our state," should be fully represented. And I fell back to that charming life which in boyhood one dreams of, when he supposes he shall do his own duty and make his own sacrifices, without being tied up with those of other people. My rusty Sanskrit, Arabic, Hebrew, Greek, Latin, French, Italian, Spanish, German, and English began to take polish. Heavens! how little I had done with them while I attended to my *public* duties! My calls on my parishioners became the friendly frequent, homelike sociabilities they were meant to be, instead of the hard work of a man goaded to desperation by the sight of his lists of arrears. And preaching! what a luxury preaching was when I had on Sunday the whole result of an individual, personal week, from which to speak to a people whom all that week I had been meeting as hand-to-hand friend;—I, never tired on Sunday, and in condition to leave the sermon at home, if I chose, and preach it extempore, as all men should do always. Indeed, I wonder, when I think that a sensible people, like ours—really more attached to their clergy than they were in the lost days, when the Mathers and Nortons were noblemen—should choose to neutralize so much of their ministers' lives, and destroy so much of their early training, by this undefined passion for seeing them in public. It springs from our balancing of sects. If a spirited Episcopalian takes an interest in the almshouse, and is put on the Poor Board, every other denomination must have a minister there, lest the poorhouse be changed into St. Paul's Cathedral. If a Sandemanian is chosen president of the Young Men's Library, there must be a Methodist vice-president and a Baptist secretary. And if a Universalist Sunday-School Convention collects five hundred delegates, the next Congregationalist Sabbath-School Conference must be as large "lest 'they'—whoever *they* may be—should think 'we'—whoever *we* may be—are going down."

Freed from these necessities, that happy year I began to know my wife by sight. We saw each other sometimes. In those long mornings, when Dennis was in the study explaining to map-peddlers that I had eleven maps of Jerusalem already, she and I were at work together, as in those old dreamy days, and in these of our log-cabin again. But all this could not last; and at length poor Dennis, my double, overtasked in turn, undid me.

It was thus it happened. There is an excellent fellow, once a minister, —I will call him Isaacs,—who deserves well of the world till he dies, and after, because he once, in a real exigency, did the right thing, in the right way, at the right time, as no other man could do it. In the world's great football match, the ball by chance found him loitering on the outside of the field; he closed with it, "camped" it, charged it home—yes, right through the other side—not disturbed, not frightened by his own success —and, breathless, found himself a great man, as the Great Delta rang applause. But he did not find himself a rich man; and the football has never come in his way again. From that moment to this moment he has been of no use, that one can see at all. Still, for that great act we speak of Isaacs gratefully and remember him kindly; and he forges on, hoping to meet the football somewhere again. In that vague hope he had arranged a "movement" for a general organization of the human family into Debating Clubs, County Societies, State Unions, etc., etc., with a view of inducing all children to take hold of the handles of their knives and forks, instead of the metal. Children have bad habits in that way. The movement, of course, was absurd; but we all did our best to forward, not it, but him. It came time for the annual county meeting on this subject to be held at Naguadavick. Isaacs came round, good fellow! to arrange for it—got the town-hall, got the Governor to preside (the saint! —he ought to have triplet doubles provided him by law), and then came to get me to speak. "No," I said, "I do not beleive in the enterprise. If I spoke it should be to say children should take hold of the prongs of the forks and the blades of the knives. I would subscribe ten dollars, but I would not speak a mill." So poor Isaacs went his way sadly, to coax Auchmuty to speak, and Delafield. I went out. Not long after he came back, and told Polly that they had promised to speak, the Governor would speak, and he himself would close with the quarterly report, and some interesting anecdotes regarding Miss Biffin's way of handling her knife and Mr. Nellis's way of footing his fork. "Now if Mr. Ingham will only come and sit on the platform, he need not say one word; but it will show well in the paper—it will show that the Sandemanians take as much interest in the movement as the Armenians or the Mesopotamians, and will be a great favor to me." Polly, good soul! was tempted, and she promised. She knew Mrs. Isaacs was starving, and the babies,—she knew Dennis was at home,—and she promised! Night came, and I returned. I heard her story. I was sorry. I doubted. But Polly had promised to beg me, and I dared all! I told Dennis to hold his peace, under all circumstances, and sent him down.

It was not half an hour more before he returned, wild with excitement,—in a perfect Irish fury,—which it was long before I understood. But I knew at once that he had undone me!

What happened was this. The audience got together, attracted by Governor Gorges' name. There were a thousand people. Poor Gorges was late from Augusta. They became impatient. He came in direct from the train at last, really ignorant of the object of the meeting. He opened it in the fewest possible words, and said other gentlemen were present who would entertain them better than he. The audience were disappointed, but waited. The Governor, prompted by Isaacs, said, "The Honorable Mr. Delafield will address you." Delafield! He had forgotten the knives and forks, and was playing the Ruy Lopez opening at the chess-club. "The Rev. Mr. Auchmuty will address you." Auchmuty had promised to speak late, and was at the school-committee. "I see Dr.

Stearns in the hall; perhaps he will say a word." Dr. Stearns said he had come to listen and not to speak. The Governor and Isaacs whispered. The Governor looked at Dennis, who was resplendent on the platform; but Isaacs, to give him his due, shook his head. But the look was enough. A miserable lad, ill-bred, who had once been in Boston, thought it would sound well to call for me, and peeped out, "Ingham!" A few more wretches cried, "Ingham! Ingham!" Still Isaacs was firm; but the Governor, anxious, indeed, to prevent a row, knew I would say something, and said, "Our friend Mr. Ingham is always prepared; and, though we had not relied upon him, he will say a word perhaps." Applause followed, which turned Dennis's head. He rose, fluttered, and tried No. 3. "There has been so much said, and, on the whole, so well said, that I will not occupy the time!" and sat down, looking for his hat; for things seemed squally. But the people cried, "Go on! go on!" and some applauded. Dennis, still confused, but flattered by the applause, to which neither he nor I are used, rose again, and this time tried No. 2: "I am very glad you liked it!" in a sonorous, clear delivery. My best friends stared. All the people who did not know me personally yelled with delight at the aspect of the evening; the Governor was beside himself, and poor Isaacs thought he was undone! Alas, it was I! A boy in the gallery cried in a loud tone, "It's all an infernal humbug," just as Dennis, waving his hand, commanded silence, and tried No. 4: "I agree, in general, with my friend the other side of the room." The poor Governor doubted his senses and crossed to stop him—not in time, however. The same gallery-boy shouted, "How's your mother?" and Dennis, now completely lost, tried, as his last shot, No. 1, vainly: "Very well, thank you. And you?"

I think I must have been undone already. But Dennis, like another Lockhard, chose "to make sicker." The audience rose in a whirl of amazement, rage, and sorrow. Some other impertinence, aimed at Dennis, broke all restraint, and, in pure Irish, he delivered himself of an address to the gallery, inviting any person who wished to fight to come down and do so—stating, that they were all dogs and cowards, and the sons of dogs and cowards—that he would take any five of them single-handed. "Shure, I have said all his Riverence and the Misthress bade me say," cried he, in defiance; and, seizing the Governor's cane from his hand, brandished it, quarter-staff fashion, above his head. He was, indeed, got from the hall only with the greatest difficulty by the Governor, the city marshal, who had been called in, and the superintendent of my Sunday-School.

The universal impression, of course, was that the Rev. Frederic Ingham had lost all command of himself in some of those haunts of intoxication which for fifteen years I have been laboring to destroy. Till this moment, indeed, that is the impression in Naguadavick. This number of the *Atlantic* will relieve from it a hundred friends of mine who have been sadly wounded by that notion now for years; but I shall not be likely ever to show my head there again.

No! My double has undone me.

We left town at seven the next morning. I came to No. 9 in the Third Range, and settled on the Minister's Lot. In the new towns of Maine, the first settled minister has a gift of a hundred acres of land. I am the first settled minister in No. 9. My wife and little Paulina are my parish. We raise corn enough to live on in summer. We kill bear's meat enough to carbonize it in winter. I work on steadily on my "Traces of Sandemanianism in the Sixth and Seventh Centuries," which I hope to persuade Phillips, Samson & Co. to publish next year. We are very happy, but the world thinks we are undone.

FRANCIS PARKMAN (1823–1893)

From THE CONSPIRACY OF PONTIAC

INDIAN PREPARATION

I INTERRUPT the progress of the narrative to glance for a moment at the Indians in their military capacity, and observe how far they were qualified to prosecute the formidable war into which they were about to plunge.

A people living chiefly by the chase, and therefore, of necessity, thinly and widely scattered; divided into numerous tribes, held together by no strong principle of cohesion, and with no central government to combine their strength, could act with little efficiency against such an enemy as was now opposed to them. Loose and disjointed as a whole, the government even of individual tribes, and of their smallest separate communities, was too feeble to deserve the name. There were, it is true, chiefs whose office was in a manner hereditary; but their authority was wholly of a moral nature, and enforced by no compulsory law. Their province was to advise, and not to command. Their influence, such as it was, is chiefly to be ascribed to the principle of hero-worship, natural to the Indian character, and to the reverence for age, which belongs to a state of society where a patriarchal element largely prevails. It was their office to declare war and make peace; but when war was declared, they had no power to carry the declaration into effect. The warriors fought if they chose to do so; but if, on the contrary, they preferred to remain quiet, no man could force them to raise the hatchet. The war-chief, whose part it was to lead them to battle, was a mere partisan, whom his bravery and exploits had led to distinction. If he thought proper, he sang his war-song and danced his war-dance; and as many of the young men as were disposed to follow him gathered around and enlisted themselves under him. Over these volunteers he had no legal authority, and they could desert him at any moment, with no other penalty than disgrace. When several war-parties, of different bands or tribes, were united in a common enterprise, their chiefs elected a leader, who was nominally to command the whole; but unless this leader was a man of uncommon reputation and ability, his commands were disregarded, and his authority was a cipher. Among his followers, every latent element of discord, pride, jealousy, and ancient half-smothered feuds, were ready at any moment to break out, and tear the whole asunder. His warriors would often desert in bodies; and many an Indian army, before reaching the enemy's country, has been known to dwindle away until it was reduced to a mere scalping-party.

To twist a rope of sand would be as easy a task as to form a permanent and effective army of such materials. The wild love of freedom, and impatience of all control, which mark the Indian race, render them utterly intolerant of military discipline. Partly from their individual character, and partly from this absence of subordination, spring results highly unfavorable to continued and extended military operations. Indian warriors, when acting in large masses, are to the last degree wayward, capricious, and unstable; infirm of purpose as a mob of children, and devoid of providence and foresight. To provide supplies for a campaign forms no part of their system. Hence the blow must be struck at once, or not struck at all; and to postpone victory is to insure defeat. It is when acting in small, detached parties that the Indian warrior puts forth his energies, and displays his admirable address, endurance, and intrepidity. It is then that he becomes a truly formidable enemy. Fired with the hope of winning scalps, he is stanch as a bloodhound. No hardship can divert him from his purpose, and no danger subdue his patient and cautious courage.

From their inveterate passion for war, the Indians are always prompt enough to engage in it; and on the present occasion, the prevailing irritation gave ample assurance that they would not remain idle. While there was little risk that they would capture any strong and well-defended fort, or carry any important position, there was, on the other hand, every reason to apprehend wide-spread havoc, and a destructive war of detail. That the war might be carried on with effect, it was the part of the Indian leaders to work upon the passions of their people, and keep alive their irritation; to whet their native appetite for blood and glory, and cheer them on to the attack; to guard against all that might quench their ardor, or cool their fierceness; to avoid pitched battles; never to fight except under advantage; and to avail themselves of all the aid which craft and treachery could afford. The very circumstances which unfitted the Indians for continued and concentrated attack were, in another view, highly advantageous, by preventing the enemy from assailing them with vital effect. It was no easy task to penetrate tangled woods in search of a foe, alert and active as a lynx, who would seldom stand and fight, whose deadly shot and triumphant whoop were the first and often the last tokens of his presence, and who, at the approach of a hostile force, would vanish into the black recesses of forests and pine swamps, only to renew his attacks with unabated ardor. There were no forts to capture, no magazines to destroy, and little property to seize upon. No warfare could be more perilous and harassing in its prosecution, or less satisfactory in its results.

The English colonies at this time were but ill fitted to bear the brunt of the impending war. The army which had conquered Canada was broken up and dissolved; the provincials were disbanded, and most of the regulars sent home. A few fragments of regiments, miserably wasted by war and sickness, had just arrived from the West Indies; and of these, several were already ordered to England, to be disbanded. There remained barely troops enough to furnish feeble garrisons for the various forts on the frontier and in the Indian country. At the head of this dilapidated army was Sir Jeffrey Amherst, who had achieved the reduction of Canada, and clinched the nail which Wolfe had driven. In some respects he was well fitted for the emergency; but, on the other hand, he held the Indians in supreme contempt, and his arbitrary treatment of them and total want of every quality of conciliation where they were concerned, had had no little share in exciting them to war.

While the war was on the eve of breaking out, an event occurred which had afterwards an important effect upon its progress,—the signing of the treaty of peace at Paris, on the tenth of February, 1763. By this treaty France resigned her claims to the territories east of the Mississippi, and that great river now became the western boundary of the British colonial possessions. In portioning out her new acquisitions into separate governments, England left the valley of the Ohio and the adjacent regions as an Indian domain, and by the proclamation of the seventh of October following, the intrusion of settlers upon these lands was strictly prohibited. Could these just and necessary measures have been sooner adopted, it is probable that the Indian war might have been prevented, or, at all events, rendered less general and violent, for the treaty would have made it apparent that the French could never repossess themselves of Canada, and would have proved the futility of every hope which the Indians entertained of assistance from that quarter, while, at the same time, the royal proclamation would have tended to tranquillize their minds, by removing the chief cause of irritation. But the remedy came too late, and served only to inflame the evil. While the sovereigns of France, England, and Spain were signing the treaty at Paris, countless Indian warriors in the American forests were singing the war-song, and whetting their scalping-knives.

Throughout the western wilderness, in a hundred camps and villages, were celebrated the savage rites of war. Warriors, women, and children were alike eager and excited; magicians consulted their oracles, and prepared charms to insure success; while the war-chief, his body painted black from head to foot, concealed himself in the solitude of rocks and caverns, or the dark recesses of the forest. Here, fasting and praying, he calls day and night upon the Great Spirit, consulting his dreams, to draw from them auguries of good or evil; and if, perchance, a vision of the great war-eagle seems to hover over him with expanded wings, he exults in the full conviction of triumph. When a few days have elapsed, he emerges from his retreat, and the people discover him descending from the woods, and approaching their camp, black as a demon of war, and shrunken with fasting and vigil. They flock around and listen to his wild harangue. He calls on them to avenge the blood of their slaughtered relatives; he assures them that the Great Spirit is on their side, and that victory is certain. With exulting cries they disperse to their wigwams, to array themselves in the savage decorations of the war-dress. An old man now passes through the camp, and invites the warriors to a feast in the name of the chief. They gather from all quarters to his wigwam, where they find him seated, no longer covered with black, but adorned with the startling and fantastic blazonry of the war-paint. Those who join in the feast pledge themselves, by so doing, to follow him against the enemy. The guests seat themselves on the ground, in a circle around the wigwam, and the flesh of dogs is placed in wooden dishes before them, while the chief, though goaded by the pangs of his long, unbroken fast, sits smoking his pipe with unmoved countenance, and takes no part in the feast.

Night has now closed in; and the rough clearing is illumined by the blaze of fires and burning pine-knots, casting their deep red glare upon the dusky boughs of the surrounding forest, and upon the wild multitude who, fluttering with feathers and bedaubed with paint, have gathered for the celebration of the war-dance. A painted post is driven into the ground, and the crowd form a wide circle around it. The chief leaps into the vacant space, brandishing his hatchet as if rushing upon an enemy, and, in a loud, vehement tone, chants his own exploits and those of his ancestors, enacting the deeds which he describes, yelling the war-whoop, throwing himself into all the postures of actual fight, striking the post as if it were an enemy, and tearing the scalp from the head of the imaginary victim. Warrior after warrior follows his example, until the whole assembly, as if fired with sudden frenzy, rush together into the ring, leaping, stamping, and whooping, brandishing knives and hatchets in the fire-light, hacking and stabbing the air, and breaking at intervals into a burst of ferocious yells, which sounds for miles away over the lonely midnight forest.

In the morning, the warriors prepare to depart. They leave the camp in single file, still decorated with all their finery of paint, feathers, and scalplocks; and, as they enter the woods, the chief fires his gun, the warrior behind follows his example, and the discharges pass in slow succession from front to rear, the salute concluding with a general whoop. They encamp at no great distance from the village, and divest themselves of their much-prized ornaments, which are carried back by the women, who have followed them for this purpose. The warriors pursue their journey, clad in the rough attire of hard service, and move silently and stealthily through the forest towards the hapless garrison, or defenceless settlement, which they have marked as their prey.

The woods were now filled with war-parties such as this, and soon the first tokens of the approaching tempest began to alarm the unhappy settlers of the frontier. At first, some trader or hunter, weak and emaciated, would come in from the forest, and relate that his companions had been butchered in the Indian villages, and that he alone had escaped. Next succeeded vague and uncertain rumors of forts attacked and garrisons slaughtered; and soon after, a report gained ground that every post throughout the Indian country had been taken, and every soldier killed. Close upon these tidings came the enemy himself. The Indian war-parties broke out of the woods like gangs of wolves, murdering, burning, and laying waste; while hundreds of terror-stricken families, abandoning their homes, fled for refuge towards the older settlements, and all was misery and ruin.

Passing over, for the present, this portion of the war, we will penetrate at once into the heart of the Indian country, and observe those passages of the conflict which took place under the auspices of Pontiac himself,—the siege of Detroit, and the capture of the interior posts and garrisons.

THE COUNCIL AT THE RIVER ECORCES.

To begin the war was reserved by Pontiac as his own peculiar privilege. With the first opening of spring his preparations were complete. His light-footed messengers, with their wampum belts and gifts of tobacco, visited many a lonely hunting-camp in the gloom of the northern woods, and called chiefs and warriors to attend the general meeting. The appointed spot was on the banks of the little river Ecorces, not far from Detroit. Thither went Pontiac himself, with his squaws and his children. Band after band came straggling in from every side, until the meadow was thickly dotted with their frail wigwams. Here were idle warriors smoking and laughing in groups, or beguiling the lazy hours with gambling, feasting, or doubtful stories of their own martial exploits. Here were youthful gallants, bedizened with all the foppery of beads, feathers, and hawks' bells, but held as yet in light esteem, since they had slain no enemy, and taken no scalp. Here too were young damsels, radiant with bears' oil, ruddy with vermilion, and versed in all the arts of forest coquetry; shrivelled hags, with limbs of wire and the voices of screech-owls; and troops of naked children, with small, black, mischievous eyes, roaming along the outskirts of the woods.

The great Roman historian observes of the ancient Germans that when summoned to a public meeting, they would lag behind the appointed time in order to show their independence. The remark holds true, and perhaps with greater emphasis, of the American Indians; and thus it happened that several days elapsed before the assembly was complete. In such a motley concourse of barbarians, where different bands and different tribes were mustered on one common camp-ground, it would need all the art of a prudent leader to prevent their dormant jealousies from starting into open strife. No people are more prompt to quarrel, and none more prone, in the fierce excitement of the present, to forget the purpose of the future; yet, through good fortune, or the wisdom of Pontiac, no rupture occurred; and at length the last loiterer appeared, and further delay was needless.

The council took place on the twenty-seventh of April. On that morning, several old men, the heralds of the camp, passed to and fro among the lodges, calling the warriors, in a loud voice, to attend the meeting.

In accordance with the summons, they issued from their cabins: the tall, naked figures of the wild Ojibwas, with quivers slung at their backs, and light war-clubs resting in the hollow of their arms; Ottawas, wrapped close in their gaudy blankets; Wyandots, fluttering in painted shirts, their heads adorned with feathers, and their leggings garnished with bells. All were soon seated in a wide circle upon the grass, row within row, a grave and silent assembly. Each savage countenance seemed carved in wood, and none could have detected the ferocious passions hidden beneath that immovable mask. Pipes with ornamented stems were lighted, and passed from hand to hand.

Then Pontiac rose, and walked forward into the midst of the council. According to Canadian tradition, he was not above the middle height, though his muscular figure was cast in a mould of remarkable symmetry and vigor. His complexion was darker than is usual with his race, and his features, though by no means regular, had a bold and stern expression; while his habitual bearing was imperious and peremptory, like that of a man accustomed to sweep away all opposition by the force of his impetuous will. His ordinary attire was that of the primitive savage,—scanty cincture girt about his loins, and his long, black hair flowing loosely at his back; but on occasions like this he was wont to appear as befitted his power and character, and he stood doubtless before the council plumed and painted in the full costume of war.

Looking round upon his wild auditors he began to speak, with fierce gesture, and a loud, impassioned voice; and at every pause, deep, guttural ejaculations of assent and approval responded to his words. He inveighed against the arrogance, rapacity, and injustice of the English, and contrasted them with the French, whom they had driven from the soil. He declared that the British commandant had treated him with neglect and contempt; that the soldiers of the garrison had abused the Indians; and that one of them had struck a follower of his own. He represented the danger that would arise from the supremacy of the English. They had expelled the French, and now they only waited for a pretext to turn upon the Indians and destroy them. Then, holding out a broad belt of wampum, he told the council that he had received it from their great father the King of France, in token that he had heard the voice of his red children; that his sleep was at an end; and that his great war canoes would soon sail up the St. Lawrence, to win back Canada, and wreak vengeance on his enemies. The Indians and their French brethren would fight once more side by side, as they had always fought; they would strike the English as they had struck them many moons ago, when their great army marched down the Monongahela, and they had shot them from their ambush, like a flock of pigeons in the woods.

Having roused in his warlike listeners their native thirst for blood and vengeance, he next addressed himself to their superstition, and told the following tale. Its precise origin is not easy to determine. It is possible that the Delaware prophet, mentioned in a former chapter, may have had some part in it; or it might have been the offspring of Pontiac's heated imagination, during his period of fasting and dreaming. That he deliberately invented it for the sake of the effect it would produce, is the least probable conclusion of all; for it evidently proceeds from the superstitious mind of an Indian, brooding upon the evil days in which his lot was cast, and turning for relief to the mysterious Author of his being. It is, at all events, a characteristic specimen of the Indian legendary tales, and, like many of them, bears an allegoric significancy. Yet he who endeavors to interpret an Indian allegory through all its erratic windings and puerile inconsistencies, has undertaken no enviable task.

"A Delaware Indian," said Pontiac, "conceived an eager desire to learn wisdom from the Master of Life; but, being ignorant where to find him, he had recourse to fasting, dreaming, and magical incantations. By these means it was revealed to him, that, by moving forward in a straight, undeviating course, he would reach the abode of the Great Spirit. He told his purpose to no one, and having provided the equipment of a hunter,—gun, powder-horn, ammunition, and a kettle for preparing his food,—he set out on his errand. For some time he journeyed on in high hope and confidence. On the evening of the eighth day, he stopped by the side of a brook at the edge of a meadow, where he began to make ready his evening meal, when, looking up, he saw three large openings in the woods before him, and three well-beaten paths which entered them. He was much surprised; but his wonder increased, when, after it had grown dark, the three paths were more clearly visible than ever. Remembering the important object of his journey, he could neither rest nor sleep; and, leaving his fire he crossed the meadow, and entered the largest of the three openings. He had advanced but a short distance into the forest, when a bright flame sprang out of the ground before him, and arrested his steps. In great amazement, he turned back, and entered the second path, where the same wonderful phenomenon again encountered him; and now, in terror and bewilderment, yet still resolved to persevere, he took the last of the three paths. On this he journeyed a whole day without interruption, when at length, emerging from the forest, he saw before him a vast mountain, of dazzling whiteness. So precipitous was the ascent that the Indian thought it hopeless to go farther, and looked around him in despair: at that moment, he saw, seated at some distance above, the figure of a beautiful woman arrayed in white, who arose as he looked upon her, and thus accosted him: 'How can you hope, encumbered as you are, to succeed in your design? Go down to the foot of the mountain, throw away your gun, your ammunition, your provisions, and your clothing, wash yourself in the stream which flows there, and you will then be prepared to stand before the Master of Life.' The Indian obeyed, and again began to ascend among the rocks, while the woman, seeing him still discouraged, laughed at his faintness of heart, and told him, that, if he wished for success, he must climb by the aid of one hand and one foot only. After great toil and suffering, he at length found himself at the summit. The woman had disappeared, and he was left alone. A rich and beautiful plain lay before him, and at a little distance he saw three great villages, far superior to the squalid wigwams of the Delawares. As he approached the largest, and stood hesitating whether he should enter, a man gorgeously attired stepped forth, and, taking him by the hand, welcomed him to the celestial abode. He then conducted him into the presence of the Great Spirit, where the Indian stood confounded at the unspeakable splendor which surrounded him. The Great Spirit bade him be seated, and thus addressed him:—

"'I am the Maker of heaven and earth, the trees, lakes, rivers, and all things else. I am the Maker of mankind; and because I love you, you must do my will. The land on which you live I have made for you, and not for others. Why do you suffer the white men to dwell among you? My children, you have forgotten the customs and traditions of your forefathers. Why do you not clothe yourselves in skins, as they did, and use the bows and arrows, and the stone-pointed lances, which they used? You have bought guns, knives, kettles, and blankets, from the white men, until you can no longer do without them; and, what is worse, you have drunk the poison fire-water, which turns you into fools. Fling all these things away; live as your wise forefathers lived before you. And as for these English,—these dogs dressed in red, who have come to rob you of your hunting-grounds, and drive away the game,—you must lift the hatchet against them. Wipe them from the face of the earth, and then you will win my favor back again, and once more be happy and prosperous. The children of your great father, the King of France, are not like the English. Never forget that they are your brethren. They are very dear to me, for they love the red men, and understand the true mode of worshipping me.' "

The Great Spirit next gave his hearer various precepts of morality and religion, such as the prohibition to marry more than one wife; and a warning against the practice of magic, which is worshipping the devil. A prayer, embodying the substance of all that he had heard, was then presented to the Delaware. It was cut in hieroglyphics upon a wooden stick, after the custom of his people; and he was directed to send copies of it to all the Indian villages.

The adventurer now departed, and returning to the earth, reported all the wonders he had seen in the celestial regions.

Such was the tale told by Pontiac to the council; and it is worthy of notice that not he alone, but many of the most notable men who have arisen among the Indians have been opponents of civilization, and stanch advocates of primitive barbarism. Red Jacket and Tecumseh would gladly have brought back their people to the rude simplicity of their original condition. There is nothing progressive in the rigid, inflexible nature of an Indian. He will not open his mind to the idea of improvement; and nearly every change that has been forced upon him has been a change for the worse.

Many other speeches were doubtless made in the council, but no record of them has been preserved. All present were eager to attack the British fort; and Pontiac told them, in conclusion, that on the second of May he would gain admittance, with a party of his warriors, on pretence of dancing the calumet dance before the garrison; that they would take note of the strength of the fortification; and that he would then summon another council to determine the mode of attack.

The assembly now dissolved, and all the evening the women were employed in loading the canoes, which were drawn up on the bank of the stream.

The encampments broke up at so early an hour that when the sun rose, the savage swarm had melted away; the secluded scene was restored to its wonted silence and solitude, and nothing remained but the slender framework of several hundred cabins, with fragments of broken utensils, pieces of cloth, and scraps of hide, scattered over the trampled grass; while the smouldering embers of numberless fires mingled their dark smoke with the white mist which rose from the little river.

Every spring, after the winter hunt was over, the Indians were accustomed to return to their villages, or permanent encampments, in the vicinity of Detroit; and, accordingly, after the council had broken up, they made their appearance as usual about the fort. On the first of May, Pontiac came to the gate with forty men of the Ottawa tribe, and asked permission to enter and dance the calumet dance, before the officers of the garrison. After some hesitation, he was admitted; and proceeding to the corner of the street, where stood the house of the commandant, Major Gladwyn, he and thirty of his warriors began their dance, each recounting his own exploits, and boasting himself the bravest of mankind. The officers and men gathered around them; while, in the meantime, the remaining ten of the Ottawas strolled about the fort, observing everything it contained. When the dance was over, they all quietly withdrew, not a suspicion of their designs having arisen in the minds of the English.

After a few days had elapsed, Pontiac's messengers again passed among the Indian cabins, calling the principal chiefs to another council, in the Pottawattamie village. Here there was a large structure of bark, erected for the public use on occasions like the present. A hundred chiefs were seated around this dusky council-house, the fire in the centre shedding its fitful light upon their dark, naked forms, while the pipe passed from hand to hand. To prevent interruption, Pontiac had stationed young men as sentinels, near the house. He once more addressed the chiefs; inciting them to hostility against the English, and concluding by the proposal of his plan for destroying Detroit. It was as follows: Pontiac would demand a council with the commandant concerning matters of great importance; and on this pretext he flattered himself that he and his principal chiefs would gain ready admittance within the fort. They were all to carry weapons concealed beneath their blankets. While in the act of addressing the commandant in the council-room, Pontiac was to make a certain signal, upon which the chiefs were to raise the war-whoop, rush upon the officers present, and strike them down. The other Indians, waiting meanwhile at the gate, or loitering among the houses, on hearing the yells and firing within the building, were to assail the astonished and half-armed soldiers; and thus Detroit would fall an easy prey.

In opening this plan of treachery, Pontiac spoke rather as a counsellor than as a commander. Haughty as he was, he had too much sagacity to wound the pride of a body of men over whom he had no other control than that derived from his personal character and influence. No one was hardy enough to venture opposition to the proposal of their great leader. His plan was eagerly adopted. Hoarse ejaculations of applause echoed his speech; and, gathering their blankets around them, the chiefs withdrew to their respective villages, to prepare for the destruction of the unsuspecting garrison.

DETROIT.

To the credulity of mankind each great calamity has its dire prognostics. Signs and portents in the heavens, the vision of an Indian bow, and the figure of a scalp imprinted on the disk of the moon, warned the New England Puritans of impending war. The apparitions passed away, and Philip of Mount Hope burst from the forest with his Narragansett warriors. In October, 1762, thick clouds of inky blackness gathered above the fort and settlement of Detroit. The river darkened beneath the awful shadows, and the forest was wrapped in double gloom. Drops of rain began to fall, of strong, sulphurous odor, and so deeply colored that the people, it is said, collected them and used them for writing. A literary and philosophical journal of the time seeks to explain this strange phenomenon on some principle of physical science; but the simple Canadians held a different faith. Throughout the winter, the shower of black rain was the foremost topic of their fireside talk; and forebodings of impending evil disturbed the breast of many a timorous matron.

La Mothe-Cadillac was the founder of Detroit. In the year 1701, he planted the little military colony, which time has transformed into a thriving American city. At an earlier date, some feeble efforts had been made to secure the possession of this important pass; and when La Hontan visited the lakes, a small post, called Fort St. Joseph, was standing near the present site of Fort Gratiot. The wandering Jesuits, too, made frequent sojourns upon the borders of the Detroit, and baptized the savage children whom they found there.

Fort St. Joseph was abandoned in the year 1688. The establishment of Cadillac was destined to a better fate, and soon rose to distinguished importance among the western outposts of Canada. Indeed, the site was formed by nature for prosperity; and a bad government and a thriftless people could not prevent the increase of the colony. At the close of the French war, as Major Rogers tells us, the place contained twenty-five hundred inhabitants. The centre of the settlement was the fortified town, currently called the Fort, to distinguish it from the straggling dwellings along the river-banks. It stood on the western margin of the river, covering a small part of the ground now occupied by the city of Detroit, and contained about a hundred houses, compactly pressed together, and surrounded by a palisade. Both above and below the fort, the banks of the stream were lined on both sides with small Canadian dwellings, extending at various intervals for nearly eight miles. Each had its garden and its orchard, and each was enclosed by a fence of rounded pickets. To the soldier or the trader, fresh from the harsh scenery and ambushed perils of the surrounding wilds, the secluded settlement was welcome as an oasis in the desert.

The Canadian is usually a happy man. Life sits lightly upon him; he laughs at its hardships, and soon forgets its sorrows. A lover of roving and adventure, of the frolic and the dance, he is little troubled with thoughts of the past or the future, and little plagued with avarice or ambition. At Detroit, all his propensities found ample scope. Aloof from the world, the simple colonists shared none of its pleasures and excitements, and were free from many of its cares. Nor were luxuries wanting which civilization might have envied them. The forest teemed with game, the marshes with wild fowl, and the rivers with fish. The apples and pears of the old Canadian orchards are even to this day held in esteem. The poorer inhabitants made wine from the fruit of the wild grape, which grew profusely in the woods, while the wealthier class procured a better quality from Montreal, in exchange for the canoe-loads of furs which they sent down with every year. Here, as elsewhere in Canada, the long winter was a season of social enjoyment; and when, in summer and autumn, the traders and *voyageurs,* the *coureurs de bois* and half-breeds, gathered from the distant forests of the northwest, the whole settlement was alive with dancing and feasting, drinking, gaming, and carousing.

Within the limits of the settlement were three large Indian villages. On the western shore, a little below the fort, were the lodges of the Pottawattamies; nearly opposite, on the eastern side, was the village of the Wyandots; and on the same side, five miles higher up, Pontiac's band of Ottawas had fixed their abode. The settlers had always maintained the best terms with their savage neighbors. In truth, there was much congeniality between the red man and the Canadian. Their harmony was seldom broken; and among the woods and wilds of the northern lakes roamed many a lawless half-breed, the mongrel offspring of the colonists of Detroit and the Indian squaws.

We have already seen how, in an evil hour for the Canadians, a party of British troops took possession of Detroit, towards the close of the year 1760. The British garrison, consisting partly of regulars and partly of provincial rangers, was now quartered in a well-built range of barracks within the town or fort. The latter, as already mentioned, contained about a hundred small houses. Its form was nearly square, and the palisade which surrounded it was about twenty-five feet high. At each corner was a wooden bastion, and a blockhouse was erected over each gateway. The houses were small, chiefly built of wood, and roofed with bark or a thatch of straw. The streets also were extremely narrow, though a wide passage-way, known as the *chemin du ronde,* surrounded the town, between the houses and the palisade. Besides the barracks, the only public buildings were a council-house and a rude little church.

The garrison consisted of a hundred and twenty soldiers, with about forty fur-traders and *engagés;* but the latter, as well as the Canadian inhabitants of the place, could little be trusted, in the event of an Indian outbreak. Two small, armed schooners, the "Beaver" and the "Gladwyn," lay anchored in the stream, and several light pieces of artillery were mounted on the bastions.

Such was Detroit,—a place whose defences could have opposed no resistance to a civilized enemy; and yet, far removed as it was from the hope of speedy succor, it could only rely, in the terrible struggles that awaited it, upon its own slight strength and feeble resources.

Standing on the water bastion of Detroit, a pleasant landscape spread before the eye. The river, about half a mile wide, almost washed the foot of the stockade; and either bank was lined with the white Canadian cottages. The joyous sparkling of the bright blue water; the green luxuriance of the woods; the white dwellings, looking out from the foliage; and, in the distance, the Indian wigwams curling their smoke against the sky,—all were mingled in one broad scene of wild and rural beauty.

Pontiac, the Satan of this forest paradise, was accustomed to spend the early part of the summer upon a small island at the opening of the Lake St. Clair, hidden from view by the high woods that covered the intervening Isle-au-Cochon. "The king and lord of all this country," as Rogers calls him, lived in no royal state. His cabin was a small, oven-shaped structure of bark and rushes. Here he dwelt, with his squaws and children; and here, doubtless, he might often have been seen, lounging, half-naked, on a rush mat, or a bear-skin, like any ordinary warrior. We may fancy the current of his thoughts, the turmoil of his uncurbed passions, as he revolved the treacheries which, to his savage mind, seemed fair and honorable. At one moment, his fierce heart would burn with the anticipation of vengeance on the detested English; at another, he would meditate how he best might turn the approaching tumults to the furtherance of his own ambitious schemes. Yet we may believe that Pontiac was not a stranger to the high emotion of the patriot hero, the champion not merely of his nation's rights, but of the very existence of his race. He did not dream how desperate a game he was about to play. He hourly flattered himself with the futile hope of aid from France, and thought in his ignorance that the British colonies must give way before the rush of his savage warriors; when, in truth, all the combined tribes of the forest might have chafed in vain rage against the rock-like strength of the Anglo-Saxon.

Looking across an intervening arm of the river, Pontiac could see on its eastern bank the numerous lodges of his Ottawa tribesmen, half hidden among the ragged growth of trees and bushes. On the afternoon of the fifth of May, a Canadian woman, the wife of Saint-Aubin, one of the principal settlers, crossed over from the western side, and visited the Ottawa village, to obtain from the Indians a supply of maple sugar and venison. She was surprised at finding several of the warriors engaged in filing off the muzzles of their guns, so as to reduce them, stock and all, to the length of about a yard. Returning home in the evening, she mentioned what she had seen to several of her neighbors. Upon this, one of them, the blacksmith of the village, remarked that many of the Indians had lately visited his shop, and attempted to borrow files and saws for a purpose which they would not explain. These circumstances excited the suspicion of the experienced Canadians. Doubtless there were many in the settlement who might, had they chosen, have revealed the plot; but it is no less certain that the more numerous and respectable class in the little community had too deep an interest in the preservation of peace to countenance the designs of Pontiac. M. Gouin, an old and wealthy settler, went to the commandant, and conjured him to stand upon his guard; but Gladwyn, a man of fearless temper, gave no heed to the friendly advice.

In the Pottawattamie village, if there be truth in tradition, lived an Ojibwa girl, who could boast a larger share of beauty than is common in the wigwam. She had attracted the eye of Gladwyn. He had formed a connection with her, and she had become much attached to him. On the afternoon of the sixth, Catharine—for so the officers called her—came to the fort, and repaired to Gladwyn's quarters, bringing with her a pair of elk-skin moccasons, ornamented with porcupine work, which he had requested her to make. There was something unusual in her look and manner. Her face was sad and downcast. She said little, and soon left the room; but the sentinel at the door saw her still lingering at the street corner, though the hour for closing the gates was nearly come. At length she attracted the notice of Gladwyn himself; and calling her to him, he pressed her to declare what was weighing upon her mind. Still she remained for a long time silent, and it was only after much urgency and many promises not to betray her, that she revealed her momentous secret.

To-morrow, she said, Pontiac will come to the fort with sixty of his chiefs. Each will be armed with a gun, cut short, and hidden under his blanket. Pontiac will demand to hold a council; and after he has delivered his speech, he will offer a peace-belt of wampum, holding it in a reversed position. This will be the signal of attack. The chiefs will spring up and fire upon the officers, and the Indians in the street will fall upon the garrison. Every Englishman will be killed, but not the scalp of a single Frenchman will be touched.

Such is the story told in 1768 to the traveller Carver at Detroit, and preserved in local tradition, but not sustained by contemporary letters or diaries. What is certain is, that Gladwyn received secret information, on the night of the sixth of May, that an attempt would be made on the morrow to capture the fort by treachery. He called some of his officers, and told them what he had heard. The defences of the place were feeble and extensive, and the garrison by far too weak to repel a general assault. The force of the Indians at this time is variously estimated at from six hundred to two thousand; and the commandant greatly feared that some wild impulse might precipitate their plan, and that they would storm the fort before the morning. Every preparation was made to meet the sudden emergency. Half the garrison were ordered under arms. and all the officers prepared to spend the night upon the ramparts.

The day closed, and the hues of sunset faded. Only a dusky redness lingered in the west, and the darkening earth seemed her dull self again. Then night descended, heavy and black, on the fierce Indians and the sleepless English. From sunset till dawn, an anxious watch was kept from the slender palisades of Detroit. The soldiers were still ignorant of the danger; and the sentinels did not know why their numbers were doubled, or why, with such unwonted vigilance, their officers repeatedly visited their posts. Again and again Gladwyn mounted his wooden ramparts, and looked forth into the gloom. There seemed nothing but repose and peace in the soft, moist air of the warm spring evening, with the pipings of frogs along the river-bank, just roused from their torpor by the genial influence of May. But, at intervals, as the night wind swept across the bastion, it bore sounds of fearful portent to the ear, the sullen booming of the Indian drum and the wild chorus of quavering yells, as the warriors, around their distant camp-fires, danced the war-dance, in preparation for the morrow's work.

TREACHERY OF PONTIAC.

The night passed without alarm. The sun rose upon fresh fields and newly budding woods, and scarcely had the morning mists dissolved, when the garrison could see a fleet of birch canoes crossing the river from the eastern shore, within range of cannon-shot above the fort. Only two or three warriors appeared in each, but all moved slowly, and seemed deeply laden. In truth, they were full of savages, lying flat on their faces, that their numbers might not excite the suspicion of the English.

At an early hour the open common behind the fort was thronged with squaws, children, and warriors, some naked, and others fantastically arrayed in their barbarous finery. All seemed restless and uneasy, moving hither and thither, in apparent preparation for a general game of ball. Many tall warriors, wrapped in their blankets, were seen stalking towards the fort, and casting malignant furtive glances upward at the palisades. Then with an air of assumed indifference, they would move towards the gate. They were all admitted; for Gladwyn, who, in this instance at least, showed some knowledge of Indian character, chose to convince his crafty foe that, though their plot was detected, their hostility was despised.

The whole garrison was ordered under arms. Sterling, and the other English fur-traders, closed their storehouses and armed their men, and all in cool confidence stood waiting the result.

Meanwhile, Pontiac, who had crossed with the canoes from the eastern shore, was approaching along the river road, at the head of his sixty chiefs, all gravely marching in Indian file. A Canadian settler, named Beaufait, had been that morning to the fort. He was now returning homewards, and as he reached the bridge which led over the stream then called Parent's Creek, he saw the chiefs in the act of crossing from the farther bank. He stood aside to give them room. As the last Indian passed, Beaufait recognized him as an old friend and associate. The savage greeted him with the usual ejaculation, opened for an instant the folds of his blanket, disclosed the hidden gun, and, with an emphatic gesture towards the fort, indicated the purpose to which he meant to apply it.

At ten o'clock, the great war-chief, with his treacherous followers, reached the fort, and the gateway was thronged with their savage faces. All were wrapped to the throat in colored blankets. Some were crested with hawk, eagle, or raven plumes; others had shaved their heads, leaving only the fluttering scalp-lock on the crown; while others, again, wore their long, black hair flowing loosely at their backs, or wildly hanging about their brows like a lion's mane. Their bold yet crafty features, their cheeks besmeared with ochre and vermilion, white lead and soot, their keen, deep-set eyes gleaming in their sockets, like those of rattlesnakes, gave them an aspect grim, uncouth, and horrible. For the most part, they were tall, strong men, and all had a gait and bearing of peculiar stateliness.

As Pontiac entered, it is said that he started, and that a deep ejaculation half escaped from his breast. Well might his stoicism fail, for at a glance he read the ruin of his plot. On either hand, within the gateway, stood ranks of soldiers and hedges of glittering steel. The swarthy *engagés* of the fur-traders, armed to the teeth, stood in groups at the street corners, and the measured tap of a drum fell ominously on the ear. Soon regaining his composure, Pontiac strode forward into the narrow street; and his chiefs filed after him in silence, while the scared faces of women and children looked out from the windows as they passed. Their rigid muscles betrayed no sign of emotion; yet, looking closely, one might have seen their small eyes glance from side to side with restless scrutiny.

Traversing the entire width of the little town, they reached the door of the council-house, a large building standing near the margin of the river. On entering, they saw Gladwyn, with several of his officers, seated in readiness to receive them, and the observant chiefs did not fail to remark that every Englishman wore a sword at his side, and a pair of pistols in his belt. The conspirators eyed each other with uneasy glances. "Why," demanded Pontiac, "do I see so many of my father's young men standing in the street with their guns?" Gladwyn replied through his interpreter, La Butte, that he had ordered the soldiers under arms for the sake of exercise and discipline. With much delay and many signs of distrust, the chiefs at length sat down on the mats prepared for them; and, after the customary pause, Pontiac rose to speak. Holding in his hand the wampum belt which was to have given the fatal signal, he addressed the commandant, professing strong attachment to the English, and declaring, in Indian phrase, that he had come to smoke the pipe of peace, and brighten the chain of friendship. The officers watched him keenly as he uttered these hollow words, fearing lest, though conscious that his designs were suspected, he might still attempt to accomplish them. And once, it is said, he raised the wampum belt as if about to give the signal of attack. But at that instant Gladwyn signed slightly with his hand. The sudden clash of arms sounded from the passage without, and a drum rolling the charge filled the council-room with its stunning din. At this, Pontiac stood like one confounded. Some writers will have it that Gladwyn, rising from his seat, drew the chief's blanket aside, exposed the hidden gun, and sternly rebuked him for his treachery. But the commandant wished only to prevent the consummation of the plot, without bringing on an open rupture. His own letters affirm that he and his officers remained seated as before. Pontiac, seeing his unruffled brow and his calm eye fixed steadfastly upon him, knew not what to think, and soon sat down in amazement and perplexity. Another pause ensued, and Gladwyn commenced a brief reply. He assured the chiefs that friendship and protection should be extended towards them as long as they continued to deserve it, but threatened ample vengeance for the first act of aggression. The council then broke up; but, before leaving the room, Pontiac told the officers that he would return in a few days, with his squaws and children, for he wished that they should all shake hands with their fathers, the English. To this new piece of treachery Gladwyn deigned no reply. The gates of the fort, which had been closed during the conference, were again flung open, and the baffled savages were suffered to depart, rejoiced, no doubt, to breathe once more the free air of the open fields.

Gladwyn has been censured, and perhaps with justice, for not detaining the chiefs as hostages for the good conduct of their followers. An entrapped wolf meets no quarter from the huntsman; and a savage, caught in his treachery, has no claim to forbearance. Perhaps the commandant feared lest, should he arrest the chiefs when gathered at a public council, and guiltless as yet of open violence, the act might be interpreted as cowardly and dishonorable. He was ignorant, moreover, of the true nature of the plot. In his view, the whole affair was one of those impulsive outbreaks so common among Indians; and he trusted that, could an immediate rupture be averted, the threatening clouds would soon blow over.

Here, and elsewhere, the conduct of Pontiac is marked with the blackest treachery; and one cannot but lament that a commanding and magnanimous nature should be stained with the odious vice of cowards and traitors. He could govern, with almost despotic sway, a race unruly as the winds. In generous thought and deed, he rivalled the heroes of ancient story; and craft and cunning might well seem alien to a mind like his. Yet Pontiac was a thorough savage, and in him stand forth, in strongest light and shadow, the native faults and virtues of the Indian race. All children, says Sir Walter Scott, are naturally liars; and truth and honor are developments of later education. Barbarism is to civilization what childhood is to maturity; and all savages, whatever may be their country, their color, or their lineage, are prone to treachery and deceit. The barbarous ancestors of our own frank and manly race are no less obnoxious to the charge than those of the cat-like Bengalee; for in this childhood of society brave men and cowards are treacherous alike.

The Indian differs widely from the European in his notion of military virtue. In his view, artifice is wisdom; and he honors the skill that can circumvent, no less than the valor that can subdue, an adversary. The object of war, he argues, is to destroy the enemy. To accomplish this end, all means are honorable; and it is folly, not bravery, to incur a needless risk. Had Pontiac ordered his followers to storm the palisades of Detroit, not one of them would have obeyed him. They might, indeed, after their strange superstition, have reverenced him as a madman, but, from that hour, his fame as a war-chief would have sunk forever.

Balked in his treachery, the great chief withdrew to his village, enraged and mortified, yet still resolved to persevere. That Gladwyn had suffered him to escape, was to his mind an ample proof either of cowardice or ignorance. The latter supposition seemed the more probable; and he resolved to visit the English once more, and convince them, if possible, that their suspicions against him were unfounded. Early on the following morning, he repaired to the fort with three of his chiefs, bearing in his hand the sacred calumet, or pipe of peace, its bowl carved in stone, and its stem adorned with feathers. Offering it to the commandant, he addressed him and his officers to the following effect: "My fathers, evil birds have sung lies in your ear. We that stand before you are friends of the English. We love them as our brothers; and, to prove our love, we have come this day to smoke the pipe of peace." At his departure, he gave the pipe to Captain Campbell, second in command, as a further pledge of his sincerity.

That afternoon, the better to cover his designs, Pontiac called the young men of all the tribes to a game of ball, which took place, with great noise and shouting, on the neighboring fields. At nightfall, the garrison were startled by a burst of loud, shrill yells. The drums beat to arms, and the troops were ordered to their posts; but the alarm was caused only by the victors in the ball play, who were announcing their success by these discordant outcries. Meanwhile, Pontiac was in the Pottawattamie village, consulting with the chiefs of that tribe, and with the Wyandots, by what means they might compass the ruin of the English.

Early on the following morning, Monday, the ninth of May, the French inhabitants went in procession to the principal church of the settlement, which stood near the river-bank, about half a mile above the fort. Having heard mass, they all returned before eleven o'clock, without discovering any signs that the Indians meditated an immediate act of hostility. Scarcely, however, had they done so, when the common behind the fort was once more thronged with Indians of all the four tribes; and Pontiac, advancing from among the multitude, approached the gate. It was closed and barred against him. He shouted to the sentinels, and demanded why he was refused admittance. Gladwyn himself replied, that the great chief might enter, if he chose, but that the crowd he had brought with him must remain outside. Pontiac rejoined that he wished all his warriors to enjoy the fragrance of the friendly calumet. Gladwyn's answer was more concise than courteous, and imported that he would have none of his rabble in the fort. Thus repulsed, Pontiac threw off the mask which he had worn so long. With a grin of hate and rage, he turned abruptly from the gate, and strode towards his followers, who, in great multitudes, lay flat upon the ground, just beyond reach of gunshot. At his approach, they all leaped up and ran off, "yelping," in the words of an eye-witness, "like so many devils."

Looking out from the loopholes, the garrison could see them running in a body towards the house of an old English woman, who lived, with her family, on a distant part of the common. They beat down the doors, and rushed tumultuously in. A moment more, and the mournful scalp-yell told the fate of the wretched inmates. Another large body ran, yelling, to the river-bank, and, leaping into their canoes, paddled with all speed to the Isle-au-Cochon, where dwelt an Englishman, named Fisher, formerly a sergeant of the regulars.

They soon dragged him from the hiding-place where he had sought refuge, murdered him on the spot, took his scalp, and made great rejoicings over this miserable trophy of brutal malice. On the following day, several Canadians crossed over to the island to inter the body, which they accomplished, as they thought, very effectually. Tradition, however, relates, as undoubted truth, that when, a few days after, some of the party returned to the spot, they beheld the pale hands of the dead man thrust above the ground, in an attitude of eager entreaty. Having once more covered the refractory members with earth, they departed, in great wonder and awe; but what was their amazement, when, on returning a second time, they saw the hands protruding as before. At this, they repaired in horror to the priest, who hastened to the spot, sprinkled the grave with holy water, and performed over it the neglected rites of burial. Thenceforth, says the tradition, the corpse of the murdered soldier slept in peace.

Pontiac had borne no part in the wolfish deeds of his followers. When he saw his plan defeated, he turned towards the shore; and no man durst approach him, for he was terrible in his rage. Pushing a canoe from the bank, he urged it with vigorous strokes, against the current, towards the Ottawa village, on the farther side. As he drew near, he shouted to the inmates. None remained in the lodges but women, children, and old men, who all came flocking out at the sound of his imperious voice. Pointing across the water, he ordered that all should prepare to move the camp to the western shore, that the river might no longer interpose a barrier between his followers and the English. The squaws labored with eager alacrity to obey him. Provisions, utensils, weapons, and even the bark covering to the lodges, were carried to the shore; and before evening all was ready for embarkation. Meantime, the warriors had come dropping in from their bloody work, until, at nightfall, nearly all had returned. Then Pontiac, hideous in his war-paint, leaped into the central area of the village. Brandishing his tomahawk, and stamping on the ground, he recounted his former exploits, and denounced vengeance on the English. The Indians flocked about him. Warrior after warrior caught the fierce contagion, and soon the ring was filled with dancers, circling round and round with frantic gesture, and startling the distant garrison with unearthly yells.

The war-dance over, the work of embarkation was commenced, and long before morning the transfer was complete. The whole Ottawa population crossed the river, and pitched their wigwams on the western side, just above the mouth of the little stream then known as Parent's Creek, but since named Bloody Run, from the scenes of terror which it witnessed.

During the evening, fresh tidings of disaster reached the fort. A Canadian, named Desnoyers, came down the river in a birch canoe, and, landing at the water gate, brought news that two English officers, Sir Robert Davers and Captain Robertson, had been waylaid and murdered by the Indians, above Lake St. Clair. The Canadian declared, moreover, that Pontiac had just been joined by a formidable band of Ojibwas, from the Bay of Saginaw. These were a peculiarly ferocious horde, and their wretched descendants still retain the character.

Every Englishman in the fort, whether trader or soldier, was now ordered under arms. No man lay down to sleep, and Gladwyn himself walked the ramparts throughout the night.

All was quiet till the approach of dawn. But as the first dim redness tinged the east, and fields and woods grew visible in the morning twilight, suddenly the war-whoop rose on every side at once. As wolves assail the wounded bison, howling their gathering cries across the wintry prairie, so the fierce Indians, pealing their terrific yells, came bounding naked to the assault. The men hastened to their posts. And truly it was time; for not the Ottawas alone, but the whole barbarian swarm—Wyandots, Pottawattamies, and Ojibwas—were upon them, and bullets rapped hard and fast against the palisades. The soldiers looked from the loopholes, thinking to see their assailants gathering for a rush against the feeble barrier. But, though their clamors filled the air, and their guns blazed thick and hot, yet very few were visible. Some were ensconced behind barns and fences, some skulked among bushes, and some lay flat in hollows of the ground; while those who could find no shelter were leaping about with the agility of monkeys, to dodge the shot of the fort. Each had filled his mouth with bullets, for the convenience of loading, and each was charging and firing without suspending these agile gymnastics for a moment. There was one low hill, at no great distance from the fort, behind which countless black heads of Indians alternately appeared and vanished; while, all along the ridge, their guns emitted incessant white puffs of smoke. Every loophole was a target for their bullets; but the fire was returned with steadiness, and not without effect. The Canadian *engagés* of the fur-traders retorted the Indian war-whoops with outcries not less discordant, while the British and provincials paid back the clamor of the enemy with musket and rifle balls. Within half gunshot of the palisades was a cluster of outbuildings, behind which a host of Indians found shelter. A cannon was brought to bear upon them, loaded with red-hot spikes. They were soon wrapped in flames, upon which the disconcerted savages broke away in a body, and ran off yelping, followed by a shout of laughter from the soldiers.

For six hours, the attack was unabated; but as the day advanced, the assailants grew weary of their futile efforts. Their fire slackened, their clamors died away, and the garrison was left once more in peace, though from time to time a solitary shot, or lonely whoop, still showed the presence of some lingering savage, loath to be balked of his revenge. Among the garrison, only five men had been wounded, while the cautious enemy had suffered but trifling loss.

FRANK RICHARD STOCKTON (1834-1902)

The Lady, or the Tiger?

IN the very olden time, there lived a semi-barbaric king, whose ideas, though somewhat polished and sharpened by the progressiveness of distant Latin neighbors, were still large, florid, and untrammelled, as became the half of him which was barbaric. He was a man of exuberant fancy, and, withal, of an authority so irresistible that, at his will, he turned his varied fancies into facts. He was greatly given to self-communing; and, when he and himself agreed upon anything, the thing was done. When every member of his domestic and political systems moved smoothly in its appointed course, his nature was bland and genial; but whenever there was a little hitch, and some of his orbs got out of their orbits, he was blander and more genial still, for nothing pleased him so much as to make the crooked straight, and crush down uneven places.

Among the borrowed notions by which his barbarism had become semified was that of the public arena, in which, by exhibitions of manly and beastly valor, the minds of his subjects were refined and cultured.

But even here the exuberant and barbaric fancy asserted itself. The arena of the king was built, not to give the people an opportunity of hearing the rhapsodies of dying gladiators, nor to enable them to view the inevitable conclusions of a conflict between religious opinions and hungry jaws, but for purposes far better adapted to widen and develop the mental energies of the people. This vast amphitheatre, with its encircling galleries, its mysterious vaults, and its unseen passages, was an agent of poetic justice, in which crime was punished, or virtue rewarded, by the decrees of an impartial and incorruptible chance.

When a subject was accused of a crime of sufficient importance to interest the king, public notice was given that on an appointed day the fate of the accused person would be decided in the king's arena,—a structure which well deserved its name; for, although its form and plan were borrowed from afar, its purpose emanated solely from the brain of this man, who, every barleycorn a king, knew no tradition to which he owed more allegiance than pleased his fancy, and who ingrafted on every adopted form of human thought and action the rich growth of his barbaric idealism.

When all the people had assembled in the galleries, and the king, surrounded by his court, sat high up on his throne of royal state on one side of the arena, he gave a signal, a door beneath him opened, and the accused subject stepped out into the amphitheatre. Directly opposite him, on the other side of the enclosed space, were two doors, exactly alike and side by side. It was the duty and the privilege of the person on trial, to walk directly to these doors and open one of them. He could open either door he pleased: he was subject to no guidance or influence but that of the aforementioned impartial and incorruptible chance. If he opened the one, there came out of it a hungry tiger, the fiercest and most cruel that could be procured, which immediately sprang upon him, and tore him to pieces, as a punishment for his guilt. The moment that the case of the criminal was thus decided, doleful iron bells were clanged, great wails went up from the hired mourners posted on the outer rim of the arena, and the vast audience, with bowed heads and downcast hearts, wended slowly their homeward way, mourning greatly that one so young and fair, or so old and respected, should have merited so dire a fate.

But, if the accused person opened the other door, there came forth from it a lady, the most suitable to his years and station that his majesty could select among his fair subjects; and to his lady he was immediately married, as a reward of his innocence. It mattered not that he might already possess a wife and family, or that his affections might be engaged upon an object of his own selection: the king allowed no such subordinate arrangements to interfere with his great scheme of retribution and reward. The exercises, as in the other instance, took place immediately, and in the arena. Another door opened beneath the king, and a priest, followed by a band of choristers, and dancing maidens blowing joyous airs on golden horns and treading an epithalamic measure, advanced to where the pair stood, side by side; and the wedding was promptly and cheerily solemnized. Then the gay brass bells rang forth their merry peals, the people shouted glad hurrahs, and the innocent man, preceded by children strewing flowers on his path, led his bride to his home.

This was the king's semi-barbaric method of administering justice. Its perfect fairness is obvious. The criminal could not know out of which door would come the lady: he opened either he pleased, without having the slightest idea whether, in the next instant, he was to be devoured or married. On some occasions the tiger came out of one door, and on some out of the other. The decisions of this tribunal were not only fair, they were positively determinate: the accused person was instantly punished if he found himself guilty; and, if innocent, he was rewarded on the spot, whether he liked it or not. There was no escape from the judgments of the king's arena.

The institution was a very popular one. When the people gathered together on one of the great trial days, they never knew whether they were to witness a bloody slaughter or a hilarious wedding. This element of uncertainty lent an interest to the occasion which it could not otherwise have attained. Thus, the masses were entertained and pleased, and the thinking part of the community could bring no charge of unfairness against this plan; for did not the accused person have the whole matter in his own hands?

This semi-barbaric king had a daughter as blooming as his most florid fancies, and with a soul as fervent and imperious as his own. As is usual in such cases, she was the apple of his eye, and was loved by him above all humanity. Among his courtiers was a young man of that fineness of blood and lowness of station common to the conventional heroes of romance who love royal maidens. This royal maiden was well satisfied with her lover, for he was handsome and brave to a degree unsurpassed in all this kingdom; and she loved him with an ardor that had enough of barbarism in it to make it exceedingly warm and strong. This love affair moved on happily for many months, until one day the king happened to discover its existence. He did not hesitate nor waver in regard to his duty in the premises. The youth was immediately cast into prison, and a day was appointed for his trial in the king's arena. This, of course, was an especially important occasion; and his majesty, as well as all the people, was greatly interested in the workings and development of this trial. Never before had such a case occurred; never before had a subject dared to love the daughter of a king. In after-years such things became commonplace enough; but then they were, in no slight degree, novel and startling.

The tiger-cages of the kingdom were searched for the most savage and relentless beasts, from which the fiercest monster might be selected for the arena; and the ranks of maiden youth and beauty throughout the land were carefully surveyed by competent judges, in order that the young man might have a fitting bride in case fate did not determine for him a different destiny. Of course, everybody knew that the deed with which the accused was charged had been done. He had loved the princess, and neither he, she, nor any one else thought of denying the fact; but the king would not think of allowing any fact of this kind to interfere with the workings of the tribunal, in which he took such great delight and satisfaction. No matter how the affair turned out, the youth would be disposed of; and the king would take an æsthetic pleasure in watching the course of events, which would determine whether or not the young man had done wrong in allowing himself to love the princess.

The appointed day arrived. From far and near the people gathered, and thronged the great galleries of the arena; and crowds, unable to gain admittance, massed themselves against its outside walls. The king and his court were in their places, opposite the twin doors,—those fateful portals, so terrible in their similarity.

All was ready. The signal was given. A door beneath the royal party opened, and the lover of the princess walked into the arena. Tall, beautiful, fair, his appearance was greeted with a low hum of admiration and anxiety. Half the audience had not known so grand a youth had lived among them. No wonder the princess loved him! What a terrible thing for him to be there!

As the youth advanced into the arena, he turned, as the custom was, to bow to the king: but he did not think at all of that royal personage; his eyes were fixed upon the princess, who sat to the right of her father. Had it not been for the moiety of barbarism in her nature, it is probable that lady would not have been there; but her intense and fervid soul would not allow her to be absent on an occasion in which she was so terribly interested. From the moment that the decree had gone forth, that her lover should decide his fate in the king's arena, she had thought of nothing, night or day, but this great event and the various subjects connected with it. Possessed of more power, influence, and force of character than any one who had ever before been interested in such a case, she had done what no other person had done,—she had possessed herself of the secret of the doors. She knew in which of the two rooms, that lay behind those doors, stood the cage of the tiger, with its open front, and in which waited the lady. Through these thick doors, heavily curtained with skins on the inside, it was impossible that any noise or suggestion should come from within to the person who should approach to raise the latch of one of them; but gold, and the power of a woman's will, had brought the secret to the princess.

And not only did she know in which room stood the lady ready to emerge, all blushing and radiant, should her door be opened, but she knew who the lady was. It was one of the fairest and loveliest of the damsels of the court who had been selected as the reward of the accused youth, should he be proved innocent of the crime of aspiring to one so far above him; and the princess hated her. Often had she seen, or imagined that she had seen, this fair creature throwing glances of admiration upon the person of her lover, and sometimes she thought these glances were perceived and even returned. Now and then she had seen them talking together; it was but for a moment or two, but much can be said in a brief space; it may have been on most unimportant topics, but how could she know that? The girl was lovely, but she had dared to raise her eyes to the loved one of the princess; and, with all the intensity of the savage blood transmitted to her through long lines of wholly barbaric ancestors, she hated the woman who blushed and trembled behind that silent door.

When her lover turned and looked at her, and his eye met hers as she sat there paler and whiter than any one in the vast ocean of anxious faces about her, he saw, by that power of quick perception which is given to those whose souls are one, that she knew behind which door crouched the tiger, and behind which stood the lady. He had expected her to know it. He understood her nature, and his soul was assured that she would never rest until she had made plain to herself this thing, hidden to all other lookers-on, even to the king. The only hope for the youth in which there was any element of certainty was based upon the success of the princess in discovering this mystery; and the moment he looked upon her, he saw she had succeeded, as in his soul he knew she would succeed.

Then it was that his quick and anxious glance asked the question: "Which?" It was as plain to her as if he shouted it from where he stood. There was not an instant to be lost. The question was asked in a flash; it must be answered in another.

Her right arm lay on the cushioned parapet before her. She raised her hand, and made a slight, quick movement toward the right. No one but her lover saw her. Every eye but his was fixed on the man in the arena.

He turned, and with a firm and rapid step he walked across the empty space. Every heart stopped beating, every breath was held, every eye was fixed immovably upon that man. Without the slightest hesitation, he went to the door on the right, and opened it.

Now, the point of the story is this: Did the tiger come out of that door, or did the lady?

The more we reflect upon this question, the harder it is to answer. It involves a study of the human heart which leads us through devious mazes of passion, out of which it is difficult to find our way. Think of it, fair reader, not as if the decision of the question depended upon yourself, but upon that hot-blooded, semi-barbaric princess, her soul at a white heat beneath the combined fires of despair and jealousy. She had lost him, but who should have him?

How often, in her waking hours and in her dreams, had she started in wild horror, and covered her face with her hands as she thought of her lover opening the door on the other side of which waited the cruel fangs of the tiger!

But how much oftener had she seen him at the other door! How in her grievous reveries had she gnashed her teeth, and torn her hair, when she saw his start of rapturous delight as he opened the door of the lady! How her soul had burned in agony when she had seen him rush to meet that woman, with her flushing cheek and sparkling eye of triumph; when she had seen him lead her forth, his whole frame kindled with the joy of recovered life; when she had heard the glad shouts from the multitude, and the wild ringing of the happy bells; when she had seen the priest, with his joyous followers, advance to the couple, and make them man and wife before her very eyes; and when she had seen them walk away together upon their path of flowers, followed by the tremendous shouts of the hilarious multitude, in which her one despairing shriek was lost and drowned!

Would it not be better for him to die at once, and go to wait for her in the blessed regions of semi-barbaric futurity?

And yet, that awful tiger, those shrieks, that blood!

Her decision had been indicated in an instant, but it had been made after days and nights of anguished deliberation. She had known she would be asked, she had decided what she would answer, and, without the slightest hesitation, she had moved her hand to the right.

The question of her decision is one not to be lightly considered, and it is not for me to presume to set myself up as the one person able to answer it. And so I leave it with all of you: Which came out of the opened door,—the lady, or the tiger?

MARK TWAIN (1835-1910)

The Notorious Jumping Frog of Calaveras County

IN compliance with the request of a friend of mine, who wrote me from the East, I called on good-natured, garrulous old Simon Wheeler, and inquired after my friend's friend, Leonidas W. Smiley, as requested to do, and I hereunto append the result. I have a lurking suspicion that *Leonidas W.* Smiley is a myth; that my friend never knew such a personage; and that he only conjectured that if I asked Wheeler about him, it would remind him of his infamous *Jim* Smiley, and he would go to work and bore me to death with some exasperating reminiscence of him as long and as tedious as it should be useless to me. If that was the design, it succeeded.

I found Simon Wheeler dozing comfortably by the barroom stove of the dilapidated tavern in the decaying mining camp of Angel's, and I noticed that he was fat and bald-headed, and had an expression of winning gentleness and simplicity upon his tranquil countenance. He roused up, and gave me good-day. I told him a friend of mine had commissioned me to make some inquiries about a cherished companion of his boyhood named *Leonidas* W. Smiley—*Rev. Leonidas W.* Smiley, a young minister of the Gospel, who he had heard was at one time a resident of Angel's Camp. I added that if Mr. Wheeler could tell me anything about this Rev. Leonidas W. Smiley, I would feel under many obligations to him.

Simon Wheeler backed me into a corner and blockaded me there with his chair, and then sat down and reeled off the monotonous narrative which follows this paragraph. He never smiled, he never frowned, he never changed his voice from the gentle-flowing key to which he turned his initial sentence, he never betrayed the slightest suspicion of enthusiasm; but all through the interminable narrative there ran a vein of impressive earnestness and sincerity, which showed me plainly that, so far from his imagining that there was anything ridiculous or funny about his story, he regarded it as a really important matter, and admired its two heroes as men of transcendent genius in *finesse*. I let him go on in his own way, and never interrupted him once.

"Rev. Leonidas W. H'm, Reverend Le—well, there was a feller here once by the name of *Jim* Smiley, in the winter of '49—or maybe it was the spring of '50—I don't recollect exactly, somehow, though what makes me think it was one or the other is because I remember the big flume warn't finished when he first come to the camp; but anyway, he was the curiosest man about always betting on anything that turned up you ever see, if he could get anybody to bet on the other side; and if he couldn't he'd change sides. Any way that suited the other man would suit *him*—any way just so's he got a bet, *he* was satisfied. But still he was lucky, uncommon lucky; he most always came out winner. He was always ready and laying for a chance; there couldn't be no solit'ry thing mentioned but that feller'd offer to bet on it, and take ary side you please, as I was just telling you. If there was a horse-race, you'd find him flush or you'd find him busted at the end of it; if there was a dog-fight, he'd bet on it; if there was a cat-fight, he'd bet on it; if there was a chicken-fight, he'd bet on it; why, if there was two birds setting on a fence, he would bet you which one would fly first; or if there was a camp-meeting, he would be there reg'lar to bet on Parson Walker, which he judged to be the best exhorter about here, and so he was, too, and a good man. If he even see a straddle-bug start to go anywheres, he would bet you how long it would take him to get to—to wherever he was going to, and if you took him up, he would foller that straddle-bug to Mexico but what he would find out where he was bound for and how long he was on the road. Lots of the boys here has seen that Smiley, and can tell you about him. Why, it never made no difference to *him*—he'd bet on *any* thing—the dangdest feller. Parson Walker's wife laid very sick once, for a good while, and it seemed as if they warn't going to save her; but one morning he come in, and Smiley up and asked him how she was, and he said she was considerable better—thank the Lord for his inf'nite mercy—and coming on so smart that with the blessing of Prov'dence she'd get well yet; and Smiley, before he thought, says: 'Well, I'll resk two-and-a-half she don't anyway.'

"Thish-yer Smiley had a mare—the boys called her the fifteen-minute nag, but that was only in fun, you know, because, of course, she was faster than that—and he used to win money on that horse, for all she was so slow and always had the asthma, or the distemper, or the consumption, or something of that kind. They used to give her two or three hundred yards start, and then pass her under way; but always at the fag end of the race she'd get excited and desperate like, and come cavorting and straddling up, and scattering her legs around limber, sometimes in the air, and sometimes out to one side among the fences, and kicking up m-o-r-e dust and raising m-o-r-e racket with her coughing and sneezing and blowing her nose—and *always* fetch up at the stand just about a neck ahead, as near as you could cipher it down.

"And he had a little small bull-pup, that to look at him you'd think he warn't worth a cent but to set around and look ornery and lay for a chance to steal something.   But as soon as money was up on him he was a different dog; his under-jaw'd begin to stick out like the fo'castle of a steamboat, and his teeth would uncover and shine like the furnaces.   And a dog might tackle him and bully-rag him, and bite him, and throw him over his shoulder two or three times, and Andrew Jackson—which was the name of the pup—Andrew Jackson would never let on but what *he* was satisfied, and hadn't expected nothing else—and the bets being doubled and doubled on the other side all the time, till the money was all up; and then all of a sudden he would grab that other dog jest by the j'int of his hind leg and freeze to it—not chaw, you understand, but only just grip and hang on till they throwed up the sponge, if it was a year.   Smiley always come out winner on that pup, till he harnessed a dog once that didn't have no hind legs, because they'd been sawed off in a circular saw, and when the thing had gone along far enough, and the money was all up, and he come to make a snatch for his pet holt, he see in a minute how he'd been imposed on, and how the other dog had him in the door, so to speak, and he 'peared surprised, and then he looked sorter discouraged-like and didn't try no more to win the fight, and so he got shucked out bad.   He give Smiley a look, as much as to say his heart was broke, and it was *his* fault, for putting up a dog that hadn't no hind legs for him to take holt of, which was his main dependence in a fight, and then he limped off a piece and laid down and died.   It was a good pup, was that Andrew Jackson, and would have made a name for hisself if he'd lived, for the stuff was in him and he had genius—I know it, because he hadn't no opportunities to speak of, and it don't stand to reason that a dog could make such a fight as he could under them circumstances if he hadn't no talent.   It always makes me feel sorry when I think of that last fight of his'n, and the way it turned out.

"Well, thish-yer Smiley had rat-tarriers, and chicken cocks, and tomcats and all them kind of things, till you couldn't rest, and you couldn't fetch nothing for him to bet on but he'd match you.   He ketched a frog one day, and took him home, and said he cal'lated to educate him; and so he never done nothing for three months but set in his back yard and learn that frog to jump.   And you bet you he *did* learn him, too.   He'd give him a little punch behind, and the next minute you'd see that frog whirling in the air like a doughnut—see him turn one summerset, or maybe a couple, if he got a good start, and come down flat-footed and all right, like a cat.   He got him up so in the matter of ketching flies, and kep' him in practice so constant, that he'd nail a fly every time as fur as he could see him.   Smiley said all a frog wanted was education, and he could do 'most anything—and I believe him.   Why, I've seen him set Dan'l Webster down here on this floor—Dan'l Webster was the name of the frog—and sing out, "Flies, Dan'l, flies!" and quicker'n you could wink he'd spring straight up and snake a fly off'n the counter there, and flop down on the floor ag'in as solid as a gob of mud, and fall to scratching the side of his head with his hind foot as indifferent as if he hadn't no idea he'd been doin' any more'n any frog might do. You never see a frog so modest and straightfor'ard as he was, for all he was so gifted. And when it come to fair and square jumping on a dead level, he could get over more ground at one straddle than any animal of his breed you ever see. Jumping on a dead level was his strong suit, you understand; and when it come to that, Smiley would ante up money on him as long as he had a red. Smiley was monstrous proud of his frog, and well he might be, for fellers that had travelled and been everywheres all said he laid over any frog that ever *they* see.

"Well, Smiley kep' the beast in a little lattice box, and he used to fetch him down town sometimes and lay for a bet. One day a feller—a stranger in the camp, he was—come acrost him with his box, and says:

" 'What might it be that you've got in the box?'

"And Smiley says, sorter indifferent-like: 'It might be a parrot, or it might be a canary, maybe, but it ain't—it's only just a frog.'

"And the feller took it, and looked at it careful, and turned it round this way and that, and says: 'H'm—so 'tis. Well, what's *he* good for?'

" 'Well,' Smiley says, easy and careless, 'he's good enough for *one* thing, I should judge—he can out-jump any frog in Calaveras county.'

"The feller took the box again, and took another long, particular look, and give it back to Smiley, and says, very deliberate, 'Well,' he says, 'I don't see no p'ints about that frog that's any better'n any other frog.'

" 'Maybe you don't,' Smiley says. 'Maybe you understand frogs and maybe you don't understand 'em; maybe you've had experience, and maybe you ain't only a amature, as it were. Anyways, I've got *my* opinion, and I'll resk forty dollars that he can outjump any frog in Calaveras county.'

"And the feller studied a minute, and then says, kinder sad like, 'Well, I'm only a stranger here, and I ain't got no frog; but if I had a frog, I'd bet you.'

"And then Smiley says, 'That's all right—that's all right—if you'll hold my box a minute, I'll go and get you a frog.' And so the feller took the box, and put up his forty dollars along with Smiley's, and set down to wait.

"So he set there a good while thinking and thinking to hisself, and then he got the frog out and prized his mouth open and took a teaspoon and filled him full of quail-shot—filled him pretty near up to his chin—and set him on the floor. Smiley he went to the swamp and slopped around in the mud for a long time, and finally he ketched a frog, and fetched him in, and give him to this feller, and says:

" 'Now, if you're ready, set him alongside of Dan'l, with his forepaws just even with Dan'l's, and I'll give the word.' Then he says, 'One—two—three—*git!*' and him and the feller touched up the frogs from behind, and the new frog hopped off lively, but Dan'l give a heave, and hysted up his shoulders—so—like a Frenchman, but it warn't no use—he couldn't budge; he was planted as solid as a church, and he couldn't no more stir than if he was anchored out. Smiley was a good deal surprised, and he was disgusted too, but he didn't have no idea what the matter was, of course.

"The feller took the money and started away; and when he was going out at the door, he sorter jerked his thumb over his shoulder—so—at Dan'l, and says again, very deliberate, 'Well,' he says, '*I* don't see no p'ints about that frog that's any better'n any other frog.'

"Smiley he stood scratching his head and looking down at Dan'l a long time, and at last he says, 'I do wonder what in the nation that frog throw'd off for—I wonder if there ain't something the matter with him—he 'pears to look mighty baggy, somehow.' And he ketched Dan'l by the nap of the neck, and hefted him, and says, 'Why, blame my cats if he don't weigh five pound!' and turned him upside down and he belched out a double handful of shot. And then he see how it was, and he was the maddest man—he set the frog down and took out after that feller, but he never ketched him. And—"

[Here Simon Wheeler heard his name called from the front yard, and got up to see what was wanted.] And turning to me as he moved away, he said: "Just set where you are, stranger, and rest easy—I ain't going to be gone a second."

But, by your leave, I did not think that a continuation of the history of the enterprising vagabond *Jim* Smiley would be likely to afford me much information concerning the Rev. *Leonidas W.* Smiley, and so I started away.

At the door I met the sociable Wheeler returning, and he buttonholed me and re-commenced:

"Well, thish-yer Smiley had a yaller one-eyed cow that didn't have no tail, only just a short stump like a bannanner, and—"

However, lacking both time and inclination, I did not wait to hear about the afflicted cow, but took my leave.

From LIFE ON THE MISSISSIPPI

A Daring Deed

WHEN I returned to the pilot-house St. Louis was gone, and I was lost. Here was a piece of river which was all down in my book, but I could make neither head nor tail of it: you understand, it was turned around. I had seen it when coming up-stream, but I had never faced about to see how it looked when it was behind me. My heart broke again, for it was plain that I had got to learn this troublesome river *both ways*.

The pilot-house was full of pilots, going down to "look at the river." What is called the "upper river" (the two hundred miles between St. Louis and Cairo, where the Ohio comes in) was low; and the Mississippi changes its channel so constantly that the pilots used to always find it necessary to run down to Cairo to take a fresh look, when their boats were to lie in port a week; that is, when the water was at a low stage. A deal of this "looking at the river" was done by poor fellows who seldom had a berth, and whose only hope of getting one lay in their being always freshly posted and therefore ready to drop into the shoes of some reputable pilot, for a single trip, on account of such pilot's sudden illness, or some other necessity. And a good many of them constantly ran up and down inspecting the river, not because they ever really hoped to get a berth, but because (they being guests of the boat) it was cheaper to "look at the river" than stay ashore and pay board. In time these fellows grew dainty in their tastes, and only infested boats that had an established reputation for setting good tables. All visiting pilots were useful, for they were always ready and willing, winter or summer, night or day, to go out in the yawl and help buoy the channel or assist the boat's pilots in any way they could. They were likewise welcomed because all pilots are tireless talkers, when gathered together, and as they talk only about the river they are always understood and are always interesting. Your true pilot cares nothing about anything on earth but the river, and his pride in his occupation surpasses the pride of kings.

We had a fine company of these river inspectors along this trip. There were eight or ten, and there was abundance of room for them in our great pilot-house. Two or three of them wore polished silk hats, elaborate shirt-fronts, diamond breastpins, kid gloves, and patent-leather boots. They were choice in their English, and bore themselves with a dignity proper to men of solid means and prodigious reputation as pilots. The others were more or less loosely clad, and wore upon their heads tall felt cones that were suggestive of the days of the Commonwealth.

I was a cipher in this august company, and felt subdued, not to say torpid. I was not even of sufficient consequence to assist at the wheel when it was necessary to put the tiller hard down in a hurry; the guest that stood nearest did that when occasion required—and this was pretty much all the time, because of the crookedness of the channel and the scant water. I stood in a corner; and the talk I listened to took the hope all out of me. One visitor said to another:

"Jim, how did you run Plum Point, coming up?"

"It was in the night, there, and I ran it the way one of the boys on the *Diana* told me; started out about fifty yards above the wood-pile on the false point, and held on the cabin under Plum Point till I raised the reef—quarter less twain—then straightened up for the middle bar till I got well abreast the old one-limbed cottonwood in the bend, then got my stern on the cottonwood, and head on the low place above the point, and came through a-booming—nine and a half."

"Pretty square crossing, an't it?"

"Yes, but the upper bar's working down fast."

Another pilot spoke up and said:

"I had better water than that, and ran it lower down; started out from the false point—mark twain—raised the second reef abreast the big snag in the bend, and had quarter less twain."

One of the gorgeous ones remarked:

"I don't want to find fault with your leadsmen, but that's a good deal of water for Plum Point, it seems to me."

There was an approving nod all around as this quiet snub dropped on the boaster and "settled" him. And so they went on talk-talk-talking. Meantime, the thing that was running in my mind was, "Now, if my ears hear aright, I have not only to get the names of all the towns and islands and bends, and so on, by heart, but I must even get up a warm personal acquaintanceship with every old snag and one-limbed cottonwood and obscure wood-pile that ornaments the banks of this river for twelve hundred miles; and more than that, I must actually know where these things are in the dark, unless these guests are gifted with eyes that can pierce through two miles of solid blackness. I wish the piloting business was in Jericho and I had never thought of it."

At dusk Mr. Bixby tapped the big bell three times (the signal to land), and the captain emerged from his drawing-room in the forward end of the "texas," and looked up inquiringly. Mr. Bixby said:

"We will lay up here all night, captain."

"Very well, sir."

That was all. The boat came to shore and was tied up for the night.

It seemed to me a fine thing that the pilot could do as he pleased, without asking so grand a captain's permission. I took my supper and went immediately to bed, discouraged by my day's observations and experiences. My late voyage's note-booking was but a confusion of meaningless names. It had tangled me all up in a knot every time I had looked at it in the daytime. I now hoped for respite in sleep; but no, it revelled all through my head till sunrise again, a frantic and tireless nightmare.

Next morning I felt pretty rusty and low-spirited. We went booming along, taking a good many chances, for we were anxious to "get out of the river" (as getting out to Cairo was called) before night should overtake us. But Mr. Bixby's partner, the other pilot, presently grounded the boat, and we lost so much time getting her off that it was plain the darkness would overtake us a good long way above the mouth. This was a great misfortune, especially to certain of our visiting pilots, whose boats would have to wait for their return, no matter how long that might be. It sobered the pilot-house talk a good deal. Coming up-stream, pilots did not mind low water or any kind of darkness; nothing stopped them but fog. But down-stream work was different; a boat was too nearly helpless, with a stiff current pushing behind her; so it was not customary to run down-stream at night in low water.

There seemed to be one small hope, however: if we could get through the intricate and dangerous Hat Island crossing before night, we could venture the rest, for we would have plainer sailing and better water. But it would be insanity to attempt Hat Island at night. So there was a deal of looking at watches all the rest of the day, and a constant ciphering upon the speed we were making; Hat Island was the eternal subject; sometimes hope was high and sometimes we were delayed in a bad crossing, and down it went again. For hours all hands lay under the burden of this suppressed excitement; it was even communicated to me, and I got to feeling so solicitous about Hat Island, and under such an awful pressure of responsibility, that I wished I might have five minutes on shore to draw a good, full, relieving breath, and start over again. We were standing no regular watches. Each of our pilots ran such portions of the river as he had run when coming up-stream, because of his greater familiarity with it; but both remained in the pilot-house constantly.

An hour before sunset Mr. Bixby took the wheel, and Mr. W. stepped aside. For the next thirty minutes every man held his watch in his hand and was restless, silent, and uneasy. At last somebody said, with a doomful sigh:

"Well, yonder's Hat Island—and we can't make it."

All the watches closed with a snap, everybody sighed and muttered something about its being "too bad, too bad—ah, if we could *only* have got here half an hour sooner!" and the place was thick with the atmosphere of disappointment. Some started to go out, but loitered, hearing no bell-tap to land. The sun dipped behind the horizon, the boat went on. Inquiring looks passed from one guest to another; and one who had his hand on the door-knob and had turned it, waited, then presently took away his hand and let the knob turn back again. We bore steadily down the bend. More looks were exchanged, and nods of surprised admiration —but no words. Insensibly the men drew together behind Mr. Bixby, as the sky darkened and one or two dim stars came out. The dead silence and sense of waiting became oppressive. Mr. Bixby pulled the cord, and two deep, mellow notes from the big bell floated off on the night. Then a pause, and one more note was struck. The watchman's voice followed, from the hurricane-deck:

"Labboard lead, there! Stabboard lead!"

The cries of the leadsmen began to rise out of the distance, and were gruffly repeated by the word-passers on the hurricane-deck.

"M-a-r-k three! M-a-r-k three! Quarter-less-three! Half twain! Quarter twain! M-a-r-k twain! Quarter-less—"

Mr. Bixby pulled two bell-ropes, and was answered by faint jinglings far below in the engine-room, and our speed slackened. The steam began to whistle through the gauge-cocks. The cries of the leadsmen went on—and it is a weird sound, always, in the night. Every pilot in the lot was watching now, with fixed eyes, and talking under his breath. Nobody was calm and easy but Mr. Bixby. He would put his wheel down and stand on a spoke, and as the steamer swung into her (to me) utterly invisible marks—for we seemed to be in the midst of a wide and gloomy sea—he would meet and fasten her there. Out of the murmur of half-audible talk, one caught a coherent sentence now and then—such as:

"There; she's over the first reef all right!"

After a pause, another subdued voice:

"Her stern's coming down just *exactly* right, by *George!*"

"Now she's in the marks; over she goes!"

Somebody else muttered:

"Oh, it was done beautiful—*beautiful!*"

Now the engines were stopped altogether, and we drifted with the current. Not that I could see the boat drift, for I could not, the stars being all gone by this time. This drifting was the dismalest work; it held one's heart still. Presently I discovered a blacker gloom than that which surrounded us. It was the head of the island. We were closing right down upon it. We entered its deeper shadow, and so imminent seemed the peril that I was likely to suffocate; and I had the strongest impulse to do *something*, anything, to save the vessel. But still Mr. Bixby stood by his wheel, silent, intent as a cat, and all the pilots stood shoulder to shoulder at his back.

"She'll not make it!" somebody whispered.

The water grew shoaler and shoaler, by the leadsman's cries, till it was down to:

"Eight-and-a-half! E-i-g-h-t feet! E-i-g-h-t feet! Seven-and—"

Mr. Bixby said warningly through his speaking-tube to the engineer: "Stand by, now!"

"Ay, ay, sir!"

"Seven-and-a-half! Seven feet! *Six*-and—"

We touched bottom! Instantly Mr. Bixby set a lot of bells ringing, shouted through the tube, *"Now,* let her have it—every ounce you've got!" then to his partner, "Put her hard down! snatch her! snatch her!" The boat rasped and ground her way through the sand, hung upon the apex of disaster a single tremendous instant, and then over she went! And such a shout as went up at Mr. Bixby's back never loosened the roof of a pilot-house before!

There was no more trouble after that. Mr. Bixby was a hero that night; and it was some little time, too, before his exploit ceased to be talked about by river-men.

Fully to realize the marvelous precision required in laying the great steamer in her marks in that murky waste of water, one should know that not only must she pick her intricate way through snags and blind reefs, and then shave the head of the island so closely as to brush the overhanging foliage with her stern, but at one place she must pass almost within arm's reach of a sunken and invisible wreck that would snatch the hull timbers from under her if she should strike it, and destroy a quarter of a million dollars' worth of steamboat and cargo in five minutes, and maybe a hundred and fifty human lives into the bargain.

The last remark I heard that night was a compliment to Mr. Bixby, uttered in soliloquy and with unction by one of our guests. He said:

"By the Shadow of Death, but he's a lightning pilot!"

A Pilot's Needs

BUT I am wandering from what I was intending to do; that is, make plainer than perhaps appears in the previous chapters some of the peculiar requirements of the science of piloting. First of all, there is one faculty which a pilot must incessantly cultivate until he has brought it to absolute perfection. Nothing short of perfection will do. That faculty is memory. He cannot stop with merely thinking a thing is so and so; he must *know* it; for this is eminently one of the "exact" sciences. With what scorn a pilot was looked upon, in the old times, if he ever ventured to deal in that feeble phrase "I think," instead of the vigorous one, "I know!" One cannot easily realize what a tremendous thing it is to know every trivial detail of twelve hundred miles of river and know it with absolute exactness. If you will take the longest street in New York, and travel up and down it, conning its features patiently until you know every house and window and lamp-post and big and little sign by heart, and know them so accurately that you can instantly name the one you are abreast of when you are set down at random in that street in the middle of an inky black night, you will then have a tolerable notion of the amount and the exactness of a pilot's knowledge who carries the Mississippi River in his head. And then, if you will go on until you know every street-crossing, the character, size, and position of the crossing-stones, and the varying depth of mud in each of these numberless places, you will have some idea of what the pilot must know in order to keep a Mississippi steamer out of trouble. Next, if you will take half of the signs in that long street, and *change their places* once a month, and still manage to know their new positions accurately on dark nights, and keep up with these repeated changes without making any mistakes, you will understand what is required of a pilot's peerless memory by the fickle Mississippi.

I think a pilot's memory is about the most wonderful thing in the world. To know the Old and New Testaments by heart, and be able to recite them glibly, forward or backward, or begin at random anywhere in the book and recite both ways and never trip or make a mistake, is no extravagant mass of knowledge, and no marvelous facility, compared to a pilot's massed knowledge of the Mississippi and his marvelous facility in handling of it. I make this comparison deliberately, and believe I am not expanding the truth when I do it. Many will think my figure too strong, but pilots will not.

And how easily and comfortably the pilot's memory does its work; how placidly effortless is its way; how *unconsciously* it lays up its vast stores, hour by hour, day by day, and never loses or mislays a single valuable package of them all! Take an instance. Let a leadsman cry, "Half twain! half twain! half twain! half twain! half twain!" until it becomes as monotonous as the ticking of a clock; let conversation be going on all the time, and the pilot be doing his share of the talking, and no longer consciously listening to the leadsman; and in the midst of this endless string of half twains let a single "quarter twain!" be interjected, without emphasis, and then the half-twain cry go on again, just as before: two or three weeks later that pilot can describe with precision the boat's position in the river when that quarter twain was uttered, and give you such a lot of head-marks, stern-marks, and side-marks to guide you, that you ought to be able to take the boat there and put her in that same spot again yourself! The cry of "quarter twain" did not really take his mind from his talk, but his trained faculties instantly photographed the bearings, noted the change of depth, and laid up the important details for future reference without requiring any assistance from *him* in the matter. If you were walking and talking with a friend, and another friend at your side kept up a monotonous repetition of the vowel sound A, for a couple of blocks, and then in the midst interjected an R, thus, A, A, A, A, A, R, A, A, A, etc., and gave the R no emphasis, you would not be able to state, two or three weeks afterward, that the R had been put in, nor be able to tell what objects you were passing at the moment it was done. But you could if your memory had been patiently and laboriously trained to do that sort of thing mechanically.

Give a man a tolerably fair memory to start with, and piloting will develop it into a very colossus of capability. But *only in the matters it is daily drilled in.* A time would come when the man's faculties could not help noticing landmarks and soundings, and his memory could not help holding on to them with the grip of a vise; but if you asked that same man at noon what he had had for breakfast, it would be ten chances to one that he could not tell you. Astonishing things can be done with the human memory if you will devote it faithfully to one particular line of business.

At the time that wages soared so high on the Missouri River, my chief, Mr. Bixby, went up there and learned more than a thousand miles of that stream with an ease and rapidity that were astonishing. When he had seen each division *once* in the daytime and *once* at night, his education was so nearly complete that he took out a "daylight" license; a few trips later he took out a full license, and went to piloting day and night—and he ranked A 1, too.

Mr. Bixby placed me as steersman for a while under a pilot whose feats of memory were a constant marvel to me. However, his memory was born in him, I think, not built. For instance, somebody would mention a name. Instantly Mr. Brown would break in:

"Oh, I knew *him.* Sallow-faced, red-headed fellow, with a little scar on the side of his throat, like a splinter under the flesh. He was only in the Southern trade six months. That was thirteen years ago. I made a trip with him. There was five feet in the upper river then; the *Henry*

Blake grounded at the foot of Tower Island drawing four and a half; the *George Elliott* unshipped her rudder on the wreck of the *Sunflower—*"

"Why, the *Sunflower* didn't sink until—"

"*I* know when she sunk; it was three years before that, on the 2d of December; Asa Hardy was captain of her, and his brother John was first clerk; and it was his first trip in her, too; Tom Jones told me these things a week afterward in New Orleans; he was first mate of the *Sunflower*. Captain Hardy stuck a nail in his foot the 6th of July of the next year, and died of the lockjaw on the 15th. His brother John died two years after—3d of March—erysipelas. I never saw either of the Hardys—they were Alleghany River men—but people who knew them told me all these things. And they said Captain Hardy wore yarn socks winter and summer just the same, and his first wife's name was Jane Shook—she was from New England—and his second one died in a lunatic asylum. It was in the blood. She was from Lexington, Kentucky. Name was Horton before she was married."

And so on, by the hour, the man's tongue would go. He could *not* forget anything. It was simply impossible. The most trivial details remained as distinct and luminous in his head, after they had lain there for years, as the most memorable events. His was not simply a pilot's memory; its grasp was universal. If he were talking about a trifling letter he had received seven years before, he was pretty sure to deliver you the entire screed from memory. And then, without observing that he was departing from the true line of his talk, he was more than likely to hurl in a long-drawn parenthetical biography of the writer of that letter; and you were lucky indeed if he did not take up that writer's relatives, one by one, and give you their biographies, too.

Such a memory as that is a great misfortune. To it, all occurrences are of the same size. Its possessor cannot distinguish an interesting circumstance from an uninteresting one. As a talker, he is bound to clog his narrative with tiresome details and make himself an insufferable bore. Moreover, he cannot stick to his subject. . He picks up every little grain of memory he discerns in his way, and so is led aside. Mr. Brown would start out with the honest intention of telling you a vastly funny anecdote about a dog. He would be "so full of laugh" that he could hardly begin; then his memory would start with the dog's breed and personal appearance; drift into a history of his owner; of his owner's family, with descriptions of weddings and burials that had occurred in it, together with recitals of congratulatory verses and obituary poetry provoked by the same; then this memory would recollect that one of these events occurred during the celebrated "hard winter" of such-and-such a year, and a minute description of that winter would follow, along with the names of people who were frozen to death, and statistics showing the high figures which pork and hay went up to. Pork and hay would suggest corn and fodder; corn and fodder would suggest cows and horses; cows and horses would suggest the circus and certain celebrated bare-back riders; the transition from the circus to the menagerie was easy and natural; from the elephant to equatorial Africa was but a step; then of course the heathen savages would suggest religion; and at the end of three or four hours' tedious jaw, the watch would change, and Brown would go out of the pilot-house muttering extracts from sermons he had heard years before about the efficacy of prayer as a means of grace. And the original first mention would be all you had learned about that dog, after all this waiting and hungering.

A pilot must have a memory; but there are two higher qualities which he must also have. He must have good and quick judgment and decision, and a cool, calm courage that no peril can shake. Give a man the merest trifle of pluck to start with, and by the time he has become a pilot he cannot be unmanned by any danger a steamboat can get into; but one cannot quite say the same for judgment. Judgment is a matter of brains, and a man must *start* with a good stock of that article or he will never succeed as a pilot.

The growth of courage in the pilot-house is steady all the time, but it does not reach a high and satisfactory condition until some time after the young pilot has been "standing his own watch" alone and under the staggering weight of all the responsibilities connected with the position. When the apprentice has become pretty thoroughly acquainted with the river, he goes clattering along so fearlessly with his steamboat, night or day, that he presently begins to imagine that it is *his* courage that animates him; but the first time the pilot steps out and leaves him to his own devices he finds out it was the other man's. He discovers that the article has been left out of his own cargo altogether. The whole river is bristling with exigencies in a moment; he is not prepared for them; he does not know how to meet them; all his knowledge forsakes him; and within fifteen minutes he is as white as a sheet and scared almost to death. Therefore pilots wisely train these cubs by various strategic tricks to look danger in the face a little more calmly. A favorite way of theirs is to play a friendly swindle upon the candidate.

Mr. Bixby served me in this fashion once, and for years afterward I used to blush, even in my sleep, when I thought of it. I had become a good steersman; so good, indeed, that I had all the work to do on our watch, night and day. Mr. Bixby seldom made a suggestion to me; all he ever did was to take the wheel on particularly bad nights or in particularly bad crossings, land the boat when she needed to be landed, play gentleman of leisure nine-tenths of the watch, and collect the wages. The lower river was about bank-full, and if anybody had questioned my ability to run any crossing between Cairo and New Orleans without help or instruction, I should have felt irreparably hurt. The idea of being afraid of any crossing in the lot, in the *daytime,* was a thing too preposterous for contemplation. Well, one matchless summer's day I was bowling down the bend above Island 66, brimful of self-conceit and carrying my nose as high as a giraffe's, when Mr. Bixby said:

"I am going below awhile. I suppose you know the next crossing?"

This was almost an affront. It was about the plainest and simplest crossing in the whole river. One couldn't come to any harm, whether he ran it right or not; and as for depth, there never had been any bottom there. I knew all this, perfectly well.

"Know how to *run* it? Why, I can run it with my eyes shut."

"How much water is there in it?"

"Well, that is an odd question. I couldn't get bottom there with a church steeple."

"You think so, do you?"

The very tone of the question shook my confidence. That was what Mr. Bixby was expecting. He left, without saying anything more. I began to imagine all sorts of things. Mr. Bixby, unknown to me, of course, sent somebody down to the forecastle with some mysterious instructions to the leadsmen, another messenger was sent to whisper among the officers, and then Mr. Bixby went into hiding behind a smoke-stack where he could observe results. Presently the captain stepped out on the hurricane-deck; next the chief mate appeared; then a clerk. Every moment or two a straggler was added to my audience; and before I got to the head of the island I had fifteen or twenty people assembled down there under my nose. I began to wonder what the trouble was. As I started across, the captain glanced aloft at me and said, with a sham uneasiness in his voice:

"Where is Mr. Bixby?"

"Gone below, sir."

But that did the business for me. My imagination began to construct dangers out of nothing, and they multiplied faster than I could keep the run of them. All at once I imagined I saw shoal water ahead! The wave of coward agony that surged through me then came near dislocating every joint in me. All my confidence in that crossing vanished. I seized the bell-rope; dropped it, ashamed; seized it again; dropped it once more; clutched it tremblingly once again, and pulled it so feebly that I could hardly hear the stroke myself. Captain and mate sang out instantly, and both together:

"Starboard lead there! and quick about it!"

This was another shock. I began to climb the wheel like a squirrel; but I would hardly get the boat started to port before I would see new dangers on that side, and away I would spin to the other; only to find perils accumulating to starboard, and be crazy to get to port again. Then came the leadsman's sepulchral cry:

"D-e-e-p four!"

Deep four in a bottomless crossing! The terror of it took my breath away.

"M-a-r-k three! M-a-r-k three! Quarter-less-three! Half twain!"

This was frightful! I seized the bell-ropes and stopped the engines.

"Quarter twain! Quarter twain! *Mark* twain!"

I was helpless. I did not know what in the world to do. I was quaking from head to foot, and I could have hung my hat on my eyes, they stuck out so far.

"Quarter-*less*-twain! Nine-and-a-*half!*"

We were *drawing* nine! My hands were in a nerveless flutter. I could not ring a bell intelligibly with them. I flew to the speaking-tube and shouted to the engineer:

"Oh, Ben, if you love me, *back* her! Quick, Ben! Oh, back the immortal *soul* out of her!"

I heard the door close gently. I looked around, and there stood Mr. Bixby, smiling a bland, sweet smile. Then the audience on the hurricane-deck sent up a thundergust of humiliating laughter. I saw it all, now, and I felt meaner than the meanest man in human history. I laid in the lead, set the boat in her marks, came ahead on the engines, and said:

"It was a fine trick to play on an orphan, *wasn't* it? I suppose I'll never hear the last of how I was ass enough to heave the lead at the head of 66."

"Well, no, you won't, maybe. In fact I hope you won't; for I want you to learn something by that experience. Didn't you *know* there was no bottom in that crossing?"

"Yes, sir, I did."

"Very well, then. You shouldn't have allowed me or anybody else to shake your confidence in that knowledge. Try to remember that. And another thing: when you get into a dangerous place don't turn coward. That isn't going to help matters any.'

It was a good enough lesson, but pretty hardly learned. Yet about the hardest part of it was that for months I so often had to hear a phrase which I had conceived a particular distaste for. It was, "Oh, Ben, if you love me, back her!"

From A Connecticut Yankee at the Court of King Arthur

In 1879, Hank Morgan was superintendent of an arms factory in Hartford, in the state of Connecticut. Engaging in "a misunderstanding conducted with crowbars" with a workman known as Hercules, Hank was laid out "with a crusher alongside the head that made everything crack." He awoke under a tree near Camelot, the seat of King Arthur's court, in the year 528. He was captured and brought to Camelot by Sir Kay the Seneschal, and condemned to be burned at the stake. The execution was to take place at noon on the twenty-first of June, 528. In his former existence he had somehow learned that this was the exact day and hour of an eclipse. He therefore threatened to blot out the sun if he was harmed; and as the torch was about to be applied, the eclipse occurred, while he pretended to command it. Overcome, the King made the Yankee his minister, with the title of Sir Boss. The magician Merlin resented bitterly such success on the part of a rival, and endeavored by every means to destroy him. But through triumph after triumph, though often in the utmost danger, Sir Boss went on, introducing inventions and reforms. Not least interesting among the conflicts between him and the existing order was the tournament here related.

The Yankee's Fight with the Knights

HOME again, at Camelot. A morning or two later I found the paper, damp from the press, by my plate at the breakfast-table. I turned to the advertising columns, knowing I should find something of personal interest to me there. It was this:

DE PAR LE ROI.

Know that the great lord and illustrious Knight, SIR SAGRAMOR LE DESIROUS having condescended to meet the King's Minister, Hank Morgan, the which is surnamed The Boss, for satisfaction of offence anciently given, these will engage in the lists by Camelot about the fourth hour of the morning of the sixteenth day of this next succeeding month. The battle will be à l outrance, sith the said offence was of a deadly sort, admitting of no composition.

DE PAR LE ROI

Clarence's editorial reference to this affair was to this effect:

thdrew.
work maintained
there since, soon
lastic have witq
oked interest
npon the es**n**-
ve been m **ï** d
by the an**ó**ns,
ent out ch**é**y by
gterian *B*n, and
e some y**u**ng men
of our under the
l guidance of tha
óor aid in a**°**known
ór great enterprise
of making pure;
escn**i**
movement had its
origin in preven-
his ever been a
sions id our
on the **m**is-
other one
ospel,
by-
e
The
the same
Co represent
ized thirty of
needs and hear-
which,**°**years age!
twresgn was osgan-
ing, the missions,
mo that both had
to withdraw' and
much to their
grief,

It will be observed, by a gl**y**nce at our advertising columns, that the community is to be favored **m**ith a treat of unusual interest in the tournament line. The n ames of the artists are warrant of good enter**t**amment. The box-office will be open at noon of the 13th; admission 3 cents, reserve**d** seats 5; proceeds to go to the hospital fund **i**he royal pair and all **t**ne Court will be present. With these exceptions, and the press and the clergy, **t**he free list is strictly sus**T**ended. Parties are hereby warned against buying tickets of speculators; they will not be good at the door. Everybody knows and **l**ikes The Boss, everybody knows and likes Sir Sag.; come, let us give tne lads a good send-off. ReMember, tne proceeds go to a great and free charity, and one whose broad begevolence stretches out its helping hand, warm with the blood of a loving heart, to all that su**y**er, regardless of race, creed, condition or color—the only charity yet established in tne earth which has no politico-religious stopcock on its compassion, but says Here flows **t**the stream, let *all* come and drink! **i**urn out, all hands! fet**ct** along your dou**z**hnuts and your gum-drops and have a good time. Pie for sale on the groun**d**s, and rocks to crack it with; also ci**R**cus-lemonade—three drops of lime juice to a barrel of water.

N. B. *This is the first tou**rn**amen**t** under the new law, whi**d**h allo**w** each combatant to use any weapon he may prefer. You want to make a note of **t**ha**t.**

our disappo**inted**
promptly and—**i**
two of their fel**o**
e**r**lain, and oth**er**
ers have **a**lrea**dy**
spoken, you **in**
furnished for
their use, **m**
make and
the **x**ind
letters
o**f** introd
duction whi
they are unin
ing friends to **u**
ried, and leave t**he**
thot**°**kind words **are**
which you my yo**r**
hind; and it is **a**
home matter of b
it is our dur**y**
direct them to
now under the
g fields as are
These **°**youn**g**
are warm-hear**ted**
az**r**l, regions b**ut**
not to "build **a**
ond,'**¸** and the
der instructi
ons of our
another man
founhati's **o**n**,**
ociety, which
They go un-
say t**y**at "**m**
ionaries to mon
say sending mi**s**

Up to the day set, there was no talk in all Britain of anything but this combat. All other topics sank into insignificance and passed out of men's thoughts and interest. It was not because a tournament was a great matter; it was not because Sir Sagramor had found the Holy Grail, for he had not, but had failed; it was not because the second (official) personage in the kingdom was one of the duelists; no, all these features were commonplace. Yet there was abundant reason for the extraordinary interest which this coming fight was creating. It was born of the fact that all the nation knew that this was not to be a duel between mere men, so to speak, but a duel between two mighty magicians; a duel not of muscle but of mind, not of human skill but of superhuman art and craft; a final struggle for supremacy between the two master enchanters of the age. It was realized that the most prodigious achievements of the most renowned knights could not be worthy of comparison with a spectacle like this; they could be but child's play, contrasted with this mysterious and awful battle of the gods. Yes, all the world knew it was going to be in reality a duel between Merlin and me, a measuring of his magic powers against mine. It was known that Merlin had been busy whole days and nights together, imbuing Sir Sagramor's arms and armor with supernal powers of offence and defence, and that he had procured for him from the spirits of the air a fleecy veil which would render the wearer invisible to his antagonist while still visible to other men. Against Sir Sagramor, so weaponed and protected, a thousand knights could accomplish nothing; against him no known enchantments could prevail. These facts were sure; regarding them there was no doubt, no reason for doubt. There was but one question: might there be still other enchantments, *unknown* to Merlin, which could render Sir Sagramor's veil transparent to me, and make his enchanted mail vulnerable to my weapons? This was the one thing to be decided in the lists. Until then the world must remain in suspense.

So the world thought there was a vast matter at stake here, and the world was right, but it was not the one they had in their minds. No a far vaster one was upon the cast of this die: *the life of knight-errantry.* I was a champion, it was true, but not the champion of the frivolous black arts, I was the champion of hard unsentimental common sense and reason. I was entering the lists to either destroy knight-errantry or be its victim.

Vast as the show-grounds were, there were no vacant spaces in them outside of the lists, at ten o'clock on the morning of the 16th. The mammoth grand-stand was clothed in flags, streamers, and rich tapestries, and packed with several acres of small-fry tributary kings, their suites, and the British aristocracy; with our own royal gang in the chief place, and each and every individual a flashing prism of gaudy silks and velvets —well, I never saw anything to begin with it but a fight between an Upper Mississippi sunset and the aurora borealis. The huge camp of beflagged and gay-colored tents at one end of the lists, with a stiff-standing sentinel at every door and a shining shield hanging by him for challenge, was another fine sight. You see, every knight was there who had any ambition or any caste feeling; for my feeling toward their order was not much of a secret, and so here was their chance. If I won my fight with Sir Sagramor, others would have the right to call me out as long as I might be willing to respond.

Down at our end there were but two tents; one for me, and another for my servants. At the appointed hour the king made a sign, and the heralds, in their tabards, appeared and made proclamation, naming the combatants and stating the cause of quarrel. There was a pause, then a ringing bugle-blast, which was the signal for us to come forth. All the multitude caught their breath, and an eager curiosity flashed into every face.

Out from his tent rode great Sir Sagramor, an imposing tower of iron, stately and rigid, his huge spear standing upright in its socket and grasped in his strong hand, his grand horse's face and breast cased in steel, his body clothed in rich trappings that almost dragged the ground —oh, a most noble picture. A great shout went up, of welcome and admiration.

And then out I came. But I didn't get any shout. There was a wondering and eloquent silence for a moment, then a great wave of laughter began to sweep along that human sea, but a warning bugle-blast cut its career short. I was in the simplest and comfortablest of gymnast costumes—flesh-colored tights from neck to heel, with blue silk puffings about my loins, and bareheaded. My horse was not above medium size, but he was alert, slender-limbed, muscled with watch-springs, and just a greyhound to go. He was a beauty, glossy as silk, and naked as he was when he was born, except for bridle and ranger-saddle.

The iron tower and the gorgeous bed-quilt came cumbrously but gracefully pirouetting down the lists, and we tripped lightly up to meet them. We halted; the tower saluted, I responded; then we wheeled and rode side by side to the grand-stand and faced our king and queen, to whom we made obeisance. The queen exclaimed:

"Alack, Sir Boss, wilt fight naked, and without lance or sword or—"

But the king checked her and made her understand, with a polite phrase or two, that this was none of her business. The bugles rang again; and we separated and rode to the ends of the lists, and took position. Now old Merlin stepped into view and cast a dainty web of gossamer threads over Sir Sagramor which turned him into Hamlet's ghost; the king made a sign, the bugles blew, Sir Sagramor laid his great lance in rest, and the next moment here he came thundering down the course with his veil flying out behind, and I went whistling through the air like an arrow to meet him—cocking my ear the while, as if noting the invisible knight's position and progress by hearing, not sight. A chorus of encouraging shouts burst out for him, and one brave voice flung out a heartening word for me—said:

"Go it, slim Jim!"

It was an even bet that Clarence had procured that favor for me —and furnished the language, too. When that formidable lance-point was within a yard and a half of my breast I twitched my horse aside without an effort, and the big knight swept by, scoring a blank. I got plenty of applause that time. We turned, braced up, and down we came again. Another blank for the knight, a roar of applause for me. The same thing was repeated once more; and it fetched such a whirlwind of applause that Sir Sagramor lost his temper, and at once changed his tactics and set himself the task of chasing me down. Why, he hadn't any show in the world at that; it was a game of tag, with all the advantage on my side; I whirled out of his path with ease whenever I chose, and once I slapped him on the back as I went to the rear. Finally I took the chase into my own hands; and after that, turn, or twist, or do what he would, he was never able to get behind me again; he found himself always in front at the end of his manœuver. So he gave up that business and retired to his end of the lists. His temper was clear gone now, and he forgot himself and flung an insult at me which disposed of mine. I slipped my lasso from the horn of my saddle, and grasped the coil in my right hand. This time you should have seen him come!—it was a business trip, sure; by his gait there was blood in his eye. I was sitting my horse at ease, and swinging the great loop of my lasso in wide circles about my head; the moment he was under way, I started for him; when the space between us had narrowed to forty feet, I sent the snaky spirals of the rope a-cleaving through the air, then darted aside and faced about and brought my trained animal to a halt with all his feet braced under him for a surge. The next moment the rope sprang taut and yanked Sir Sagramor out of the saddle! Great Scott, but there was a sensation!

Unquestionably, the popular thing in this world is novelty. These people had never seen anything of that cowboy business before, and it carried them clear off their feet with delight. From all around and everywhere, the shout went up:

"Encore! encore!"

I wondered where they got the word, but there was no time to cipher on philological matters, because the whole knight-errantry hive was just humming now, and my prospect for trade couldn't have been better. The moment my lasso was released and Sir Sagramor had been assisted to his tent, I hauled in the slack, took my station and began to swing my loop around my head again. I was sure to have use for it as soon as they could elect a successor for Sir Sagramor, and that couldn't take long where there were so many hungry candidates. Indeed, they elected one straight off—Sir Hervis de Revel.

Bzz! Here he came, like a house afire; I dodged: he passed like a flash, with my horse-hair coils settling around his neck; a second or so later, *fst!* his saddle was empty.

I got another encore; and another, and another, and still another. When I had snaked five men out, things began to look serious to the ironclads, and they stopped and consulted together. As a result, they decided that it was time to waive etiquette and send their greatest and best against me. To the astonishment of that little world, I lassoed Sir Lamorak de Galis, and after him Sir Galahad. So you see there was simply nothing to be done now, but play their right bower—bring out the superbest of the superb, the mightiest of the mighty, the great Sir Launcelot himself!

A proud moment for me? I should think so. Yonder was Arthur, King of Britain; yonder was Guinevere; yes, and whole tribes of little provincial kings and kinglets; and in the tented camp yonder, renowned knights from many lands; and likewise the selectest body known to chivalry, the Knights of the Table Round, the most illustrious in Christendom; and biggest fact of all, the very sun of their shining system was yonder couching his lance, the focal point of forty thousand adoring eyes; and all by myself, here was I laying for him. Across my mind flitted the dear image of a certain hello-girl of West Hartford, and I wished she could see me now. In that moment, down came the Invincible, with the rush of a whirlwind—the courtly world rose to its feet and bent forward—the fateful coils went circling through the air, and before you could wink I was towing Sir Launcelot across the field on his back, and kissing my hand to the storm of waving kerchiefs and the thunder-crash of applause that greeted me!

Said I to myself, as I coiled my lariat and hung it on my saddle-horn, and sat there drunk with glory, "The victory is perfect—no other will venture against me—knight-errantry is dead." Now imagine my astonishment—and everybody else's, too—to hear the peculiar bugle-call which announces that another competitor is about to enter the lists! There was a mystery here; I couldn't account for this thing. Next, I noticed Merlin gliding away from me; and then I noticed that my lasso was gone! The old sleight-of-hand expert had stolen it, sure, and slipped it under his robe.

The bugle blew again. I looked, and down came Sagramor riding again, with his dust brushed off and his veil nicely rearranged. I trotted up to meet him, and pretended to find him by the sound of his horse's hoofs. He said:

"Thou'rt quick of ear, but it will not save thee from this!" and he touched the hilt of his great sword. "An ye are not able to see it, because of the influence of the veil, know that it is no cumbrous lance, but a sword—and I ween ye will not be able to avoid it."

His visor was up; there was death in his smile. I should never be able to dodge his sword, that was plain. Somebody was going to die this time. If he got the drop on me, I could name the corpse. We rode forward together, and saluted the royalties. This time the king was disturbed. He said:

"Where is thy strange weapon?"

"It is stolen, sire."

"Hast another at hand?"

"No, sire, I brought only the one."

Then Merlin mixed in:

"He brought but the one because there was but the one to bring. There exists none other but that one. It belongeth to the king of the Demons of the Sea. This man is a pretender, and ignorant; else he had known that that weapon can be used in but eight bouts only, and then it vanisheth away to its home under the sea."

"Then is he weaponless," said the king. "Sir Sagramor, ye will grant him leave to borrow."

"And I will lend!" said Sir Launcelot, limping up. "He is as brave a knight of his hands as any that be on live, and he shall have mine."

He put his hand on his sword to draw it, but Sir Sagramor said:

"Stay, it may not be. He shall fight with his own weapons; it was his privilege to choose them and bring them. If he has erred, on his head be it."

"Knight!" said the king. "Thou'rt overwrought with passion; it disorders thy mind. Wouldst kill a naked man?"

"An he do it, he shall answer it to me," said Sir Launcelot.

"I will answer it to any he that desireth!" retorted Sir Sagramor hotly.

Merlin broke in, rubbing his hands and smiling his low-downest smile of malicious gratification:

"'Tis well said, right well said! And 'tis enough of parleying, let my lord the king deliver the battle signal."

The king had to yield. The bugle made proclamation, and we turned apart and rode to our stations. There we stood, a hundred yards apart, facing each other, rigid and motionless, like horsed statues. And so we remained, in a soundless hush, as much as a full minute, everybody gazing, nobody stirring. It seemed as if the king could not take heart to give the signal. But at last he lifted his hand, the clear note of a bugle followed, Sir Sagramor's long blade described a flashing curve in the air, and it was superb to see him come. I sat still. On he came. I did not move. People got so excited that they shouted to me:

"Fly, fly! Save thyself! This is murther!"

I never budged so much as an inch till that thundering apparition had got within fifteen paces of me; then I snatched a dragoon revolver out of my holster, there was a flash and a roar, and the revolver was back in the holster before anybody could tell what had happened.

Here was a riderless horse plunging by, and yonder lay Sir Sagramor, stone dead.

The people that ran to him were stricken dumb to find that the life was actually gone out of the man and no reason for it visible, no hurt upon his body, nothing like a wound. There was a hole through the breast of his chain-mail, but they attached no importance to a little thing like that; and as a bullet-wound there produces but little blood, none came in sight because of the clothing and swaddlings under the armor. The body was dragged over to let the king and the swells look down upon it. They were stupefied with astonishment naturally. I was requested to come and explain the miracle. But I remained in my tracks, like a statue, and said:

"If it is a command, I will come, but my lord the king knows that I am where the laws of combat require me to remain while any desire to come against me."

I waited. Nobody challenged. Then I said:

"If there are any who doubt that this field is well and fairly won, I do not wait for them to challenge me, I challenge them."

"It is a gallant offer," said the king, "and well beseems you. Whom will you name first?"

"I name none, I challenge all! Here I stand, and dare the chivalry of England to come against me—not by individuals, but in mass!"

"What!" shouted a score of knights.

"You have heard the challenge. Take it, or I proclaim you recreant knights and vanquished, every one!"

It was a "bluff" you know. At such a time it is sound judgment to put on a bold face and play your hand for a hundred times what it is worth; forty-nine times out of fifty nobody dares to "call," and you rake in the chips. But just this once—well, things looked squally! In just no time, five hundred knights were scrambling into their sad-dles, and before you could wink a widely scattering drove were under way and clattering down upon me. I snatched both revolvers from the holsters and began to measure distances and calculate chances.

Bang! One saddle empty. Bang! another one. Bang—bang, and I bagged two. Well, it was nip and tuck with us, and I knew it. If I spent the eleventh shot without convincing these people, the twelfth man would kill me, sure. And so I never did feel so happy as I did when my ninth downed its man and I detected the wavering in the crowd which is premonitory of panic. An instant lost now could knock out my last chance. But I didn't lose it. I raised both revolvers and pointed them—the halted host stood their ground just about one good square moment, then broke and fled.

The day was mine. Knight-errantry was a doomed institution. The march of civilization was begun. How did I feel? Ah, you never could imagine it.

And Brer Merlin? His stock was flat again. Somehow, every time the magic of fol-de-rol tried conclusions with the magic of science, the magic of fol-de-rol got left.

THOMAS BAILEY ALDRICH
(1836-1907)

Sargent's Portrait of Edwin Booth at "The Players"

THAT face which no man ever saw
And from his memory banished quite,
With eyes in which are Hamlet's awe
And Cardinal Richelieu's subtle light
Looks from this frame. A master's hand
Has set the master-player here,
In the fair temple that he planned
Not for himself. To us most dear
This image of him! "It was thus
He looked; such pallor touched his cheek;
With that same grace he greeted us—
Nay, 'tis the man, could it but speak!"
Sad words that shall be said some day—
Far fall the day! O cruel Time,
Whose breath sweeps mortal things away,
Spare long this image of his prime,

That others standing in the place
Where, save as ghosts, we come no more,
May know what sweet majestic face
The gentle Prince of Players wore!

An Ode on the Unveiling of the Shaw Memorial on Boston Common

I

NOT with slow, funereal sound
Come we to this sacred ground;
Not with wailing fife and solemn muffled
    drum,
Bringing a cypress wreath
    To lay, with bended knee,
On the cold brows of Death—
    Not so, dear God, we come,
But with the trumpets' blare
And shot-torn battle-banners flung to air,
    As for a victory!

Hark to the measured tread of martial
     feet,
The music and the murmurs of the
     street!
  No bugle breathes this day
  Disaster and retreat!—
  Hark how the iron lips
  Of the great battle-ships
Salute the City from her azure Bay!

II

Time was—time was, ah, unforgotten
     years!—
We paid our hero tribute of our tears.
   But now let go
All sounds and signs and formulas of
     woe:
  'Tis Life, not Death, we celebrate;
  To Life, not Death, we dedicate
This storied bronze, whereon is
     wrought
The lithe immortal figure of our
     thought,
  To show forever to men's eyes,
  Our children's children's children's
     eyes,
   How once he stood
   In that heroic mood,
  He and his dusky braves
  So fain to glorious graves!—
  One instant stood, and then
Drave through that cloud of purple steel
     and flame,
Which wrapt him, held him, gave him not
     again,
But in the trampled ashes left to Fame
  An everlasting name!

III

That was indeed to live—
  At one bold swoop to wrest

From darkling death the best
That death to life can give.
He fell as Roland fell
That day at Roncevaux,
With foot upon the ramparts of the
     foe!
  A pæan, not a knell,
  For heroes dying so!
  No need for sorrow here,
  No room for sigh or tear,
Save such rich tears as happy eyelids
     know.
  See where he rides, our Knight!
  Within his eyes the light
Of battle, and youth's gold about his
     brow;
Our Paladin, our Soldier of the
     Cross,
  Not weighing gain with loss—
  World-loser, that won all
  Obeying duty's call!
  Not his, at peril's frown,
  A pulse of quicker beat;
  Not his to hesitate
  And parley hold with Fate,
  But proudly to fling down
  His gauntlet at her feet.
O soul of loyal valor and white truth,
  Here, by this iron gate,
Thy serried ranks about thee as of yore,
  Stand thou for evermore
  In thy undying youth!

  The tender heart, the eagle eye!
   Oh, unto him belong
   The homages of Song;
   Our praises and the praise
   Of coming days
   To him belong—
To him, to him, the dead that shall not
     die!